Corporate Governance

Marc Moore
University of Cambridge, UK

Martin Petrin
University College London, UK

Corporate Governance

Law, Regulation and Theory

First published 2017 by
PALGRAVE

Palgrave in the UK is an imprint of Macmillan Publishers Limited, registered in England, company number 785998, of 4 Crinan Street, London, N1 9XW.

Palgrave® and Macmillan® are registered trademarks in the United States, the United Kingdom, Europe and other countries.

ISBN 978–1–137–40331–5 paperback

This book is printed on paper suitable for recycling and made from fully managed and sustained forest sources. Logging, pulping and manufacturing processes are expected to conform to the environmental regulations of the country of origin.

A catalogue record for this book is available from the British Library.

A catalog record for this book is available from the Library of Congress.

CONTENTS

FOREWORD

The authors of this book have been teaching corporate governance related courses for a number of years, and at a number of different law schools both domestically and overseas. Throughout this time we have each encountered difficulties sourcing appropriate materials on which to base our lectures and seminars, due in large part to the absence of a reliable textbook for this purpose.

While there is no shortage of excellent primary sources, academic articles and research monographs in this field, the bulk of good theoretical readings on corporate governance tend to derive from the United States. Although this by no means negates their usefulness for UK based readers (and, indeed, in our teaching and in this book we often apply a comparative UK-US perspective), it does present something of a challenge for students and lecturers in terms of seeking to re-contextualize these concepts and arguments for a somewhat different national regulatory environment. Moreover, in view of the fragmented nature of much of the field of literature, there is a distinct scarcity of reliable core readings geared to tying these various strands of material together for the benefit of those who are new to the subject.

Admittedly, there are a number of good economics and management texts available on corporate governance, which are of some assistance to law students. However, we have long felt that these books – while helpful to an extent – are nonetheless excessively focused on the *practices* of corporate governance. As such, they tend to afford only very limited (if any) consideration to the *legal and regulatory framework* within which such practices are conducted, rendering them of limited value to law students. We also believe that many of the more management oriented corporate governance texts on the market provide relatively little in the way of the intellectual and theoretical 'meat' that top law students tend to thrive on.

After struggling without a satisfactory core text in our respective teachings for a number of years, we eventually decided to take matters into our own hands by attempting to write the sort of corporate governance text that we would ideally wish to use in class. Accordingly, what you have in front of you just now is the end result of our efforts in this regard. In short, this is a book that has been written *by* enthusiastic teachers of UK and Anglo-American corporate governance law, *for* fellow students and teachers of the subject. In as much as it has been written to make the lives of ourselves and our students easier, we likewise hope that it will make your own experience of studying, teaching, and/or researching and writing on this fascinating subject a little smoother. If so, then it will have undoubtedly served its principal purpose.

Of course, we do not purport to cover every single potential detail or angle of this vast and multi-faceted subject, and no doubt some readers will have cause to quibble with particular aspects of how we have chosen to set the material out. This is, alas, an inevitable occupational hazard of working without the sort of tried and tested template that exists for many of the more established law curriculum subjects. Our more modest objective is rather to provide a clear, concise and accessible introduction to the study of corporate governance as a subject of distinctly *legal* enquiry. At the same time, we have sought wherever possible to trigger readers' critical opinions on some of the most controversial corporate governance issues, and to draw them into the thick of some of the ongoing academic debates in this field.

In writing this book we have been assisted by a number of individuals and organizations, without whose support the project would not have been possible. We are grateful in particular to Rob Gibson (formerly of Palgrave Macmillan) for initially enabling us to get this project off the ground; and, latterly, to Aléta Bezuidenhout, Helen Bugler and Elizabeth Holmes at Palgrave, and also Indumathy Gunasekaran at Integra, for helping us to see the book through to completion. We are further thankful to Chris Riley and the anonymous Palgrave reviewer for their extremely insightful and constructive comments on an earlier draft of our manuscript for this book. The former author would also like to thank the Leverhulme Trust for kindly funding part of his time involved in the writing of this work. Needless to say, the opinions expressed in this book together with any outstanding errors are those of the authors alone, although we have taken every effort to ensure that the material set out herein is fully accurate and up to date as of 1 January 2017.

A special word of thanks is due to the many excellent graduate students who we have had the pleasure of teaching corporate governance to over the course of our respective academic careers: without the benefit of these stimulating and inspiring intellectual exchanges, we would not have been capable of formulating the thoughts and ideas that lie behind this book. Last but not least, we are eternally grateful to our respective families, for their unending support and toleration of the many long and sleepless nights that were involved in finalizing this book. We hope that our time and energies expended on it have been worthwhile.

Marc Moore and Martin Petrin,
6 March 2017,
Cambridge/London

PART I

Introduction to Corporate Governance

CHAPTER 1

What Is Corporate Governance?

'Corporate Governance' Defined

Despite its rapidly growing academic popularity and practical relevance in recent years, 'corporate governance' remains a somewhat uncertain and contested term of reference. Indeed, if we were to ask a group of scholars or students to each specify what they understand the term to mean, it is likely that a number of highly varied attempted definitions would be offered.

The most commonly cited definition of corporate governance in the UK is that provided in the influential 1992 Report of the Cadbury Committee on the Financial Aspects of Corporate Governance. The Cadbury Report is widely regarded as the nucleus of the modern regulatory framework for corporate governance both domestically and – to a large extent – globally. According to Cadbury, '[c]orporate governance is the system by which companies are directed and controlled', for which boards of directors bear principal responsibility.[1] Expanding on this basic theme, the most recent (2016) edition of the UK Corporate Governance Code – in effect, the Cadbury Report's contemporary incarnation – asserts that '[t]he purpose of corporate governance is to facilitate effective, entrepreneurial and prudent management that can deliver the long-term success of the company'.[2] Meanwhile, the internationally applicable G20/OECD Principles of Corporate Governance explain how, on a fundamental level, corporate governance 'provides the structure through which the objectives of the company are set, and the means of attaining those objectives and monitoring performance are determined'.[3]

Each of the above definitions is helpful in providing a degree of illumination over what corporate governance essentially entails as a matter of business practice. However, in terms of identifying the nature and focus of corporate governance as an area of *academic* enquiry, all of the above practical depictions are necessarily limited. As such, they tend to throw up as many questions

---

[1] The Cadbury Committee, Report of the Committee on the Financial Aspects of Corporate Governance (1 December 1992), para. 2.5.

[2] Financial Reporting Council, *The UK Corporate Governance Code* (April 2016), 1.

[3] Organisation for Economic Co-operation and Development, G20/OECD Principles of Corporate Governance: OECD Report to G20 Finance Ministers and Central Bank Governors (September 2015), 9.

as answers, at least for those beginning their study of the subject for the first time. Indeed, on one view corporate governance – at least as described above – comes across as a heavily procedural and bureaucratic field of study, involving the painstaking perusal of a burgeoning body of codes, committee structures and consultation documents. From another perspective, though, the notion of corporate governance – as described in the same general terms – can contrarily seem like a heavily theoretical and largely *extra*-legal subject, involving open-ended engagement with fundamental questions such as the nature and rightful beneficiaries of business corporations within a wider social context. Accordingly, corporate governance tends to be contrasted with company (or, to use US parlance, 'corporate') law: the former dealing with the conceptual 'big issues' from a reformist standpoint, and the latter with the doctrinal minutiae of business entities regulation viewed in (small 'c') conservative terms.

While both of the above understandings of corporate governance contain a certain element of truth, neither quite encapsulates the distinct essence of the subject matter. Rather, as a general social-scientific phenomenon, corporate governance is concerned – first and foremost – with the problem of *power*. In particular, corporate governance is essentially an enquiry into *the causes and consequences of the allocation of decision-making power* within large, socially significant business organizations. This is broadly consistent with how the concept of 'governance' is typically understood within its traditional political domain, as relating to the various means by which the authority and decisions of powerful public officeholders are checked, counterbalanced, or otherwise rendered legitimate within society.[4]

In defining corporate governance in this way, we seek to distinguish it from company law more generally, which deals with numerous issues additional to the core allocation of corporate decision-making power including company formation, capital structure, or procedural rules on conducting shareholders' and board meetings. Accordingly, except to the limited extent that these and other extraneous concerns have indirect ramifications for corporate 'governance' in the sense described above, they lie outside the scope of the present work. However, some other aspects of company law undoubtedly *do* have a direct bearing on the allocation of corporate decision-making power, and therefore *are* of immediate concern to us here. Included within this latter category are shareholders' rights of intervention in corporate decision-making,[5] and also the key rules and principles relating to the monitoring responsibilities of directors,[6]

---

[4] Indeed, in her introduction to the UK government's recent (at time of writing) Green Paper on corporate governance reform, the Prime Minister Theresa May emphasizes that '[g]ood corporate governance is about having the right checks and balances within big business to strengthen decision-making and accountability'. See Department for Business, Energy and Industrial Strategy, *Corporate Governance Reform: Green Paper* (November 2016) ('Green Paper'), 'Introduction from the Prime Minister'.
[5] See Chapter 4.
[6] See Chapter 7.

internal financial control,[7] executive remuneration[8] and takeovers.[9] Meanwhile, certain important elements of securities law, such as the periodic financial reporting requirements applicable to publicly listed companies,[10] likewise fall within the purview of this book on account of their centrality to prevailing corporate power dynamics.

UNDERSTANDING CORPORATE POWER

Power is a ubiquitous phenomenon: according to one influential corporate governance scholar it 'is perhaps the oldest social phenomenon in human history'.[11] But power is also an opaque and highly contested notion, and it has been said that '[f]ew words are used so frequently with so little seeming need to reflect on their meaning'.[12] Even within the specific corporate domain, the origins, nature and significance of power remain largely ambiguous issues. Pinning down a relevant and workable definition of the term for present purposes is therefore highly difficult.

Large and socially significant corporations can be regarded as exercising power in two key general respects. The first of these is the 'external' or public dimension of corporate power, and the second is the 'internal' or private dimension.[13] As we will see below, external or public manifestations of corporate power within society are conventionally regarded as controllable via orthodox regulatory state interventions, as opposed to meriting direct consideration within the realm of corporate governance itself. Consequently, corporate governance – at least within the Anglo-American environment – has tended to focus almost exclusively on mitigating the principal internal or private manifestations of corporate power, particularly as they pertain to the interests of shareholders. We will now briefly examine each of these two core aspects of corporate power in turn, and will also explain our preference for concentrating on the latter (internal) dimension for the purposes of this book.

The External/Public Dimension of Corporate Power

In essence, the external or public dimension of corporate decision-making power denotes the practical capacity that large corporations have to make substantially unconstrained choices that have significant effects on the lives

---

[7] See Chapter 8.
[8] See Chapter 9.
[9] See Chapter 10.
[10] See Chapter 5.
[11] A.A. Berle, *Power Without Property: A New Development in American Political Economy* (Harcourt, Brace & World 1959), 77.
[12] J.K. Galbraith, *The Anatomy of Power* (Houghton Mifflin 1983), 1.
[13] On the 'internal' v. 'external' corporate power dichotomy generally, see S.R. Bowman, *The Modern Corporation and American Political Thought: Law, Power and Ideology* (Penn State University Press 1996).

of others.[14] Hence 'power', as viewed in this sense, can be defined – in Carl Kaysen's words – as 'the scope of significant choice' open to a person or organization, with 'power over others' representing 'the scope of his choices which affect them significantly'.[15]

As Parkinson notes, at the heart of this understanding of the term lies the concept of *discretion* as a source of unilateral decisional prerogative, whereby 'companies are able to make choices which have important social consequences: they make private decisions which have public results'.[16] The normative implication of this conception of corporate power is that, in some very important respects, large business organizations can be said to exert a degree of power and influence over our quality and patterns of living *not dissimilar* from that exhibited by government itself. However, in contrast to orthodox governmental agents, the individual officers who occupy senior positions within large corporations are not elected in accordance with ordinary public-democratic methods. *Prima facie*, this gives rise to a curious democratic deficit problem that would appear to challenge the legitimacy of such power from a general social standpoint.[17]

Large business organizations typically possess a significant sphere of discretion over a wide array of socio-economic issues. On a micro (i.e. individual firm[18]) level, these include choices over the selection and pricing of goods and services, and also the allocation and termination of employment opportunities, both geographically and in terms of relevant skills categories. On a sectorial or macro (i.e. economy-wide) level, meanwhile, external corporate decision-making power extends collectively over broader-reaching concerns such as the intensity and focus of research and development activity, the extent and rate of automation of production methods, and the degree to which technological advances will be accommodated by the re-skilling (as opposed to de-skilling) of workers. It also has significant ramifications for the ways in which we commonly communicate with each other as human beings: indeed, we need only imagine how different our global society would be without Facebook, Twitter and Instagram to appreciate the sheer pervasiveness of these companies' influence over our lives.

Nominally 'private' corporate decisions on such matters, moreover, frequently impact considerably beyond the firm's immediate productive relations,

---

[14] On this, see J.E. Parkinson, *Corporate Power and Responsibility: Issues in the Theory of Company Law* (OUP 1993), 10.

[15] C. Kaysen, 'The Corporation: How Much Power? What Scope?' in E.S. Mason (ed.), *The Corporation in Modern Society* (Harvard University Press 1959), Ch. 5, 85.

[16] Parkinson, above n. 14, 10.

[17] On the importance of legitimacy in sustaining social and organizational power relations generally, see M.T. Moore, *Corporate Governance in the Shadow of the State* (Hart Publishing 2013), 31–33.

[18] In this book, we will tend to use the word 'company' (or, occasionally, 'corporation') to refer exclusively to incorporated for-profit business entities, whereas we will generally use the term 'firm' to denote capitalistic business enterprises (whether incorporated or unincorporated) more broadly.

and can have a determinative influence over the welfare of local communities including supply chains, tertiary service providers and public infrastructure networks. Meanwhile, higher level decisions with respect to the future development of relevant product and process technologies can have a significant bearing on the general level and direction of skills development and educational policy, both nationally and even, in some instances, globally. This is not to mention the longer-term effects of those corporate activities and decisions affecting the welfare of future generations, such as the extent (if any) that companies invest in the development of 'cleaner' or more environmentally sustainable methods of production, energy provision and transportation.

Of course, in an important sense *all* corporations, regardless of the scale and scope of their operations, can ultimately be regarded as the product of our own perpetual (re)making, albeit in a diffuse and disorderly way. This is because in contrast to sovereign state organs, capitalistic business organizations are subject to the competitive constraints of their surrounding *market* environment, which ordinarily inhibits the ambit of decisional discretion enjoyed by their managerial officers. Moreover, in cases where competitive market pressures fail to hold external corporate power sufficiently in check, it is generally accepted that the state has a crucial role to play in 'correcting' the underlying market failures via targeted regulatory interventions.[19] Such interventions include (*inter alia*) competition law measures aimed at curtailing particularly uncompetitive product market structures and practices, tort[20] and criminal law[21] principles that restrict the freedom of corporations to cause wrongful harm to persons outside of their immediate contractual networks, and domestic and international environmental laws designed to curtail firms' capacity to inflict negative externalities on their physical and ecological surroundings.[22]

Against this background, it is difficult to discern what precise 'value' – if any – corporate governance is capable of adding to the extraneous regulatory framework, in terms of providing an effective corporate power-checking mechanism that would not otherwise exist. Largely for this reason, the control of external corporate power is ordinarily not viewed as being within the remit of corporate governance, at least according to orthodox understandings of the

---

[19] See A.I. Ogus, *Regulation: Legal Form and Economic Theory* (Hart 2004), Ch. 2.

[20] See H. Hansmann and R. Kraakman, 'Towards Unlimited Shareholder Liability for Corporate Torts' (1991) 100 *Yale Law Journal* 1879; J. Armour, 'Corporate Personality and Assumption of Responsibility' (1999) *Lloyds' Maritime & Commercial Law Quarterly* 246 M. Petrin, 'Assumption of Responsibility in Corporate Groups: *Chandler v Cape plc*' (2013) 76 *Modern Law Review* 603.

[21] See C. Wells, *Corporations and Criminal Responsibility* (2nd ed., OUP 2001); C. Wells, 'Corporate Criminal Liability: A Ten Year Review' (2014) *Criminal Law Review* 849.

[22] See A. Perry-Kessaris, 'Corporate Liability for Environmental Harm' in M. Fitzmaurice and D.M. Ong (eds), *Research Handbook on International Environmental Law* (Edward Elgar 2007), Ch. 17; D.M. Ong, 'The Impact of Environmental Law on Corporate Governance: International and Comparative Perspectives' (2001) 12 *European Journal of International Law* 685.

subject. Notwithstanding, consistent with more contextual or 'progressive' views of corporate governance,[23] we will pay consideration at certain points in this book to some of the principal ramifications of external corporate power as it affects the interests of employees[24] and (to a lesser extent) other key corporate governance constituencies.[25]

The Internal/Private Dimension of Corporate Power

In the most basic and general sense of the word, 'power' can be understood – in the words of the economist John Kenneth Galbraith – as a state of affairs enabling the imposition by some person or group of 'its will and purpose on others, including on those who are reluctant or adverse'.[26] Building on Galbraith's definition, in this book we will understand internal or private corporate power essentially in terms of *inter-personal discretion*: that is to say, the discretion that certain individuals or groups within the firm enjoy to affect the interests of others in ways that the latter have not directly agreed to. Specifically, internal corporate power denotes the discretion that high-level corporate officeholders enjoy to administer the resources or funds of others in the pursuit of unilaterally determined objectives that the contributors may *or may not* commonly share.

Whilst both the external and the internal dimensions of corporate power are founded at root on the notion of managerial discretion, there is a notable distinction between them. On the one hand, external corporate power denotes general managerial discretion vis-à-vis all persons or interests in society potentially affected by a firm's operations, irrespective of whether they have a direct legal or economic relation with the firm. On the other hand, the discretionary element of internal corporate power pertains specifically to management's capacity to administer resources or funds entrusted to the firm by its contractual counterparties, and thus rests ultimately on a private-transactional basis.

Although numerous types of economic actor associated with corporations can – to varying extents – lay claim to being subject to internal corporate power in the above sense, one particular category of corporate participant nonetheless stands out as meriting special attention in this regard: that is, a firm's ordinary *shareholders* or equity holders. As we will explain further in Chapter 2, the resources of shareholders are – at least under normal circumstances – exposed to the vagaries of discretionary managerial decisions in a qualitatively more

---

[23] See, e.g. K. Greenfield, *The Failure of Corporate Law: Fundamental Flaws and Progressive Possibilities* (University of Chicago Press 2006); L.E. Mitchell (ed.), *Progressive Corporate Law (New Perspectives on Law, Culture & Society)* (Westview Press 1995); D. Millon, 'Communitarians, Contractarians, and the Crisis in Corporate Law' (1993) 50 *Washington and Lee Law Review* 1373.

[24] See Chapter 6.

[25] On the main corporate governance constituencies (or 'actors'), see below.

[26] Galbraith, above n. 12, 2.

significant way than those of any other type of economic actor connected with the firm, whether employees, lenders or trade creditors. This is because shareholders are in the unique position of being so-called 'incomplete' contractors with the firms in which their risk capital is invested, in the sense that neither (i) the specific productive uses to which their capital is put by management nor (ii) the compensatory rate of return on their invested capital is contractually specifiable in advance.

As we will see in Chapter 2, this creates a perceived need for alternative *extra*-contractual protections within the realm of corporate governance, whereby shareholders can gain a credible assurance that management will be motivated to exercise its discretion in a manner that is generally conducive to promoting shareholders' collective interests. Accordingly, when we speak about 'corporate power' in this book, unless indicated otherwise we will generally use the term to refer to the extent and forms of discretion exercised by senior corporate officeholders in making decisions outside of the direct control or oversight of shareholders. This is what economists commonly refer to as the core 'agency' problem lying at the heart of corporate governance (at least as in its so-called 'Anglo-American'[27] form), and which we will analyze further in the next chapter.

As the logical counterpart to determining how power is allocated within the firm, an effective corporate governance system must additionally ensure that such power is kept in check. In other words, those individuals or groups responsible for exercising corporate power must be held *accountable* for their discretionary decisions, as a prerequisite to maintaining the legitimacy of their decision-making authority from the perspective of those principally affected by it.[28] Indeed, it has been observed that 'modern governance – public as well as private – is at its core based on some form of accountability'.[29] Moreover, it has been shown that formal accountability mechanisms – particularly in the form of disclosure requirements – have tended historically to evolve as a natural counterbalance to discretionary decision-making authority within large organizations, and as an essential means of ensuring the subjection of power-holders to effective outside scrutiny.[30] Hence the need for effective norms and processes to ensure that senior corporate officeholders are continuously answerable to shareholders for their discretionary decisions concerning the ongoing administration of the firm's business and financial assets. We will discuss the specific corporate governance mechanisms that are customarily available in this regard throughout the book.

---

[27] On this term of reference, see below.

[28] On this, see Moore, above n. 17, 36–39.

[29] M.J. Dubnick, '*Sarbanes-Oxley* and the Search for Accountable Corporate Governance' in J. O'Brien (ed.), *Private Equity, Corporate Governance and the Dynamics of Capital Market Regulation* (Imperial College Press 2007) Ch. 9, 228.

[30] See *ibid*. On the general notion of counterbalance via 'countervailing power', see J.K. Galbraith, *American Capitalism: The Concept of Countervailing Power* (Houghton Mifflin 1952).

CORPORATE GOVERNANCE AS A PROBLEM OF PARTICULAR RELEVANCE FOR PUBLIC COMPANIES

In examining the allocation of decision-making power within large and socially significant business organizations, we will restrict the focus of our attention exclusively to so-called 'public' companies: that is, companies whose ordinary shares or equity securities are traded on a regulated public investment market. This is partly due to the especially vexing governance challenges that such firms pose in comparison to their 'private' or non-publicly-traded corporate counterparts,[31] and also on account of the general (albeit not universal) synonymy of 'public' and 'largeness' when it comes to correlating companies by status and relative size respectively. Indeed, although public companies constitute only a very small minority of the overall number of incorporated firms in the UK, in terms of collective market share and overall economic impact they are undoubtedly a dominant societal presence. This is unsurprising, given the unique capacity of public companies to attract capital from the many notionally 'passive' investors who lack the personal inclination, time or managerial acumen to undertake any sort of active entrepreneurial role within investee firms.

The (Normal) Ownership-Control Dynamic of Non-Anglo-American Public Companies

That the great majority of the largest-scale business organizations in the UK tend to take the form of publicly traded (as opposed to purely privately held) companies is, in itself, not especially unique or remarkable when viewed from a comparative point of view. Indeed, within almost any developed corporate ownership environment, it can be expected that the perceived exigencies of business growth will – to a greater or lesser extent – compel larger enterprises occasionally to 'tap' available equity capital resources outside of their immediate entrepreneurial, family or other associational networks. Generally speaking, whilst raising external capital on public investment markets will naturally expand a firm's shareholding base considerably, it need not necessarily occasion any seismic change to its basic ownership structure and dynamic.

Indeed, in the majority of developed corporate governance systems around the world, large-scale corporations have tended in general to retain their original family ownership model, with either the original founders or their familial descendants maintaining a dominant dual ownership-management – or, at least, ownership-control[32] – presence within the firm.[33] The persistence of

---

[31] As the government itself has recently acknowledged, '[t]he UK's strongest corporate governance and reporting standards are focused on public companies where the owners or shareholders are distant from the executives running the company. These standards provide independent shareholders with reassurance that the company is being run in their interests and that they have the information needed to hold the executive to account.' See Green Paper, above n. 4, 43.

[32] On the precise distinction between 'ownership' and 'control' as corporate governance attributes, see below.

[33] See C.A. Mallin, *Corporate Governance* (5th ed., OUP 2015), Ch. 5.

concentrated family ownership and control is a particularly prominent charac-
teristic of large corporations in most Southern European, Latin American and
South-East Asian countries, including (*inter alia*) Italy, Spain, Brazil, Mexico,
Hong Kong and South Korea.[34]

In other countries where family ownership is less proportionally widespread,
large corporations still tend to retain some form of dominant ownership presence, in the form of a single majority shareholder or at least a heavily concentrated
group of so-called 'blockholding' investors.[35] For instance, in the 'socialist market economy' of the People's Republic of China, the nation's largest and most
strategically important business enterprises (so-called state-owned enterprises or
'SOEs') – whilst set up ostensibly in the form of public companies – nonetheless
tend to operate under *de facto* government control via an extensive network of
indirect state majority shareholdings.[36] In Germany, meanwhile, large-scale commercial lending banks have traditionally (albeit to a decreasing extent today)
operated as the principal blockholder presence within large domestic industrial corporations, whether on an individual or collective basis.[37] Arguably the
world's most institutionally sophisticated blockholder system of large-scale corporate ownership, though, is the much studied 'keiretsu' (or 'network') ownership
model observed in Japan, which essentially features an elaborate system of cross-
shareholdings enabling major industrial corporations to forge relatively informal
vertical linkages with their principal suppliers, distributors and/or lending banks.[38]

In spite of their significant structural, cultural and political differences, all of
the above corporate ownership models are united in sharing a common fundamental feature: that is, the preservation within large corporations – and even
within those constituted as public companies – of some sort of loosely unified
entrepreneurial or quasi-entrepreneurial presence. In other words, the dominant equity ownership interest group within the firm is the same as – or closely
affiliated with – the firm's high-level managerial or controlling agents.[39] A dual
ownership-control interest grouping is thus retained at the heart of the firm,
albeit that the precise constitution and boundaries of this coalition within any
particular firm may often be difficult to discern precisely. Accordingly, the principal corporate governance problem in such systems has traditionally tended

---

[34] See *ibid.*, part 4; A.M. Fleckner and K.J. Hopt, *Comparative Corporate Governance: A
Functional and International Analysis* (Cambridge University Press 2013).
[35] On this notion generally, see A. Edmans, 'Blockholders and Corporate Governance' (2014)
6 *Annual Review of Financial Economics* 23.
[36] See G. Yu, *Comparative Corporate Governance in China: Political Economy and Legal
Infrastructure* (Routledge 2007), 25–27; I. MacNeil, 'Adaptation and Convergence in
Corporate Governance: The Case of Chinese Listed Companies' (2002) 2 *Journal of Corporate
Law Studies* 298, 298–301.
[37] See S. Vitols, 'Changes in Germany's Bank-Based Financial System: Implications for
Corporate Governance' (2005) 13 *Corporate Governance: An International Review* 386.
[38] See T. Hoshi, 'Japanese Corporate Governance as a System' in K.J. Hopt, H. Kanda, M.J.
Roe, E. Wymeersch and S. Prigge (eds), *Comparative Corporate Governance: The State of the
Art and Emerging Research* (OUP 1998), Ch. 11(a).
[39] R. La Porta, F. Lopez-de-Silanes, A. Shleifer and R. Vishny, 'Investor Protection and
Corporate Governance' (2000) 58 *Journal of Financial Economics* 3, 13–15.

to be the challenge of ensuring that the majority or controlling ownership influence does not abuse its dominant position in a manner that is oppressive towards, or manifestly inconsiderate of, minority (or 'outside') shareholder interests (the so-called 'majority v. minority' conflict). However, for reasons that shall become apparent below, this is not a problem that has traditionally tended to afflict Anglo-American public companies given their fundamentally different ownership and control dynamics.[40]

The (Abnormal) Ownership-Control Dynamic of Anglo-American Public Companies

However, if concentrated (and especially family) ownership and control is, in terms of international popularity, justifiably regarded as the world's 'normal' corporate governance model, then it follows that the United Kingdom and United States together represent the outlying 'abnormal' group of countries in this regard.[41] Indeed, the basic defining feature of the so-called 'Anglo-American' corporate ownership and governance model[42] resides in the fact that the equity securities of large-scale public corporations in the United Kingdom and United States, in stark distinction from those of their international peers, are *almost wholly* subject to 'outside' or non-entrepreneurial ownership. That is to say, the dominant pattern of shareholding observed within UK and US public companies is extremely wide ownership dispersion involving a multitude of small-scale investors, who typically fulfil no materially significant management or direct control function.[43]

The flip-side to this comparatively unique ownership model is that direct powers of control over large corporations tend to be entrusted not to traditional entrepreneurial owners, but rather to specialized managerial personnel. Such officeholders receive a contractual remuneration in fundamentally the same vein as any other employee of the firm, and are selected principally on grounds of professional expertise or merit as opposed to any pre-existing proprietary, familial or commercial relationship with their employer firms.[44] This effective 'de-entrepreneurialization' of Anglo-American public companies is undoubtedly the most peculiar structural characteristic of large-scale UK and US corporations when viewed from an international perspective. Moreover, it

---

[40] Although majority v. minority conflicts do, of course, remain a significant potential problem within closely-held or private companies in the United Kingdom (and, likewise, the United States).

[41] R. La Porta, F. Lopez-de-Silanes, A. Shleifer and R. Vishny, 'Corporate Ownership around the World' (1999) 54 *The Journal of Finance* 471, 474.

[42] On this notion generally, see M.T. Moore and A. Rebérioux, 'Revitalizing the Institutional Roots of Anglo-American Corporate Governance' (2011) 40 *Economy and Society* 84, 86–90.

[43] For the classical academic exposition of this phenomenon, see A.A. Berle and G. Means, *The Modern Corporation and Private Property* (revised ed., Harcourt, Brace & World 1968; first published 1932), Book I.

[44] See *ibid.*, Ch. VI.

has for a long time been a major source of concern for effective governance of large business organizations within these two countries.[45]

Curiously, one of the earliest recorded critiques of the institution that we would today refer to as the Anglo-American public company came from a writer who is commonly regarded as the intellectual forefather of free market capitalism itself, namely Adam Smith. In spite of Smith's general support of international free trade and other market-liberal economic policies, he was deeply sceptical of the functionality and longevity of the so-called 'joint-stock' companies that were becoming an increasingly prominent feature of early industrial Britain in the late 1700s. According to Smith:

> The directors of such companies … being the managers rather of other people's money than of their own, it cannot well be expected, that they should watch over it with the same anxious vigilance with which the partners in a private copartnery frequently watch over their own.[46]

Smith claimed that the basic misalignment of personal incentives between investors and directors meant that 'negligence and profusion, therefore, must always prevail, more or less, in the management of the affairs of such a company'.[47] Smith's only consolation in this regard was his apparent belief that the then-fledgling breed of British joint-stock companies would before long be eradicated by competition from their more highly focused and incentivized entrepreneurial counterparts.[48]

Whilst Adam Smith was proved right on many things by the course of time, his predicted premature death of the joint-stock company never occurred. In fact, little did Smith know that these remarkable business entities would – over the course of the next two centuries – go on to reach previously unimaginable heights in terms of their operational scale and bureaucratic complexity. As it transpired, though, the ultimate modern manifestation of the joint-stock company was to appear not in early industrial Britain, but rather in the much more technologically and organizationally advanced setting of the twentieth-century American economy.[49] A number of commentators in the early part of the twentieth century – most notable amongst these the esteemed US corporate lawyer and statesman Adolf Berle – picked up on a latent but highly

---

[45] See, e.g. A.A. Berle, 'For Whom Corporate Managers *Are* Trustees: A Note' (1932) 45 *Harvard Law Review* 1365; M. Friedman, 'The Social Responsibility of Business Is to Increase Its Profits' in T. Beauchamp and N. Bowie (eds), *Ethical Theory and Business* (Pearson 2004; article originally published in *The New York Times Magazine* (1970)).

[46] A. Smith, *An Inquiry into the Nature and Causes of the Wealth of Nations*, R.H. Campbell and A.S. Skinner (eds) (Clarendon Press 1976; first published 1776), 741.

[47] *ibid.*

[48] *ibid.* Smith claimed that 'joint stock companies … have seldom been able to maintain the competition against private adventurers'.

[49] On this generally, see A.D. Chandler, *Scale and Scope: The Dynamics of Industrial Capitalism* (new ed., Harvard University Press 1994; first published 1990), Part II.

remarkable structural development that seemed to have occurred within the largest American industrial organizations of the time.[50]

In many of the larger-scale manufacturing concerns of the so-called 'first' industrial revolution that took place in late-eighteenth- and nineteenth-century Britain, the separation of business ownership from direct enterprise *management* would certainly appear to have occurred to some extent, as manifested in relatively primitive forms of professional managerial personnel such as the Victorian factory foreman. However, in such organizations, the relevant entrepreneurial or family ownership body typically retained ultimate powers of enterprise *control*, in the sense of being readily able to (i) determine the general goals and strategic direction of the business and (ii) supervise, discipline and, where necessary, replace underperforming or otherwise undesired managerial agents.

By contrast, in the rapidly evolving American corporate behemoths of the early twentieth century's 'second' industrial revolution – such as General Electric, General Motors, and the American Telephone and Telegraph Company – shareholding had become so widespread and fragmented that there could be said to exist *no remotely coordinated control presence* within these companies' respective ownership bases, resulting in a substantially complete separation of corporate ownership from corporate control.[51]

The Separation of Ownership and Control

Writing in 1932, Berle (in conjunction with his co-author Gardiner Means) described this remarkable phenomenon in the following succinct terms:

> The separation of ownership from control produces a condition where the interests of owner and of *ultimate* manager may, and often do, diverge, and where many of the checks which formerly operated to limit the use of power disappeared.[52]

From a shareholder perspective, the so-called 'separation of ownership from control' in widely-held public companies derives from a combination of collective supervisory inertia and (understandable) business ineptitude. As regards the former of these factors, it can be said that – *prima facie* – broadly dispersed and diversified (i.e. invested in multiple companies) minority shareholders individually have no compelling incentive or effective means to mobilize themselves in collective opposition to powerful corporate managers. This is because any prospective shareholder gains from such efforts in terms of consequently improved business performance and profitability – once shared amongst the company's broad shareholder base as a whole – will likely be individually miniscule and thus, in general, not worth the candle.[53]

---

[50] See Berle and Means, above n. 43.
[51] *ibid.*, 112–13.
[52] *ibid.*, 7.

In terms of the latter factor, meanwhile, even to the limited extent that coordinated shareholder control efforts *are* feasible from a collective-incentive point of view, whether or not such action is generally *beneficial* for shareholders (let alone society as a whole) is a highly contested issue, given professional managers' typical decision-making advantages over their shareholder counterparts in terms of access to relevant knowledge, information and business acumen.[54]

That this peculiar organizational governance structure was – by 1932 – becoming economically *inevitable* did not, in Berle and Means' view, necessarily render it socially *desirable*. Indeed, Berle and Means identified a number of highly concerning economic and socio-political implications of this potentially divergent dual ownership-control model, centred on the effective extinction of the classical owner-entrepreneur as the pivotal proprietary interest within the modern business firm. In particular, they explained how:

> the organization under the system of private enterprise has rested upon the self-interest of the property owner – a self-interest held in check by competition and the conditions of supply and demand. Such self-interest has long been regarded as the best guarantee of economic efficiency. It has been assumed that, if the individual is protected in the right both to use his property as he sees fit and to receive the full fruits of its use, his desire for personal gain, for profits, can be relied upon as an effective incentive to his efficient use of any industrial property he may possess.[55]

As against this, however, the separation of ownership and control within modern public companies entailed that the managers of such firms – insofar as they lacked any obvious proprietary or prudential motivation to make productive use of the firm's assets – could no longer be regarded as having their decision-making power held effectively 'in check' by the standard entrepreneurial precept of competitive self-interest pursuit.[56] Berle and Means feared that if this new breed of professional managers were to pursue what they perceived as their rational self-interest when exercising corporate decision-making functions, the outcome for shareholders (and indeed society generally) would be undesirable,

---

[53] This is the essential logic of the classical 'collective action' problem afflicting the coordinated activity of large groups (including – *inter alia* – public company shareholders), whereby the rational passivity of individual group members leads – en masse – to a collectively detrimental outcome for the group as a whole. The ensuing hypothesis is that, at least absent appropriate extraneous interventions, '*rational, self-interested individuals will not act to achieve their common or group interests*'. See M. Olson, *The Logic of Collective Action: Public Goods and the Theory of Groups* (Harvard University Press 1971; first published 1965), 2.

[54] For a fuller analysis of this issue, see Chapter 4. See also S.M. Bainbridge, 'Director Primacy: The Means and Ends of Corporate Governance' (2003) 97 *Northwestern University Law Review* 547.

[55] Berle and Means, above n. 43, 9.

[56] *ibid.*

given the very different incentives of (proprietary) shareholders and (non-proprietary) managers respectively.[57]

In sketching the dominant governance features of the modern public company in their epochal 1932 work *The Modern Corporation and Private Property*,[58] Berle and Means were writing about what was at the time a distinctly American phenomenon. Indeed, with limited exceptions, large-scale *British* business organizations would generally remain the province of dominant entrepreneurial or family controllers throughout at least the first half of the twentieth century, notwithstanding the influence of the London Stock Exchange in engendering widespread public share ownership.[59] As Brian Cheffins' work has demonstrated, it was not until the latter half of that century – in particular, the period from the 1950s through to the 1970s – that truly separate ownership and control in the Berle-Means sense became a characteristic feature of the UK's corporate governance landscape.[60]

As a result of the above developments, though, it is with considerable empirical justification today that corporate governance commentators (including the present authors) have tended to refer – somewhat generically – to the so-called 'Anglo-American' corporate governance model when alluding to UK and US public companies' peculiar but mutually common ownership-control dynamic.[61] Accordingly, we will likewise make reference to this term in the chapters that follow. At the same time, though, we would urge a degree of caution in accepting the empirical validity of the 'Anglo-American' descriptor too readily at face value, at least without being alert to the significant outstanding differences between the UK and the US corporate governance systems in terms of the effect of their respective legal, market and political environments.[62] Where relevant, we will make reference to the most important of these differences throughout the book.

DISTINGUISHING THE MAIN CORPORATE GOVERNANCE CONSTITUENCIES (OR 'ACTORS')

Given this book's predominant focus on the UK corporate governance framework, we are specifically concerned with the principal groups of corporate governance 'actors' as they are typically constituted within Anglo-American public

[57] *ibid.*, 113–14. An assessment of the fascinating theoretical debate on whether the separation of ownership from control in Anglo-American public companies should be regarded principally as a positive (beneficial) or negative (problematic) phenomenon – and the correspondingly appropriate responses thereto – will be reserved for the following chapter.
[58] Above n. 43.
[59] See Chandler, above n. 49, Ch. 7; B.R. Cheffins, *Corporate Ownership and Control: British Business Transformed* (OUP 2008), esp. Ch. 8.
[60] See Cheffins, *ibid.*, esp. Chs 9 and 10.
[61] See e.g. Moore and Rebérioux, above n. 42; T. Clarke, 'Recurring Crises in Anglo-American Corporate Governance' (2010) 29 *Contributions to Political Economy* 9; S. Deakin, 'Anglo-American Corporate Governance and the Employment Relation: A Case to Answer' (2006) 4 *Socio-Economic Review* 155.
[62] On this, see C.M. Bruner, *Corporate Governance in the Common-Law World: The Political Foundations of Shareholder Power* (Cambridge University Press 2013); Moore, above n. 17, Chs 4 and 5.

companies. Of particular concern – both here and elsewhere in the book – is the distinction between what are conventionally perceived as the three central corporate governance constituencies within the Anglo-American model, namely: (i) shareholders, (ii) directors and (iii) managers. However, we will also pay due regard to employees and the general public as broader social constituencies, which – whilst ordinarily not as directly implicated as the above groups in the core allocation of corporate decision-making power – nonetheless are significantly affected by corporate governance laws and norms.[63] Finally, we include regulators as a somewhat peculiar class of corporate governance constituency. As we will see, regulators' interests are in some cases broadly aligned with those of the general public, although in other instances they can diverge.

The 'Core' Constituencies: Shareholders, Directors and Managers

In simpler business entities, including many private or closely-held companies, the above roles tend to be more or less fused together. Accordingly, the same person or affiliated group of persons will simultaneously manage the day-to-day running of the business (in their managerial capacity), determine the firm's general strategic direction and business policies (in their directorial capacity) and provide the firm's sole or main source of 'ownership' or equity capital (in their shareholder capacity).

As discussed above, this basic unified structure also persists – albeit in much greater bureaucratic complexity – within the large family-controlled and other blockholder concerns that are characteristic of most non-Anglo-American corporate governance systems. However, in Anglo-American public companies, the above three core governance functions are typically trifurcated, with the effect that business management, direction and ownership are vested in the hands of three largely separate constituencies, which each bring a correspondingly distinct set of attributes and interests to the firm's proverbial governance table. It is therefore imperative to understand the unique contributions provided by managers, directors and shareholders respectively to an effective corporate governance system.

While the term 'manager' is to a large extent self-explanatory, it nonetheless potentially encapsulates a very broad and multifarious range of personnel within large business organizations, from 'top' corporate or group management right down to lower-level branch managers and team supervisors. We should therefore make clear that, in using this generic term, we are referring specifically to senior managerial or executive officeholders, who hold a significant ambit of power and responsibility in seeking to ensure that the firm's high-level strategic objectives are successfully *executed*: that is to say, that the firm's day-to-day business operations and policies (whether as an individual company or multi-corporate group) are conducive to fulfilment of those objectives, and also to the achievement of any corresponding financial or non-financial performance targets.

---

[63] On the status of employees vis-à-vis UK corporate governance, see Chapter 6.

In addition to the Chief Executive Officer (or 'CEO'), this category of officeholders customarily also includes the firm's Chief Finance Officer (or 'CFO'), Chief Operating Officer (or 'COO'), and – particularly in the case of large banking and other financial concerns today – the Chief Risk Officer (or 'CRO').[64] Additional senior managerial offices, or variations on the above office titles, can commonly be observed in practice. Whilst in UK public companies the majority of such so-called 'top' managers will tend simultaneously to sit on the board of directors of the firm that they lead, this need not necessarily be so. Indeed, it is often the case that certain sub-board executive officeholders can wield particularly significant power within the firm's managerial hierarchy, notwithstanding their formal absence from the board of directors itself.[65]

Whereas management is charged principally with ensuring the effective *execution* of the firm's high-level strategic objectives, the collective function of the board of directors[66] is essentially to *formulate* those objectives, and subsequently *supervise* management's execution thereof.[67] Crucially, though, supervision of management's performance of its executive functions is *not* the same as – or even tantamount to – the actual *assumption* of those functions by the board of directors itself. Rather, directors' collective supervisory activities are, within public companies at least, carried out on an *intermittent* and *periodic* basis.[68] This is in contrast to management's executive activities, which are of an ongoing nature. Moreover, with limited exceptions (most notably the CEO and the CFO), the composition of a firm's board of directors is distinct from the corresponding composition of its senior management team.[69]

Hence the board of directors is ordinarily the principal high-level corporate *control* organ, in distinction from the senior executive team which comprises the firm's main top-level *management* organ. Accordingly, to revert back to our above discussion of the separation of ownership and control in Anglo-American

---

[64] On this particular function, see Sir D. Walker, *A Review of Corporate Governance in UK Banks and Other Financial Industry Entities: Final Recommendations* (26 November 2009), paras 6.21–6.25; M.T. Moore, 'The Evolving Contours of the Board's Risk Management Function in UK Corporate Governance (2010) 10 *Journal of Corporate Law Studies* 279, 296–97; M. Power, 'Organizational Responses to Risk: The Rise of the Chief Risk Officer' in B. Hutter and M. Power (eds), *Organizational Encounters with Risk* (Cambridge University Press 2005), 132.

[65] This has notably been so in the case of the heads of investment banking divisions of major financial conglomerates, particularly prior to the 2007–08 financial crisis.

[66] For a more detailed examination of the monitoring functions of boards of directors, see Chapter 7.

[67] See UK Corporate Goverance Code, above n. 2, Supporting Principle A.1; *Equitable Life Assurance Society v Bowley* [2004] 1 BCLC 180.

[68] For the classical (albeit now somewhat outdated) judicial dictum to this effect, see *Re City Equitable Fire Insurance Company Ltd* [1925] 1 Ch 407 *per* Romer J, 429: 'A director is not bound to give continuous attention to the affairs of his company. His duties are of an intermittent nature to be performed at periodical board meetings.'

[69] On this, see UK Corporate Governance Code, above n. 2, Code Provision B.1.2 (examined in greater detail in Chapter 7).

public companies, it is strictly speaking the *board of directors*, rather than management itself, which assumes the crucial corporate 'control' function historically ceded by shareholders. The specific details of the board of directors' key role in corporate governance will be addressed further in Chapter 7.

As regards the customary governance role of shareholders, meanwhile, a more detailed demographic analysis of this large and diverse corporate governance constituency will follow in Chapter 5. For present purposes, though, we should emphasize that it is fundamentally debatable whether the purported ownership 'function' of shareholders should really be described as 'functional' in any meaningful sense of the term.[70] Moreover, as we will explore further in Chapter 4, it is even questionable as to whether public company shareholders can properly be referred to as corporate 'owners' in any legally or economically valid respect, given the artificial and highly attenuated nature of their proprietary relation with investee companies.[71] We do not believe this to be the case, notwithstanding recent policy initiatives aimed at reinvigorating shareholders' perceived 'ownership' responsibilities in UK public companies.[72]

In the following chapter, we will analyze a particularly influential theoretical claim today to the effect that shareholders fulfil a structurally crucial 'residual risk bearing' function within public companies, given the uniquely uncertain and contractually open-ended nature of their economic relation with investee firms. For present purposes, though, we will proceed on the basic premise that corporate shareholding – like any aspect of ownership – is, first and foremost, a species of positive *right* rather than negative responsibility. Shareholders are therefore most appropriately regarded as relatively passive *beneficiaries* of public companies' productive and wealth-generating activities, as opposed to active and engaged participants therein.

As an important point of clarification, it should be noted that the terms 'shareholders' and 'investors' are often erroneously used synonymously with each another. However, the latter group of actors is considerably wider than the former, and potentially includes common types of public company investor other than standard equity capital investors, such as debt investors (whether commercial lenders or bondholders) and purchasers of equity derivatives.[73] Moreover, the broader definitional category of 'investors' – particularly as it is commonly used within the securities or capital markets law domain – tends to

---

[70] On this, see P. Ireland, 'Defending the *Rentier*: Corporate Theory and the Reprivatisation of the Public Company' in J. Parkinson, A. Gamble and G. Kelly, *The Political Economy of the Company* (Hart Publishing 2000), Ch. 7, 171.

[71] See P. Ireland, 'Company Law and the Myth of Shareholder Ownership' (1999) 62 *Modern Law Review* 32.

[72] On this, see Chapter 5.

[73] These include so-called contracts-for-difference or 'CfDs', which essentially give their 'purchaser' indirect exposure to equity investment risk in a particular company without the accompanying need to hold actual shares in that firm. On this, see Chapter 5, fn. 15. See also Financial Conduct Authority, *Consultation Paper: Enhancing conduct of business rules for firms providing contract for difference products to retail clients* (December 2016).

refer not just to the present holders of a particular company's shares, but rather to the broader public investment community *in general*. Given the more micro focus of corporate governance law, on the other hand, it is more customary in this latter context to use the term 'shareholders', which typically denotes a particular company's *existing* ownership base. In view of the above considerations, this book will therefore normally use the term 'shareholder' in preference to 'investor', unless the context demands otherwise.

Finally, we would highlight that – when referring to 'shareholders' in the book – we are referring specifically to 'ordinary' shareholders or equity investors, whose relationship with the firm is essentially of a risk capitalist nature. This is in distinction from other formal legal classes of shareholder, such as preference and deferred shareholders.[74] Whilst such alternative shareholder classes – and especially preference shareholders – are by no means uncommon in UK public companies, their typical legal characteristics (including, in the case of most preference shareholders, the lack of corporate voting rights) are such as to render them of limited direct relevance to core corporate governance practices.

Other Key Constituencies: Employees, the General Public and Regulators

As should become apparent from reading Part II of this book, a further comparatively noteworthy feature of the Anglo-American corporate governance system is its traditional exclusion of employee interests as a perceived direct concern of corporate governance.[75] Rather – as will be explained throughout this book – the central normative thrust of corporate governance law in both the United Kingdom and the United States dictates that public company boards, in exercising their high-level control and managerial-supervisory responsibilities – should be held accountable first and foremost to a company's general body of *shareholders*. This fundamental notion – which, as we will see, is derived in some part from established legal principles and in other part from prevailing capital market pressures – is frequently referred to as the 'shareholder primacy' norm.[76]

Consideration of the specific nature, origins and ramifications of the shareholder primacy norm within Anglo-American corporate governance will be reserved for later in the book.[77] At present, though, it is important to highlight

---

[74] For a detailed analysis of the principal classes of share in UK companies, see P.L. Davies and S. Worthington, *Gower and Davies' Principles of Modern Company Law* (9th ed., Sweet & Maxwell 2012), 865–72.

[75] On this, see Chapter 6 in particular.

[76] See e.g. J. Armour, S. Deakin and S.J. Konzelmann, 'Shareholder Primacy and the Trajectory of UK Corporate Governance' (2003) 41 *British Journal of Industrial Relations* 531; P. Ireland, 'Shareholder Primacy and the Distribution of Wealth' (2005) 68 *Modern Law Review* 49; L.A. Stout, 'Bad and Not-So-Bad Arguments for Shareholder Primacy' (2002) 75 *Southern California Law Review* 1189.

[77] See, in particular, Chapter 6.

the curiosity of the fact that employees are afforded limited direct considera-tion within UK corporate governance law. Indeed, this may strike some readers as remarkable, given the centrality of employment to our day-to-day relations with corporations as citizens, coupled with the direct subjection to corporate power that our employment capacity frequently entails.[78] Accordingly, it might reasonably be expected that, if there is any particular 'actor' guise in which cit-izens ought to be able to hold corporate decision-making power effectively to account, then surely it should be in their *employee* (rather than shareholder) capacity?

Indeed, as we will discuss further in Chapter 6, the Anglo-American sys-tem's near-exclusive focus on shareholders as the perceived rightful beneficiary of corporate governance norms and processes puts it at odds with a number of major European systems in this regard, including those of Germany, the Netherlands and Sweden. In those jurisdictions, by contrast, the dual incorpo-ration of shareholders and employees (albeit in slightly varying, country-specific ways) into the core decision-making processes of larger scale corporations – via a sophisticated legal phenomenon known as 'co-determination' – has been a long established and firmly entrenched feature of the national corporate gov-ernance landscape.[79] Some explanations, both conceptual and historical, for Anglo-American corporate governance law's traditional and characteristic resistance to co-determination and other formal worker involvement mecha-nisms will be offered in Chapters 2 and 6 of this book, respectively.

Anglo-American corporate governance law has not only been traditionally resistant to direct worker involvement in corporate decision-making specifi-cally, but also to the factoring of broader 'public interest' considerations into corporate decision-making more generally. That is not to deny that corpo-rations should be of benefit to the general public. However, as we will see in Chapter 2, the orthodox approach to understanding corporate governance regards the general public as benefitting from effective corporate governance processes in a largely *indirect* way.

Essentially, the theory goes that where a corporation is efficiently run and thereby generates high profits for its shareholders, the resultant wealth created by its management will – in some way or other – produce a number of 'trickle down' material benefits for the public at large in their overlapping economic capacities as shareholders, consumers, employees and/or beneficiaries of corporation tax revenues. This arguably precludes the need for direct regulatory determination of the social-distributional outcomes of corporate activity. It likewise purportedly precludes the need for direct legal or social articulation of any generally accepted

---

[78] On this, see Chapter 6.

[79] See K.J. Hopt, 'Comparative Corporate Governance: The State of the Art and International Regulation' in Fleckner and Hopt, above n. 34, Ch. 1, 75–80; S. Vitols, 'Varieties of Corporate Governance: Comparing Germany and the UK' in P.A. Hall and D. Soskice, *Varieties of Capitalism: The Institutional Foundations of Comparative Advantage* (OUP 2001), Ch. 10.

understanding of the public interest in economic organization, or at least one that is independent of the narrow prudential interest of shareholders in ensuring an efficient and privately profitable corporate sector *per se*.[80]

Of course, it may reasonably be expected that – to the extent corporate governance practices and processes are effectively regulated – then they will be designed in a manner that is broadly conducive to the public interest *in any event*, given the apparently natural correlation within democratic law-making environments between the respective interests of regulators and the general public. However, this is not always the case. Indeed, as we will explain further in Chapter 3, the regulatory landscape in UK corporate governance is considerably more complex and multi-faceted than a traditionally state-centric, 'command and control' understanding of regulation would suggest. Rather, the 'regulator' constituency encapsulates a range of different rule-making bodies, of varying levels of administrative formality and situated at differing linear points on the public-to-private spectrum.

In particular, certain of the most influential rule-making bodies in UK corporate governance, such as the Financial Reporting Council[81] and the Takeover Panel,[82] are – both constitutionally and operationally – situated very close (relative to standard public law-making bodies) to the private business and market actors who are subject to their regulatory authority. This has significant implications in terms of how these bodies perceive the proper bounds of their regulatory remit, as well as in relation to the scope of social interests which are conventionally encapsulated within such bodies' policymaking activities and decisions.

A final important point of note with respect to the role of regulators in corporate governance concerns the inherently limited role of law as an effective behavioural influence within this field. We will see throughout the book that in the corporate governance context, law tends in general (although by no means always) to operate less as a directly coercive state 'command' mechanism, and more as an indirect (or 'reflexive'[83]) stimulant for other salient social-institutional pressures. Such 'soft' pressures include market forces; prevailing social, moral or political opinions; or, commonly, a combination of the above. However, far from negating or even undermining the role of the lawyer in corporate governance, the complex and multi-layered social dynamic of the field calls for the development of a broader, more sophisticated and more inter-disciplinary toolkit of skills than has traditionally been required on the part of commercial lawyers. And it is to the task of developing this particular 'toolkit' in readers that the book is principally geared.

---

[80] For a fuller discussion of this general (so-called 'contractarian') line of thought, see Chapter 2.

[81] See www.frc.org.uk/.

[82] See www.thetakeoverpanel.org.uk/.

[83] On the notion of legal reflexivity generally, see G. Teubner, *Law as an Autopoietic System* (Blackwell 1993). For an application of this theoretical concept to the specific field of corporate governance, see G. Teubner, 'Corporate Fiduciary Duties and Their Beneficiaries: A Functional Approach to the Legal Institutionalization of Corporate Responsibility' in K.J. Hopt and G. Teubner (eds), *Corporate Governance and Directors' Liabilities* (De Gruyter 1985), 149.

CHAPTER 2

Corporate Governance and Theory of the Firm

In the previous chapter, we defined corporate governance from an academic perspective in terms of an enquiry into the causes and consequences of the allocation of corporate decision-making power. In particular, we explained how Anglo-American corporate governance is centrally concerned with how discretionary decision-making power is allocated within widely-held public companies, and – correspondingly – how senior corporate officeholders are held accountable for their continuing exercise of such power. We believe that this general understanding of corporate governance is shared more or less by all those who study and write about the subject academically in the United Kingdom and the United States, regardless of their particular normative disposition.

Notwithstanding, a major argumentative fault line has long existed with respect to precisely how the above goals should be achieved. Accordingly, one's perspective on how corporate power is most appropriately allocated and held in check is, on a fundamental level, conditioned implicitly by how one perceives the essential nature of a business corporation. That is to say, from a conceptual or meta-physical viewpoint, essentially *what is* a corporation in terms of the basic matter of its existence as a social institution? Only when we have dealt with the above question are we subsequently in a position to enquire as to the rightful allocation of corporate power. This complex and often controversial sub-field of interdisciplinary debate in corporate governance is referred to as corporate theory or, more commonly, *theory of the firm.*

As we will see below, there are – generally speaking – two overarching theoretical paradigms of the corporation or 'firm', which condition our basic understanding of what a corporation is, and also our corresponding view as to the most appropriate way of allocating corporate power within society. The first of these paradigms is the so-called 'entity' theory of the firm, which essentially depicts the corporation as a distinct and autonomous entity 'in itself', whose existence and corresponding responsibilities transcend the various private identities and interests of any of its human component 'parts', acquiring something of a collectivist or quasi-public quality. The second of these paradigms is the 'contractarian' theory of the firm, which contrarily views the corporation as having no distinct existence or interests in itself. That is, at least independently of the aggregate private identities and interests of its various human constituents as expressed via their consensual market interactions with one another.

The entity paradigm tends to be responsive to the perceived 'wider' social responsibilities of corporations beyond the private imperatives of their immediate market environment. The contractarian paradigm, by contrast, is generally hostile to the recognition of corporate social responsibilities, at least beyond those perceived responsibilities that emanate either directly or indirectly from market pressures. Chief amongst these, as we will show, is the so-called 'shareholder wealth maximization' norm that represents the normative centrepiece of the contractarian corporate governance model.

Whilst the contractarian theory of the firm undoubtedly remains the dominant ideological reference point for students and scholars of Anglo-American corporate governance today, its core propositions have by no means gone unchallenged in recent years. In particular, as we will see, the alternative 'stakeholder' variant of contractarianism has – somewhat paradoxically – sought to exploit the theory's underlying logic to support prescriptive conclusions that are generally averse to those favoured by orthodox proponents of the contractarian paradigm. Nonetheless, the continuing ideological dominance of the contractarian perspective, coupled with its general descriptive relevance when applied to rationalize the UK's corporate governance landscape, arguably justifies our adoption of this particular thought paradigm as the central conceptual reference point for our discussion in the remainder of the book.

THE IMPORTANCE[1] OF THEORY TO THE STUDY OF CORPORATE GOVERNANCE

The word 'theory' is frequently misunderstood and tends to mean different things to different people, especially in the field of law.[2] In essence, a theory is an academic characterization of a particular phenomenon, which is intended to influence how that subject matter is conventionally perceived and understood. The way in which a phenomenon is characterized academically is of enormous

---

[1] Although we believe that most corporate governance scholars would regard theoretical questions concerning the essential nature of the business firm as being important, there is nonetheless a particular line of scholarship that doubts the purported practical relevance of such issues. That is, at least in relation to (arguably more important) functional or consequentialist questions concerning the actual real-world *effects* of corporate activity when viewed from an economic and/or social standpoint. On this, see M. Petrin, 'Reconceptualizing the Theory of the Firm: From Nature to Function' (2013) 118 *Penn State Law Review* 1; J. Dewey, 'The Historic Background of Corporate Legal Personality' (1926) 35 *Yale Law Journal* 655. Notwithstanding these dissenting perspectives on the matter, though, we believe that the continuing academic influence and popularity of traditional theories of the firm justifies their analysis in this chapter. However, readers should feel free to form their own critical opinions as to the descriptive relevance and normative appeal of each of the principal strands of thought that we will discuss here.

[2] On this, see B.R. Cheffins, 'Using Theory to Study Law: A Company Law Perspective' (1999) 58 *The Cambridge Law Journal* 197.

and often underappreciated significance. How we tend to characterize some-thing affects how we customarily think about it, write about it and teach it. Crucially, it also affects our *normative* perspective on that subject. That is to say, it determines what we regard to be its strengths and weaknesses, its 'rights' and 'wrongs', and the appropriate course of its future development.

Just as the purpose of an artistic caricature is to accentuate the most distinc-tive or noteworthy features of a person rather than portray their every literal detail, the objective of an academic characterization is to emphasize and draw on the key distinguishing features of a subject, rather than to document that phe-nomenon in all of its complexity. Inevitably, therefore, the process of academic characterization – in law as elsewhere – involves some marginal degree of papering over the empirical cracks. That is to say, the occasional outlying or idiosyncratic feature is conveniently (and quite acceptably) elided so as not to detract from the essential qualities of the subject that the writer is seeking to accentuate. Therefore an academic characterization, like an artistic caricature, need not be one hundred per cent comprehensive in documenting a subject, nor sensitive to its every empir-ical nuance. As a minimum requirement, however, the characterization must be capable of incorporating *all materially significant* features of its subject matter, or else the ensuing model will lose its essential representational quality.

Moreover, the process of academically characterizing a subject involves not just an empirical but also a normative dimension. These two elements necessarily overlap and reinforce one other. Inevitably, the answer to the empirical question – that is, what essentially *is* a given phenomenon – affects our answer to the ensuing normative question – that is, what essential form or qualities *should* that phenomenon embody? Thus in any field of social science (including law), con-structive academic debate involves scholars providing competing characteriza-tions of the essential (empirical) nature of a thing on a definitional level, in order to establish (or change) the points of references in accordance with which the effi-cacy or desirability of that phenomenon can subsequently be judged from a more critical perspective. In other words, *ought* judgements are ultimately dependent to a large extent on *is* judgements, because in order to be able to critically evalu-ate a subject we must first of all understand its key attributes and qualities.[3]

As we explained above, the most basic theoretical issue in the field of cor-porate governance concerns the essential nature of the corporation (or 'firm') as a social phenomenon, on which there are two prevailing (and conflicting) general views. Your particular opinion on this first issue tends, moreover, to inform your corresponding view of what the core function of corporate gov-ernance *should* be – that is, as to how corporate power should generally be allo-cated within society. We will now proceed to examine each of these dominant theories of the firm in turn, focusing in particular on their respective implica-tions for corporate governance.

---

[3] On this generally, see N. MacCormick, *Institutions of Law: An Essay in Legal Theory* (OUP 2007), Chs 1 and 2; N. MacCormick, *Questioning Sovereignty: Law, State, and Nation in the European Commonwealth* (OUP 1999), Ch. 1.

THE ENTITY THEORY OF THE FIRM

What we here term the 'entity' theory of the firm is admittedly shorthand for a very rich and multi-dimensional array of theories and ideas, as developed by numerous thinkers within different national and historical settings. What follows is, therefore, a necessarily crude summary of some core and unifying themes running through this loosely affiliated school of thought, centring principally on the work of arguably the most influential exponent of this understanding of the corporation within the Anglo-American environment: namely, the twentieth-century US lawyer and statesman Adolf A. Berle.[4]

The essence of the entity theory of the firm, as explained by Berle, is that 'the entity commonly known as "corporate entity" takes its being *from the reality of the underlying enterprise*, formed on its formation'.[5] In other words, the corporation constitutes a distinct entity 'in itself' which, although in many respects intangible, is nonetheless in a fundamental sense every bit as 'real' as any natural living and breathing organism. Moreover, on a metaphysical level, it can be said that the identity and corresponding interests of the corporation as an entity entirely *transcend* the aggregate private identities and interests of its various human participants, including (*inter alia*) its shareholders. It follows that the corporation, as understood in this sense, is not just something more than the sum of its various human component 'parts', in the sense that a functioning vehicle has an integral use value in excess of the aggregate value of its separable mechanical components. More fundamentally, the corporation can be said to constitute something different *in kind* from its constituents entirely, and thus – in metaphorical terms – is akin to an organic 'offspring' of its founders rather than a synthetic 'product' as such.[6]

Central to the entity conception of the corporation is the idea that the shareholders of a widely-held public company – in acquiring a 'bare' ownership interest without any associated managerial or control capacity – have, in effect, opted for the benefit of *liquidity* (denoting the ability to transfer their shares readily in return for cash on an open capital market) in preference to

---

[4] Whilst Berle is arguably the most well-known exponent of the entity theory of the firm within English-speaking (and particularly American) legal scholarship, he was by no means the original progenitor of the theory. Rather, Berle's thinking on this issue would appear to have been heavily influenced by earlier Germanic scholarship in this regard, especially the work of Otto Von Gierke, Johann Caspar Bluntschli, Georg Beseler and Walter Rathenau. See e.g. O. Von Gierke, *Die Genossenschaftstheorie Und Die Deutsche Rechtsprechung* (Weidmann 1887). On this general line of thought, see Petrin, above n. 1, 6–8; M. Gelter, 'Taming or Protecting the Modern Corporation? Shareholder-Stakeholder Debates in a Comparative Light' (2011) 7 *New York University Journal of Law and Business* 641, 665–66.

[5] A.A. Berle, 'The Theory of Enterprise Entity' (1947) 47 *Columbia Law Review* 343, 344 (emphasis added).

[6] On this generally, see G. Schnyder and M. Luepold, 'Horse, Cow, Sheep, or "Thing-In-Itself"? The Cognitive Origins of Corporate Governance in Switzerland, Germany, and the U.S., 1910s–1930s' (Working Paper 2008), at https://ssrn.com/abstract=1018413.

control.[7] Shareholders consequently become – in effect – 'externalized' from the business firm as a productive and wealth-generating unit, which correspondingly assumes a 'neutral' or autonomous corporeal identity in itself,[8] independent of any previously-underlying proprietary influence or interest.[9]

The ultimate outcome of the above process is that the business firm – in undertaking this transition – becomes transformed from a notionally 'passive' object of ownership (according to the traditional logic of *property*), to a notionally 'active' locus of social power in its own right (according to the entirely separate logic of *institution*). In short, the firm is no longer an object of property, but rather a social institution or organization that must be governed as such. And, whereas the logic of property dictates that a person (e.g. a shareholder or manager) has private-dispositive power over a given object (e.g. a firm), the logic of institution – from which the entity paradigm essentially derives – contrarily dictates that a holder of organizational power should not be free to exercise it in their own interest, but rather *in the interests of those affected by it*. Accordingly, if the corporation is an institution – meaning that proprietary interest no longer provides a justificatory basis for the exercise of private-dispositive power over it – then it is necessary to set limits on corporate (managerial) power to ensure that it is exercised on behalf of the corporation's affected social 'subjects'.[10]

In the case of large-scale business organizations whose operations wield a significant social footprint, such affected 'subjects' potentially include the general public (whether domestically or internationally) in their various and frequently overlapping capacities as employees, consumers, investors, trading partners and/or impacted local community members; or, at least, a broad cross-section thereof who can reasonably lay claim to being directly or indirectly affected by the firm's productive and wealth-generating activities. Thus corporate *accountability*, according to this view, essentially denotes the accountability of corporate controllers to *the public at large*.[11]

Correspondingly, corporate officeholders' discretionary managerial decisions are recognized as legitimate only in the presence of an effective framework of checks (whether legal or otherwise) whereby such discretion can be

---

[7] A.A. Berle and G. Means, *The Modern Corporation and Private Property* (revised ed., Harcourt, Brace & World 1968; first published 1932), 251.

[8] In this regard, it is worth noting that – within the entity paradigm – the formally separate legal personality of the corporation under company law is not *in itself* the defining characteristic of its autonomous 'realness' as an entity or institution. Rather, according to this particular view, the corporation's purportedly 'real' physical identity arguably *transcends* any purely technical factors pertaining to its artificial identity on a juridical level.

[9] Berle and Means, above n. 7, 312.

[10] See M.T. Moore and A. Rebérioux, 'The Corporate Governance of the Firm as an Entity: Old Issues for the New Debate' in Y. Biondi, A. Canziani and T. Kirat, *The Firm as an Entity: Implications for Economics, Accounting and the Law* (Routledge 2007), Ch. 18, 357–59.

[11] See J.E. Parkinson, *Corporate Power and Responsibility: Issues in the Theory of Company Law* (OUP 1993), 21–25.

channelled in the service of objectives that are, in the last place, determined *publicly* (which, in the standard case, means *democratically*).[12] In this way – to quote the German industrialist and statesman Walter Rathenau – 'the enterprise becomes transformed into an institution which resembles the state in character'.[13] Correspondingly, the process of governing large-scale business organizations comes to resemble that of controlling the powers of government itself, whereas the function of corporate management evolves essentially into one of 'economic statesmanship'.[14]

The entity paradigm's progressive, quasi-public conception of corporate governance is encapsulated succinctly by Berle and Means, who consequently advocated that '[t]he "control" … of the great corporations should develop into a purely neutral technocracy, balancing a variety of claims by various groups in the community and assigning to each a portion of the income stream on the basis of public policy rather than private cupidity'.[15] On a juridical level, meanwhile, such notional 'neutrality' of the corporate control function within the entity paradigm is perhaps best encapsulated by the sophisticated German legal concept of 'Unternehmensinteresse' (translating into 'the interest of the company'). As Lord Wedderburn explains, this concept 'is not necessarily quite the same as an undifferentiated lump of "stakeholder interests"' but, rather, encapsulates the 'broader social expectations of economic organization',[16] or – put somewhat differently – 'the public interest in economic organization'.[17]

It follows that corporate governance, as a means of allocating corporate power within society, should be designed so as to best reflect the broad 'public consensus': that is to say (in the words of Berle), 'the existence of a set of ideas, widely held by the community, and often by the organization itself and the men who direct it, that certain uses of power are "wrong", that is, contrary to the established interest and value system of the community'.[18] In particular, this entails that the traditional entrepreneurial tenet of private (shareholder) profit-maximization should, in the case of large and socially significant business organizations at least, be legally *superseded* where its demands come into conflict with the perceived broader public interest in economic organization, however defined or enunciated.[19]

---

[12] *ibid.*, 23.

[13] As quoted in Berle and Means, above n. 7, 309. In a similar vein, Berle (writing in 1967) observed that '[t]here is an increasing recognition of the fact that collective operations, and those predominantly conducted by large corporations, are like operations carried on by the state itself. Corporations are essentially political constructs.' See *ibid.*, preface to 1967 edition, xxvi.

[14] *ibid.*, 312.

[15] *ibid.*

[16] B. Wedderburn, *The Future of Company Law: Fat Cats, Corporate Governance and Workers* (Institute of Employment Rights 2004), 36.

[17] This term is attributable to the German legal theorist Gunther Teubner, as quoted in Wedderburn, *ibid.*, 24.

[18] A.A. Berle, *Power Without Property: A New Development in American Political Economy* (Harcourt, Brace & World 1959), 90.

[19] Parkinson, above n. 11, 22.

In a nutshell, then, the essential normative claim of the entity theory of the firm is that corporate power in an advanced capitalist economy – whilst formally 'private' in the sense of being possessed and exercised outside of direct governmental control – is nonetheless substantively 'public', insofar as the continuing social licence of corporate officeholders to exercise such power is dependent on their conformance to publicly constituted norms of fair dealing and responsible economic statesmanship.

THE CONTRACTARIAN THEORY OF THE FIRM

The contractarian theory of the firm was developed initially by US-based financial economists and corporate lawyers over the course of the late twentieth century,[20] as part of a more general ideological transition in the Anglo-American political economy: from the mid- and post-war consensus of state-centric corporatism, towards the market-centric neo-liberalism that became an increasingly pervasive reference point for intellectuals and policy-makers in the century's latter half. As a microcosm of this broader movement, corporate contractarianism represented a crucial antidote to the modern business corporation's progressive intellectual removal over previous decades from the orthodox field of economic analysis.[21]

Against the above historical and intellectual background, the contractarian paradigm essentially sought to reinvigorate the business corporation as a subject of orthodox economic analysis, and thus to portray the modern 'public' corporation as being continually subject to the 'invisible hand' of market governance as opposed to the 'visible hand'[22] of technocratic managerial or state control. In this regard, the theory can be regarded as a key and characteristic component of a more general turn in Western social science, which essentially sought – ultimately with widespread success – to assert the purported

---

[20] The seminal works of this school of thought include A.A. Alchian and H. Demsetz, 'Production, Information Costs, and Economic Organization' (1972) 62 *American Economic Review* 777; M.C. Jensen and W.H. Meckling, 'Theory of the Firm: Managerial Behaviour, Agency Costs and Ownership Structure' (1976) 3 *Journal of Financial Economics* 305; E.F. Fama, 'Agency Problems and the Theory of the Firm' (1980) 88 *Journal of Political Economy* 288; E.F. Fama and M.C. Jensen, 'Separation of Ownership and Control' (1983) 26 *Journal of Law and Economics* 301; F.H. Easterbrook and D.R. Fischel, 'The Corporate Contract' (1989) 89 *Columbia Law Review* 1416; F.H. Easterbrook and D.R. Fischel, *The Economic Structure of Corporate Law* (Harvard University Press 1991). Although the foundational piece of scholarship in the contractarian tradition is commonly regarded to be Ronald Coase's landmark article 'The Nature of the Firm' (1937) 4 *Economica* 386, this work is arguably better regarded as a significant influence for the (later) contractarian movement, rather than as a constituent part of that movement itself.

[21] For a statement of intent to this effect by two early protagonists of the contractarian position, see Jensen and Meckling, *ibid.*, 307.

[22] This latter term is attributable to the American business historian Alfred Chandler, who developed it as a modern counterpose to the well-known former notion as developed in Adam Smith's classical 1776 economic text *The Wealth of Nations*. See A.D. Chandler, *The Visible Hand: The Managerial Revolution in American Business* (Harvard University Press 1977).

superiority of decentralized markets over technocratic organizations (both statist and non-statist) in achieving effective control over modern economic activity.[23]

The influence of the contractarian position has undoubtedly been most profound within the United States, where for the past three decades it has constituted the mainstream scholarly take on corporate governance as a subject of academic enquiry.[24] At the same time, the spread of influential US-inspired contributions to British scholarship over recent decades,[25] coupled with a shortage of viable home-grown counter-theories,[26] have together ensured the prevalence of contractarian logic to a large extent within UK corporate governance thinking and policymaking today.[27]

The contractarian theory of the firm is derived from an extensive and often complex body of inter-disciplinary literature, much of which would likely be more familiar to economists than lawyers. Notwithstanding, we believe that the theory as a whole can be distilled down into three reasonably straightforward propositions. These are: (i) that the corporation (or 'firm') is essentially nothing more than a 'nexus of contracts' linking together individual economic actors; (ii) that, in general, the exclusive objective of corporate management should be to maximize the residual wealth of a firm's shareholders; and (iii) that the most appropriate way of controlling (and, in turn, legitimizing) managerial power in public companies is to ensure that corporate managers are subject at all times to the constraints of competitive market pressures. We will now analyze each of these three key propositions of the contractarian paradigm in turn.

The Corporation as a Nexus of Contracts

The conceptual starting point of the contractarian theory of the firm is at first sight somewhat paradoxical. In stark contrast to the abovementioned entity paradigm, it asserts that – analytically speaking – the institution known as the business corporation is not an 'institution' at all in any meaningful metaphysical

---

[23] The foundational academic texts in this tradition are commonly regarded to be Milton Friedman's *Capitalism and Freedom* (University of Chicago Press 1962) and Friedrich von Hayek's *The Road to Serfdom* (Routledge 1944), although as a political force the movement did not begin to attain significant influence until the 1970s.

[24] Amongst the most influential academic expositions of this model of corporate law and governance are Easterbrook and Fischel, *The Economic Structure of Corporate Law*, above n. 18; Kraakman *et al.*'s *The Anatomy of Corporate Law: A Comparative and Functional Approach* (2nd ed., OUP 2009; first published 2004), and Stephen Bainbridge's *The New Corporate Governance in Theory and Practice* (OUP 2008).

[25] Most notably Brian Cheffins' excellent book *Company Law: Theory, Structure and Operation* (OUP 1997) and, more recently, David Kershaw's *Company Law in Context: Text and Materials* (2nd ed., OUP 2012; first published 2009).

[26] One notable exception to this general trend is John Parkinson's *Corporate Power and Responsibility*, above n. 11, which provides a comprehensive and path-breaking critical polemic on corporate law theory in a British context.

[27] P. Ireland, 'Property and Contract in Contemporary Corporate Theory' (2003) 23 *Legal Studies* 453, 454.

sense.[28] Rather, a corporation (or 'firm') is from a practical point of view composed of nothing more than the particular collection of individuals who are at any one time involved in the carrying on of its productive and wealth-generating operations.[29] These individuals will typically include equity and debt investors, employees (including directors and managers), trade creditors and customers.

Accordingly, if the corporation deserves any independent recognition as a 'thing' in itself, it is merely the notional 'nexus' or 'hub' around which these various micro-agents contract with one another, each offering their respective 'inputs' to the production process (e.g. equity, debt, physical or human capital) in exchange for a corresponding 'output' (e.g. dividend, interest, price or wage).[30] For this reason, the contractarian paradigm is commonly referred to in the alternative as 'nexus of contracts' theory.[31]

In reality, of course, the 'nexus' or 'hub' will be represented either by the firm's board of directors or by its senior management team, as the party that is (at least theoretically) common to the negotiations with all input-providers. However, directors and managers are ultimately themselves no more than mere input-providers to the firm's production process (insofar as they supply their human capital) like everyone else, so that it arguably makes no sense at all to speak of 'the corporation' in the sense of an autonomous, reified institution 'in itself'. Rather, in the words of Jensen and Meckling, the corporation is ultimately just a 'legal fiction which serves as a nexus for contracting relationships'.[32]

The key descriptive quality of the contractarian paradigm is its capacity to explain the structure and operation of the corporation anatomically in terms of the collective pattern of economic incentives purportedly motivating its various individual participants. Through this neo-classical economic lens, it becomes possible to ascribe theoretically rational behavioural modes to a corporation's various constituent groups based on the conceptual framework of an implicit and ongoing 'bargain' over their respective entitlements to share in the wealth generated by the firm's productive operations.[33]

Allied to this contractual bargaining hypothesis is a passive-instrumental conception of corporate governance, whereby governance structures and supporting legal rules are essentially flexible and facilitative 'tools'. As two of the leading proponents of the contractarian theory of the firm put it:

> The corporation and its securities are products in financial markets to as great an extent as the sewing machines or other things the firm makes. Just as the founders

---

[28] P. Ireland, 'Recontractualising the Corporation: Implicit Contract as Ideology' in D. Campbell, H. Collins and J. Wightman (eds), *Implicit Dimensions of Contract* (Hart 2003), 255, 260.

[29] P. Ireland, 'The Myth of Shareholder Ownership' (1999) 62 *Modern Law Review* 32, 56.

[30] See Easterbrook and Fischel, *The Economic Structure of Corporate Law*, above n. 20, 11–12.

[31] Although now a generic term of reference, the literal phrase would appear to be attributable to the financial economist Eugene Fama, who coined it in his 1980 article 'Agency Problems and the Theory of the Firm', above n. 20, 290.

[32] See Jensen and Meckling, above n. 20, 311. See also Cheffins, above n. 25, 31–41.

[33] See Fama, above n. 20, 289.

of a firm have incentives to make the kind of sewing machines people want to buy, they have incentives to create the kind of firm, governance structure, and securities the customers in capital markets want.[34]

Accordingly, prevailing corporate governance norms and structures – even where enshrined in law or regulation – are regarded as merely 'mimicking' the commercially expedient arrangements which corporate participants would otherwise tend to establish with one another via private contracting. From a contractarian viewpoint, corporate governance arrangements are thus regarded as being impelled by pressures of a fundamentally private and economic nature.

Managerial Accountability and the Shareholder Wealth Maximization Objective

We explained above how, according to the competing entity theory of the firm, the effective accountability of corporate power-holders is predicated on the regulatory control of private decision-making power directly in the interests of the public at large. In stark contrast, the contractarian theory of the firm asserts that the accountability of corporate power-holders is effectively and appropriately achieved by ensuring that they are held privately accountable to shareholders *exclusively*: that is, for the notionally 'efficient' running of the company's business as reflected in managerial conformance to the so-called 'shareholder wealth maximization' objective. This is not to say that the contractarian paradigm is entirely unconcerned with the wider public interest in economic organization, beyond the narrow private-prudential concerns of a company's shareholders. Rather, as we touched upon in Chapter 1, its key normative contention is that the general economic welfare of the public at large is most effectively enhanced in the long run *indirectly*, via the collateral social benefits that follow from directors' and managers' *exclusive* promotion of the shareholder wealth maximization goal.

Whilst such a claim might initially strike readers as somewhat counter-intuitive, on closer consideration it is not quite as outlandish a notion as may first seem. Indeed, as long ago as 1776, Adam Smith made the now-famous remark that 'I have never known much good done by those who affected to trade for the public good',[35] but rather that '[b]y pursuing his own interest [an individual] frequently promotes that of the society more effectually than when he really intends to promote it'[36] (Smith's so-called 'invisible hand'[37] of capitalistic economic progress). Moreover, Smith's observation in this regard has its modern counterpart in Milton Friedman's well-known 1970 proposition that 'the social responsibility of business is to increase its profits'.[38]

---

[34] See Easterbrook and Fischel, *The Economic Structure of Corporate Law*, above n. 20, 4–6.

[35] A. Smith, *The Wealth of Nations* (Everyman 1921; first published 1776), 399.

[36] *ibid.*

[37] *ibid.*

[38] See M. Friedman, 'The Social Responsibility of Business Is to Increase Its Profits' in T. Beauchamp and N. Bowie (eds), *Ethical Theory and Business* (Pearson 2004; article originally published in *The New York Times Magazine* (1970)).

As we discussed in Chapter 1, such arguments about the purported indirect link between businesspersons' pursuit of private profit and the general public good may be intuitively plausible in the case of closely-held entrepreneurial or family concerns. However, they are less immediately convincing when considered in respect of widely-held public companies exhibiting a separation of ownership and control (in the Anglo-American sense), where a distinct entrepreneurial presence in the classical sense is typically non-existent. Indeed, it may reasonably be asked why the orthodox private-profit-seeking maxim should continue to apply within this comparatively peculiar corporate-organizational context, where Smith's invisible hand axiom has no readily apparent application.

Furthermore, on the contractarian presumption that the shareholder wealth maximization objective *must* be generally preferable to alternative methods of ensuring managerial accountability (otherwise corporate participants would not rationally have been inclined to 'agree' to it in their hypothetical mutual 'contract' embedded in the law), an additional question arises as to why this could plausibly be so. While it is fairly obvious why shareholders themselves would rationally opt for such an arrangement, it is less clear – indeed, at first sight, somewhat perplexing – why other participant groups in the firm (especially employees) would agree in a hypothetical bargaining scenario to sacrifice their own potential entitlement to preferential status in this regard, opting instead to vest it in shareholders alone.

In providing a normative explanation as to why the shareholder wealth maximization objective nonetheless retains prominence within managerially-controlled public companies, the contractarian paradigm reinvents the classical economic concept of entrepreneurial risk-taking in a revised form appropriate to the characteristics of modern *corporate* – as opposed to individual or family – enterprise.[39] Hence the contractarian paradigm portrays the modern corporate equity investor as a 'residual risk bearer', who voluntarily undertakes the risk of periodic business underperformance by entering into a notionally 'incomplete'[40] contract with the firm under which her periodic economic returns are unspecified. By contrast, other corporate constituent groups, notably workers and lenders, are (in theory at least) usually able to specify in advance their economic return from the firm plus the conditions

---

[39] On the inappropriateness of classical entrepreneurial concepts as a means of rationalizing large-scale corporate enterprise generally, see D. Campbell, 'Adam Smith, Farrar on the Company and the Economics of the Corporation' (1990) 19 *Anglo-American Law Review* 185.

[40] In economic theory, a contract is notionally 'incomplete' when the parties to it are incapable of providing in advance for all of the various contingencies that will affect their continuing economic relationship with one another. The inevitable outcome is that at least one party to the contract will be forced to incur the risk of future losses arising from unforeseeable events, which they are unable to 'price' accurately in advance due to limited information and foresight. On this, see I.R. Macneil, 'Contracts: Adjustment of Long-Term Economic Relations under Classical, Neoclassical, and Relational Contract Law' (1978) 72 *Northwestern University Law Review* 854; O.E. Williamson, *The Mechanisms of Governance* (OUP 1999), Chs 3 and 7.

upon which they agree to advance their respective inputs to the firm's production process.[41]

As compensation for bearing the 'downside' risk of receiving little or nothing in the event of the firm being loss-making, it is said that the equity investor will rationally bargain for the corresponding 'upside' entitlement to the whole of the 'residual' profit generated by the firm over a successful period: that is to say, for any outstanding net returns remaining once all other factors of production (e.g. employees, lenders, suppliers) have been paid their respective fixed contractual entitlements.[42] Furthermore, in order to exert a degree of influence over how directors and managers use their invested funds, equity investors as a group will purportedly tend also to demand both (i) the exclusive right of appointment over the company's board of directors and (ii) the accompanying right to hold its directors individually to account *ex post facto* for breach of their legal-fiduciary duties.[43]

Meanwhile, other corporate constituent groups (and especially employees) will in the typical case be able to achieve satisfactory protection for their various investments under their respective 'complete' contracts with the firm, thus rendering the above governance rights unnecessary for them. Moreover, non-shareholder groups (including employees) will purportedly be prepared to concede governance entitlements to equity investors on the understanding that this arrangement will on the whole prove to be mutually beneficial for them. This is because equity investors are – it is claimed – uniquely placed to diversify their capital on an economy-wide basis and thus 'hedge' against the risk of individual firm failure, meaning that the failure of any one firm in which a shareholder is invested will generally not be catastrophic for their overall economic position.[44]

Equity investors are consequently said to be much more capable than other groups at absorbing the occasional losses resulting from risky but potentially path-breaking ventures which, although liable to increase temporarily the likelihood of firm failure, if successful will generate long-term economic benefits for the firm and its participants as a whole. However, other corporate constituent groups, such as workers and suppliers, are by nature 'over-invested' in

---

[41] For a concise summary and critical analysis of the dual notions of residual risk-bearing and incomplete contracting within corporate-contractarian theory, see G. Kelly and J. Parkinson, 'The Conceptual Foundations of the Company: A Pluralist Approach' in J. Parkinson, A. Gamble and G. Kelly (eds), *The Political Economy of the Company* (Hart Publishing 2000), Ch. 6, esp. 114–21.

[42] Fama and Jensen, 'Separation of Ownership and Control', above n. 20, 302–03. As Easterbrook and Fischel put it, '[i]nvestors bear most of the risk of business failure, in exchange for which they are promised most of the rewards of success'. See *The Economic Structure of Corporate Law*, above n. 20, 11.

[43] On the significance of the director's fiduciary duty of loyalty in prioritizing the interests of shareholders relative to those of other corporate constituents (and, in particular, employees) in the UK, see Chapter 6.

[44] Fama, 'Agency Problems', above n. 20, 291; Easterbrook and Fischel, *The Economic Structure of Corporate Law*, above n. 20, 29.

specific firms in the sense that they usually stand to lose considerably in the event of individual corporate failure. Such groups, therefore, if vested with corporate governance rights would arguably not be prone to support risky strategies by management even where they promise positive risk-adjusted returns for the firm as a whole.

Furthermore, to the extent that making boards of directors answerable to multiple constituencies is arguably prone to engender conflicts of interest and thus undermine consensus decision-making,[45] it is claimed to be universally preferable from the viewpoint of the firm's participants as a whole to establish a system of clear and unitary directorial accountability to one single, roughly homogenous group.[46] And, for the above reason, shareholders generally stand out as the most desirable collective candidate in this regard. It follows that a company's various participants will – in the standard case – thus have a mutual incentive to support management's exclusive furtherance of the shareholder wealth maximization objective, as this is the only method of ensuring managerial accountability which is consistent with the advancement of the productive dynamism and overall wealth-generating capacity of the firm's business.

Accordingly, the contractarian paradigm establishes an instrumental rationale for the shareholder wealth maximization objective in corporate governance, based on the logic of implicit bargain and private ordering. In doing so, it seeks to highlight the purportedly key productive function of equity investors in efficiently underwriting entrepreneurial risks, notwithstanding the typical absence of direct shareholder involvement in the internal managerial affairs of Anglo-American public companies.

The 'Agency Costs' Understanding of Corporate Governance

As explained above, the contractarian paradigm portrays the corporation as a decentralized network of consensual bargaining relations, and its prevailing corporate governance framework (including any supporting legal rules) as the outcome of a mutual agreement between corporate participants emanating therefrom. As a key part of this notional corporate governance 'agreement', the shareholder wealth maximization objective purportedly represents the most efficient – and thus collectively desirable – way of apportioning participants' relative entitlements to the firm's periodic profit streams, while also ensuring effective managerial accountability within the firm.

However, there remains an outstanding question as to how, precisely, a system of managerial accountability premised on conformance to the shareholder wealth maximization objective can be said to secure the *legitimacy* of corporate managers' discretionary decision-making power. That is to say, irrespective

---

[45] On this problem, see further below.
[46] See Easterbrook and Fischel, above n. 20, 38; Bainbridge, *The New Corporate Governance*, above n. 24, 66–67; M.C. Jensen, 'Value Maximisation, Stakeholder Theory, and the Corporate Objective Function' (2001) 7 *European Financial Management* 297, 301.

of its (purported) economic efficiency, is the shareholder wealth maximization objective an overall *appropriate* or *desirable* criterion of corporate-managerial accountability from a general public perspective? In large part, of course, the answer to this question depends on one's particular ideological predisposition, and therefore is inherently subjective. However, before developing a definite opinion on this matter, it is important for readers to appreciate how, from a contractarian perspective, the discretionary decision-making power of senior corporate officeholders is conventionally deemed to be legitimized by adherence to the shareholder wealth maximization goal.

Consistent with its general understanding of corporate governance as the outcome of consensual bargaining dynamics, contractarian theory views the shareholder wealth maximization objective as a fundamentally *market*-driven phenomenon. Indeed, this is a basic tenet of its influential 'agency' conception of the relation between shareholders and managers of public companies, which posits that market pressures are capable of reducing managers' discretionary decision-making power to unproblematic levels.

'Agency costs' – according to the financial economists Jensen and Meckling – are the losses that a company's shareholders (as notional 'principals') will tend to incur due to managers (as their 'agents') failing to promote shareholders' best interests when running the business.[47] Specifically, agency costs represent the sum of three distinct categories of expense and/or loss borne by shareholders as a result of managerial recalcitrance. These are: (i) the direct monitoring costs incurred by shareholders in seeking to ensure that managers are acting in their best interests at all times; (ii) the so-called 'bonding' expenses incurred by the firm (and, indirectly, its shareholders) due to managers voluntarily introducing self-oversight mechanisms (such as independent monitoring boards[48]) designed to secure shareholders' continuing trust and confidence in them; and (iii) any outstanding residual losses incurred by shareholders – whether due to undetected fraud or managerial self-enrichment at the firm's expense, or managers withholding optimal work effort (so-called 'shirking') – to the extent that the above mechanisms are unsuccessful in eradicating scope for such recalcitrance.[49]

Against the above background, the agency costs approach – operating within an overarching contractarian frame of reference – identifies the competitive market as the principal social mechanism (or, more accurately, *set of* social mechanisms) for incentivizing and disciplining corporate managers in line with shareholders' interests. According to this view, the most powerful such discipline acting on managers is not their firm's relevant product market(s), but rather the markets for the financial (and especially equity) securities of companies themselves (i.e. the capital markets), which is regarded as a much more

---

[47] See Jensen and Meckling, above n. 20.
[48] On this, see Chapter 7.
[49] Jensen and Meckling, above n. 20, 308.

compelling factor motivating continual improvements in managerial performance from a shareholder point of view.[50]

Indeed, from the above perspective, capital markets are not only of direct importance as a medium through which firms must compete to raise fresh external finance at low cost. They are also a necessary prelude to the effective functioning of the market for corporate control, whereby especially severe or prolonged managerial underperformance (and resultant share price depreciation) can prompt the 'wholesale' purchase of a company's share capital by a prospective outside control-acquirer, which will almost inevitably entail the subsequent outright displacement of its incumbent management team.[51] It follows that the mere threat of such an eventuality will – in theory at least – provide corporate managers with a powerful discipline to maximize shareholder wealth on an ongoing basis, even at times when resort to outside capital markets is not necessary to sustain the firm's continuing business operations.[52]

At the same time, by means of performance-based pay structures linked to a company's share price performance, managers are theoretically given a compelling incentive to work at all times with a view to maximizing shareholder wealth.[53] The overall effect of the above mechanisms is to ensure that managers' discretionary decision-making power – as manifested in the scope that they would otherwise enjoy to impose agency costs on shareholders – is eradicated or, at the very least, mitigated to a level that is economically unproblematic.

In terms of demonstrating the purported legitimacy of corporate-managerial power, the agency costs approach is highly significant. In particular, it is premised on the implicit understanding that purely market-driven pressures are capable of constraining discretionary decision-making power within generally acceptable bounds. Accordingly, managers who are compliant with the dictates of the capital markets are deemed to be *accountable* (to shareholders at least), with the normative outcome that their continuing exercise of discretionary decision-making power is implicitly rendered legitimate.

In the above way, corporate power is presented as an inherently self-correcting problem when set within the broader context of a market-based governance framework. It follows that any regulatory interventions by the state in corporate governance, apart from its limited role as a surrogate provider of efficient default 'contract' terms, is both unnecessary and – moreover – economically inferior to the alternative of simply deferring the resolution of corporate governance problems to the workings of the market.

---

[50] See A.A. Alchian, 'Corporate Management and Property Rights' in H. Manne (ed.), *Economic Policy and the Regulation of Corporate Securities* (American Enterprise Institute 1969).

[51] See H.G. Manne, 'Mergers and the Market for Corporate Control' (1965) 73 *Journal of Political Economy* 110. On the significance of the market for corporate control within corporate governance, see Chapter 10.

[52] See Fama, above n. 20.

[53] On performance-related managerial pay generally, see Chapter 9.

CONTRACTARIANISM *WITHOUT* SHAREHOLDER WEALTH MAXIMIZATION: THE 'STAKEHOLDER' THEORY OF THE FIRM

We explained above how the key structural quality of the contractarian theory of the firm is its assertion that no particular corporate governance arrangement is proverbially 'set in stone'. Rather, notional corporate 'contractors' are purportedly at liberty to allocate decision-making power and other key entitlements as the perceived exigencies of competitive business demand. Remarkably, this means that even the central normative feature of the contractarian model of the firm – namely the shareholder wealth maximization objective – is itself potentially vulnerable to override in appropriate instances via firm-level private ordering. Indeed, this would appear to be the core prescriptive argument of the popular 'stakeholder' theory of the firm. Somewhat paradoxically, stakeholder theory exploits the basic logic of the contractarian position to support normative conclusions that most orthodox contractarian theorists have customarily been averse to.

The normative essence of the stakeholder approach, for which the theory is most well-known, is its basic contention that corporations should be managed not only for the benefit of their shareholders, but also directly in the interests of various non-propertied 'stakeholder' groups – including employees, suppliers and customers – who can each be said to hold a material 'stake' in the firm's continuing success and prosperity.[54] At the heart of the stakeholder theory of the firm is a rejection of the traditional neo-liberal assumption that a corporation's perceived 'economic' versus 'social' responsibilities are inherently conflicted.

In this regard, the economist John Kay – one of the foremost academic proponents of the stakeholder paradigm – draws an analogy between the guiding objective of a successful corporation and that of a good doctor. Kay claims that just as a good doctor strives to 'serve their patients through the innovative and responsible application of medical science',[55] the corresponding goal of a successful business corporation is the multi-faceted one of 'satisfying the needs of customers, meeting the reasonable expectations of employees and developing their capabilities'.[56] Whilst 'generating returns for investors' remains essential to the stakeholder-oriented corporation, Kay makes equally clear that 'profit is not its object'[57]; in the same way that a doctor focused primarily on maximizing her earnings would be not only morally irresponsible, but also *economically*

---

[54] On this school of thought generally, see R.E. Freeman, J.S. Harrison, A.C. Wicks, B.L. Parmar and S. De Colle (eds), *Stakeholder Theory: The State of the Art* (Cambridge University Press 2010); G. Kelly, D. Kelly and A. Gamble (eds), *Stakeholder Capitalism* (Macmillan 1997).

[55] J. Kay, 'A Stakeholding Society – What Does It Mean for Business?' (1997) 44 *Scottish Journal of Political Economy* 425, 426.

[56] *ibid.*, 434.

[57] *ibid.* For a fuller exposition of this argument, see J. Kay, *Obliquity: Why Our Goals Are Best Achieved Indirectly* (Profile 2010), Ch. 3.

unsuccessful by virtue of failing to elicit the trust and resultant 'custom' of patients.

Despite its differing normative implications, the stakeholder theory of the firm is ultimately grounded in the same conceptual premises as the contractarian paradigm, specifically: (i) a view of the corporation not as an autonomous and reified entity in itself, but rather as a complex *'network of relationships'*[58] binding together its various individual participants; (ii) a central focus on economic success and *wealth creation* as the ultimate criteria for determining the effectiveness of any given set of corporate governance arrangements; and (iii) an acceptance of *residual risk* as the principal determinant of corporate participants' relative economic and legal entitlements within the firm. We will now examine each of these three conceptual components of corporate stakeholder theory in turn.

The Corporation as a 'Network of Relationships'

In beginning her exposition of the stakeholder model of corporate governance, Margaret Blair posits – in conspicuously contractarian terms – that '[c]orporations are legal devices for assembling and organizing capital, labour and other resources to sell goods and services'.[59] Blair claims that, although corporations are 'protected and sanctioned by government, they are generally *private* enterprises'.[60] Accordingly, the state's role in their creation is merely 'indirect, providing the legal and institutional environment to encourage and support wealth-creating economic activity'.[61] Meanwhile, in one of the most respected academic expositions of the stakeholder position written in the UK, Gavin Kelly and John Parkinson likewise accept 'the value of viewing the company as a set of contractual relationships for the purpose of analysing the welfare effects of different allocations of risk, returns and governance rights'.[62] In a similar vein, John Kay based his influential stakeholder-oriented work *The Foundations of Corporate Success* on a fundamental understanding of the corporation as 'part of a rich network of relationships'.[63]

However, Blair (in a subsequent article co-authored with Lynn Stout) emphasizes the fact that 'human behaviour can be influenced in a number of ways that are not captured by standard nexus-of-contracts analysis'.[64] Blair and Stout therefore call for 'a more tempered approach to analysing corporate law'

---

[58] This term is attributable to J. Kay, *The Foundations of Corporate Success: How Business Strategies Add Value* (OUP 1993), 9 (emphasis added).

[59] M.M. Blair, *Ownership and Control, Rethinking Corporate Governance for the Twenty-First Century* (Brookings Institute 1995), 2.

[60] *ibid.* (emphasis added).

[61] *ibid.*

[62] Kelly and Parkinson, above n. 41, 122.

[63] See above n. 58.

[64] M.M. Blair and L.A. Stout, 'Trust, Trustworthiness and the Behavioral Foundations of Corporate Law' (2001) 149 *University of Pennsylvania Law Review* 1735, 1808.

which 'recognizes the multidimensional quality of human nature' and, in particular, the fact that '[h]uman beings are individualistic *and* social creatures'.[65] In this regard, Kay identifies the essence of the corporation as residing in its unique capacity to enable individual economic actors to cooperate with one another in forming a distinct productive organization. Accordingly, the corporation 'adds value' by enabling investors, managers, employees and suppliers to combine their respective productive inputs in such a way as to yield a greater amount of wealth than that resulting from the sum of their individual efforts alone.[66]

Kay argues that the capacity of a successful corporation to add value to market relationships in this way derives from the uniqueness of its 'architecture': that is to say, the established organizational systems and routines by which the firm's various participants collectively coordinate their respective productive inputs. Crucially, in Kay's view, a successful corporate architecture – as a complex organic phenomenon – is inherently incapable of being reduced to a series of pre-determinable contracts between individual corporate participants, as the contractarian theory of the firm would seem to aver. Otherwise a firm's architecture would be readily replicable by competitors and thus of no distinct competitive advantage.[67]

According to stakeholder theory, a successful corporate architecture is a key structural tool for engendering *trust* between the firm and its various participants.[68] As Kay and Silberston explain, '[b]usinesses are defined by a nexus of long established trust relationships', whereas 'the principal agent model' characteristic of the contractarian theory of the firm 'sees only a group of people who find it expedient every morning to renew their contracts with one another'.[69] Kay explains the economic value of trust to a corporation in terms of its propensity to encourage corporate participants (whether employees, suppliers, lenders or customers) 'systematically [to] … undertake relationships on terms which they would not make available to other people'.[70] Of course, *quid pro quo*, the firm must be able to offer its participants a corresponding above-market return on their respective economic inputs, given that 'one goal in designing a [corporate] governance system is to motivate those investments that are not properly rewarded in the marketplace'.[71]

Contrary to what the orthodox contractarian theory of the firm suggests, it has been found that the willingness of participants in successful corporations to

---

[65] *ibid.*, 1809–10.

[66] J. Kay, 'The Stakeholder Corporation' in Kelly *et al.*, above n. 54, 125, 131.

[67] Kay, above n. 58, 9.

[68] See UK Company Law Review Steering Group, Modern Company Law for a Competitive Economy: The Strategic Framework (DTI 1999), 42–43.

[69] J. Kay and A. Silberston, 'Corporate Governance' (1995) *National Institute Economic Review* 84, 91.

[70] Kay, above n. 58, 64.

[71] L. Zingales, 'Corporate Governance' in P. Newman (ed.), *The New Palgrave Dictionary of Economics and the Law* (Macmillan 1998), 497, 499.

depend upon one another over time as reliable commercial partners cannot be explained by the existence of prudential market incentives alone. Rather, the extent to which a productive and sustainable network of economic relations is possible within any firm requires the additional presence of what Blair and Stout term 'internalized trust': that is, the willingness of corporate participants to render themselves vulnerable to potential exploitation by the firm, in the absence of any concrete legal or contractual assurance that they will be compensated for doing so.[72] For example, an employee who agrees to work extra unpaid hours during an especially busy period, or a supplier who voluntarily agrees to accept a 'below-contract' price from a major customer during difficult trading conditions, each subjects themselves to potential exploitation by their contractual counterparty. Indeed, in either case, the relevant stakeholder (whether employer or supplier) risks having their relationship with the firm unilaterally terminated in future, without receiving any compensatory reward for their previous generosity.

Thus the willingness of stakeholders to go above and beyond the contractual call of duty in such ways depends, in turn, on whether the relevant firm's management is capable of being 'trustworthy': in other words, is the firm (via its management) capable of making a credible long-term promise to its stakeholders that it will refrain from exploiting their vulnerabilities for the short-term benefit of shareholders?[73] Ultimately, though, the degree and complexity of firm commitment – and corresponding stakeholder expectation – that are necessary to make such a promise credible cannot be engendered by means of orthodox legal and contractual protections, consequently rendering the respective contracts of *all* economic participants in the firm (and not just those of shareholders) to varying extents implicit or 'incomplete'.[74]

Corporate Governance as a Framework for Facilitating 'Total Wealth Creation'

Similarly to orthodox contractarianism, stakeholder theory attaches considerable importance to the separation of ownership and control within the typical Anglo-American public company. However, whereas orthodox contractarianism views this separation as a negative problem (i.e. of agency costs) that calls for a corresponding solution, stakeholder theory by contrast sees this feature of the corporation as a *positive attribute*, which should thus be *exploited* (rather than mitigated).[75] That is insofar as a public company's management, in being

---

[72] See Blair and Stout, above n. 64, 1750–53.

[73] See Blair and Stout, *ibid*. On this notion, see also C. Mayer, *Firm Commitment: Why the Corporation Is Failing Us and How to Restore Trust in It* (OUP 2013), Ch. 7.

[74] Kay, above n. 58, 134; Mayer, *ibid.*, 34.

[75] On the dichotomy between (i) mitigation and (ii) exploitation of the separation of ownership and control in Anglo-American public companies, see M.T. Moore and A. Rebérioux, 'Revitalizing the Institutional Roots of Anglo-American Corporate Governance' (2011) 40 *Economy and Society* 84, 87–100.

purportedly 'liberated' from the day-to-day control or oversight of shareholders, will consequently enjoy the freedom to promote the general development of the corporate enterprise in addition to just the narrow financial interest of shareholders.[76]

Unlike entity theorists, though, who in general regard the structural detachment of shareholders from corporate management and control as a prelude to the outright 'socialization' of managerial decision-making; stakeholder theorists – like their orthodox contractarian counterparts – tend to view the progressive potential of the corporate form from a functional-economic standpoint.[77] For instance, in distinctly contractarian terms, Margaret Blair argues that the laws and other institutions to which corporations are subject 'should foster the development of ... systems of corporate governance that lead to the most efficient use of resources to create wealth for society as a whole'.[78]

However, Blair emphasizes that, contrary to popular supposition, the stakeholder approach is not just about making corporations behave more 'socially responsibly', in whatever way this nebulous notion might be defined, measured or enforced. Rather, in Blair's view, the stakeholder theory of the firm demands specifically 'that corporations exist to create wealth for society', necessitating a corporate governance framework that is designed for the purpose of 'maximizing the wealth-producing potential of the enterprise as a whole'.[79] In order to attain this objective in any particular instance, Parkinson suggests that 'directors should balance the relevant interests, without giving priority to those of shareholders, with a view to *maximizing the welfare of the parties in aggregate*'.[80]

Stakeholder theorists accept that, in many instances, the wealth of the corporate enterprise as a whole will be maximized by directly maximizing the wealth of shareholders exclusively.[81] However, there is said to be a distinct range of cases where the respective objectives of (i) *shareholder* wealth maximization and (ii) *total* wealth maximization will each demand differing courses of action from management, thereby putting the interests of shareholders and other stakeholders starkly into conflict with one another. In such situations, a management that is required to maximize only shareholder wealth will be expected to terminate the firm's productive operations on the basis of their economic unviability, regardless of whether or not other stakeholders are still benefitting from those operations. By contrast, a management that is required to maximize total enterprise wealth (in the sense of the collective wealth enjoyed by all of the participating stakeholder groups) will be expected to maintain the firm's productive operations, even though shareholders are

---

[76] See J. Parkinson, 'Company Law and Stakeholder Governance' in Kelly *et al.*, above n. 54, 142, 151–52.

[77] See e.g. Kay and Silberston, above n. 69, 86, 91.

[78] Blair, above n. 59, 3.

[79] *ibid.*, 219.

[80] J. Parkinson, 'Inclusive Company Law' in J. de Lacy (ed.), *The Reform of UK Company Law* (Cavendish 2002), 43, 44 (emphasis added).

[81] See e.g. Blair, above n. 59, 203–04.

making no return on their investment. This is because the *total wealth* produced by the enterprise is still positive (insofar as outputs exceed inputs), the identity of the actual recipients of the wealth being immaterial from this particular perspective.[82]

The key point is that, so long as the overall social wealth generated by any productive project is positive, it follows that society has an interest in ensuring that that project is continued. Only when the total social wealth produced by the project is negative, in the sense that the cost of maintaining the relevant productive operations is insufficient to pay not just shareholders but also employees and suppliers for their respective inputs, will it be socially beneficial for management to cease that project.[83]

Residual Risk as the Principal Determinant of Relative Stakeholder Entitlements

The most conspicuous commonality between (i) orthodox contractarianism and (ii) stakeholder theory is the reliance that both theories place upon the notion of *residual risk* as the principal criterion for determining the relative distribution of entitlements within the firm. Indeed, it is in this regard that stakeholder theory could be said to borrow most heavily from its ideological predecessor. Blair, for example, proceeds upon the well-established contractarian assumption that:

> corporations are more likely to be managed in ways that maximize social value if those who monitor and control firms receive (at least some of) the residual gain and bear (some of) the residual risk, and, conversely, if those who share in the residual gains and risks are given the access and authority they need to monitor.[84]

In similarly contractualist terms, Kay states that it is 'clearly efficient that responsibility for creating or increasing added value should be associated with those who benefit from it'.[85] On this basis, he concedes that 'among the stakeholders in corporate activity, shareholders have a special place' insofar as they 'bear the largest part of the risks associated with corporate activity'.[86] However, whilst accepting the conceptual validity of the purported link between residual risk-bearing and efficient wealth creation, stakeholder theory disputes the empirical validity of the notion that shareholders are necessarily the *exclusive* bearers of residual risk within modern business corporations. Rather, the stakeholder position asserts that, in many instances, both employees and suppliers

---

[82] Blair, *ibid.*, 270; Kelly and Parkinson, above n. 41, 130–31.
[83] Kelly and Parkinson, *ibid.*, 130; see also Company Law Review Steering Group, above n. 68, 43.
[84] Above n. 59, 231–32.
[85] Above n. 58, 217.
[86] *ibid.*, 190, 217.

will be *at least as much* exposed as shareholders to contractually uncoverable risks arising from occasional firm failure or underperformance.[87]

As regards the former category of stakeholder, the essential argument is that in a dynamic and fluctuating modern product market environment employees are increasingly called upon to develop highly specialist skills and knowledge that, whilst useful to the particular firm by whom they are presently employed, are not readily marketable elsewhere.[88] Such so-called 'firm-specific' attributes range from 'hard' skills investments such as the ability to operate a particular piece of customized machinery, to 'soft' investments including knowledge of specialized operating procedures or language ('jargon') used within a firm, or even familiarity within particular productive teams or workplace social networks.[89]

The economic significance of these investments resides in the fact that they cannot be readily redeployed to an alternative use outside of the employer firm, thus rendering the relevant employee dependent upon the firm for the opportunity to continue to earn from the use of those attributes. Otherwise, the employee must incur the personal costs of reskilling for an alternative employment.[90] At the same time, though, the employer firm is likewise dependent on the employee, given the inability of the firm to find a substitute worker without having to incur the associated skilling (or at least specialization) costs.

Stakeholder theorists highlight that, in such a situation, the employee and the firm become 'co-specialized', in the sense that the capacity of each party to continue generating wealth from the employment relation is contingent on the continuing co-operation of their counterparty.[91] Given the inability of either party to resort to the 'outside' market to find a suitable alternative contractual partner, the employee and the firm in effect become 'locked in' to their relationship, with both parties consequently sharing a joint interest in maximizing the total long-term wealth created by their joint enterprise. Meanwhile, the particular share of joint enterprise wealth that each party is able to claim becomes dependent on the relative strength of their respective bargaining positions, which is – in turn – determined by the relative credibility of each party's threat to withdraw their respective investment from the joint enterprise at any given point in time.[92]

From a corporate governance perspective, the key point is that, within such a co-specialized arrangement, the level of wealth reaped by an employee comes to depend directly on the level of wealth reaped by their employer firm as a whole, in view of the joint interest that both the firm *and the employee* have in ensuring maximization of the total 'pie' available to share between them. In terms of risk exposure, an employee who invests in acquiring firm-specific skills

---

[87] Kelly and Parkinson, above n. 41, 121–22; Mayer, above n. 73, 34.

[88] Blair, above n. 59, 249.

[89] Kelly and Parkinson, above n. 41, 127.

[90] Blair, above n. 59, 255.

[91] *ibid.*, 251.

[92] *ibid.*, 252.

or attributes could therefore be said to put themselves in an analogous position to a shareholder, insofar as the former's future job security and earnings capacity is no longer fixed in accordance with the specific terms of their contract, but rather varies directly with the future success and wealth-generating capacity of the firm as a whole. Accordingly, the employee becomes an additional residual risk-bearer, and – as such – deserves to exercise a direct influence over the future level of residual wealth created by the firm, by means of an appropriate share of corporate decision-making power.[93]

Furthermore, on the assumption that firm-specific human capital investments are conducive to significant advancements in productive efficiency and industrial innovation, it follows that there is an economic benefit to society in affording a degree of corporate decision-making power to such types of employee. In particular, it can be surmised that giving co-specialized employees a direct influence over the strategic direction of their employer firm will empower them to protect their continuing firm-specific investments within that firm, even on occasions when the managerial imperative of generating residual wealth for shareholders might otherwise impel the unilateral termination (by the firm) of such investments in the pursuit of short-term profit gains.[94]

Although the above analysis has focused exclusively on the position of employees as potential residual risk-bearers in the firm, the issue of firm-specific investment and resultant residual risk is additionally relevant to certain other common categories of corporate stakeholder relation.[95] These include suppliers who have invested in developing customer-specific machinery or production techniques, or who have geographically located their operations close to a major customer in order to reduce transportation costs. They also include trade customers (such as franchisees or dealerships) whose facilities and other attributes have been designed specifically for selling the products of one particular major supplier. Like the category of employees discussed above, the ability of both these constituencies to survive and expand in business depends to a large extent on the success of the firm with which they are accustomed to dealing, and vice versa. It follows, therefore, that permitting both these types of stakeholder a share in corporate decision-making power will arguably be conducive to protecting the continuing joint value of their co-specialized productive relationships with the relevant firm.

THE DOMINANCE OF THE ORTHODOX CONTRACTARIAN PARADIGM

Whatever one's personal view on the normative merits or drawbacks of the orthodox contractarian paradigm relative to its principal competitors, one thing is objectively clear today: the contractarian theory of the firm is unquestionably

---

[93] See Blair, above n. 59, 245, 257; Company Law Review Steering Group, above n. 68, 36.
[94] Kelly and Parkinson, above n. 41, 125; Mayer, above n. 73, 32; L. Zingales, 'In Search of New Foundations' (2000) 55 *The Journal of Finance* 1623, 1639.
[95] See Blair, above n. 59, 262; Kelly and Parkinson, *ibid.*, 127–29.

the dominant ideological reference point for students and scholars of Anglo-American governance. Moreover, it looks likely to remain so for the foreseeable future, notwithstanding growing dissatisfaction with neo-liberal ideologies within broader political and social-scientific discourse.

One particular (negative) factor arguably underpinning the dominance of the orthodox contractarian paradigm is the obvious practical limitations of its two main ideological competitors, namely the entity and stakeholder theories of the firm. Both of these alternative positions are premised on the normative idea that managers should be held directly accountable to more than just the one corporate constituency (that is, shareholders). However, in this regard, the entity and stakeholder paradigms fall prey to the common contractarian criticism that (in the words of Easterbrook and Fischel) 'a manager told to serve two masters ... has been freed of both and is answerable to neither'.[96] Consequently, '[f]aced with a demand from either group, the manager can appeal to the interests of the other', with the outcome that '[a]gency costs rise and social wealth falls'.[97]

Whilst we believe that Easterbrook and Fischel's claims as to the perceived dangers of multi-constituency accountability are somewhat exaggerated, their basic worry is nonetheless a valid one. Moreover, such concerns have a long history,[98] with Adolf Berle warning as long ago as 1932 that providing corporate managers with freedom to deviate from their exclusive service of shareholders' interests would be akin to granting them 'uncontrolled power'.[99] The inevitable result of this, according to Berle, would be 'the massing of group after group to assert their private claims by force or threat'.[100] For this reason, Berle believed that the 'shareholder versus stakeholder' debate in corporate governance could only ever be a normative zero-sum game, whereby '[e]ither you have a system based on individual ownership of property or you do not'.[101]

It is arguable that the stakeholder theory of the firm – insofar as it argues for an objective (albeit substantively broad) corporate-managerial goal of ensuring 'total wealth creation' – is somewhat less open to the above charges than the entity paradigm, wherein the lack of any such unifying criterion clearly renders corporations more susceptible to the potential vagaries of unchecked managerial discretion. Moreover, it would appear that leading proponents of the stakeholder position are fully cognizant of such concerns, and indeed have

---

[96] Easterbrook and Fischel, above n. 20, 38.

[97] *ibid*. On this, see references cited above n. 46.

[98] See H. Wells, 'The Cycles of Corporate Social Responsibility' (2002) 51 *University of Kansas Law Review* 77.

[99] A.A. Berle, 'For Whom Corporate Managers *Are* Trustees: A Note' (1932) 45 *Harvard Law Review* 1365, 1372. This piece was a critical response to a then-recently published article by Berle's contemporary, Edwin Merrick Dodd, in the same journal edition. See E.M. Dodd, 'For Whom Are Corporate Managers Trustees?' (1932) 45 *Harvard Law Review* 1145.

[100] *ibid*., 1368.

[101] *ibid*.

sought as best as possible to defuse them. Indeed, partly in response to the pur-ported 'two masters' problem at the heart of the stakeholder paradigm, Blair and Stout have developed an influential variant of this position in the form of their 'team production' model of corporate governance.[102] In essence, Blair and Stout's team production theory posits that a corporation's board of direc-tors should be understood not as the agents of either shareholders or any other particular corporate constituency, but rather as a 'neutral mediating hierarch'[103] whose function is 'to coordinate the activities of the team members, allocate the resulting production, and mediate disputes among team members over that allocation'.[104]

Blair and Stout argue that corporate law, by ascribing legal ownership over the corporation's business assets to the corporate entity itself (rather than its shareholders), serves the (proper) purpose of 'insulating corporate directors from the direct command of *any* of the groups that comprise the corporate team, including its shareholders'.[105] In balancing the competing claims of different stakeholder groups in this way, Blair and Stout recommend that directors should in particular seek to prevent any one constituency (e.g. share-holders or employees) from exploiting its relative bargaining advantage in order to demand a greater share of wealth from the firm than their respective input should merit (so-called 'rent-seeking' behaviour).[106] According to Blair and Stout, a board that fulfils this task successfully will 'balance team members' competing interests in a fashion that keeps everyone happy enough that the productive coalition stays together'.[107]

Undoubtedly, Blair and Stout's team production approach to apportion-ing corporate decision-making power has significantly enriched the ongoing 'shareholder versus stakeholder' debate in corporate governance, while providing additional conceptual ammunition to those sympathetic to the stakeholder approach. However, whether it has done enough to refute the tra-ditional criticisms of multi-constituency models of corporate responsibility is at least questionable, and we will leave readers to form their own conclusions in this regard.

Finally, we should note what we believe to be an additional important reason for the contractarian paradigm's prominence within the specific context of UK corporate governance scholarship today. This is the fact that – on a descriptive level – contractarianism would appear to provide a reasonably accurate (albeit by no means perfect) theoretical characterization of the underlying substance

---

[102] See M.M. Blair and L.A. Stout, 'A Team Production Theory of Corporate Law' (1999) 85 *Virginia Law Review* 247. For a further examination of this theory from the (alternative) perspective of determining the proper scope of the board's decision-making authority, see Chapter 4.
[103] *ibid.*, 250.
[104] *ibid.*, 251.
[105] *ibid.*, 255.
[106] *ibid.*, 292.
[107] *ibid.*, 281.

and dynamics of UK corporate governance law and regulation today. Therefore in rationalizing the main rules and institutions of UK corporate governance throughout the remainder of this book, we will tend to refer exclusively to the contractarian paradigm. However, this is not to imply that we as authors necessarily sympathize with all (or even most) of the typical normative implications that tend to follow from adherence to this particular thought paradigm, nor to deny that there are other valid approaches to understanding the nature of large business organizations together with their associated responsibilities within society.

CHAPTER 3

The Corporate Governance Regulatory Architecture

In the previous two chapters, we have sought to explain the essential nature of corporate governance as a subject of academic enquiry, and also the comparative uniqueness of the Anglo-American corporate governance paradigm. We have also highlighted the principal ways in which large business corporations are theoretically rationalized, and the implications of such views insofar as prevalent academic understandings of corporate governance are concerned. Accordingly, in this chapter, we begin to set out the contours of the applicable law itself concerning the governance of UK public companies.

Whereas the subsequent parts of the book will examine the substance of the key laws and regulations pertaining to UK corporate governance, the present chapter is focused on the main *sources* and *forms* of law in this field. In other words, here we are concerned less with what the relevant rules and principles actually are, and more with the important preliminary concerns of: (i) where we should look to find the main aspects of UK corporate governance law; (ii) what essential form(s) those provisions take; and (iii) the principal ways in which the applicable regulatory framework is enforced in practice.

As should hopefully become clear from the following discussion, on a formal level one of the most remarkable aspects of UK corporate governance law is the fact that the term itself is arguably something of a misnomer. Whilst many key norms of UK corporate governance do ultimately emanate from orthodox statutory and case law, a significant proportion of the applicable rules and principles in this field take the form of so-called 'soft law' provisions that lack the coercive force of orthodox laws, at least in the sense of being formally enforceable by recourse to the courts. Rather, in the UK as in many other jurisdictions today, corporate governance norms are typically enshrined in non-statutory codes of so-called 'best practice', violation of which elicits no direct judicial sanction in the sense of a fine, injunction or compensatory damages award.

To a large extent, the phenomenon of non-legally-binding soft law is consistent with the rationality of the contractarian understanding of corporate governance, as described in the previous chapter. Indeed, contractarianism is generally hostile to what it deems as regulatory 'interference' in corporate governance on public policy grounds, seeing any such deliberate state intervention as a clumsy intrusion into what is rightfully the domain of firm-specific private ordering. Accordingly, within the contractarian paradigm, the role of the courts and regulatory state in corporate governance is restricted to that of providing – on an 'off-the-shelf' basis – those 'default' rules and structures that are likely to be adopted in the majority of hypothetical agreements concerning the governance of individual firms. This purportedly saves incorporators the extensive transaction costs that would otherwise be involved in establishing those rules on an ad hoc contractual basis. At the same time, those firms for whom the default norms are unsuitable in any respect(s) are theoretically permitted to 'opt out' of the standard system and put in place their own alternative corporate governance arrangements instead.[1]

As alluded to in Chapter 1, the influential UK Corporate Governance Code[2] – first promulgated as the Cadbury Committee Code of Best Practice[3] back in 1992 and administered today by the Financial Reporting Council – represents the international archetype of this flexible and decentralized approach to regulation in practice. In the discussion that follows, we will show how the UK Corporate Governance Code, despite its ostensibly 'soft law' nature, is in practice a highly influential and respected regulatory instrument which public issuers ignore at their peril, not least on account of its dynamic 'comply or explain' enforcement method. Meanwhile, in a similar way, certain aspects of the UK Takeover Code[4] demonstrate that so-called 'soft law'[5] – if designed in the right way and backed up by appropriate market-based sanctions – can in practice wield considerable coercive force. Indeed, in some respects notionally 'soft' methods of corporate governance regulation can be much more effective than their orthodox 'hard law' counterparts, as the experience of the above two regulatory instruments in the UK has arguably shown.

At least insofar as UK public companies are concerned, one notable outcome of the above phenomenon has been the evolution of a complex and somewhat disparate regulatory architecture pertaining to corporate governance, encapsulating aspects of standard companies legislation, non-statutory codes of best practice and also the Listing Rules of the London Stock Exchange. Moreover, as mentioned in Chapter 1, at the helm of this architecture sits a collection

---

[1] See F.H. Easterbrook and D.R. Fischel, 'The Corporate Contract' (1989) 89 *Columbia Law Review* 1416, 1444; S.M. Bainbridge, *The New Corporate Governance in Theory and Practice* (OUP 2008), 35–37.
[2] Financial Reporting Council, *The UK Corporate Governance Code* (April 2016) ('UKCGC'), at www.frc.org.uk/Our-Work/Codes-Standards/Corporate-governance/UK-Corporate-Governance-Code.aspx.
[3] See The Cadbury Committee, Report of the Committee on the Financial Aspects of Corporate Governance (1 December 1992).
[4] The Panel on Takeovers and Mergers, *The Takeover Code* (September 2016), at www.thetakeoverpanel.org.uk/the-code/download-code.
[5] On the phenomenon of 'soft law' in corporate governance generally, see E. Ferran, 'Corporate Law, Codes and Social Norms Finding the Right Regulatory Combination and Institutional Structure' (2001) 1 *Journal of Corporate Law Studies* 381; E. Wymeersch, 'The Enforcement of Corporate Governance Codes' (2006) 6 *Journal of Corporate Law Studies* 113.

of varied regulatory authorities, ranging from traditional state lawmakers to quasi-public and even entirely non-governmental regulatory actors. At the same time, as we will show, in sophisticated capital market environments the informal sanction of competitive and reputational pressures can often prove *at least as* compelling as standard court-imposed sanctions in eliciting compliance from those organizations and individuals who are subject to the applicable rules framework.

As we will further explain below, it is even arguable that market-based forces have had the effect in some instances of pressuring *excessive* compliance by companies with prescribed corporate governance regulatory norms over recent years. This has had the curious effect of undermining the flexibility that is lauded as one of the key practical benefits of the UK's relatively informal enforcement framework, thereby calling into question UK corporate governance's purported comparative advantage in this regard over competitor systems.[6]

Sources of UK Corporate Governance Law

Standard Companies Legislation and Case Law

One thing that immediately strikes law students who are studying corporate governance for the first time is the perception that relatively little of the subject matter comprises 'real' law in the orthodox sense of legislation and case law. This is undoubtedly true. However, it would be erroneous to conclude from this that statutory and judicial sources of law are consequently irrelevant for students of corporate governance. On the contrary, as we will see in subsequent chapters of this book, some of the most fundamental and significant features of UK corporate governance law derive from one or other of these traditional forms of law. Moreover, in the case of statutory aspects of UK corporate governance in particular, the applicable legal provisions are typically established on a *mandatory* and thus *irreversible* legal footing, which at first sight would appear inconsistent with the law's arguably dominant contractarian footing in this field.

On closer inspection, though, it would seem that the widespread presence of mandatory (and especially statutory) legal rules in UK corporate governance is not quite as averse to contractarian rationality as might initially appear to be the case. Rather (and, it may be said, somewhat paradoxically), a popular and convincing contractarian explanation for the existence of mandatory corporate

---

[6] On the purported advantages of the UK's relatively informal corporate governance law enforcement framework, particularly as viewed from a comparative UK-US perspective, see J. Armour, B. Black, B. Cheffins and R. Nolan, 'Private Enforcement of Corporate Law: An Empirical Comparison of the UK and US' (2009) 6 *Journal of Empirical Legal Studies* 687; J. Armour, 'Enforcement Strategies in UK Corporate Governance: A Roadmap and Empirical Assessment' in J. Armour and J. Payne (eds), *Rationality in Company Law: Essays in Honour of DD Prentice* (Hart Publishing 2009), 71.

governance rules actually exists in the form of what may broadly be referred to as the 'market mimicking' rationale. Essentially, the argument is that despite the overall economic benefits of private rule selection, there are inevitably occasions when rules will be 'mispriced' by investors: that is to say, when investors will fail to discount adequately the projected returns from a corporate equity investment to reflect latent weaknesses or inefficiencies in the relevant firm's governance structure. Rule mispricing is prone to occur in situations where the 'search' costs that investors must incur in order to ascertain the importance of any particular corporate governance 'term' are prohibitively high. In particular, this could be said to be true in respect of complex, niche or infrequently used governance rights of shareholders.[7]

Accordingly, the function of mandatory state regulation of corporate governance affairs is, in effect, to tease out the purportedly optimal bargaining outcomes that are liable to ensue in the absence of transaction costs and other impediments to efficient contracting, so that contracts can be made to work. That is to say, the regulatory state – via appropriately targeted interventions in private ordering – can succeed in providing what the parties (counterfactually) *would have wanted* as the outcome to their mutual bargain, but for whatever reason were unable to arrive at – or perhaps even recognize as optimal – under the given circumstances. In other words, the purpose of regulation is in effect to 'mimic'[8] the operation of an efficiently functioning market, whereby contracting parties are impulsively inclined towards those agreements that are best calculated to advance their respective material interests.[9]

Whilst only relatively limited parts of standard British companies legislation pertain directly to corporate governance matters in the sense defined in this book, those that *do* certainly merit consideration in a work of this nature. In particular, the primary source of general company law in the UK, namely the Companies Act 2006, deals with the fundamentally important topic of directors' general statutory duties, including (inter alia) the three directors' duties that are arguably most significant from a corporate governance perspective, namely: (i) the director's general duty under section 171 of the Act to (*inter alia*) exercise their powers for a proper purpose;[10] (ii) the director's general

---

[7] Easterbrook and Fischel, above n. 1, 1436. For arguable examples of some such rights, see in particular Chapter 4.

[8] On the alleged 'market-mimicking' function of corporate governance law within the contractarian thought paradigm generally, see Chapter 2.

[9] See J.N. Gordon, 'The Mandatory Structure of Corporate Law' (1989) 89 *Columbia Law Review* 1549, 1554, 1549; L.A. Bebchuk, 'The Debate on Contractual Freedom in Corporate Law' (1989) 89 *Columbia Law Review* 1395. For a critical perspective on this argument, see M.T. Moore, 'Private Ordering and Public Policy: The Paradoxical Foundations of Corporate Contractarianism' (2014) 34 *Oxford Journal of Legal Studies* 693, 711–14.

[10] This duty will be discussed further, and specifically in a takeover context, in Chapter 10.

duty to promote the success of the company under section 172;[11] and (iii) the director's general duty of care, skill and diligence under section 174.[12]

The 2006 Act also notably deals with the crucial matter of shareholders' rights of intervention in corporate decision-making, which are central to determining the formal balance of decision-making power between directors and shareholders in public companies.[13] Additionally, the Act contains important provisions that address corporate takeovers and other control transactions such as schemes of arrangement.[14] To varying extents, moreover, the specific ramifications of the above statutory principles are dependent on their precise interpretation in individual problem scenarios, especially in cases concerning the application of directors' duties. This highlights the parallel importance of supplementary case law to the study of corporate governance, at least insofar as the subject is taught from a specifically legal (as opposed to purely economic or management-oriented) point of reference.

The Companies Act 2006 applies to all companies registered in the UK regardless of whereabouts in the world they subsequently conduct their business activities. Moreover, despite the United Kingdom formally comprising four separate national legislatures[15] today, the 2006 Act applies (with only very limited exceptions) uniformly throughout the UK as a whole. Likewise, notwithstanding that the UK is composed of two formally distinct judicial legal systems,[16] the companies case law of the English (and, to a significant extent, wider Commonwealth) courts is generally regarded to be applicable across the UK as a whole. For these reasons, it is therefore by and large accurate to say that, functionally speaking, the UK possesses one single and broadly homogenous system of company (and, by implication, corporate governance) law, which is contrary to the case with most other aspects of domestic private or commercial law.

Stock Exchange Listing Rules

Some noteworthy corporate governance related rules pertaining to large public companies are contained in the UK listing rules[17] promulgated by the Financial Conduct Authority (FCA), which apply to all companies whose shares are listed on the Main Market of the London Stock Exchange. Where relevant, these will be discussed in subsequent chapters of this book.

---

[11] This duty will be discussed further in Chapter 6.

[12] This duty will be discussed further, and specifically in an internal control context, in Chapter 9.

[13] These rights will be discussed further in Chapter 4.

[14] See Companies Act 2006, Parts 26–28 (addressing, respectively, schemes of arrangement, mergers and takeovers).

[15] Namely, the UK Parliament at Westminster, the Scottish Parliament in Edinburgh, the National Assembly for Wales in Cardiff and the Northern Irish Assembly at Stormont.

[16] These are the formally independent national legal systems of: (i) England and Wales (as traditionally applicable also to Northern Ireland); and (ii) Scotland.

[17] See Financial Conduct Authority, *FCA Handbook*, 'LR Listing Rules', at www.handbook.fca. org.uk/handbook.

One important point to highlight at present is the multi-tiered corporate listings regime that exists for prospective public securities issuers today, and the variety of options that this offers. First, a company wishing to issue its equity shares on a public investment marketplace in the UK can opt for a Main Market stock exchange listing, thereby rendering it subject to the regulatory purview of the FCA as the UK's official listing authority.[18] Alternatively, it can elect to issue its shares on another investment platform such as the London Stock Exchange's Alternative Investment Market (or 'AIM'), which operates its own regulatory framework as a less onerous and costly alternative to the FCA's Main Market regime.[19]

Second, those companies who opt for a Main Market listing have the additional choice today of undertaking a standard listing, or else a so-called 'premium listing'.[20] The latter type of listing entails a considerably more demanding regulatory burden than the former type, especially with respect to continuing public disclosure requirements.[21] The general logic here is that those issuers who envisage raising particularly large amounts of equity capital on the public market might find it worthwhile subjecting themselves to a higher disclosure and general compliance burden. This is in anticipation of the greater credibility and trustworthiness that a premium listing notionally represents from the viewpoint of prospective investors, thereby enabling the relevant issuer to secure cheaper and more extensive access to capital than would otherwise be possible.[22]

Of particular interest for immediate purposes is the important continuing disclosure obligation in the UK listing rules concerning publication of a company's conformance with the UK Corporate Governance Code,[23] which forms

---

[18] The FCA's official power to formulate listing rules is formally delegated to it by government under section 73A of the Financial Services and Markets Act ('FSMA') 2000.

[19] See London Stock Exchange, *AIM Rules for Companies* (July 2016), at www.londonstock exchange.com/companies-and-advisors/aim/advisers/rules/regulation.htm.

[20] See *FCA Handbook*, above n. 12, LR 1.5 'Standard and Premium Listing'.

[21] In particular, only premium listed companies are required to disclose, and obtain formal shareholder approval of, significant transactions and related party transactions under Listing Rules 10 and 11 respectively. See *ibid*.

[22] The US securities lawyer John Coffee has developed what he calls a 'bonding' rationale to explain the apparent ability of companies whose shares are listed in particularly rigorous regulatory regimes to attract a comparatively high valuation premium for their shares, relative to those companies subject to less stringent financial-regulatory requirements. Coffee argues that by submitting to an onerous regulatory environment (such as the New York Stock Exchange), a securities issuer sends a strong 'signal' to the stock market as to both the propriety of its internal controls and the superiority of its future business prospects. The ensuing assumption of investors is that only a company with sound future prospects, and thus requiring extensive capital access, would ever wish to subject itself to such a costly and demanding legal regime. See J.C. Coffee, 'Law and the Market: The Impact of Enforcement' (2007) 156 *University of Pennsylvania Law Review* 229, 291–92. On this, see also L. Ribstein, 'International Implications of Sarbanes-Oxley: Raising the Rent on US Law' (2003) 3 *Journal of Corporate Law Studies* 299, 317–18.

[23] See *FCA Handbook*, above n. 12, LR 9.8.6(5)–(6), analyzed further below.

the institutional backbone of much of Britain's dynamic corporate governance regulatory regime. This requirement is applicable to all UK-incorporated
issuers listed on the Main London Market (regardless of whether they are
standard or premium listed), and additionally to any overseas-incorporated
issuers with a premium listing thereon.[24] The precise nature and ramifications
of this requirement will be discussed in further detail below.

Finally, it should be noted that just because a company happens to be incorporated in the UK does not preclude it from issuing equity shares or other securities in an overseas listings environment, such as the New York Stock Exchange
(NYSE), the Nasdaq Stock Market or the Hong Kong Stock Exchange.
Interestingly, some of the UK's biggest and most well-known corporate names –
including BP, Barclays and GlaxoSmithKline – have a dual listing on both the
London and the New York markets. This provides them with the capacity to raise
potential capital in two separate public investment marketplaces, albeit at the
corresponding cost of submitting to the combined regulatory purview of two
different listings authorities.[25] In particular, listing on a US-based market such
as NYSE or Nasdaq entails subjection to the United States' highly demanding
system of federal securities law, including extensive periodic financial-disclosure
rules and also a number of highly onerous corporate governance requirements.
Especially salient in this regard are the notorious internal control requirements
imposed on US stock market participants (regardless of their particular country
of incorporation) by the Sarbanes-Oxley Act of 2002.[26]

For the most part, though, our principal focus in this book will be on
the key corporate governance laws and regulations applicable to those companies incorporated in the United Kingdom, who additionally have a standard or premium listing on the London Stock Exchange. Such companies are
accordingly subject both to the general rules of UK company law applicable to
domestically incorporated entities and to the additional corporate governance
related requirements emanating from the London listing rules regime (including conformance with the UK Corporate Governance Code and the Takeover
Code[27]). However, readers should nonetheless be aware of the many exceptions that are permissible from this general norm in practice.

The UK Corporate Governance Code

The UK Corporate Governance Code is the main source of regulation in relation to public company board structures in the United Kingdom. As we mentioned above (and will explain further below), the Code applies to all listed UK

---

[24] *ibid.*, LR 9.8.6–9.8.7.

[25] On the phenomenon of overseas listing generally, and the key regulatory implications
thereof, see I. Macneil and A. Lau, 'International Corporate Regulation: Listing Rules and
Overseas Companies' (2001) 50 *International & Comparative Law Quarterly* 787.

[26] See HR 5070 (107th): the Public Company Accounting Reform and Investor Protection Act
of 2002 ('Sarbanes-Oxley'), at www.govtrack.us/congress/bills/107/hr5070.

[27] On this, see further below.

companies and also to all premium-listed overseas companies on the London Stock Exchange.[28] The regulatory body vested with official responsibility for promulgating and periodically updating the Code is the Financial Reporting Council (FRC), which is additionally responsible for regulating the accounting, auditing and actuarial professions in the UK.[29]

The FRC is formally a non-governmental body that is constituted on a private sector basis in the form of a limited company. However, it operates under indirect government influence insofar as its Chair and Deputy Chair are appointed by the Secretary of State for Business, Energy and Industrial Strategy. The Chair and Deputy Chair in turn appoint the Council's other board members, who are typically from an institutional investment, industry, accounting or legal-professional background. A more detailed discussion of the extraordinary form and structure of the UK Corporate Governance Code, and – in particular – its dynamic 'comply or explain' enforcement method, will be reserved for later in this chapter.

The Takeover Code

The regulatory framework for transactions involving the transfer of control over UK public companies is governed in large part by the influential City Code on Takeovers and Mergers, otherwise known as the Takeover Code.[30] The Takeover Code is a non-statutory body of rules and principles, which essentially applies to all takeovers where the target (or 'offeree') entity is either: (i) a UK-incorporated company whose shares are traded on a regulated market in the UK or any other European Economic Area (EEA) country; or (ii) a company incorporated in an EEA country other than the UK, whose shares are traded on a regulated market in the UK.[31] Generally speaking, the Takeover Code's six General Principles and 38 Supplementary Rules are designed to ensure the efficiency and procedural fairness of a bid from the perspective of the target company's shareholders.[32]

One particular issue dealt with by the Takeover Code is the crucial question of which corporate constituency has the ultimate right to decide on the outcome of a takeover bid. As we will explain further in Chapter 10, the Takeover Code – once a takeover bid is imminent – allocates this right unquestionably to shareholders, in preference to directors or indeed any other competing stakeholder group.[33] As we will see later, this has considerable

---

[28] See above n. 24 and accompanying text.

[29] See www.frc.org.uk/Home.aspx.

[30] See above n. 4.

[31] *ibid.*, 'Introduction', A3–A4.

[32] J. Armour and D.A. Skeel, 'Who Writes the Rules for Hostile Takeovers, and Why? The Peculiar Divergence of US and UK Takeover Regulation' (2007) 95 *Georgetown Law Journal* 1727, 1730.

[33] This is principally by virtue of the so-called 'board neutrality' rule emanating from General Principle 3 and Rule 21 of the Takeover Code, on which see Chapter 10.

implications for the character and normative impetus of the UK's corporate governance system as a whole.

The Takeover Code is promulgated and administered by the Panel on Takeovers and Mergers (or Takeover Panel): a non-governmental rulemaking and executive body, which mainly comprises secondees from financial institutions that are broadly representative of the City of London's institutional shareholder and associated professional communities. The Panel administers and adjudicates on the application of the Takeover Code, and also publishes regular updates to the Code in response to developing market practices. Compliance with the Takeover Code is policed flexibly by means of informal 'real-time' communication between the Panel executive and professional intermediaries to tender offers. At the same time, the Code's application is reinforced mainly by the threat of reputational administrative sanctions for non-compliance[34] (most commonly in the form of publicized statements of public censure[35]), with only limited available recourse to the formal courts.

Whilst the Takeover Code was originally administered by the Panel on an entirely extra-legal basis,[36] this is no longer the case today. Further to the UK's implementation of the EU Takeover Directive, the existence and functions of the Panel are now statutorily formalized under domestic legislation.[37] As a consequence, the Takeover Code's ongoing enforcement is today underpinned by a residual avenue of recourse to the courts, which may be invoked on the application of the Panel[38] in the event of a failure to comply with any of its rules or administrative enforcement rulings.

A further notable connection between the Takeover Code and the English courts derives from the Court of Appeal's ruling in the landmark *Datafin*[39] case, where it was held that the inherently public function performed by the Takeover Panel (in spite of its non-governmental and financially independent status) rendered its decisions potentially susceptible to judicial review, albeit on a historical rather than contemporaneous basis so as to preclude scope for tactical litigation aimed at stalling the course of a bid in progress. This is in notable contrast to the US system of takeover regulation, which is significantly

---

[34] Armour and Skeel, above n. 32, 1731.

[35] One of the most noteworthy recent examples of such was the Panel's well-publicized public censure in November 2015 of the investment bank Credit Suisse and the international law firms Freshfields Bruckhaus Deringer and Holman Fenwick Willan, for breaches of the Takeover Code committed in connection with their respective advisory roles in a major mining industry acquisition back in 2011. See the Takeover Panel, 'Asia Resource Minerals plc (formerly Bumi plc): Statement of Public Criticism of Credit Suisse, Freshfields and Holman Fenwick Willan' (5 November 2015), at www.thetakeoverpanel.org.uk/wp-content/uploads/2014/12/2015-15.pdf; M. Dakers and J. Yeomans, 'Takeover Panel delivers public wrist-slap to Bumi advisers', *The Telegraph*, 5 November 2015.

[36] On the historical origins and early development of the Takeover Code, see A. Johnston, *The City Take-over Code* (OUP 1980).

[37] Specifically, under sections 942–956 of the Companies Act 2006.

[38] Under section 955 of the Companies Act 2006.

[39] *R v Panel on Takeovers and Mergers, ex parte Datafin Ltd* [1987] QB 815.

formalized under both federal legislation and Delaware common law. As a result, courts in the United States (unlike their English counterparts[40]) are often heavily involved in determining the outcome of bids, especially those that are carried out on a hostile or contested basis.[41]

THE 'COMPLY OR EXPLAIN' PRINCIPLE IN UK CORPORATE GOVERNANCE

Economic Rationality of the UK Corporate Governance Code and 'Comply or Explain'

It is generally acknowledged today that the quality and suitability of a company's corporate governance arrangements are material factors contributing to its economic performance.[42] It is likewise widely accepted that what constitutes efficient or 'good' governance for any particular company cannot readily be ascertained in the abstract, but rather depends on the specific characteristics of the relevant firm and also the strategic challenges facing its business at any point in time.[43]

Where a company installs an inappropriate corporate governance structure, it incurs the dual cost of: (i) unnecessary expenditure on ineffective or unsuitable monitoring mechanisms that fail to add value to the firm's organizational structure; and (ii) the loss of a more suitable alternative governance structure, which might have equipped the company more readily for securing competitive advantage in its various markets. Therefore instead of promoting a uniform or universalistic approach to corporate governance, it is strongly arguable that policymakers – to the extent that they intervene in this domain at all – should instead deploy relatively informal or reflexive regulatory techniques that are sensitive to the need to strike a balance between: on the one hand, promoting

---

[40] On the comparative informality and administrative efficiency of the UK regulatory framework in this regard, see Armour and Skeel, above n. 32, 1729; B.R. Cheffins, *Company Law: Theory, Structure and Operation* (OUP 1997), 370.

[41] Armour and Skeel, *ibid.*, 1743–44.

[42] For instance, the OECD has emphasized that '[g]ood corporate governance is not an end in itself', but rather 'is a means to support economic efficiency, sustainable growth and financial stability.' See OECD, 'G20/OECD Principles of Corporate Governance: About the Principles' (2015) at www.oecd.org/corporate/principles-corporate-governance.htm. In a similar vein, the World Bank has stressed that '[w]ell-governed companies carry lower financial and non-financial risks and generate higher shareholder returns', and 'also have better access to external finance and reduce systemic risks due to corporate crises and financial scandals'. See World Bank, 'Corporate Governance: The Development Challenges' (24 February 2016), at www.worldbank.org/en/topic/financialmarketintegrity/brief/corporate-governance.

[43] Organisation for Economic Co-Operation and Development, G20/*OECD Principles of Corporate Governance: OECD Report to G20 Finance Ministers and Central Bank Governors* (September 2015), 10–11; S. Bhagat and B. Black, 'The Uncertain Relationship between Board Composition and Firm Performance' (1999) 54 *Business Lawyer* 921.

governance best practice; while, on the other hand, preserving a sufficient degree of institutional flexibility at the individual firm level. This notionally 'light-touch' philosophy lies at the heart of the characteristic UK approach to corporate governance regulation generally.[44]

Underpinning this approach is the UK Corporate Governance Code, by virtue of which Britain has succeeded in preserving a set of corporate governance norms that are non-legally binding in form, relatively broad-based in substance and readily comprehensible by boards without the need for extensive professional assistance. Arguably the most crucial institutional contributor to the Code's comparative advantage in the above regards is the principle of 'comply or explain', whereby conformant companies are exempted from the need to adopt a prescriptive 'one-size-fits-all' model of internal organizational control. In theory, this regulatory technique permits a company to opt out, in effect, from any one or more requirements of the Code that its board considers to be cost-ineffective or otherwise inappropriate for that company's specific circumstances, on the condition that the board provides investors with a valid and reasoned justification for non-compliance in its annual directors' report at the end of the financial year.[45]

The economic rationale for 'comply or explain', as articulated succinctly by Arcot and Bruno, centres on the notion that the reasons cited by boards for deviating from any Code provision (at least where genuine) 'reveal information about why adherence to the Code provisions is not necessarily the optimal choice for a company'.[46] This implies that 'companies which provide informative justifications for their non-compliance are more likely to have weighed the pros and cons of complying before arriving at their decision ... and are thus likely to be well-governed, which is reflected in their performance'.[47] Of course, the effectiveness of 'comply or explain' in enhancing corporate performance in the above way is not an automatic given. Rather, it depends on the extent to which the 'comply or explain' approach to corporate governance norm conformance is meaningfully carried out in practice, by institutional shareholders and boards of directors alike. Indeed, the Code itself emphasizes that, in order for the 'comply or explain' approach to work properly, the particular reasons that are forwarded by a company for not complying with a particular Code provision 'should be explained clearly and carefully to shareholders'.[48] Additionally, 'the company should aim to illustrate how its actual [alternative] practices are consistent with the principle to which the particular provision relates, contribute to good governance and promote delivery of business objectives'.[49]

---

[44] On this, see Financial Reporting Council, *The UK Approach to Corporate Governance* (October 2010).

[45] On 'comply or explain' generally, see UKCGC, above n. 2, 4; Financial Reporting Council, *Comply or Explain: 20th Anniversary of the UK Corporate Governance Code* (2012).

[46] S.R. Arcot and V.G. Bruno, 'One Size Does Not Fit All, After All: Evidence from Corporate Governance', London School of Economics Working Paper (2007), 9.

[47] *ibid.*, 9, 4.

[48] UKCGC, above n. 2, 4.

[49] *ibid.*

In a similar vein, the Code recommends that, '[i]n their responses to explanations, shareholders should pay due regard to companies' individual circumstances and bear in mind in particular the size and complexity of the company and the nature of the risks and challenges it faces'.[50] In particular, it implores that '[w]hilst shareholders have every right to challenge companies' explanations if they are unconvincing, they should not be evaluated in a mechanistic way and departures from the Code should not be automatically treated as breaches'.[51] Rather, under the Code shareholders are expected 'to respond to the statements from companies in a manner that supports the "comply or explain" process and bearing in mind the purpose of good corporate governance', on the premise that '[s]atisfactory engagement between company boards and investors is crucial to the health of the UK's corporate governance regime'.[52]

Origins and Historical Development of 'Comply or Explain'

The principle of 'comply or explain' was pioneered in the landmark 1992 Report by Sir Adrian Cadbury's Committee on the Financial Aspects of Corporate Governance.[53] As the basis for its inaugural Code of Best Practice on governance, the Cadbury Committee proposed a system of voluntary compliance by corporate boards with certain recommended norms of best practice, backed up by a mandatory disclosure requirement to be contained in UK Listing Rules.

All listed companies registered in the UK were accordingly urged to comply with the Code's initial 19 provisions covering the four overarching (and overlapping) issues of the board of directors, non-executive directors, executive directors, and reporting and controls. In respect of each relevant company the board was required to make a statement about the firm's compliance with the Code as part of its annual directors' report and, in the event of non-compliance with any one or more provisions, to provide supporting reasons for the deviation(s) from the Code. Meanwhile, institutional shareholders and/or their professional advisors were encouraged to use their ownership influence to pressure companies towards compliance with the Code's provisions.

This novel 'soft' approach was justified on the basis that a mandatory and legalistic set of standards would be likely to encourage a perfunctory form of compliance by companies with the minimum standard, whereby boards and their legal advisors would aim to satisfy the strict letter of the law while nevertheless negating the Committee's key policy goals.[54] The Cadbury Committee was also very keen to enable a degree of flexibility in implementation of the Code, and emphatically rejected the notion that it should take a uniform, 'one-size-fits-all' approach to prescribing what constitutes an appropriate governance

---

[50] ibid.
[51] ibid.
[52] ibid.
[53] Above n. 3.
[54] ibid., para. 1.10.

system for any company. Accordingly, the Committee recommended that '[t]he Code [should] be followed by individuals and companies in the light of their own specific circumstances and in interpreting it they should give preference to substance over form'.[55]

When the Cadbury Committee's recommendations underwent their first comprehensive review in 1998, the overriding concern of Sir Ronnie Hampel's review committee was 'the need to restrict the regulatory burden on companies, and to substitute principles for detail wherever possible'.[56] This necessitated a reconfiguration of the balance that had previously been struck between the dual criteria of compliance and flexibility, with the Hampel Committee recommending an even stronger emphasis on the latter goal and a correspondingly reduced focus by boards on ensuring blind compliance with the Code absent proper regard for the particular circumstances of the relevant company. As the Hampel Committee explained:

> Good corporate governance is not just a matter of prescribing particular corporate structures and complying with a number of hard and fast rules. There is a need for broad principles. All concerned should then apply these flexibly and with common sense to the varying circumstances of individual companies.[57]

The Hampel Committee accordingly recommended a significant change in the process whereby companies report to shareholders and the public on their record of conformance with the Code's Provisions, together with a complementary alteration to the Code's underlying structure, both of which were subsequently adopted within the first Combined Code on Corporate Governance in 2000.[58] Meanwhile, in the more recent editions of the Code which followed the publication of the Higgs[59] and Smith[60] reports in 2003, the compliance task was further complicated with the insertion of an additional third layer of norms into the Code's basic regulatory structure. The key mechanics of this sophisticated compliance and reporting structure, which remains in place today subject to only very limited tweaks since 2003, will be analyzed in detail below.

Since its inception in the Cadbury Committee's inaugural recommendations 25 years ago, the 'comply or explain' principle has been exported from the UK to provide a basis for numerous other countries' corporate governance systems, including those of Australia, Canada, Mexico, Singapore and, to a very limited extent, even the United States.[61] Moreover, in 2013 the EU

---

[55] *ibid.*, para. 3.10.
[56] Committee on Corporate Governance, Final Report ('The Hampel Report') (January 1998), para. 1.6.
[57] *ibid.*, para. 1.11.
[58] See *The Combined Code: Principles of Best Practice and Code of Best Practice* (May 2000).
[59] See *The Higgs Report: Review of the Role and Effectiveness of Non-Executive Directors* (January 2003).
[60] See *Audit Committees: Combined Code Guidance* ('The Smith Report') (January 2003).
[61] P. Coombes and S. Wong, 'Why Codes of Governance Work' (2004) 2 *The McKinsey Quarterly* 48, 51.

Accounting Directive in effect extended the mandatory application of 'comply or explain' corporate governance reporting to companies incorporated in any EU Member State whose shares are traded on a regulated market within the European Union.[62] 'Comply or explain' has since also been adopted as a basis for numerous other important regulatory initiatives in the UK's corporate and financial domains, including the Financial Reporting Council's influential Stewardship Code[63] applicable to institutional investors in UK public companies today, the Private Equity Reporting Group's self-regulatory Good Practice Reporting Guide for Portfolio Companies[64] and the Hedge Fund Standards Board's standards of best practice for hedge funds.[65] Overall, then, it suffices to say that the Cadbury Committee's brainchild of 'comply or explain' has come a long way within its relatively short life span.

The Regulatory Mechanics of 'Comply or Explain'

In its contemporary (post-2003) structural format, the UK Corporate Governance Code is divided into three different but adjoining levels of prescription, today comprising: (i) a set of 18 relatively open-ended Main Principles together dealing with the five overarching themes of corporate leadership, board effectiveness, board accountability, directors' remuneration and relations with shareholders; (ii) a supplementary group of 27 mid-level Supporting Principles; and (iii) a larger number of more detailed explanatory Provisions.[66]

Contrary to common misunderstanding, the Code is not a self-regulatory instrument anymore, despite its original self-regulatory foundations. Rather, its functionality is underpinned by a formally binding public enforcement mechanism contained in the UK listing rules. In this regard, Listing Rule 9.8.6(5)–(6)[67] provides that listed UK companies and, likewise, premium-listed overseas companies[68] are obliged to include within their annual published financial reports a corporate governance statement detailing (inter alia): (i) how the company has applied the Main Principles of the Code, in a manner that enables shareholders to evaluate how those principles have been applied; and (ii) whether, throughout its most recent financial year, the company has complied with all relevant Code Provisions together with accompanying *reasons* to explain any specified instances of non-compliance.

---

[62] See Directive 2013/34/EU, Article 20 ('Corporate governance statement').

[63] On this, see Chapter 5.

[64] See Private Equity Reporting Group, *Improving Transparency and Disclosure: Good Practice Reporting for Portfolio Companies* (March 2016), 4, at http://privateequityreportinggroup. co.uk/wp-content/uploads/2016/03/Improving-Transparency-and-Disclosure---Good-Practice-Reporting-by-Portfolio-Companies---March-2016.pdf.

[65] See http://www.hfsb.org/standards/comply-or-explain/.

[66] See UKCGC, above n. 2.

[67] Above n. 23.

[68] See LR 9.8.7, above n. 24.

Crucially, whereas direct compliance with the actual substantive provisions of the Code is not formally obligatory for listed companies, compliance with the underpinning procedural requirement to disclose a company's recent Code conformance record undoubtedly *is* a mandatory listing condition. Where the latter obligation is breached, due to a board either failing outright to publish a corporate governance statement or else preparing a statement that is materially inadequate in its informational coverage, the company in question can potentially be sanctioned by the FCA in accordance with the standard statutory penalties regime for listing rule breaches.[69] In theory at least, a recalcitrant company could thereby be fined,[70] publicly censured[71] or, in extreme instances, suspended or even delisted from the market entirely.[72]

Notwithstanding the punitive armoury at its disposal, the Financial Conduct Authority (FCA) and, likewise, its predecessor body the Financial Services Authority (FSA) have customarily refrained from imposing sanctions on corporate issuers in instances of apparent breach of the above obligation.[73] Indeed, we are aware of no recorded instance of the FCA or the FSA having taken formal enforcement action against a company on account of having an inadequate corporate governance statement in its annual report, in spite of there being numerous documented instances of issuers failing to explain deviation from Code Provisions as required. However, it is not inconceivable that the FCA could for whatever reason choose to adopt a more interventionist stance in this regard in future, which in itself should provide a sufficient reason for responsible boards to remain vigilant about the quality and comprehensiveness of their corporate governance related disclosures to the market.

For the most part, though, it is the private dynamics of the stock market, rather than the public dynamics of administrative enforcement, that are the main driving force behind the Code as an effective regulatory instrument and behavioural influence. Accordingly the expectation is that, where shareholders are dissatisfied with the reasons that are given by a company in its attempted justification of any incidence of Code non-compliance, they can, in the first place, communicate this dissatisfaction to its board with a view to entering into a mutual dialogue aimed at resolving those concerns.[74] Where the board of a

---

[69] Penalties available to the FCA for sanctioning listing rule breaches are set out in section 91 of FSMA 2000.

[70] FSMA 2000, s 91(1).

[71] FSMA 2000, s 91(3).

[72] Under section 77(1) of FSMA 2000, the FCA is empowered, in accordance with listing rules, to discontinue the listing of any securities if satisfied that there are special circumstances which preclude normal regular dealings in them. Section 77(2) further empowers the FCA, in the alternative, to suspend the listing of any securities.

[73] See Armour, above n. 6, 103. In this regard it has notably been observed that, as a sanction for corporate governance related disclosure breaches, delisting of a recalcitrant company's shares is 'impracticable' in that 'it inflicts damage on the innocent shareholders'. See E. Wymeersch, 'The Enforcement of Corporate Governance Codes' (2006) 6 *Journal of Corporate Law Studies* 113, 131.

[74] On this, see UKCGC, above n. 2, 4.

non-compliant company is unwilling to engage with dissatisfied shareholders in this way, or fails to deal with their concerns adequately, those (large) shareholders can ultimately take the 'nuclear' step of disposing of their respective holding in that company on the market, which can potentially drive down the relevant company's share price and, in turn, undermine the relative standing of its board in the eyes of the market at large. In this way, the functionality of 'comply or explain' is predicated on the competitive discipline of public equity markets which, operating in tandem with the reputational capital of corporate boards, in effect provide a surrogate lever of rule enforcement in place of the traditional medium of the courts.

However, whilst the effective operation of 'comply or explain' as a quasi-enforcement technique is inherently dependent on such market-based dynamics, this does not render it a purely private or non-state-driven phenomenon. Rather, its pivotal reliance on the abovementioned Listing Rules disclosure requirement means that, formally speaking, the foundation of the Code's coerciveness lies in the FCA's delegated statutory powers (as the governmentally-designated UK Listing Authority[75]) to enforce the underlying conformance-disclosure obligation, without which the Code's practical impact would almost certainly be nullified. Adopting Professor Melvin Eisenberg's terminology, the Code is therefore best described as a body of 'organizational rules' which, although not legal rules in the standard sense of the term, nevertheless 'tend to operate in many ways like legal rules'.[76] That is insofar as they are 'adopted by private organizations' (in this context, the Financial Reporting Council) and also are 'directly or indirectly backed by formal sanctions'.[77]

It follows that the 'comply or explain' phenomenon, like the UK Corporate Governance Code in general, should be regarded as neither exclusively public *nor* purely private in nature. Instead, it should be understood as a complex hybrid of mutually reinforcing state and market pressures, designed to facilitate the achievement of what are, in the last place, publicly sanctioned policy goals, albeit by recourse to the private incentives and disciplines of key corporate and market actors. As such, it is an archetypical example of private ordering in the shadow of the state.[78]

Practical Impediments to the Effective Functioning of 'Comply or Explain'

In spite of the generally positive reception that the 'comply or explain' principle has received within both corporate and investor communities in the UK, there are nonetheless some serious outstanding concerns as to whether its

---

[75] See above n. 18.

[76] See M. Eisenberg, 'Corporate Law and Social Norms' (1999) 99 *Columbia Law Review* 1253, 1255.

[77] *ibid.*, 1256.

[78] On this phenomenon generally within Anglo-American corporate governance, see M.T. Moore, *Corporate Governance in the Shadow of the State* (Hart Publishing 2013).

central promise of nurturing institutional diversity is being effectively achieved in practice. We believe that two developments in particular over recent years have conspired to undermine the characteristic flexibility of the Code's innovative regulatory-conformance method.

The first main factor that has increasingly hampered the Code's flexibility is the common tendency of institutional investors and their professional corporate governance advisors to adopt a 'box ticking' approach towards monitoring companies' compliance with the Code. Accordingly, deviation from any Code provision is treated automatically as a breach regardless of the reasons cited by a company's board in justification of its non-compliance decision.

The practice of investor 'box ticking' was initially highlighted by the Hampel Committee in its 1998 Review of the early operation of the Code. According to the Committee:

> Too often [companies] believe that the codes have been treated as sets of prescriptive rules. The shareholders or their advisers would be interested only in whether the letter of the rule has been complied with – yes or no. A 'yes' would receive a tick.[79]

The Committee expressed concern about the detrimental effect of this practice on the promised flexibility of the 'comply or explain' approach:

> Box ticking takes no account of the diversity of circumstances and experience among companies, and within the same company over time ... Where practices are approved by the board after due consideration, it is not conducive to good corporate governance for the company's explanations to be rejected out of hand and for its reputation to suffer as a result.[80]

Hampel's comments in this regard have been echoed on an academic level by Arcot and Bruno, who observe that investors do not adequately pressure managers to provide effective justifications for non-compliance.[81] They explain how 'if all the boxes are ticked, in the sense that the company does comply with respect to all provisions of the Code, then the conclusion is that the company is well governed'.[82]

The popularity of this practice is understandable, given the obvious extra cost to investors of analyzing and verifying the reasons given for non-compliance. However, it destroys the intended flexibility of the Code by enshrining an inappropriate 'one-size-fits-all' approach towards the design of governance mechanisms. The effect is that the principle of 'comply or explain' is instead interpreted by investors and boards as that of 'comply or breach', with box

---

[79] Above n. 56, para. 1.12.

[80] *ibid.*, para. 1.13.

[81] S.R. Arcot and V.G. Bruno, 'In Letter but Not in Spirit: An Analysis of Corporate Governance in the UK' (2006) London School of Economics Working Paper.

[82] *ibid.*, 32.

ticking of uniform criteria ousting any more fundamental analysis of compa-nies' explanations for deviation from Code Provisions.[83]

It would appear that a significant catalyst in this regard over recent years has been the rapidly growing influence in the UK of specialized corporate gov-ernance advisory firms, known colloquially by their American name of 'proxy advisors'.[84] The market leaders in this burgeoning professional sub-industry include Institutional Shareholder Services (ISS), Glass Lewis, Manifest, Pensions Investment Research Consultants (PIRC) and the Institutional Voting Information Service (IVIS). In theory, the presence of these informed and spe-cialist consultancies should help to mitigate the collective action difficulties brought about by a public company's dispersed share ownership structure.[85]

However, corporate governance advisory firms are often seriously inhibited in their own monitoring activities as a result of inevitable resource limitations. Furthermore, the tendency of listed companies to bunch their Annual General Meetings around seasonal peaks often presents advisors with extremely short deadlines within which to turn around companies' governance statements at the request of shareholders. It has been recorded that, partly as a result of the above factors, corporate governance advisory firms are often either unwilling or unable to afford qualitative consideration to companies' explanations for non-compliance with the Code, but instead opt to treat reasoned deviation from any Code pro-vision as tantamount to simple breach.[86] Also, many corporate governance advi-sory firms have a practice of superimposing their own governance requirements on companies over and above those provided by the Code itself. These standards are often more substantively onerous and/or formally absolute than the corre-sponding Code Provisions, thus effectively undercutting the 'comply or explain' principle altogether in respect of the particular issues covered.[87]

A second major factor that has arguably undermined the utility of the 'comply or explain' approach in recent years has been the attitudes towards Code con-formance adopted by corporate boards themselves, who have become accus-tomed in many cases to providing perfunctory or 'boiler-plate' explanations for non-compliance with Code Provisions. This has had the adverse effect of reducing

---

[83] Coombes and Wong, above n. 61, 53. In a similar vein, MacNeil and Li have suggested that the basic regulatory dilemma for companies subject to the UK Code can in practice be characterized as that of 'comply or perform', in the sense that the inability and/or unwillingness of investors and analysts to evaluate properly a company's reasons for non-compliance has led them to adopt that firm's financial performance (by share price) as a routine proxy for reasoned explanations by its board. See I. MacNeil and X. Li, '"Comply or Explain": Market Discipline and Non-Compliance with the Combined Code' (2006) 14 *Corporate Governance: An International Review* 486, 492.
[84] On the role of proxy advisors in corporate governance generally, see S. Choi, J.E. Fisch and M. Kahan, 'The Power of Proxy Advisors: Myth or Reality?' (2010) 59 *Emory Law Journal* 869.
[85] On collective action problems generally as they affect Anglo-American corporate ownership and governance, see Chapter 5.
[86] Financial Reporting Council, *2007 Review of the Combined Code: Summary of Responses to Consultation* (November 2007), paras 12–13, 23; Financial Reporting Council, *Developments in Corporate Governance and Stewardship 2015* (January 2016), 15.
[87] On this, see M.T. Moore, '"Whispering Sweet Nothings": The Limitations of Informal Conformance in UK Corporate Governance' (2009) 9 *Journal of Corporate Law Studies* 95, 123–25.

the merit of explanation as a substitute for full Code compliance by boards and, in turn, undermining investors' trust in the genuineness of those explanations for non-compliance that *are* actually motivated by valid strategic reasons.[88]

A so-called 'boiler-plate' corporate governance statement is one that contains only generic and/or perfunctory remarks which make little or no reference to the specific circumstances of the relevant company: for example, that non-compliance with a particular Code Provision is 'of commercial benefit' or 'in the best interests of the company'. As an informative guide to shareholders, such statements are virtually useless on account of their inherent subjectivity and generality, which preclude investors from undertaking any sort of serious evaluation of the basis for the directors' belief in this regard.[89] By contrast, a genuine explanation for non-compliance should include detailed and verifiable company-specific information, on the basis of which investors can form their own independent assessment of the matter in question.[90]

To some extent the practice of 'boiler-plating' is understandable, given the sheer length of public company annual reports today and the correspondingly large administrative burden involved in their preparation. However, where investor disinterest in the quality of explanations given for non-compliance discourages companies from devoting any more than minimal resources towards this task, there results something of a vicious circle whereby poor-quality corporate reporting and investor disengagement become mutually reinforcing phenomena. The natural and unfortunate consequence is that boards increasingly come to view corporate governance as a purely procedural endeavour, which is external to the company's 'real' business affairs. In other words, governance is seen mainly as a negative issue of compliance or regulatory risk management, rather than as a positive contributor to enhanced corporate performance in itself.[91]

ANTICIPATED IMPLICATIONS OF BREXIT FOR THE UK'S CORPORATE GOVERNANCE ARCHITECTURE

Given the highly uncertain political and legal climate at the time of writing, it is difficult to predict with any precision what the likely outcome of the UK's recent 'Brexit' vote will be, at least insofar as the future shape of the country's corporate governance regulatory architecture is concerned. However, without wishing to sound glib or lackadaisical about the undoubted challenges that lie ahead in this

---

[88] On this practice generally, see Arcot and Bruno, above n. 81. Recent evidence would suggest that, whilst 'boiler-plating' of corporate governance statements remains a problem, its frequency would appear to be decreasing. Indeed, the FRC in 2016 recorded a material improvement in the number of companies providing comprehensive reasons in support of incidences of Code non-compliance. See Financial Reporting Council, *Developments*, above n. 86, 6.

[89] MacNeil and Li, above n. 83, 489–90.

[90] Financial Reporting Council, What Constitutes an Explanation under 'Comply or Explain': Report of Discussions between Companies and Investors (February 2012), 5–6.

[91] Curiously, such beliefs are entirely averse to the fundamental ethos of the UK Corporate Governance Code, as expressed in its salient preliminary assertion that '[t]he purpose of corporate governance is to facilitate effective, entrepreneurial and prudent management that can deliver the long-term success of the company'. See above n. 2, 1.

area, we would tentatively surmise that, at least in the short to medium term, the implications of Brexit are likely to be fairly limited in this context.

The most significant anticipated outcome of Brexit in terms of the issues discussed above will be the ensuing disapplication of the EU Takeover Directive[92] in a domestic context. This means that the UK government will formally be at liberty, if it so chooses, to remove the statutory basis to the Takeover Panel's existence and enforcement powers.[93] The effect of such a move would be to restore the Panel's original (pre-2006) status as a uniquely private sector regulatory body, subject only to the relatively minimal constraint of having its decisions potentially subject to domestic judicial review.[94] Whether the government ultimately takes this step post-Brexit remains to be seen. However, even if it does opt to do so this would be unlikely to have much of an effect on the day-to-day operations of the Takeover Panel and Code. Indeed, the government's initial statutory formalization of the Panel's status and powers back in 2006, following the UK's implementation of the Takeover Directive,[95] would appear to have had only a limited practical impact in this regard. We see no particular reason to believe that a future post-Brexit reversal of this development would be any less disruptive to the Panel's normal activities, at least on an ongoing operational level.

One further notable effect of Brexit in the present context will be the possibility of removal (insofar as UK traded companies are concerned) of the EU-wide requirement for mandatory public statements concerning publicly traded companies' governance compliance practices.[96] However, to suggest that this might threaten the continuing operation of 'comply or explain' in the UK in any way would be preposterous, given that 'comply or explain' – and, moreover, the notion of corporate governance 'best practice' codes in general – are British-originated phenomena whose existence at domestic level long predates the abovementioned EU initiatives in this field. Furthermore, there would appear to be no particularly strong domestic political appetite at present to effect any sort of fundamental change to the UK's formal regulatory architecture in this field, notwithstanding the government's recent publication (in November 2016) of a Green Paper tentatively setting out some proposed reforms to substantive corporate governance norms on a domestic level.[97]

---

[92] See Directive 2004/25/EC on takeover bids.

[93] On this, see above n. 37.

[94] On this, see above n. 39 and accompanying text.

[95] See The Takeovers Directive (Interim Implementation) Regulations 2006 (SI 2006/1183).

[96] See above n. 62 and accompanying text.

[97] See Department for Business, Energy and Industrial Strategy, *Corporate Governance Reform: Green Paper* (November 2016). Indeed, in this document the government expressly commends the UK's 'comply or explain' regulatory framework as being a 'key strength' of its national corporate governance system, given its capacity 'to combine high standards with low burdens and the flexibility for leading businesses to innovate, rather than being unduly constrained by rules that can become rapidly outdated' (*ibid.*, 50). Interestingly, the Green Paper raises the question of whether consideration should be given to subjecting larger *privately*-held companies to a corresponding set of corporate governance regulatory standards (in addition to listed public companies), whether in the form of the main Code itself or else a more suitably designed variant version of it (see *ibid.*, 46).

PART II

Relational Aspects of Corporate Governance: Shareholders, Boards, Managers and Employees

CHAPTER 4

Board Authority and Shareholders' Rights of Intervention

This chapter will discuss the decision-making primacy of a company's board of directors as one of the most fundamental legal principles of UK (and, indeed, Anglo-American) corporate governance. The first part of the chapter sets out the main corporate-constitutional and common law rules that establish this basic principle, followed by an overview of the principal theoretical rationales for centralized board governance. The second part discusses the status and role of shareholders, focusing on rights of intervention in corporate decision-making – in particular participation in corporate voting – that shareholders are granted by virtue of company law (as opposed to shareholder engagement through additional or other means, which will be discussed in Chapter 5). This part will also discuss the practical significance of shareholders' intervention rights and, finally, conclude with an assessment of the merits of 'shareholder empowerment' as a counterbalance to board primacy.

THE PRIMACY OF THE CORPORATE BOARD

Legal Foundations

The board's primacy is reflected in both the UK's Model Articles as well as the Delaware General Corporation Law, which both make clear that the ultimate power to 'manage' or direct the company is by default vested in the board of directors.[1] This fact, as well as the 'director primacy' theory explored further below, should not confuse readers who might fairly point to the 'shareholder primacy' norm mentioned elsewhere in this book.[2] Although the terminology

---

[1] Model Articles for Public Companies and Model Articles for Private Companies Limited By Shares, article 3: 'Subject to the articles, the directors are responsible for the management of the company's business, for which purpose they may exercise all the powers of the company.'; Delaware Code Annotated, title 8, section 141(a): 'The business and affairs of every corporation organized under this chapter shall be managed by or under the direction of a board of directors, except as may be otherwise provided in this chapter or in its certificate of incorporation'. In contrast, the CA 2006 does not contain a comparable provision.

[2] See Chapters 2 and 5.

varies, 'shareholder primacy' as used in this book refers to the board's primary *accountability* to shareholders and obligation to focus on their interests, but does not normally relate to the allocation of decision-making powers.[3] Also, as we will explain in more detail in Chapter 7, 'board primacy' does not mean that boards will exercise every decision-making function themselves: directors typically delegate many tasks to corporate officers and employees, who in turn may delegate them further down the corporate hierarchy. Moreover, a company's articles (UK) or certificate of incorporation (US) may assign certain powers to the shareholders and/or limit the board's power. However, neither delegation nor, exceptionally, alterations to the default rule of the board's supreme powers within the corporation change the fundamental principle of board primacy (or board authority) that – despite the trend towards strengthening shareholder powers in the present chapter and elsewhere in this book – remains a hallmark of the Anglo-American corporate structure.

Are Directors the 'Agents' of Shareholders?

In analyzing the legal and economic dynamics of the relationship between directors and shareholders within a company, it may be convenient to think of directors as being the 'agents' of shareholders. Indeed, in Chapter 2, we also discussed the contractarian model that conceptualizes the relationship and diverging interests between shareholders and directors/managers in terms of a principal-agent model. Yet, perhaps confusingly, despite such terminology there is no 'agency' in the traditional legal sense of this term. Particularly in the context of a public company, the idea of shareholders as principals (or 'owners' of the company)[4] and directors as their agents, where directors would act according to shareholders' instructions and as their representatives, is legally and factually incorrect.

Although shareholders can assume certain powers, or even direct the board to act in a certain manner,[5] directors are not their agents. In two early cases, the UK Court of Appeal has made it clear that shareholders and directors are not in an agency relationship. In *Automatic Self-Cleansing Filter Syndicate Co. v Cunninghame*,[6] a shareholder brought an action demanding that the board should implement a shareholders' resolution, adopted with a simple majority of votes, that required the company to sell its assets to another company. However, the company's articles provided that the directors were entrusted with managing the company and the only procedure for shareholders to

---

[3] See, for example, J.E. Fisch, 'Measuring Efficiency in Corporate Law: The Role of Shareholder Primacy' (2005) 31 *Journal of Corporation Law* 637, 638 n. 4, explaining that 'shareholder primacy' can refer to (1) the principle of shareholder wealth maximization; (2) the ultimate control of shareholders over corporate decision-making; or (3) the idea that boards and managers owe fiduciary duties (exclusively or mainly) to shareholders.

[4] As will be discussed in more detail below, shareholders do not 'own' the company.

[5] On the shareholders' so-called 'reserve power', see text further below.

[6] [1906] 2 Ch 34 (CA).

influence the board's decision-making was through a special resolution (passed with a 75 per cent majority of votes). The Court of Appeal thus refused the claim as an invalid attempt to instruct the board by sidestepping the company's constitutional separation of powers. In this context, the court stated that directors are not the agents of the shareholders, and that the only way for shareholders to 'direct' the board was through the procedure as outlined in the company's articles.

Shortly thereafter, in *Gramophone and Typewriter Co v Stanley*,[7] the Court of Appeal again referred to its decision in *Automatic Self-Cleansing* and affirmed the previously stated position on the legal nature of the shareholder-director relationship. As Buckley LJ stated:

> The directors are not servants to obey directions given by the shareholders as individuals; they are not agents appointed by and bound to serve the shareholders as their principals. They are persons who may by the [articles] be entrusted with the control of the business, and if so entrusted they can be dispossessed from that control only by the statutory majority which can alter the articles. Directors are not, I think, bound to comply with the directions even of all the corporators acting as individuals. Of course the corporators have it in their power by proper resolutions, which would generally be special resolutions, to remove directors who do not act as they desire, but this in no way answers the question ... whether the corporators are engaged in carrying on the business of the corporation. In my opinion they are not. To say that they are involves a complete confusion of ideas.[8]

As these two cases and their strong reliance on the articles demonstrates, the division and allocation of corporate powers in UK companies is governed by contractarian principles. The Companies Act 2006 reflects this basic principle in section 33(1), which provides that the 'provisions of a company's constitution bind the company and its members to the same extent as if there were covenants on the part of the company and of each member to observe those provisions'. Of course, while shareholders can alter the corporate constitution[9] at any time, they can only do so in accordance with prescribed constitutional procedure, which requires a special resolution with a heightened majority requirement of three-quarters.[10]

Again, the *Automatic Self-Cleansing* decision provides a good illustration of this point. There, alluding to the partnership roots of English company law,[11] the court compared the position of directors to those of 'managing partners appointed to fill that post by a mutual arrangement between all the shareholders'.[12] It also stated that, as in the case of a partnership, the internal arrangements

---

[7] [1908] 2 KB 89 (CA).
[8] This sentiment was also expressed in *John Shaw & Sons v Shaw & Shaw* [1935] 2 KB 113.
[9] As defined in section 17 of the Companies Act 2006.
[10] *ibid.*, sections 21 and 283(1).
[11] See L.C.B Gower, 'Some Contrasts between British and American Law' (1956) 69 *Harvard Law Review* 1369, 1370–72.
[12] [1906] 2 Ch 34 (CA), per Cozens-Hardy LJ.

between the parties making up a company are 'mutual stipulations for their common benefit' and that, in the case at hand, there was 'no ground for saying that the mere majority can put an end to the express stipulations contained in the bargain which they have made'.[13] In other words, shareholders should lie in the bed that they have made for themselves: they are bound by the corporate constitution, which is akin to an agreement or 'contract' and which they cannot simply override by giving instructions to directors as their 'agents'. As one commentator has observed, English company law is thus based on a 'simple – but very flexible – empowering, facultative principle, through which shareholders can establish in a company's articles … how they will interact with each other, and with other participants in the company. This principle … [gives] enduring legal effect to shareholders' bargains as to how their company is to be run.'[14]

Under English law, therefore, the board's supreme executive authority stems from the contractarian principle of consensus or agreement between shareholders via the corporate constitution. Under US law, in contrast, the board's authority is traditionally regarded to emanate directly from the state as the formal grantor of corporate status (the 'concession' theory of corporate law).[15] Under this latter view, the directors are also not regarded as agents of the shareholders given that they receive their powers directly from the state. The Court of Appeals of New York, for example, has expressed this idea in *Hoyt v Thompson's Executor*:[16]

> The board of directors of a corporation do not stand in the same relation to the corporate body which a private agent holds toward his principal. In the strict relation of principal and agent, all the authority of the latter is derived by legislation from the former … But in corporate bodies the powers of the board of directors are, in a very important sense, original and undelegated … in the sense of being received from the State in the act of incorporation.

Thus, in continuance of the traditional roots of their respective company laws both the UK and US states such as Delaware do not conceptualize shareholders and directors as principals and agents in a technical legal sense. Indeed, in Delaware – in contrast to UK corporate law – the law does not even permit shareholders to initiate amendments to the company's charter of incorporation in order to remove executive authority from the board. In this and other respects,[17] UK shareholders may exercise greater influence over directors than their US counterparts.

---

[13] *ibid.*

[14] R. Nolan, 'The Continuing Evolution of Shareholder Governance' (2006) 65 *Cambridge Law Journal* 95.

[15] On the concession theory, see M. Petrin, 'From Nature to Function: Reconceptualizing the Theory of the Firm' (2013) 118 *Penn State Law Review* 1, 5–6.

[16] 19 N.Y. 207 (N.Y. 1859), per Comstock J. See also *People ex rel. Manice v Powell*, 201 N.Y. 194 (N.Y. 1911), where Chase J found that 'the individual directors making up the board are not mere employees, but a part of an elected body of officers constituting the executive agents of the corporation'.

[17] See the discussion further below in this chapter.

Theoretical Rationales for Board Primacy

In the 1970s, John Kenneth Galbraith developed a managerial or techno-cratic justification for centralized corporate decision-making.[18] Essentially, Galbraith argued that organizational, group decision-making must necessar-ily be authoritarian in order to protect the organization (or 'technostructure') from poorly informed outsiders. While Galbraith argued that power therefore had to pass from the shareholders to the corporate organization itself, he also observed – in keeping with the weak position of boards during the time of his writing – that it was management, not the board of directors, that held *de facto* decision-making power.

Subsequently, corporate theorists have developed various explanations for authoritative corporate decision-making, now, however, with a focus on the board's primacy.[19] As it turned out, the dominant contractarian paradigm (discussed in Chapter 2) was particularly well suited to explain the directors' elevated position, namely by reference to hypothetical negotiations between the board and shareholders, with board primacy representing the most effi-cient outcome of such negotiations. Under this view, the law – in order to avoid the need for actual negotiations, which would be time consuming and costly – simply provides for this decision-making arrangement as the (pre-sumed) best – because most efficient – option for all parties involved. For example, Stephen Bainbridge refers to this contractarian or consent-based jus-tification for board autonomy when he notes that 'the rights of shareholders are established through bargaining, even though the form of the bargain typi-cally is a take-it-or-leave-it standard form contract provided off-the-rack by the default rules of corporate law and the corporation's organic documents'.[20] This consent-based approach provides the basis for Bainbridge's director primacy theory, which presently represents one of the most prominent descriptive and normative accounts of the board's authority.

Under director primacy theory, the focus is not on a company's purported nature as being a nexus of contracts.[21] Instead, the guiding idea is that the firm *has* a central nexus of contracts, which is a board of directors equipped with ultimate power of fiat or authority. The board, in turn, negotiates with and hires the various factors of production or 'capital'. Drawing in part on the economist Kenneth Arrow's work on organizational decision-making, direc-tor primacy contends that effective corporate governance requires ultimate authority over the firm's conduct to be vested in a central place – a model that is mirrored by the typical decision-making structure of public corporations today. Thus, the board of directors, and not shareholders, is and should be

---

[18] See J.K. Galbraith, *Economics and the Public Purpose* (Houghton Mifflin 1973) and *The New Industrial State* (Princeton University Press 1976), 186.
[19] There is also an opposing movement that argues for increasing shareholders powers. For aspects of this discussion, see the section on the merits of shareholder empowerment below.
[20] S.M. Bainbridge, *The New Corporate Governance in Theory and Practice* (OUP 2008), 33.
[21] On this, see Chapter 2.

in control of the corporation, exercising almost unfettered authority. Among the model's most important claims is therefore that in order to ensure corporate decision-making efficiency, the board's decision-making authority should, subject to narrow exceptions, not be trumped by either shareholders or courts.[22] To be sure, Bainbridge also queries why shareholders should and would voluntarily consent to vest decision-making authority in the board, rather than retain it for themselves. In short, his answer is that there is a necessity of centralized authority given that shareholders in widely dispersed companies will have difficulty in reaching effective consensus, possess limited information, and may encounter conflicting interests among themselves. In this situation, centralized and specialized decision-making by the board is arguably preferable. We will return again to these apparent limitations faced by shareholders later in the chapter when we discuss the merits of shareholder empowerment.

Another notable modern theory – which is also based on contractarian ideas – is Margaret Blair and Lynn Stout's team production model, which we discussed in Chapter 2. As explained there, the corporation is described as a team-production unit that serves as a vehicle through which teams of shareholders, creditors, managers, employees and other stakeholders relinquish control over firm-specific resources to a board of directors.[23] The public firm is a 'mediating hierarchy' whose essential function, exercised through the board of directors, is to coordinate team members' activities, allocate production outputs, and mediate disputes among team members.[24] 'At the peak of this hierarchy', Blair and Stout explain, 'sits a board of directors whose authority over the use of corporate assets is virtually absolute and whose independence from individual team members … is protected by law.'[25] Because of the board's independent position, which sees it floating above the other team members and exercising a role similar to that of a trustee for the firm's assets, the team production approach tends to support policies that shield directors from being under the direct control of either shareholders or stakeholders. Thus, the team production concept also provides theoretical support for board authority or board primacy, albeit for reasons that differ from director primacy theory.[26]

---

[22] Director primacy theory also asserts that shareholders alone, as opposed to other stakeholders, are the appropriate beneficiaries of director fiduciary duties. Consequently, director primacy entrusts the board with maximizing the wealth of shareholders, whose interests should prevail over those of any other constituencies.

[23] M.M. Blair and L.A. Stout, 'A Team Production Theory of Corporate Law' (1999) 85 *Vanderbilt Law Review* 247.

[24] In contrast to the traditional contractarian approach, team production implies that the board should take into account interests other than only those of shareholders, since its responsibility is to protect the firm-specific resources for all team members.

[25] Blair and Stout, above n. 23, 753.

[26] On these reasons, see Chapter 2.

SHAREHOLDERS' RIGHTS OF INTERVENTION IN CORPORATE DECISION-MAKING

Having outlined the board's authoritative position in the modern public corporation, this part of the chapter will look more closely at the status and 'decision-making' rights of shareholders, which – as we will see – are more akin to intervention rights as opposed to rights of actual decision-making per se.

We begin by stressing the importance of rejecting the popular conception of shareholders as the legal 'owners' of a company. Once the relevance of ownership as a justification for shareholder rights is undermined, it becomes easier to appreciate the very limited extent to which shareholders are actually vested with affirmative decision-making powers under prevailing corporate governance laws. In order to provide a more complete understanding of share ownership and shareholder rights, the following discussion will also touch upon the issue of financial intermediation, that is the potentially lengthy chains between beneficial owners of shares and the companies in which they invest their capital.

The discussion will then proceed to look at the main powers that shareholders have to intervene in managerial decision-making, whether on an *ex ante* or *ex post facto* basis, affording special attention to shareholders' voting rights. The extent of shareholder rights under UK law relative to its US/Delaware counterpart will be discussed as well. To put shareholder rights as provided by the law in perspective with their relevance and use in practice, the following will also emphasize the limited extent to which shareholders' most coercive intervention powers are actually used within public companies. Finally, the chapter ends with a discussion of the merits of 'shareholder empowerment', addressing the controversial question as to whether there is a case for more expansive shareholder rights.

Shareholders as Owners of the Company?

We have, above, already clarified that shareholders are not principals and directors are not their agents. We begin this part of the discussion by addressing another common misconception: the idea that shareholders are the 'owners' of the companies of which they are members. To be sure, it is common to colloquially refer to shareholders as owners of their companies. Indeed, even economist and Nobel Prize winner Milton Friedman in a well-known essay once famously proclaimed that shareholders own the corporation.[27] Nevertheless,

---

[27] M. Friedman, 'The Social Responsibility of Business Is to Increase Its Profit', *The New York Times Magazine*, 13 September 1970. Note that Friedman made this observation in relation to the question of corporate social responsibility (and whether boards should have duties other than shareholder value maximization), which he argued against based on the idea of shareholders' ownership of companies.

this view has been shown to be incorrect, as a matter of law and even as a matter of figurative speech.

First, a basic observation is that shareholders have no proprietary interest in their company's assets. For instance, a shareholder of Apple Inc. would clearly not be entitled to walk into the company's headquarters in California and demand electronic gadgets representing the value of his shares. While this seems obvious, shareholders of smaller, closely-held companies sometimes display difficulties differentiating between their ownership of shares and the company's ownership of the assets of the business. Similarly, discussions of corporate governance issues in public companies – executive remuneration is one example – still often invoke the image of the shareholders as owners.[28] But as the House of Lords has stated in *Macaura v Northern Assurance Co*,[29] 'it is not the shareholders but the company that owns the corporate assets, and the concept of a share serves somewhat different functions'. To put it more succinctly, as the House of Lords stated in yet another case, 'shareholders are not, in the eyes of the law, part owners of the undertaking'.[30]

While not providing ownership of the company, there are three main functions that shares serve. First, a share denotes the holder's proportionate financial stake in the company. Second, a share denotes the holder's interest in the company as an 'association', which includes the rights of voting. Third, a share represents a form of property in its own right, which can be bought and sold.[31] The latter function also correctly reflects the legal nature of shares, which can be owned *themselves* but which do not convey ownership rights in the company by which they were issued.[32] The modern view is thus that only the shares – but not the company – are objects of property owned by the respective shareholder.[33]

---

[28] See B. Groom, 'Cable Warns of Curbs unless Top Companies Act over Executive Pay', *Financial Times*, 22 April 2014 (quoting a former UK business secretary as saying 'we will see how far [executives] have listened to pressure from the people who own the banks – the shareholders').

[29] [1925] AC 619.

[30] *Short v Treasury Commissioners* [1948] AC 534 (HL), per Evershed LJ.

[31] L. Sealy and S. Worthington, *Cases and Materials in Company Law* (10th ed., OUP 2013), 493. Shareholders' rights to dispose of their shares are not unlimited. Although shares are usually freely transferable in public companies, restrictions for the sale of shares may apply in private companies. Additionally, shareholders may agree to voluntary transfer restrictions in shareholders' agreements.

[32] See also *Borland's Trustee v Steel* [1901] 1 Ch 279, where Farwell J noted that '[a] share is the interest of a shareholder in the company measured by a sum of money, for the purpose of liability in the first place, and of interest in the second, but also consisting of a series of mutual covenants entered into by all the shareholders inter se in accordance with [the constitution]'.

[33] See also section 541 of the Companies Act 2006, which describes the nature of shares in terms of a member's personal property. In the UK, shares are conceptualized by reference to the property law concept of 'choses in action', that is property rights in something intangible, or which is not in one's possession, but enforceable through legal or court action. For an in-depth discussion, including philosophical aspects, of the nature of shares and their ownership, see also P. Ireland, 'Company Law and the Myth of Shareholder Ownership' (1999) 62 *Modern Law Review* 32.

Shareholders can therefore be said to have both a right *in* and *against* the company. The right *against* the company is a residual right, a right to receive whatever is left in corporate insolvency (winding up) after claims by higher-ranking creditors have been settled.[34] The right *in* the company consists of a set or bundle of rights that, to some extent, should counter-balance the board's primary decision-making authority in the company.

Intermediation and the Investment Chain

In this chapter and throughout this book we often refer to 'the shareholder' or 'the shareholders'. However, given the increasing complexity surrounding the holding of shares, it seems prudent to have a closer look at this point at what it actually means to talk about 'shareholders' before we proceed with a discussion of shareholder rights.

It is well known that there is a significant distinction between individual shareholders and institutional shareholders (the latter of which we will discuss in more detail in the next chapter). However, we should note, first, that there are additional categories of shareholder if one uses a more granular categorization. For example, the Kay Review's analysis of modern shareholder ownership divided shareholders into insurance companies, pension funds, individuals and 'other', with the 'other' category comprising charities, financials, governments, hedge funds, investment funds, investment trusts, company holdings and unclassified funds.[35] The use of these additional sub-classes may already give the reader a better sense of the heterogeneous nature of the shareholder franchise.

Second, the individual shareholder's relationship with the company is likely far less direct and more complex than a non-specialist observer might assume. Typically, due to the increasing use of intermediaries, there is an 'investment chain' between the beneficial owners of shares (who are commonly thought of as 'the shareholders') and the public companies in which they invest.[36] As the Kay Review (which refers to beneficial owners as 'investors' or 'savers') noted, '[b]etween the company and the saver are now interposed registrars, nominees, custodians, asset managers, managers who allocate funds to specialist asset managers, trustees, investment consultants, agents who "wrap" products, retail platforms, distributors and independent financial advisers'.[37] The orthodox ownership chain observed in UK public companies today will be analyzed in further detail in the next chapter. For now, though, it suffices to note some

---

[34] See also the corresponding discussion in Chapter 2 on shareholders' residual risk-bearing role.

[35] J. Kay, *The Kay Review of UK Equity Markets and Long-Term Decision Making: Final Report* (July 2012), 32. On the main types of institutional shareholder typically seen in UK public companies, see also the discussion in Chapter 5.

[36] One consequence of this is the use of proxies at the General Meeting (discussed below).

[37] Kay Review, above n. 35, 30.

important points pertaining to the difficulties involved in identifying the 'real' ownership interest underlying complex and fragmented investment chains.

The difficulty here is that despite the existence of lengthy intermediation chains, what normally counts for companies when it comes to voting and other shareholder rights is solely the legal owner – who is not necessarily the person with the relevant beneficial or economic interest – as reflected in the company's register of members. It is this registered shareholder (who may also be referred to as a 'nominee shareholder') who is the person or entity that can exercise shareholder rights.[38] Thus, by default, the registered shareholder may vote, will be the one with whom the company will communicate, etc. Given the reality of intermediation, however, the disregard of beneficial ownership may disenfranchise indirect investors. As Brenda Hannigan observes:

> Often the result is that the person with the voting rights is uninterested in exercising them (monitoring the investment remotely as it were) whereas the ultimate beneficial owner of the shares might be interested but does not have the legal right to exert any influence over the company in which his money is invested. The classic example is the pension fund investment where sums are passed from the contributor through the hands of trustees and managers in an ever-lengthening chain to the company raising capital. Even identifying shareholders, or at least those with the true economic interest, along the investment chain can be difficult as a result of stock lending practices and long chains, possibly across borders.[39]

As part of its study of equity markets and long-term decision-making, the Kay Review also considered intermediation and its impact on capital markets. It observed 'an explosion of intermediation' and noted that 'asset managers – specialist investment intermediaries – have become the dominant players in the investment chain'.[40] These asset managers, not the beneficial owners, 'typically play a key role in exercising the attributes of share ownership most relevant to company decision making: the right to vote and the right to buy or sell a given share'.[41] Indeed, the increasing popularity of investing in equity markets

---

[38] For an illustration of this principle, see *Eckerle v Widecker Westfalenstahl GmbH* [2013] 3 EWCH 68, where the court held that a minority shareholder protection mechanism did not apply to the beneficial owners of shares. But see section 793 of the Companies Act 2006, which gives public companies the opportunity to look behind legal ownership and require information about 'interests' in its shares. See also the new provisions in Part 21A of the Companies Act requiring companies to maintain a register of people with significant direct or indirect control over the company.

[39] B. Hannigan, *Company Law* (4th ed., OUP 2016), 151. Additionally, also as part of the intermediation process, the majority of shares by value in the UK are now held in multiple-ownership pooled accounts, where the true beneficiary is not easily identifiable. See also H.T.C. Hu and B.S. Black, 'The New Vote Buying: Empty Voting and Hidden (Morphable) Ownership' (2006) 79 *Southern California Law Review* 811, which describes arrangements in which economic ownership and corporate voting power are decoupled and in extreme cases can even lead to situations where the party exercising votes has an interest in reducing the company's share price.

[40] Kay Review, above n. 35, 11.

[41] *ibid.*

through mutual funds and exchange traded funds has led to prominent fund providers such as BlackRock and Vanguard becoming major (registered) shareholders in many global companies.

The Kay Review correctly noted that intermediation has both positive and negative aspects. On the positive side, it observed that effective intermediaries can provide diversification and liquidity to savers and that a 'skilled and trusted intermediary will minimise the loss of information and control which come from a more fragmented and distant relationship with companies'.[42] Intermediaries, we may add, also save the beneficial owners the immense time and effort that would be required to research each company that is part of a fund and exercise their voting rights – something that would be close to impossible for a retail investor. At the same time, the Kay Review compared intermediation with the principal-agent model that is commonly used to describe the problem of diverging interests between shareholders and corporate boards and managers. Thus, it pointed to the harmful effects of intermediation, namely added costs for the beneficial owners and the potential for conflicts of interest between them and the intermediaries.[43]

Indeed, the problem of separation of ownership and control that we described in Chapter 1 as existing between shareholders and directors also affects the relationship between beneficial owners of shares and their intermediaries. Ultimately, the beneficial owners are faced not only with the problem of agency costs at the level of their investee companies but also with an additional layer of agency costs that arise as a consequence of not holding shares directly – something that Ronald Gilson and Jeffrey Gordon have referred to as the 'agency costs of agency capitalism'.[44] In this respect, the Kay Review also noted the strong growth in the number and types of intermediaries, driven in part by the apparent need for adding new intermediaries to supervise existing intermediaries (some of which may behave badly, leading to added costs).

The law has to a certain degree reacted to these developments. In the Companies Act 2006, provisions such as those that allow companies to permit their registered members to nominate another person to enjoy or exercise members' rights and to enjoy information rights[45] are reflective of efforts to 'enfranchise' indirect shareholders. Additionally, the contractual relationship between the registered member/shareholder and the beneficial owner of shares

---

[42] ibid.

[43] ibid., 22. To illustrate the issue of costs, Kay notes that each intermediary 'must employ its own compliance staff to monitor consistency with regulation, must use the services of its own auditors and lawyers and earn sufficient to remunerate the employees and reward its own investors'. ibid., 30.

[44] The costs are caused by institutional intermediaries that prioritize their interests over those of the ultimate beneficiaries. R.J. Gilson and J.N. Gordon, 'Agency Capitalism: Further Implications of Equity Intermediation' in J.G. Hill and R.S. Thomas (eds), Research Handbook on Shareholder Power (Edward Elgar 2015), 32.

[45] Sections 145–146 of the Companies Act 2006. See also text further below on the Annual General Meeting and its proxy mechanism.

may provide the latter with various rights, such as the ability to give voting instructions to the registered shareholder.[46] For its part, the Kay Review has recommended seeking to tackle the problem on two fronts: first, by strengthening the fiduciary duties of intermediaries who manage and advise on investments; and second, by improving the engagement of indirect shareholders.[47] Thus far, however, shareholders have in practice shown little interest in exercising the various 'enfranchising' options that have already been implemented. Nevertheless, intermediation and the investment chain remain a concern and are set to be the subject of future regulatory action.

Economic and Non-Economic Rights

Shareholders' rights can be very roughly divided into economic rights (in the sense of financial rights) and non-economic rights (or non-financial rights), the latter of which can be further categorized into control and informational rights.[48] While the remainder of this chapter will be concerned with non-economic rights that allow shareholders to intervene in or influence the corporate decision-making process (in the broadest sense and including by having a say in the board's composition), we begin by briefly outlining two fundamental economic rights: the 'rights' to receive dividends and the return of capital.

It is often assumed that shareholders – given that they do not receive interest on the capital that they invest in the company – have a guaranteed right to receive a variable periodic dividend, that is a portion of the company's profits. However, there is no absolute right to a dividend. First, while it is the shareholders in general meeting that approve a dividend, the process is in great part controlled by the directors who are in charge of preparing the relevant proposal, which in view of the voting dynamics in public companies gives the board in many cases the *de facto* the power to forgo dividend payments by proposing to use profits for other purposes. In practice, it is not uncommon for companies, particularly in the technology and other growth sectors, not to pay any dividends and instead reinvest profits in the business. Second, dividend payments are subject to statutory limitations. Dividends fall under the

---

[46] *ibid.*, section 149. On the EU level, the European Commission has proposed new measures aimed at assisting companies in identifying their shareholders as well as improving intermediaries' reliability. See the proposal for amendments to the EU Shareholder Rights Directive outlined in COM (2014) 213 final (2014).

[47] For further discussion of the Kay Review, see Chapter 5.

[48] See, for example, J. Velasco, 'The Fundamental Rights of the Shareholders' (2006) 40 *UC Davis Law Review* 407. In the following, we base our discussion on the rights of equity shareholders, although the reader should note that special classes of shareholders, such as those with preference shares, may have different or additional rights. Further, readers should note that the right to inspect certain corporate documents and the right to bring shareholder actions, in particular derivative actions will not generally be examined in this book. See, however, Chapter 8 for a discussion of the board's duty to exercise oversight, which also touches upon shareholder claims alleging failures in this regard.

Companies Act rules on distributions, which generally prohibit dividend payments unless a company has freely available profits for this purpose.[49]

In addition to dividend payments, which are a return on the invested capital, shareholders have a deferred right to a return of the capital itself. Thus, shareholders as residual claimants are entitled to share in their company's surplus assets on winding up: that is, once all prior claims by higher-ranked creditors are satisfied (which may, however, well mean that there is nothing left to distribute once it is the shareholders' turn). Additionally – apart from via sale of their shares – shareholders may receive some or all of their capital back in the event that the company goes through capital reduction proceedings or redeems shares.[50]

Shareholders also have important non-economic rights, which include a limited right to participate in corporate decision-making.[51] Shareholders' decision-making is mainly exercised by attending shareholder meetings and participating in voting. Voting control (in the UK as provided for by the Companies Act and/or the FCA's Listing Rules) can pertain to a variety of issues, including decisions on changing a company's articles; the composition of the board; executive remuneration; purchase of the company's own shares; transactions where directors have a conflict of interest; or approving mergers and substantial transactions.[52] The UK Model Articles also grant shareholders a 'members' reserve power' whereby '[t]he members may, by special resolution, direct the directors to take, or refrain from taking, specified action'.[53] This allows shareholders to make binding directions on the board, although they cannot invalidate anything which the board has already done.[54]

Shareholder Voting and the General Meeting

The primary forum for the exercise of shareholders' rights of intervention in corporate decision-making is the company's Annual General Meeting (also referred to as the General Meeting or AGM, as it is commonly called in the UK) or the shareholders' meeting (which is the term used in the US). The General Meeting will normally be held annually, although shareholders in UK companies have the power to require the board to convene a General Meeting outside of the company's normal Annual General Meeting cycle

---

[49] See Part 23 of the Companies Act 2006, in particular the Accumulated Profit Test (section 830) and the Net Asset Test (section 831).

[50] Companies Act 2006, Part 17, Chapter 10.

[51] There are also certain non-interventionist information and disclosure rights, which, however, we will not examine herein.

[52] A discussion of shareholder engagement regarding remuneration can be found in Chapter 9. See also Chapter 10, which contains details on shareholders' power and role in deciding the outcome of takeover bids.

[53] Article 4(1) of the Model Articles for Public Companies.

[54] *ibid.*, 4(2). On this, see D. Kershaw, *Company Law in Context: Text and Materials* (2nd ed., OUP 2012), 193.

(a right that US/Delaware shareholders normally do not possess). Previously, this type of meeting was referred to as the Extraordinary General Meeting (EGM), a term that the Companies Act 2006 abolished although it may still be encountered today. The power to call such meetings is exercisable at the request of one or more shareholders representing at least 5 per cent of the total voting rights.[55]

At the AGM the board will present shareholders with an account of the company's performance over the previous year, which will be followed by a discussion and formal vote on each of the issues that have been proposed for resolution at the meeting. In addition to these procedures, which applicable company law provisions regulate in considerable detail, the UK Corporate Governance Code also encourages boards to use General Meetings to strengthen shareholder relations and informally communicate with their investors.[56]

All ordinary shareholders are normally entitled to attend the General Meeting and vote on each resolution proposed. Generally, UK companies follow the principle of 'one vote per share' ('one share one vote'), which means that each shareholder's voting power is proportionate to that shareholder's economic stake in the company. Nevertheless, the Companies Act does not prohibit disproportionate voting, which can be seen in companies with classes of non-voting shares, restricted voting shares, or multiple voting shares.[57] These are shares that carry no or limited rights to participate and vote in a company's General Meeting (non-voting or restricted voting shares), or shares that have votes attached to them that are a multiple of the votes attached to other shares (multiple voting shares). Companies that have such shares will have certain shareholders (often managers and other insiders) that control a proportion of the company's votes that is larger than their economic interest in the company. This is beneficial for these shareholders as they can retain control over a business with comparatively little capital investment.

Conversely, however, it can also lead to concerns related to inequality in shareholder power and prejudice to minority shareholders. For this reason, the FCA's Listing Rules have been amended to restrict the use of disproportionate voting structures for premium listed companies.[58] Additionally, even for companies that are allowed to use disproportionate voting, the practice is rare

---

[55] For details, see sections 303–305 of the Companies Act 2006.

[56] See UK Corporate Governance Code, Main Principle E.2.

[57] However, it should be noted that the Act in this respect has to be read in conjunction with the EU Takeovers Directive, which provides shareholders with an option to 'break through' provisions that establish special voting rights in the takeover context. On this, see Chapter 10.

[58] According to Premium Listing Principle 3, '[a]ll equity shares in a class that has been admitted to premium listing must carry an equal number of votes on any shareholder vote'. Under Premium Listing Principle 4, '[w]here a listed company has more than one class of equity shares admitted to premium listing, the aggregate voting rights of the shares in each class should be broadly proportionate to the relative interests of those classes in the equity of the listed company'.

in the UK given investor pressures against such structures. Conversely, there is less resistance (and an enabling regulatory environment) in the US, where notably technology and e-commerce giants Google, Facebook and Alibaba have disproportionate voting structures in place, with Alibaba having reportedly even forgone a listing in its home jurisdiction in favour of the ability to concentrate voting power among insiders.[59] Although a more detailed discussion of this issue is beyond the scope of this chapter, we should note that given the mixed empirical data and the context-specific nature of the issues surrounding disproportionate voting there does not seem to be a clear-cut case either for or against it.

The Proxy Mechanism

Since shareholders are often unwilling or unable to attend General Meetings in person, it is customary for them to cast their vote indirectly 'by proxy': this is a procedure which enables a shareholder to appoint someone else to attend the meeting and vote (as well as speak) on their behalf and according to their instructions.[60] A shareholder may appoint anyone to act as his proxy, although it is usual for some shareholders to appoint as their proxy an individual suggested by the company (for example its chairman) in its preliminary documentation.

Prior to each General Meeting, a public company will send out to each of its shareholders a form listing the various resolutions to be voted on at the meeting, and containing boxes specified 'Yes', 'No' and 'Vote Withheld' for each resolution (in the US this is known as a 'proxy card'). By ticking his chosen box for each resolution, the shareholder is not voting himself but rather is instructing his proxy to vote in accordance with his request. The proxy card will also usually be accompanied by a series of short statements in respect of each of the resolutions that have been proposed to be voted on at the meeting (known in the US as a 'proxy statement').

The board of directors, as the authorized controlling organ of the company, is normally able to determine what material is included in the company's proxy card and proxy statement. This means that, as a general rule, any shareholder wishing to challenge a proposal that will be put by the board at a meeting, or make their own counter-proposal – including regarding a new appointee to the board of directors – must send out their own proxy statement and/or proxy card to each of the company's shareholders at considerable personal expense. This process is known in the US as a 'proxy contest', which often comes up in

---

[59] See 'Shareholder rights – Out of control', *The Economist* (20 September 2014): 'Alibaba only listed in New York because Hong Kong Stock Exchange, a more natural home, insists that shareholders have a say over management in keeping with their stake. The firm's owners, who balked at this notion, took their business to a more pliable venue.' See also E. Ferran and L. Chan Ho, *Principles of Financial Regulation* (2nd ed., OUP 2014), 355–56.

[60] See sections 324–324A of the Companies Act 2006.

the context of an activist shareholder seeking to effect changes to the board's composition. In contrast to the US, proxy contests are extremely rare in UK companies.[61]

Shareholders' Power to Change the Governance Structure

Under section 21 of the Companies Act, shareholders have the express statutory power to amend the articles of association and thereby alter the company's default governance structure. This power is exercisable by special resolution: that is, by means of a resolution passed in General Meeting by a majority of not less than 75 per cent of votes.[62] Shareholders' collective power under section 21 is also mandatory and therefore applies regardless of any contrary provision in the company's articles.

Further, shareholders in UK companies have a right to initiate constitutional amendments (among other potential initiatives) by using their mandatory statutory power under section 338 of the Companies Act to propose members' resolutions to be added to the company's proxy card in advance of Annual General Meetings. A members' resolution may be proposed by one or more shareholders representing at least 5 per cent of the company's total voting rights, or alternatively by 100 or more shareholders each holding at least £100 worth of voting shares.[63] The company is obliged to include any members' resolutions so made in its proxy card for circulation to shareholders, and must also pay the expenses of the requesting members if sufficient requests for a resolution are received by the company before the end of the previous financial year.[64] The members may additionally request circulation, at the company's expense, of a written statement (of 1,000 words or less) in support of their proposed resolution to be voted on at the meeting.[65] The substance of shareholder proposals is limited only insofar as, according to section 338(2) of the Companies Act, they may not be ineffective (whether by reason of inconsistency with any enactment or the company's constitution or otherwise), defamatory, or frivolous or vexatious.

The US position in this respect notably differs from UK law. Under Delaware's General Corporation Law, amendments to a company's charter of

---

[61] In a proxy contest, shareholders nominate outsiders and solicit votes for them to be elected to the company's board. This process is onerous and costly because dissidents have to prepare and pay for their own proxy statements (which contain information for shareholders), with estimated price ranges between $30,000 to $9 million per contest in the US. See M. Kahan and E.B. Rock, 'The Insignificance of Proxy Access' (2011) 97 *Virginia Law Review* 1347, 1384; Schedule 14A, 17 CFR § 240.14a-101 (2010). Although shareholder rights proponents have long opposed this state of affairs, proposals to substantially change the proxy process have thus far proven unsuccessful.

[62] Section 283(1) of the Companies Act 2006.

[63] *ibid.*, section 338(3).

[64] *ibid.*, sections. 339–340.

[65] *ibid.*, sections 314–316.

incorporation must be proposed by the board of directors for subsequent ex post facto approval/veto by the shareholders' meeting.[66] While shareholders have authority to propose amendments to the company's bylaws without prior board approval (unless the articles of incorporation confer that power on the directors), these are subordinate to the charter of incorporation, and thus must not contain any provision contrary to the former document or to the general law.[67]

Shareholders' Power of Appointment over the Board

The UK Model Articles provide that the shareholders and the board have concurrent authority to make new directorial appointments. Shareholders may exercise this right by way of ordinary resolution in the Annual General Meeting[68] or by calling a General Meeting specifically for this purpose if time is of the essence. Shareholders can use their abovementioned right under section 338 (power to require circulation of resolutions for AGMs) to propose their own candidates for appointment to the board. This represents an unusually empowering option at least as compared to the position of US shareholders, who are allowed to make certain proposals to be voted on at a shareholders meeting but – as a general default rule – are not allowed to propose directorial candidates through this route.[69] US shareholders are instead normally restricted to the choice of either approving or vetoing the board's own nominees for election/re-election as directors, or in extreme cases staging a 'proxy contest'.[70]

All newly appointed directors in the UK must submit themselves for reappointment at the first General Meeting following their appointment. At every subsequent Annual General Meeting any directors who have been appointed by the directors since the last AGM or who were not appointed or reappointed at one of the preceding two AGMs, must retire from office and may offer themselves for reappointment by the members.[71] The UK Corporate Governance

---

[66] Delaware Code Annotated, title 8, section 242(b).

[67] ibid., section 109. The Delaware Supreme Court, in *CA, Inc. v. AFSCME Employees Pension Plan*, 953 A.2d 227 (De. 2008) held that while shareholder proposed bylaws may define the *process* and *procedures* by which boards decide substantive business decisions, they may not mandate how these decisions should be decided. Thus, given this framework, the executive authority of US/Delaware boards is to a significant extent irreversible, or at least to a much lesser degree subject to potential interference by shareholders as compared to the UK. This position is consistent with the traditional US view of the board's powers as 'original and undelegated'.

[68] Article 20 of the Model Articles for Public Companies.

[69] See Rule 14a-8 of the Securities Exchange Act of 1934.

[70] On proxy contests, see above. Even this option, however, has limitations. In US public companies, it has traditionally been customary for members of the board to have 'staggered' three-year terms of office, meaning that each year only one-third of the board will stand for reappointment.

[71] Article 21 of the Model Articles for Public Companies.

Code further provides that all directors of FTSE 350 companies should be subject to annual election by shareholders, while all other directors of companies in the Code's purview should be subject to election by shareholders at the first Annual General Meeting after their appointment, and to re-election thereafter at intervals of no more than three years. Non-executive directors who have served longer than nine years should be subject to annual re-election.[72] Finally, at a General Meeting, proposed directors are voted on individually as two or more candidates for the board cannot be proposed for appointment simultaneously unless this is unanimously agreed to by the shareholders present at the meeting.[73]

Shareholders' Power to Dismiss the Directors without Cause

Section 168 of the Companies Act 2006 provides UK shareholders with another mandatory and potentially strong power, which we may refer to as the 'shotgun' right. Accordingly, '[a] company may by ordinary resolution at a meeting remove a director before the expiration of his period of office, notwithstanding anything in any agreement between it and him'.[74] This right does not deprive a removed director of any compensation or damages due to him.[75] Also, section 169 provides directors with opportunities to protest against their removal, including the right to attend the meeting at which their removal is to be discussed and voted on; the right to make representations in writing to the company prior to the meeting; and the right to speak on the relevant resolution at the meeting.

Notably, as a matter of company law, there is the possibility of weighted voting rights in decisions on the removal of directors. In *Bushell v Faith*,[76] a company's articles provided that '[i]n the event of a resolution being proposed at any general meeting of the company for the removal from office of any director, any shares held by that director shall ... in respect of such resolution carry ... three votes per share'. This had the effect of giving a shareholder who also served as the company's director the power to block any attempts to remove him from his position, which led to an action by the other shareholders alleging that the articles violated the Companies Act (in the version as it was then enacted).

Considering the apparent conflict between the relevant provision in the articles and the statutory provision equivalent to today's section 168, the House

---

[72] UK Corporate Governance Code, Provision B.7.1.

[73] Section 160 of the Companies Act 2006.

[74] Section 141(k) of the Delaware General Corporation Law also provides shareholders with the power to dismiss the directors without cause. However, this provision provides that the right it confers is not applicable where a corporation has a classified/staggered board (unless the certificate of incorporation provides otherwise) or cumulative voting, which often will be the case.

[75] Section 168(5) of the Companies Act 2006.

[76] [1970] AC 1099 (HL).

of Lords reluctantly upheld the company's articles, thus favouring party autonomy over the 'one vote per share' principle. Nevertheless, while *Bushell* remains
good law today, similarly weighted voting would not be permissible today in
the case of premium listed companies.[77] Still, it would be possible to achieve
similar results using different share classes (each of which could have the right
to appoint a director) or via shareholder agreements.

Practical Effectiveness of Shareholder Rights

The preceding sections outlined shareholders' intervention rights as they are
'on the books': that is, as provided by laws and corporate documents. As such,
UK shareholder rights appear to be more robust and extensive than US shareholder rights. UK shareholders may influence the board's composition (which
includes a right to remove directors without cause), change the corporate constitution, veto or approve certain corporate transactions, and even instruct the
board to take (or refrain from taking) a particular cause of action. In contrast,
their US counterparts have less rights (for example, no right to give the board
binding instructions) and, insofar as both jurisdictions offer the same rights,
more restricted iterations of such rights (for example, the right to submit shareholder proposals).

Yet, examining shareholder rights solely on the basis of what is theoretically provided for is misleading. Contrary to what may have been surmised
from the discussion thus far, UK shareholders' position is in practice not as
strong as it seems 'on paper' and perhaps even weaker than the position of
US shareholders, although already the latter's powers have been described as
severely limited.[78] As Andrew Keay commented in an article assessing shareholder rights, 'while [UK] shareholders might have more legal power in technical terms to control boards, compared with their American counterparts, it
is exceedingly difficult for UK shareholders to discipline directors as a matter
of practice'.[79] Keay finds that the view that 'shareholders do not decide on

---

[77] See above n. 5.

[78] See L.A. Bebchuk, 'The Myth of the Shareholder Franchise' (2007) 93 *Virginia Law Review*
675 (finding that the possibility that US public company directors will be replaced by shareholder nominated candidates is negligible and challenging the idea of shareholders having the
'power of corporate democracy').

[79] A. Keay, 'Company Directors Behaving Poorly: Disciplinary Options for Shareholders'
(2007) *Journal of Business Law* 656, 682. In contrast, Bebchuk has suggested that the UK
shareholders' position is stronger than that of US shareholders. See L.A. Bebchuk, 'The Case
for Increasing Shareholder Power' (2005) 118 *Harvard Law Review* 833, 847–50; Bebchuk,
above n. 78, 725. Similarly, a study of shareholder proposals in the US and the UK found that
it seemed 'considerably easier for UK investors to use shareholder proposals to effect board
and corporate changes than for US investors'. B. Buchanan and others, 'Shareholder Proposal
Rules and Practice: Evidence from a Comparison of the US and UK' (2011), at http://
papers.ssrn.com/sol3/papers.cfm?abstract_id=1969606, 26. Although the study found lower
numbers of submitted proposals in the UK compared to the US, UK proposals had a greater
acceptance rate.

fundamental company issues and have few rights to veto what is going on' is correct for both the US and the UK, even though in the latter the law provides more opportunities for intervention.[80]

The reasons for the limited practical significance of UK shareholder rights are manifold and both practical and legal in nature.[81] First, shareholders will normally find it difficult to gain the support from other shareholders that is necessary to exercise most shareholder 'voice' options (the formal ones explored in this chapter as well as the informal avenues to be discussed in Chapter 5). The hurdles in terms of necessary resources, time and determination will often be insurmountable for regular shareholders and challenging even for more sophisticated investors. Second, shareholders often lack the information necessary to engage in co-ordinated action. For example, it is not always clear which shareholders should be approached, and even where this can be overcome, shareholders are not (or only with delays) privy to many important corporate decisions, which they consequently cannot effectively oppose. Third, shareholders have diverging interests, which makes it hard to agree on a common course of action for intervention. Finally, even assuming shareholders could intervene, there is always the possibility that negative publicity will adversely affect the relevant investee company, to an extent that makes intervention an irrational choice.

Under these circumstances, it is not surprising (and, indeed, might even be rational given a small shareholder's lack of influence) that shareholders often remain apathetic and do not engage in any intervention or, alternatively, choose to voice their opinion through the 'Wall Street walk' or 'voting with their feet', that is by simply selling shares in a company that they are dissatisfied with. Shareholder intervention remains a very rare occurrence, and if and when they do voice their opinion, the effect is often limited or symbolic.[82]

There are, of course, successful activist shareholder initiatives and other outbursts of shareholder discontent, but these are exceptions that confirm the general rule of non-action. Normally, shareholders vote for the directorial candidates that the incumbent board members propose, they approve remuneration policies, and they do not (successfully) propose General Meeting agenda items. They also rarely ever exercise their shotgun right and normally do not instruct the board to take or refrain from action by using their reserve power.[83] Brenda Hannigan, commenting on the situation in the UK, finds that

---

[80] Keay, above n. 79, 679.

[81] For a useful account from a UK and comparative perspective, see *ibid*. While Keay's article was written shortly before the Companies Act 2006 came into force, the basic thrust of his observations remains to hold true under the revised regime.

[82] As one commentator noted in connection with UK shareholders' right to influence the general meeting's agenda, 'it has to be acknowledged that some of these powers have always been available and shareholders have shown little interest in exercising them and that remains the position'. Hannigan, above n. 39, 144.

[83] For example, in his 2007 paper, Andrew Keay mentions only two high-profile cases of directors that were removed, one from 1994 and one from 2006. Keay, above n. 79.

'[t]here is some level of ongoing intervention, typically on the issue of executive pay and board composition, these being the two issues which are easiest for shareholders to address, but without any significant change in the role played by shareholders in the largest companies'.[84] She goes on to speculate that reasons for the limited role of UK shareholders could be that investors' interests increasingly diverge, holdings by institutional investors are declining, and because there are more shareholders from abroad,[85] meaning that geographical remoteness and reduced susceptibility to domestic political pressure to engage reduce these shareholders' influence. These reasons, together with the factors mentioned above, all seem to offer good explanations for the low efficacy of shareholder rights as observed in practice.

THE MERITS OF SHAREHOLDER EMPOWERMENT

Our discussion thus far has shown that directors are primarily in charge of governing companies, that the law provides (both mandatory and non-mandatory) shareholder rights – of which at least in the UK some appear to give shareholders a strong position – but also that theory and practice of shareholder rights differ in that such rights are for various reasons often not extensively used in practice. The final question for this chapter to engage with is whether the current balance of board and shareholder powers is justified or whether changes – in one direction or the other – are in order.

In the first part of this chapter, we looked at the board's primacy, in terms of both its descriptive reality (as evidenced in the power concentrated in this body by virtue of the current corporate governance law framework) as well as the theoretical underpinnings that seek to explain the board's dominance. Accepting this dominance means, in effect, that the separation of ownership and control in the public company is an economically rational, conscious decision based on the idea of allocating power to the party that is in the best position to exercise corporate decision-making. Economists Eugene Fama and Michael Jensen have made this argument several decades ago, pointing to the benefits of having a specialized managerial body and rebutting Berle and Means' conclusion that managerial powers need to be substantially constrained by shareholders given the modern ownership/control separation.[86] Other scholars have further developed this idea in subsequent years, focusing on elements of shareholder weakness/unsuitability for corporate decision-making and/or the advantages of hierarchical decision-making by boards and managers.[87]

---

[84] Hannigan, above n. 39, 149.

[85] According to an official estimate, beneficial ownership of UK shares by value by non-UK investors stood at 54 per cent at the end of 2014. Office of National Statistics, *Ownership of UK Quoted Shares: 2014* (2 September 2015).

[86] E.F. Fama and M.C. Jensen, 'Separation of Ownership and Control' (1983) 26 *Journal of Law and Economics* 301.

[87] See already above on selected theoretical approaches to board primacy.

Against this background, one line of argument could be to say that shareholder rights should be even more limited, perhaps with economic rights the only remaining shareholder rights. However, there is no serious case for disempowering shareholders completely and the relevant discussions in academic and regulatory circles thus revolve around the nature and degree of decisional involvement that shareholders should be allowed to have. Indeed, scholars across the spectrum agree that good corporate governance contains an element of shareholder control over the board, although it is disputed how much and what type of control is desirable. Fama and Jensen, for instance, have suggested as a broad categorization that generally ratification and monitoring of decisions is acceptable as a subject for shareholder intervention, while initiation and implementation of these decisions is not.[88] Conversely, in an effort to reduce the negative effects caused by conflicted managerial decisions, proponents of shareholder empowerment 'seek to reform the prevailing legal model of the corporation (or what might be called the Fama-Jensen corporation) to ensure that shareholder inputs directly impact both business decision making and monitoring'.[89]

In line with the latter approach, the prevailing regulatory trend – internationally – in recent years has clearly been to enlarge shareholder powers. For instance, already in 2003, the EU identified the establishment of 'real shareholder democracy' as one if its medium to long-term political goals,[90] and the push towards stronger shareholder rights has only gathered steam since then, both in Europe and the US. Among the most visible signs in this respect are enlarged shareholder rights in the area of executive remuneration, discussions surrounding short-termism and shareholder engagement, and – in the US – repeated (albeit unsuccessful) efforts to give shareholders more control over board appointments, increased opportunities to submit proposals, and means to change the corporate 'constitution'.[91]

Proponents of shareholder empowerment have promoted these and other ideas. One of the leading advocates of shareholder intervention powers, Harvard Law Professor Lucian Bebchuk has inter alia argued in favour of: (i) reformed election arrangements to bolster shareholder rights pertaining to the appointment and removal of directors; (ii) greater influence over corporate constitutional governance arrangements; (iii) increased veto powers over fundamental changes; and (iv) reduced board insulation from hostile takeovers.[92]

---

[88] See Fama and Jensen, above n. 86.

[89] W.W. Bratton and M.L. Wachter, 'The Case against Shareholder Empowerment' (2010) 158 *University of Pennsylvania Law Review* 653, 668.

[90] European Commission, 'Modernising Company Law and Enhancing Corporate Governance in the European Union – A Plan to Move Forward' COM(2003) 284, 14.

[91] See Bratton and Wachter, above n. 89, 705–16.

[92] See above n. 78 and 79. Chapter 10 will discuss the board's role in takeovers. Among others, additional US scholars favouring shareholder empowerment include Ronald Gilson, Jeffrey Gordon, John Coffee and Lisa Fairfax. See, for example, L.M. Fairfax, 'Shareholder Democracy On Trial: International Perspective on the Effectiveness of Increased Shareholder Power' (2008) 3 *Virginia Law & Business Review* 1.

According to Bebchuk, greater shareholder involvement through rights provided by company law is necessary given that market forces (such as pressures from investors or hostile takeovers) do not sufficiently monitor, discipline, and incentivize boards and managers. Furthermore, in his view, shareholder empowerment is efficient and claims that shareholders – if given more power – would make bad, poorly informed choices are overstated or speculative. Similarly, Bebchuk does not view short-termism as a valid reason for insulating boards from shareholders, but rather as an element to consider when designing the precise modalities of shareholders' decision-making opportunities and their frequency.

For proponents of shareholder empowerment, regularly occurring corporate scandals as well as the most recent 2007–08 financial crisis have further bolstered the case for stronger shareholder rights. From this perspective, directors and managers – particularly in financial institutions – and other gatekeepers are to blame for the crisis and its effects.[93] Commentators have suggested that directors and managers – emboldened by their near-absolute control – behaved inappropriately, took excessive risks, and drove their companies into the ground, sometimes enriching themselves at the shareholders' expense. Consequently, and in line with the concept of agency costs or the general need for 'owners' to monitor 'controllers', it arguably follows from this perspective that shareholders should be given more powers to control companies and keep managers in check.

But there is also an opposing view.[94] Focusing on the recent financial crisis as a test case for shareholder empowerment, William Bratton and Michael Wachter, along with numerous other scholars, for instance have argued that the financial crisis in fact supports the case for the current model, not one that would shift the balance of board and shareholder powers towards the latter.[95] They contend that shareholders push directors to an unhealthy focus on their companies' share price, which – as more risk translates into higher financial returns – leads (and has already led) to ever-increasing levels of risk. This, in itself, is not necessarily problematic, at least as long as shareholders are aware

---

[93] On this, see J.G. Hill, 'The Rising Tension between Shareholder and Director Power in the Common Law World' (2010) 18(4) *Corporate Governance: An International Review* 344, 346.

[94] As Hill has noted on the opposing views of the role of shareholders, '[t]he global financial crisis added a new layer of ambiguity, with shareholders alternatively viewed as victims or collaborators in the crisis'. J.G. Hill, 'Images of the Shareholder – Shareholder Power and Shareholder Powerlessness' in Hill and Thomas, above n. 93, 53.

[95] Bratton and Wachter, above n. 89. There is ample literature on this topic, in both the US and the UK. From the latter, see for example J. Mukwiri and M. Siems, 'The Financial Crisis: A Reason to Improve Shareholder Protection in the EU' (2014) 41 *Journal of Law and Society* 51; A. Dignam, 'The Future of Shareholder Democracy in the Shadow of the Financial Crisis' (2013) 36 *Seattle University Law Review* 639; B.R. Cheffins, 'Did Corporate Governance "Fail" During the 2008 Stock Market Meltdown? – The Case of the S&P 500' (2009) 65 *Business Lawyer* 1; A. Keay, 'Risk, Shareholder Pressure and Short-Termism in Financial Institutions: Does Enlightened Shareholder Value Offer a Panacea?', 5 *Law and Financial Markets Review* 435 (2011).

of and comfortable with these risks. But the problem, Bratton and Wachter explain, is the lack of risk internalization.

Should risk manifest itself in economic rescue costs and other negative effects, the risk-taker (shareholders who, for example, pushed companies towards aggressive lending practices) should ideally bear the entire risks. However, in the case of corporations, such risk internalization does not or not fully take place as (i) governments – ultimately the taxpayers – may step in to 'bail out' certain systemically important companies (such as banks, public utilities, etc.) and (ii) shareholders' downside risk is in any event limited due to the concept of limited liability. For Bratton and Wachter, this lack of risk internalization, coupled with shareholders' lack of information (which they argue is often limited to market pricing information), does not bode well for shareholder empowerment. As they explain:

> If managers misunderstood the quantum of risks they were taking, then shareholders with more limited access to the relevant information certainly were no better informed and accordingly had no role to play in preventing externalization. Even as managers must shoulder the blame for the crisis, current complaints about management irresponsibility can legitimately be restated as complaints about management to the market. At the same time, management's risk aversion – its long-derided willingness to accept reduced risk in exchange for institutional stability – all of a sudden holds out advantages. Managers are risk averse because they fear losing their jobs in bankruptcy. Whereas bankruptcy is a natural element in the 'winds of creative destruction,' those winds blow no good when the losses are externalized to the U.S. Treasury.[96]

In short, shareholders have less information but are willing to accept larger risks in return for increased profit than managers, which at least in the case of the financial crisis meant that giving them more power would not have led to superior outcomes. Bratton and Wachter conclude that there is no case for legal reform in the shape of new or stronger shareholder rights. Similarly, Lynn Stout contends that while board control produces both (agency) costs and benefits, the benefits prevail. She argues that governance concentrated in the board promotes efficient and informed decision-making, discourages opportunistic behaviour by large shareholders, and – alluding to the team production theory discussed earlier in this chapter – encourages specific investment in corporate team production.[97] Stephen Bainbridge's director primacy theory is, as discussed in the first part of the chapter above, also antithetical to shareholder empowerment. The case for director primacy is equally a case for limited shareholder powers.[98]

---

[96] Bratton and Wachter, above n. 89, 659 (footnote omitted).

[97] L.A. Stout, 'The Mythical Benefits of Shareholder Control' (2007) 93 *Virginia Law Review* 789.

[98] Among others, see S.M. Bainbridge, 'The Case for Limited Shareholder Voting Rights' (2006) 53 *UCLA Law Review* 601, 'Director Primacy and Shareholder Disempowerment' (2006) 119 *Harvard Law Review* 1735, and 'Preserving Director Primacy by Managing Shareholder Interventions' in Hill and Thomas (above n. 93).

In our opinion, many issues highlighted by sceptics of shareholder empowerment are convincing. The wisdom and potential for success of strategies that rely on shareholders to monitor companies, take prudent decisions, and – ultimately – fix various corporate governance issues are questionable. As David Kershaw observes, the determination of who is the better decision-maker – shareholders or directors/managers – depends on (i) the decision-maker's capability and knowledge; (ii) his incentives to pay attention to the issue at hand; and (iii) his incentives to act in the company's best interests.[99] While shareholders – in particular institutional shareholders – may score high on all counts, directors will normally still be in a superior position with regards to criteria (i) and (ii). To what extent one favours shareholder decision-making will thus depend to a large extent on the degree of self-interested (agency cost producing) behaviour on the part of directors and managers that is left after accounting for the market forces that operate so as to limit such behaviour.

Moreover, as the following chapter will discuss in greater detail, UK institutional investors at least have so far generally not proven to be willing to act as proactive and engaged stewards,[100] not to mention that they also pursue their own, often short-term-oriented goals.[101] Additionally, insofar as institutional shareholders rely on proxy advisors, shifting power to shareholders means shifting power to these advisory firms, raising a host of new accountability and conflict of interest issues.[102] At the same time, individual shareholders remain constrained by the well-known issues stemming from collective action problems, information asymmetries, and rational apathy.[103] In light of the example of the recent financial crisis and its lessons, we believe that shareholder empowerment proponents should be mindful of the fact that shareholders are among those thought to have contributed to the financial crisis, even prompting the European Commission to state that 'confidence in the model of the shareholder-owner who contributes to the company's long-term viability has been severely shaken'.[104] Giving these same shareholders, with their proven appetite for risk and quick profits, more power may lead to increased pressures on boards to justify their pay with short-term gains, eviscerating the thrust of ongoing efforts to curb short-termism.[105]

---

[99] Kershaw, above n. 53, 205.

[100] B.R. Cheffins, 'The Stewardship Code's Achilles' Heel' (2010) 73 *Modern Law Review* 1004. Note, however, the existence of evidence that the presence of institutional investors may improve alignment of pay and performance.

[101] Kay Review, above n. 35, 8 (citing evidence from the Institute of Directors).

[102] On the role of proxy advisors in corporate governance generally, see Chapter 3.

[103] On these issues, see Chapter 5.

[104] European Commission, Green Paper: Corporate Governance in financial institutions and remuneration policies, COM (2010) 284, 8. Although in the case of the EU Commission the conclusion was that more – not fewer – shareholders powers would provide the adequate cure to the malaise.

[105] See also L.A. Bebchuck and H. Spamann, 'Regulating Bankers' Pay' (2010) 98 *Georgetown Law Journal* 247 (suggesting that say on pay in financial institutions may amplify managerial risk-taking). On the problem of short-termism generally, see Chapter 5.

On this basis and in the absence of empirical evidence that would suggest otherwise,[106] we conclude that shareholders' rights of intervention in corporate decision-making are most appropriately depicted in terms of a legal 'nuclear deterrent', whose functional value resides not so much in their direct use, but rather in their indirect 'threat' capacity. Given the board's decision-making primacy, we believe that shareholder rights mainly serve the purpose of contributing to the accountability and legitimacy of the considerable powers that the law vests in the corporate board, but should not rise to the level of actual decision-making powers in themselves. We do not deny the existence of agency costs, managerial self-interest and excesses. However, additional shareholder empowerment through means of formal corporate law rules would create its own costs and would not lead to overall governance improvements either for shareholders themselves, or for society more generally.

---

[106] On this, see W.W. Bratton, 'Corporate Law Reform in the Era of Shareholder Empowerment' in B. Choudhury and M. Petrin (eds), *Understanding the Company – Corporate Governance and Theory* (CUP 2017).

CHAPTER 5

Institutional Investors and Shareholder Engagement

In the previous chapter, we discussed the various formal rights of intervention in corporate decision-making that UK corporate governance law grants to shareholders. We also remarked on the fact that, at least in the case of public companies, these rights are very seldom used by shareholders directly. However, as we highlighted by recourse to our nuclear deterrent analogy, the mere fact that shareholders' legal intervention rights are not used directly does not necessarily undermine their significant *indirect* functional value. That said, in reality the impact of those rights should not be overestimated, in light of the practical impediments to their effective implementation by shareholders.

Accordingly, the corporate decision-making framework described in the previous chapter provides the formal backdrop to the lower-level, relatively *informal* methods of communication and engagement between shareholders, directors and managers that take place on an ongoing basis within public companies. It is these latter forms of interaction between key corporate governance constituencies that are the principal focus of our attention in this chapter. Of particular interest from this perspective are the various types of professional institutional investor who typically play the principal engagement role within UK public companies.

As we will see below, an active and engaged institutional investor community is *prima facie* desirable from the standpoint of disciplining corporate managers and – in turn – mitigating agency costs within public companies. However, the extent (if any) to which institutional investors are effective managerial monitors in practice is dependent: first, on the strength of their incentives and acumen to undertake their supervisory functions; second, on the offsetting effect of any negative collateral impacts of their activities on investee companies; and, third, on the internal governance of institutional investment firms themselves, which can impinge in turn on the quality of investee companies' governance.

In particular, one of the most commonly cited adverse effects of shareholder activism in public companies is the consequently increased pressure which is (allegedly) imposed on managers to maximize short-term financial profitability, often at the expense of longer-term enterprise growth and sustainability. Of course, whether institutional investors are, on the whole, a force for good (or, conversely, ill) within UK corporate governance we will leave for readers to judge for themselves, subject to us setting out both sides of the debate below.

INSTITUTIONAL INVESTORS AND THE SEPARATION OF OWNERSHIP AND CONTROL

When Berle and Means wrote their classic exposition of the separation of ownership and control in modern US public companies back in 1932,[1] they most likely had little foresight of the significant capital market developments that would occur towards the end of that century. Admittedly for the following half-century, US public company share ownership would for the most part remain the preserve of the relatively small household or retail investor, with institutional shareholders playing only a marginal governance role. However, in the 1980s and 1990s the balance between individual/retail and institutional shareholding in the United States began to tip decisively on the latter end of the scale, changing the character of US corporate governance considerably.[2]

In the UK, by contrast, the widespread institutionalization of public company share ownership took place considerably early, such that – as Cheffins has recorded – '[b]y 1969, retail investors no longer owned a majority of shares of UK public companies' whilst '[i]nstitutional shareholders stepped into the breach'.[3] So profound was this trend that, by the early 1990s, individual (i.e. non-institutional) shareholding accounted for less than 20 per cent of UK public companies' aggregate ownership base.[4] Therefore, notwithstanding additional changes to the composition of London's investment community over the past two decades,[5] it is an incontestable fact today that UK corporate governance is firmly the preserve of the *institutional* – rather than individual – investor.

The modern prevalence of professional-institutional over individual shareholding in Anglo-American (and, in particular, UK) public companies clearly presents an empirical challenge to Berle and Means' supposed ownership-control dichotomy, although one should be wary of dismissing the continuing relevance of Berle and Means' concerns about managerial unaccountability too hastily. Certainly the percentage of any one firm's equity capital held by a typical UK institutional shareholder is ordinarily much larger than that of an individual shareholding in a widely-held company. However, in the vast

---

[1] See A.A. Berle and G. Means, *The Modern Corporation and Private Property* (revised ed., Harcourt, Brace & World 1968; first published 1932), Book I, discussed further in Chapter 1 of this book.

[2] B.R. Cheffins, *The History of Modern U.S. Corporate Governance: Volume I* (Edward Elgar 2011), xix.

[3] B.R. Cheffins, *Corporate Ownership and Control: British Business Transformed* (OUP 2008), 344.

[4] B.R. Cheffins, 'The Stewardship Code's Achilles' Heel' (2010) 73 *Modern Law Review* 1004, 1017.

[5] On this, see below.

majority of instances, a single institutional shareholders' investment still represents a relatively small (indeed, usually fractional) percentage of overall share capital, which would be dwarfed by comparison to a typical blockholder stake within a concentrated corporate ownership system.[6]

Taking into additional account the widespread diversification of most institutional share ownership portfolios, it is clear that in terms of neither influence nor incentives are Anglo-American-style institutional shareholders comparable to family or entrepreneurial owners within non-Anglo-American corporate governance environments. Therefore, whilst – as we will see below – managerial accountability (or 'agency costs'[7]) concerns are certainly mitigated to some extent in the presence of professional institutional shareholders, they are far from eradicated. Accordingly, the Berle-Means ownership-control dichotomy remains a relevant conceptual lens through which to view the basic dynamics of Anglo-American (including UK) corporate governance today, albeit that a more empirically nuanced understanding of this notion is correspondingly called for today.

Who Are the Main Types of Institutional Investor in UK Public Companies?

As an initial concern, it is important to highlight the descriptive limitations of referring to 'institutional investors' as a single homogenous group. As was mentioned in the previous chapter, in reality there are many distinct types of institutional investor, who differ considerably from one another in terms of their respective characteristics, behaviours, preferences and investment time horizons. In the discussion that follows we will thus briefly describe the *main* types of institutional investor typically observed within UK public companies today, subject to the proviso that this list is by no means an exhaustive account of the great variety and complexity of institutional forms that exist within London's globalized capital market environment.

Pension Funds

Pension funds have traditionally been one of the dominant types of institutional investor in UK public companies, and also one of the most influential corporate governance actors. The structural characteristics of individual pension funds can vary considerably depending on a range of factors. In particular, public sector pension funds are often (although not necessarily always) more extensive than their private sector counterparts in terms of financial scale and scope of coverage. Relatedly, whilst some pension funds (typically in the private sector) are set up by individual employers for the exclusive benefit of their own employees, others (most commonly in the public sector) are established on a

---

[6] On this, see Chapter 1.
[7] On this notion, see Chapter 2.

sectoral basis to cover a large pool of beneficiaries working for a number of different organizations. Notwithstanding these variations, though, most pension funds share certain common fundamental features.

Essentially, a pension fund's capital resources accrue from periodic contributions made to the fund by employees who are 'members' of the relevant scheme. In a standard occupational pension scheme, pension contributions will normally be deducted automatically from a member's salary (monthly or otherwise) at source. Each member (i.e. employee) contribution will then usually be 'matched' by a parallel contribution from the relevant employer, with the resulting total being paid into a common investment fund in conjunction with the corresponding 'matched' contributions of other scheme members. The ultimate expectation is that investments made by the fund (or, more commonly, by agents appointed to invest on the fund's behalf) using 'active' (i.e. working) members' contributions will generate ongoing financial returns. These returns will then, in effect, be 'recycled' so as to sustain regular income payments to 'passive' (i.e. non-working) members of the scheme following their eventual retirement.

In a defined benefit (or 'DB') pension scheme, each member's anticipated level of post-retirement income from the fund is contractually specified in advance, ordinarily as a fixed percentage of that individual's final (or, alternatively, career-average) salary. In a defined contribution (or 'DC') benefit scheme, on the other hand, only a member's periodic contribution level is pre-specified, whereas their post-retirement income level is contractually unguaranteed. As such, a DC beneficiary's future income-generating capacity is necessarily contingent on the long-term performance of the various investments that are made (whether directly or indirectly) by the fund throughout the period of that individual's membership of the relevant scheme.[8] Moreover, the ability of both DC and DB pension scheme members to receive income after retirement is naturally dependent on the continuing solvency of the fund, as determined in large part by the relative balance of active (contributing) to passive (receiving) scheme members over time.

Due to funding pressures and major demographic changes over recent decades (including greater longevity rates[9]), DB pension schemes appear to be becoming progressively extinct in the UK, and have all but disappeared from the private sector today. In many instances these have been replaced by more flexible DC schemes, which have consequently increased in popularity (at least from the perspective of employers). Moreover, the spread of DC

---

[8] See E.A. Zelinsky, 'The Defined Contribution Paradigm' (2004) 114 *Yale Law Journal* 451; A. Tucker, 'Retirement Revolution: Unmitigated Risks in the Defined Contribution Society' (2013) 51 *Houston Law Review* 153.

[9] On this, see United Nations Department of Economic and Social Affairs (Population Division), *World Population Ageing 2015* (2015); R. Jackson, 'The Global Retirement Crisis: The Threat to World Stability and What to Do About It' (2002) 27 *The Geneva Papers on Risk and Insurance – Issues and Practice* 486; P. Wallace, *Agequake: Riding the Demographic Rollercoaster Shaking Business, Finance and Our World* (Brealey 1999).

pension schemes looks likely to increase following the introduction of compulsory employee enrolment in occupational pension schemes (so-called 'auto-enrolment') under the Pensions Act 2008.[10]

As a matter of prudent financial practice, most pension funds will customarily invest in a broad and diverse basket of different financial instruments, including not just corporate equities (i.e. ordinary shares) but also debt instruments, property, currency, commodities and financial derivatives. However, corporate equity (i.e. public company shares) has in general tended to be the most popular investment outlet for pension funds. This is because no other class of asset has in general been capable of generating as consistently high a rate of return as shares.[11] Corporate equity has thus been crucial in helping to sustain the levels of income and capital growth that many such funds require in order to satisfy their beneficiaries' expectations.

Because pension funds are investing in part for the long-term purpose of providing income for currently active fund members (some of whom may not be due to retire for another 30 or even 40 years), they can reasonably be expected to take a long view with respect to their investment time horizons. However, this is subject to two important provisos. First, pension funds are also focused to a large extent on meeting the immediate income expectations of their current passive (i.e. already-retired) members, which in some instances might necessitate taking a shorter-term perspective when evaluating the relative viability of competing investment options. And, second, even where pension fund trustees are themselves willing to take a long-term perspective with respect to their fund's investment strategies, it does not necessarily follow that the particular agents who are hired to invest on the fund's behalf will be inclined to do so. We will return to this point below when we analyse the problem of stock market short-termism in further detail.

Due to their exclusivity to those working within individual firms or employment sectors, pension funds are perhaps not the most widely-known of investment institutions, notwithstanding their scale and impact. Amongst the largest and most influential occupational pension schemes in the UK are the BT Pension Scheme, British Steel Pensions and the Universities Superannuation Scheme.

Insurers

Alongside pension funds, insurers have also been one of the traditionally key ownership influences in UK public companies, particularly from a governance point of view. There is likewise considerable variety between different insurers in terms the particular types of insurance product that they provide.

---

[10] On this, see www.thepensionsregulator.gov.uk/doc-library/automatic-enrolment-detailed-guidance.aspx.

[11] M. Gelter, 'The Pension System and the Rise of Shareholder Primacy' (2013) 43 *Seton Hall Law Review* 909, 928.

However, most of the larger insurers today offer a broad range of different forms of coverage including home insurance, car insurance, life assurance, fire assurance and health insurance.

Generally speaking, insurers take the regular 'premiums' (i.e. policy payments) that are paid by their various policyholders and invest those funds with a view to generating a continuing return thereon. Their purpose for doing so is two-fold: first, it enables insurers to amass sufficient financial capacity to meet future claims by their policyholders, some of which (for example, in respect of storm damage to property) may be unanticipated in terms of their occasional scale and/or number; and, second, it enhances insurers' capacity to make a commercially attractive rate of return on their core business, or at least in a way that does not risk deterring potential customers via prohibitively exorbitant premiums.

Given that insurers are normally investing (at least in part) for the purpose of covering adverse contingencies that might not materialize for many years into the future, it might be expected that they will conform to correspondingly long-term investment time horizons. However, as in the case of pension funds it is possible that where (as is common) insurers delegate part of their portfolio management responsibilities to external agents (such as professional fund managers), those agents for a variety of reasons may not be inclined to adopt the same perspective. An additional factor to take into account in this regard is that many larger insurers in the UK are themselves constituted in the form of a public company (at least at 'top' holding company level), and therefore may be subject to countervailing stock market pressure to take a shorter-term view in evaluating the relative performance of their investments.

Due to their broad retail business and extensive advertising activities, many of the larger UK insurers with significant corporate governance presence are household names today. Notable examples include Legal & General, Prudential, Aviva (formerly Norwich Union) and Standard Life. Interestingly, whilst London is unquestionably the UK's hub for financial services (including insurance) generally, the UK's traditional 'capital' city for life assurance services is Edinburgh, which is home to (*inter alia*) Standard Life, Scottish Widows and Aegon.

Mutual Funds/Unit Trusts

Essentially, a mutual fund – or, to use the more customary UK parlance, a 'unit trust' – is a collective or pooled investment vehicle, whose managers have delegated authority to trade funds advanced by a typically large and diverse group of clients. The names given to this vehicle denote the fact that the clients of such a fund, rather than having a direct proprietary interest in any of the investments that are made by the fund's investment managers, are instead granted effective partial ownership of the fund itself. The expectation is that returns accruing from shares and other financial instruments held or traded by the fund will contribute to enhancing the overall asset value of the fund itself, and – in turn – the value of each individual's client's 'unit' or financial stake in the fund.

Mutual funds are most common in the United States, which is home to the biggest and most well-known global examples of such including Fidelity, BlackRock, Vanguard and Schroders. The greater prominence of mutual funds in the United States is due in part to their stronger retail presence there: that is, at least by comparison to the UK where middle-class savers have tended to exercise less direct control than their American counterparts over prospective retirement funds. However, in the UK mutual funds are also very commonly used by other institutional investors including pension funds and insurers, both of which customarily delegate a large portion of their investment portfolios to professional fund managers.

Fund managers consequently assume authority to invest and/or trade many other institutions' funds as an effective agent, which in practice gives them enormous proprietary and governance influence over individual investee companies. Indeed, as noted in the previous chapter, the Kay Review reported that fund (or 'asset') managers are typically the most influential link within corporate equity investment chains today; and, moreover, that 'the dominant players in UK equity markets are London based asset managers'.[12] However, the same review found that the largest fund manager in the UK was in fact the New York-based firm BlackRock, which in 2010 held £530 billion worth of financial assets in the UK alone.[13] By way of illustration, this is *over one-quarter* of the UK's 2015 GDP.

It follows that how fund managers behave, and in particular the time horizons that they adopt when making investment and/or trading decisions, can have significant ramifications not just for stock markets but also for the performance of the British (and, indeed, global) economy as a whole. We will examine purported problems with how fund managers are appointed and remunerated by their institutional clients in our discussion of stock market short-termism below.

Charitable/Endowment Trusts

Despite their typically (although not necessarily) smaller scale and non-commercial objectives, charitable endowment trusts are not entirely dissimilar from mutual funds in terms of their basic structure and mode of operation. Simply put, such trusts assume control over funds advanced by external donors, which they subsequently invest with a view to generating a commercially attractive rate of return thereon. The obvious principal difference to the case of a mutual fund, though, is that a charitable trust's donors will of course not expect any sort of economic return on their 'investment' consistent with

---

[12] J. Kay, *The Kay Review of UK Equity Markets and Long-Term Decision Making: Final Report* (July 2012), para. 3.17.
[13] *ibid.*, para. 3.16.

the enhanced future value of the trust, in the way that a mutual fund's investors would.

However, insofar as the authority and objectives of the trust's managers are concerned, the distinctions between the two types of vehicle are less readily apparent. Certainly one should not assume from the ultimate charitable purpose of such a trust that its motivations and preferences *qua* investor will be anything other than prudential. Indeed, over recent decades many formally 'charitable' endowment trusts have proved to be amongst the most shrewd and exacting financial market participants, in some cases surpassing their orthodox commercial peer institutions in performance terms. This has been true nowhere more so than in the case of university endowment trusts, which in the United States at least have backed some of the most pioneering and controversial financial market innovations over recent years, including the investment of endowed capital in hedge funds and private equity ventures. Note also that charitable trusts will often in turn entrust a significant portion of their funds with standard commercial fund management vehicles. However, this is typically subject to restrictions designed to prevent agents from investing in companies whose activities (e.g. tobacco or weapons production) are deemed averse to the trust's own objectives or ethos.

One further characteristic feature of a charitable trust from an investment perspective – which the additional term 'endowment' commonly denotes – is the fact that its trustees will, as a matter of prudent financial and charitable practice, tend to rely exclusively on income accruing from the trust's investments in meeting necessary organizational expenditures. Trustees will, correspondingly, tend to refrain from dissipating the trust's income-generating 'endowment' (i.e. its underlying purse of donated funds) under normal circumstances at least, and may well be prohibited from doing so under the terms of the relevant trust deed itself.

Hedge/Activist Funds

A hedge fund is a relatively unregulated alternative class of institutional investor to the above standard types.[14] Generally speaking, by advancing capital to a hedge fund – as opposed to, say, an orthodox mutual fund – an end-point investor is able to gain access to a greater degree of market risk exposure (both upside and downside) than would otherwise be possible. From this point of view, the term 'hedge' fund is in itself something of a misnomer. Whilst such funds do customarily hedge their primary risk positions to a considerable extent via purchase of offsetting financial derivative products, many are just as likely to use debt and derivatives to *amplify* their initial risk exposures: for instance, by

---

[14] On the nature and typical structure of hedge funds generally, see H. McVea, 'Hedge Funds and the New Regulatory Agenda' (2007) 27 *Legal Studies* 709, 711–17; N. Maloney, 'The EC and the Hedge Fund Challenge: A Test Case for EC Securities Policy after the Financial Services Action Plan' (2006) 6 *Journal of Corporate Law Studies* 1, 2–3.

'taking the long side' on a Contract-for-Difference (or 'CfD') referenced to a particular company's market equity price,[15] in addition to purchasing shares in the relevant company itself.

Hedge funds' regulation-light status[16] is due principally to the fact that such funds are typically domiciled offshore, in many cases within so-called 'tax haven' jurisdictions such as the Cayman Islands, the British Virgin Islands and Bermuda. However, the management of such funds will still often be conducted in – or, more commonly, *close to* – major Western financial centres, with central London's Mayfair district and the North-East US town of Greenwich, Connecticut arguably being the two most popular geographic locations for hedge fund managers today. A further distinctive (albeit somewhat trivial) feature of hedge fund management is its customarily informal work culture and casual dress code, with chinos and button-down shirts a more common form of office attire than the traditional business suits and ties that their mainstream fund management counterparts are associated with.

Hedge fund management is generally regarded as a much more lucrative and less bureaucratic occupation than orthodox fund management, hence its success over recent years in attracting some of the world's elite financial talent. This is due in large part to the fact that, whereas orthodox fund managers' fees traditionally represent a relatively small (typically 1 per cent to 2 per cent) proportion of the value of client funds under their control, hedge fund managers are remunerated by contrast on an 'absolute return' basis. Accordingly, where a hedge fund manager succeeds in creating added value for clients over and above a specified return threshold (typically in the region of 8 per cent to 10 per cent over initial capital value), they will ordinarily be entitled to a significant (typically 20 per cent) share of any additional net profits generated over the relevant time period. Given that many larger hedge funds customarily handle many billions of pounds of client money at a time, this 20 per cent profit cut will in many cases be extremely sizeable. Indeed, some individual hedge fund managers in the United States have been known to earn as much as $1 billion in a single year. To say that such figures establish powerful incentives on the part of hedge fund managers to generate optimal client returns is something of an understatement.

---

[15] A CfD is essentially a financial derivative product which gives its holder economic exposure to future changes in the price of a company's equity, without them ever actually owning any of that company's shares in the first place. The CfD holder who is 'long' stands to gain if the company's share price increases over a pre-specified time period; and, vice versa, to lose if its share price decreases over that period. CfDs have many practical advantages over shares, notably including immunity from stamp duty tax and brokerage fees. See Financial Services Authority, *Disclosure of Contracts for Difference: Consultation and Draft Handbook Text* (November 2007), 11–12.

[16] However, in the case of both hedge funds and private equity, there would appear to be a gradual trend towards increased state regulation of these sectors, at both domestic and international level. At least in comparison to more mainstream or retail-focused investment activities, though, these so-called 'alternative' investment sectors in general remain relatively lightly regulated. On this trend as it concerns private equity, see Chapter 10.

In terms of client eligibility most hedge funds have significant minimum investment thresholds, frequently in the order of £100,000 or higher. In effect, this means that they are realistically open only to institutional investors or high-net-worth personal investors, as opposed to relatively small-scale retail investors. Given their relatively wealthy and risk-tolerant client base, hedge funds ordinarily enjoy a much greater degree of discretionary leeway over the capital entrusted to them compared to their mainstream institutional investor counterparts. In particular, hedge funds frequently make use of capital 'lock-up' provisions within their investment mandates to preclude clients from withdrawing capital on demand. This correspondingly enables such funds to hold very large and illiquid ownership stakes in individual companies, in turn creating more powerful incentives for active shareholder oversight and challenge of corporate management and/or strategy in appropriate instances.[17]

Hedge fund managers' incentives in this regard are further intensified by the relatively limited scope for institutional conflicts of interest on their part. Although some hedge funds are formed as a more or less autonomously functioning part of a larger financial conglomerate (e.g. JP Morgan/Goldman Sachs Asset Management), most tend to be constituted as independent investment vehicles in their own right, and as such are free from any extraneous corporate constraints. One important implication of this is that hedge funds can occasionally intervene in matters of corporate management and strategy in individual investee companies, and even publicly challenge underperforming corporate managers, without concern for losing lucrative financial intermediation business from those particular firms.[18]

For the above reasons, it is unsurprising that some of the most aggressive incidences of institutional shareholder intervention in UK public companies over recent years have been instigated not by traditional institutions such as pension funds, insurers or orthodox fund managers; but rather by entities whose structural characteristics are much more akin to those of a hedge fund in the above sense. Such episodes include Efficient Capital Structures' relentless campaign against the then-telecommunications giant Vodafone's management strategy in 2007[19]; and, more recently, the US activist fund ValueAct Capital's high-profile 2016 campaign against Roll-Royce's management, which notably culminated in the British engineering firm granting a seat on its board to a ValueAct Capital representative.[20] Other prominent examples of hedge funds that have an active corporate governance presence today are Bridgewater Associates, Pershing Square Capital, Icahn Enterprise and Elliott Management.

---

[17] On this, see M. Kahan and E.B. Rock, 'Hedge Funds in Corporate Governance and Corporate Control' (2007) 155 *University of Pennsylvania Law Review* 1021.

[18] On this problem as it afflicts many orthodox fund managers that are part of broader conglomerate structures, see below.

[19] R. Wray, 'Vodafone Faces Investor Call for Break-Up', *The Guardian*, 7 June 2007.

[20] E. Anderson and A. Tovey, 'Rolls-Royce Caves to Pressure and Grants Activist Investor ValueAct a Seat on the Board', *The Telegraph*, 2 March 2016.

A distinctive feature of these firms' corporate governance behaviour, at least in relation to the customary approach of traditional institutional investors in this regard, is their largely unique propensity to engage in what Cheffins and Armour have termed 'offensive' shareholder activism. This term denotes many activist funds' customary practice of intervening in investee companies on an *ex ante* basis with a specific view to changing their business strategies proactively.[21] One particularly noteworthy offensive strategy favoured by certain activist funds in the United States recently has been a campaign of publicly-disclosed collaboration with a prospective hostile corporate control-acquirer,[22] geared in effect to brokering an outside takeover of the firm against the initial wishes of its management. This was exemplified most pertinently by Elliott Management's high-profile pressuring of the computing firm EMC to submit to a leveraged acquisition at the hands of its larger competitor Dell in 2015[23]; and, similarly, by Pershing Square Capital Management's coordinated prompting of Valeant's ultimately unsuccessful 2014 takeover bid for Allergan in the US pharmaceuticals sector.[24]

In contrast to the above practices, orthodox institutional investors such as pension funds and insurers have traditionally tended to intervene in investee companies' management on an *ex post facto* basis following a period of revealed underperformance, a practice referred to by Cheffins and Armour as 'defensive' shareholder activism.[25] From the perspective of disciplining poorly performing, unmotivated or misdirected corporate boards and managers, the prospective benefits of offensive (as opposed to traditional defensive) shareholder activism are readily apparent. On the other hand, though, such practices could reasonably be criticized for usurping directors' constitutionally protected autonomy over business management affairs[26]; and – relatedly – for occasioning the problematic second-guessing of management strategy by actors whose particular judgement on such matters is arguably *at least as* questionable as that of the officers at whom their criticisms are targeted.[27]

However, it should be pointed out that in relation to the global hedge fund sector as a whole, the abovementioned offensively-activist funds are more the exception than the rule as regards their strategy of systematically intervening in perceived underperforming companies. In practice, the vast majority of hedge

---

[21] See B.R. Cheffins and J. Armour, 'The Past, Present and Future of Shareholder Activism by Hedge Funds' (2011) 37 *Journal of Corporation Law* 51, 56–58.

[22] On the market for corporate control generally, see Chapter 10.

[23] P. Tanner, 'Dell Saves EMC from Elliott Management's Shareholder Activism', *Yahoo! Finance*, 16 October 2015.

[24] D. Gelles, 'No Allergan Deal, but a $2.6 Billion Profit for Ackman', *The New York Times*, 17 November 2014. The authors are thankful to Anna Christie for initially bringing the above two examples to our attention.

[25] Above n. 19, 56.

[26] On this, see Chapter 4.

[27] On this problem generally, see *ibid.* See also W. Bratton and M. Wachter, 'The Case against Shareholder Empowerment' (2010) 158 *University of Pennsylvania Law Review* 653, 662–75; S.M. Bainbridge, *Corporate Governance after the Financial Crisis* (OUP 2012), 236–38.

funds would appear to focus more or less exclusively on trading and associated asset valuation strategies. Accordingly, they seek to achieve competitive advantage principally via the development of quicker and more sophisticated methodologies and technologies in those regards,[28] rendering corporate governance and micro-management concerns largely superfluous to their perceived core activities.

Sovereign Wealth Funds

Sovereign wealth funds (or 'SWFs') are one of the most novel and also controversial types of institutional investor today. A SWF is essentially a state-owned investment fund, which is formally constituted as an autonomous private entity under independent management.[29] Well-known examples of SWFs include the Qatar Investment Authority, the China Investment Corporation and the Singaporean government's Temasek Holdings fund.

SWFs have traditionally provided a vehicle through which states with national budgetary surpluses can channel this excess capital into a variety of private asset purchases including, but by no means limited to, corporate equity holdings. Although SWFs typically claim to follow an orthodox commercial investment strategy, and in most instances would indeed appear to do so, the extent to which some SWFs are influenced by the political interests of their owner-state governments is a much-debated issue. In addition to having complex and potentially mixed investment motives, SWFs are also typically very large in scale. The world's largest SWF at the time of writing, which is owned by the Norwegian government and funded by national oil and gas revenues, has $850 billion of assets under its control.

Popular concerns about SWFs' transnational influence are magnified by their general opaqueness in comparison to orthodox commercial investment funds, albeit that recent policy initiatives have sought to increase SWFs' public transparency to some extent.[30] SWFs to date have in general shown little appetite for intervening directly in the governance or management affairs of investee public companies, in a UK context at least. However, the extent (if any) to which SWFs are likely to do so in future, and also the particular economic and

---

[28] On this phenomenon generally, see Government Office for Science, *The Future of Computer Trading in Financial Markets: An International Perspective (Final Project Report)* (2012), Ch. 2.

[29] On the essential characteristics of sovereign wealth funds generally, see International Working Group of Sovereign Wealth Funds ('IWG'), *Sovereign Wealth Funds: Generally Accepted Principles and Practice ('Santiago Principles')* (October 2008), 3; H. McVea and N. Charalambu, 'Sovereign Wealth Funds and Game Theory' (2014) 22 *Journal of Financial Regulation and Compliance* 61, 61–62.

[30] See e.g. IWG, 'Santiago Principles', *ibid.*; Sovereign Investment Lab, *The Sky Did Not Fall: Sovereign Wealth Fund Annual Report 2015* (International Forum of Sovereign Wealth Funds 2016). At domestic level, meanwhile, it is notable that the Private Equity Reporting Group's influential Good Practice Reporting Guide for Portfolio Companies is expressly applicable (*inter alia*) to UK-based companies owned or controlled by sovereign wealth funds, on the premise that SWFs constitute 'private equity-like' firms from a general financing and governance perspective. See http://privateequityreportinggroup.co.uk/qa/ ('How do you define a PE firm?')

political challenges that such interventions would likely pose, are important issues that merit the ongoing attention of domestic and international corporate governance policymakers.[31]

The Orthodox Corporate Ownership Chain

It should be apparent from the above discussion, and also from our earlier analysis of investment chains in Chapter 4, that the relationship existing between an investee public company and the ultimate beneficiary of its shares is rarely a direct binary one. Rather, more often than not a number of intermediating institutional agents are involved in the process.

In the typical case, direct ownership influence over an investee company will be exerted by a professional asset or fund manager, who will be investing as an agent for another institutional investor – such as a pension fund or insurer – holding a proprietary interest in the relevant investment fund (although likely not in the investee company's shares themselves). That institution will in turn be acting on behalf of the ultimate beneficiary of the investment in question: that is to say, the private individual advancing funds to the institution in the form of either pension fund contributions, insurance policy premiums or otherwise.

For illustrative purposes, it is helpful to refer to the fund manager[32] within the above chain as the *primary* institutional investor (because they are closest to the corporate 'action', so to speak), and to the institution entrusting them as the *secondary* institutional investor. Accordingly, the overall (orthodox) corporate ownership chain can be depicted in the following simple diagram, subject to the proviso that this basic pattern is subject to significant variation in many cases:

Ultimate beneficiary of investment

(e.g. pension fund beneficiary/insurance policyholder)

↓

Secondary institutional investor

(e.g. pension fund/insurer)

↓

Primary institutional investor

(e.g. asset/fund manager)

↓

Investee company

---

[31] Indeed, in this regard, it has curiously been observed that '[a]s a result of the SWFs' increasing level of assets invested in public and private equity holdings, they are exercising greater influence on corporate governance practices'. See IWG, *ibid.*, 3.

[32] Strictly speaking, of course, it is the relevant investment fund itself (whose entrusted assets the fund manager is employed to handle) that is the primary investing entity in the corporate ownership chain. However, on the premise that asset allocation and corporate engagement decisions will be made (whether directly or indirectly) by the actual human manager(s) of that fund, we refer here to the fund *manager* as the primary institutional investor in the chain, which we would regard as a correct observation from a functional (if not strictly formal) point of view.

The Changing Face of Britain's Institutional Investor Community

As discussed above, for much of the second half of the twentieth century UK public company ownership was dominated by institutional rather than individual shareholders. Moreover, of those institutions it was unquestionably the dominant domestic ones, and in particular the larger pension funds and insurers, that together constituted the largest ownership grouping.[33] Hence, when the issue of corporate governance first became prominent in the UK at the beginning of the 1990s, it was – naturally – those institutions that were entrusted to take up the mantle of holding boards accountable for their direction and control of listed companies.[34]

However, over the course of the intervening three decades times have undoubtedly changed, with the result that the shareholder demographic characteristic of London's contemporary stock market environment is markedly different from that of the inaugural Cadbury Code era. In particular, the opening decade of the twenty-first century witnessed the rapid internationalization of UK public companies' general ownership base,[35] such that by 2010 pension funds and insurers together accounted for less than 14 per cent of beneficial equity ownership of UK-listed companies.[36] This compared to over 40 per cent of UK equity ownership in the hands of overseas investors including offshore hedge funds, sovereign wealth funds, foreign holding companies and high-net-worth individuals.[37]

From a corporate governance perspective, one particularly noteworthy outcome of this sudden influx of foreign owners into London's stock market environment has been the increasing (albeit limited) spread of blockholder ownership[38] within the UK's listed company sector. The principal instigators of this movement have been certain Eastern European (predominantly Russian) mining and natural resources companies, which have successfully listed their shares in London in recent years despite remaining under the majority or near-majority control of overseas holding companies. Whilst

---

[33] See Kay, above n. 12, 31 ('Table 1: Historical Trends in Beneficial Ownership (Percentage Held)').

[34] For instance, in its seminal corporate governance report in 1992, the Cadbury Committee observed that '[t]he proportion of shares held by individuals and by institutions has broadly reversed over the last thirty years, so that institutional shareholders now own the majority of shares of quoted companies'. Accordingly, the Committee emphasized that '[g]iven the weight of their votes, the way in which institutional shareholders use their power to influence the standards of corporate governance is of fundamental importance'. See The Cadbury Committee, *Report of the Committee on the Financial Aspects of Corporate Governance* (1 December 1992), para. 6.9.

[35] On this trend, see Cheffins, above n. 4, 1017–20.

[36] Kay, above n. 12, 31–32.

[37] *ibid.*

[38] On this phenomenon generally, see Chapter 1.

investors have generally not been greatly perturbed by such factors, the presence of dominant corporate shareholders of this type can potentially give risk to the sorts of majority versus minority shareholder conflicts that are customarily observed within many non-Anglo-American corporate ownership environments.[39]

In response to this development, the Financial Conduct Authority (in its capacity as the official UK Listing Authority) in 2014 amended the UK Listing Rules so as to require that any new issuer with a controlling shareholder (defined as one who either individually or in concert with others exercises or controls 30 per cent or more of voting rights) will only be admitted to a Premium Listing where it can demonstrate (*inter alia*) the existence of a formal relationship agreement. For this purpose, a 'relationship agreement' is defined as a written and legally binding agreement intended to ensure: first, that the controlling shareholder transacts with the issuer on an arm's length commercial basis only; and, second, that it respects the regulatory requirement for the issuer to carry on its business independently of the former party's direct strategic and/or financial control.[40]

Due in large part to the comparative rigour of the UK's corporate governance regulatory framework, some notable blockholder-owned foreign companies have recently rejected London as a potential listing venue in favour of the seemingly more liberal climate of the New York market. As mentioned in the previous chapter, the Chinese government-owned e-commerce firm Alibaba perhaps stands out as the most pertinent example in this regard at the present moment in time.[41] In any event it would appear that, set against the backdrop of the UK's stock market environment as a whole, the abovementioned blockholder influx – whilst by all means a significant development – does not yet risk threatening the UK's characteristically dispersed corporate ownership paradigm in any fundamental way.

Notwithstanding this fact, the long-term ramifications for UK corporate governance of London's evolving shareholder populace remain highly uncertain. At least as things presently stand, though, it would appear that pension funds and insurers remain significantly influential as corporate governance actors in the UK, irrespective of their diminished relative ownership status today and the emergence of other types of institutional investor.

---

[39] On this, see B.R. Cheffins, 'The Undermining of UK Corporate Governance(?)' (2013) 33 *Oxford Journal of Legal Studies* 503.

[40] See Listing Rules 6.1.4–6.1.4D, at www.handbook.fca.org.uk/handbook/LR/. For a critique of the FCA's new relationship agreement rule from a corporate governance perspective, see M.T. Moore and E. Walker-Arnott, 'A Fresh Look at Stock Market Short-Termism' (2014) 41 *Journal of Law and Society* 416, 443–44; E. Ferran, 'Corporate Mobility and Company Law' (2016) 79 *Modern Law Review* 813, 827–29.

[41] C. Williams, 'Alibaba Chief Jack Ma Disappoints Investors with London No-Show', *The Telegraph*, 17 September 2014.

How Do Institutional Shareholders Engage with Corporate Management?

What Is Shareholder 'Engagement'?

According to Sir David Walker's influential 2009 review of corporate governance in banks and financial institutions, 'the term "engagement" relates to procedures designed to ensure that shareholders derive value from their holdings by dealing effectively with concerns about under-performance'.[42] Such procedures include (*inter alia*) arrangements for monitoring investee companies; arrangements for meeting with an investee company's chairman, senior independent director or senior management; a strategy for intervention in investee companies' management where judged appropriate; and a policy on voting and disclosure thereof.[43]

However, the Walker Review emphasizes that, whilst shareholder engagement in the above sense is generally desirable and thus worthy of encouragement, it is nonetheless 'not the role of institutional shareholders to micromanage or "second guess" the managements of their companies'.[44] Rather, as Walker explains, the focus of fund managers' monitoring activities should be on high-level issues such as ensuring the quality and capability of leadership of the company (and especially that provided by the chairman and CEO respectively); determining the composition and proper functioning of boards and committees; developing a sufficient understanding of the company's principal strategies and objectives (especially with respect to executive remuneration and the board's collective risk appetite) so as to be capable of informedly endorsing them in a broad sense; and providing an effective appraisal of corporate performance.[45]

Of course, many shareholders (of both the individual and the institutional varieties) might rationally opt not to engage with investee companies *at all* in any of the above ways, perceiving such activities as being cost-ineffective in view of the likely limited direct benefits therefrom.[46] However, for those (predominantly institutional) shareholders which *do* opt to engage in a meaningful way with investee companies' boards and/or management, there are a number of common engagement methods open to them, each of varying degrees of formality and potential sway vis-à-vis management. These range on a scale from lower-level and non-coercive ('soft') methods of engagement, to more coercive and high-level ('hard') engagement practices. Each of these two broad (and necessarily crude) categories of shareholder engagement practice will be examined in turn below.

---

[42] D. Walker, *A Review of Corporate Governance in Banks and Other Financial Industry Entities: Final Recommendations* (26 November 2009), para. 5.14.

[43] *ibid.*

[44] *ibid.*, para. 5.30.

[45] *ibid.*

[46] For a further discussion of this issue, see below.

'Softer' Engagement Practices

On the softer end of the scale, the most common and regular forms of shareholder-management engagement that typically occur within UK public companies involve relatively informal communications between: on the one hand, a company's CEO, chairman or finance director; and, on the other, a combination of professional market analysts employed by fund managers and stock brokerage firms, and journalists writing for the financial or general broadsheet press. For fund managers, the release of new information by public companies creates potential fresh trading opportunities. Thus analysts that are employed by fund managers on an in-house basis (so-called 'buy-side' analysts) will ordinarily seek fresh company-relevant information to the extent that it is conducive to influencing the stock trading activities of their employer firm. By contrast, analysts employed by stock brokerage firms (known as 'sell-side' analysts) are accustomed to collecting, generating, and disseminating fresh information and opinion, whether privately to select clients or publicly to the market community as a whole. This is with a view to precipitating the flow of share-trading activity generally, and – in turn – exploiting the ensuing broker-age fees therefrom.[47] In the case of the financial press, meanwhile, the motivating purpose of constant corporate data collection is to sustain a sufficient flow of fresh ongoing material to fill relevant print and electronic media.

Accordingly, given their common perception of company-relevant information as a (directly or indirectly) sellable commodity in itself, both brokerage analysts and financial journalists have a common rational incentive to seek to promote the generation of 'news for news' sake'. Moreover, in many instances, the activities and interests of both groups will intertwine, such as where analysts seek to advance their market profile and financial broadsheets seek to generate material by, respectively, providing and publishing 'expert' share-purchase recommendations.[48] The outcome of the combined research activities of the above groups is to create a perennial outside pressure for continuous financial performance disclosures by public companies whether in the form of interim trading statements, pre-emptive managerial earnings guidance and profit warnings, or reports on business developments that might potentially impact on future earnings performance.[49]

To this end, senior managerial officers of public companies (and, in particular, CEOs and finance directors) are more or less constantly involved in some form of communication with these groups, whether via analyst presentations, press conferences and/or more formal announcements issued via the London Stock Exchange's official information service.[50] In the case of issues of

---

[47] See T. Golding, *The City: Inside the Great Expectation Machine* (FT Prentice Hall 2002), 204–16.

[48] *ibid.*, 216–23.

[49] *ibid.*, 179.

[50] For a critical perspective on these practices, see J. Froud, S. Johal, A. Leaver and K. Williams, *Financialization and Strategy: Narrative and Numbers* (Routledge 2006), esp. Ch. 4.

particular concern, or where especially large and influential investment institutions are concerned, shareholder-management communications will occasionally take place on a one-to-one basis. However, in such instances both parties must be alert to the risk of management disclosing price-sensitive information on a selective non-public basis, which could lead to potential criminal and other liability on the part of both parties should the investor concerned subsequently trade the shares of the company concerned.[51]

To the extent that the above corporate communications are carried out for the purpose of satisfying market demand for company-relevant information,[52] rather than monitoring and disciplining managers *per se*, it might be queried whether they actually constitute 'governance' activities in the proper sense of the term. However, notwithstanding their *prima facie* 'soft' and benign nature from management's point of view, in practice such communications can have a powerful (albeit frequently indirect) disciplinary effect by compelling corporate officers to articulate and defend a firm's ongoing strategic and performance issues, whether publicly to the market in general or privately to certain major investors. In this way they fulfil an important accountability function.[53] Moreover, to the extent that such low-level communications are capable of resolving or mitigating investor concerns at an early stage, they can be effective in dissuading shareholders from adopting more coercive or adversarial forms of engagement vis-à-vis underperforming corporate boards and managers.

'Harder' Engagement Practices

However, where the above methods fail to have the desired effect from shareholders' perspective, or investors otherwise deem them to be ineffective, a somewhat more robust method of engagement (open to larger institutional shareholders at least) is the writing of so-called 'Dear CEO' or, alternatively, 'Dear Shareholder' letters. Notwithstanding their seemingly amicable overture, such communications are – in terms of their underlying tone and purpose – usually *anything but* friendly. As its colloquial name suggests, a 'Dear CEO' letter is targeted at the incumbent CEO of a particular public company, which in the sender's belief is either exhibiting performance concerns or adopting a particular strategic or financial position that arguably merits outside criticism.

Examples of issues that commonly form the subject matter of 'Dear CEO' letters include recommendations to divest (or 'spin-off') particular parts of a company's business operations that are either underperforming or diverting

---

[51] See, in particular, Criminal Justice Act 1993, Part V ('Insider dealing'); Financial Services and Markets Act, Part VIII ('Penalties for market abuse').

[52] On this generally, see Moore and Walker Arnott, above n. 40, 432.

[53] On the notion of accountability (particularly within corporate governance) as an explanatory practice involving the articulation by decision-makers (e.g. corporate directors and/or managers) of reasons in support of their discretionary decisions and conduct, see M.T. Moore, 'The (Neglected) Value of Board Accountability in Corporate Governance' (2015) 9 *Law and Financial Markets Review* 10.

from the firm's core competencies; requests to reduce the proportion of a company's free cash flow that is kept as retained earnings, in favour of a higher annual dividend or one-off stock buyback; and – in more serious instances – requests to replace a company's incumbent CEO and/or any other members of its current senior management team. A 'Dear CEO' letter can be either private or 'open' in nature. In the former case, it will be sent exclusively and discreetly to the corporate officer in question. In the latter case it will be published via freely accessible public media such as a national newspaper, website and/or social media platform. In the alternative case of a 'Dear Shareholder' letter, the written correspondence is directed instead at other shareholders of the company, and is intended to elicit their collective support for particular measures favoured by its author. In the public company environment, 'Dear Shareholder' letters tend by nature to be 'open' or public in nature.[54]

Although *prima facie* soft in nature, such communications – at least where instigated by particularly powerful or influential investors – in practice carry the implicit veiled threat that, if management fails to respond satisfactorily to the highlighted matters, a notionally 'harder' response is likely to follow in due course. This could be in the form of divestment of the relevant company's stock, or – alternatively – a more coercive intervention such as mobilization of the complaining shareholder's voting rights against the company's CEO or board at its next Annual General Meeting. However, as we highlighted in the previous chapter, irrespective of whether the dissatisfied investor intends to remain a shareholder or else divest their stock should their concerns go unaddressed, launching any sort of high-profile public campaign against an investee company's management is a highly dangerous strategy. In particular, it risks having a negative collateral impact on share price by exposing previously latent problems to the stock market at large, which could – paradoxically – ultimately inflict greater overall harm on an underperforming company's shareholders than the very issues that motivated the campaign in the first place.

---

[54] One of the most high profile instances of an open 'Dear Shareholder' letter in relation to a UK public company was the communication issued to Vodafone's shareholders by the activist fund Efficient Capital Structures (ECS) in June 2007, which was simultaneously published in the *Financial Times* newspaper. In this letter ECS sought to elicit widespread shareholder support for a number of proposed strategic initiatives including: (i) the divestment or 'spin-off' of Vodafone's (then) 45% holding in the American telecommunications firm Verizon Wireless; (ii) the return of a significant amount of Vodafone's free cash flow to shareholders via an issue of interest-bearing bonds to the company's existing shareholders; and (iii) the alteration of the company's constitutional governance structure under its articles, so as to empower shareholders to direct management by ordinary resolution (instead of by way of special resolution, as is standard under Model Article 4, discussed in Chapter 4), and also to place a cap on the amount that can be spent by management on acquisitions in any single year without prior shareholder approval. See 'The Vodafone Letter to Shareholders: Message from the Chairman of Efficient Capital Structures', *Financial Times*, 6 June 2007; R. Wray, 'Vodafone Faces Investor Call for Break-Up', *The Guardian*, 7 June 2007; D. Kershaw, *Company Law in Context: Text and Materials* (2nd ed., OUP 2012), 198–99.

As mentioned above, on a sliding scale from soft to hard methods of share-holder engagement vis-à-vis management, the exercise by shareholders of their legal voting rights against the board at an AGM lies very much towards the latter (i.e. more stringent) end of the spectrum. As such, it is usually an avenue of last resort should other, lower-level methods of voicing shareholder opinion fail to have the desired effect. Nowadays, negative shareholder votes in AGMs are frequently instigated in the first place not by institutional share-holder themselves, but rather on the professional recommendation of proxy advisory agencies.[55]

In the most extreme scenario, a negative vote recommendation could poten-tially take the form of an instruction to shareholders to withhold their approval of the incumbent directors' reappointment, although this would likely only occur in the event of outright loss of confidence in a company's current board. A much more common focus of proxy advisors' voting recommendations today is the annual directors' remuneration (or 'say on pay') vote,[56] especially in instances where boards are perceived to have sanctioned the payment of exorbitant remuneration packages to CEOs of poorly performing companies (known colloquially as 'rewards for failure'). Insofar as such votes – at least in the case of larger public companies – are widely reported in the broadsheet (and, in some instances, popular) press,[57] they can have potentially grave reper-cussions for a CEO or board's reputational capital.[58]

Such adverse reputational consequences for directors and managers of a successfully executed shareholder engagement campaign ordinarily consti-tute sufficient sanctions against the targeted officers in themselves. It follows that resort by shareholders to the notional 'nuclear' option of utilizing their formal legal rights of intervention in corporate decision-making (as outlined in the previous chapter) is usually rendered unnecessary. However, such rights remain potentially exercisable in appropriate instances, should alternative managerial-disciplinary measures prove to be inadequate for any reason.

Accordingly, it pays corporate managements to take careful heed of the expressed sentiments of their major shareholders in relation to executive pay and other contentious matters. Otherwise, what might initially have appeared a

---

[55] On the general role and influence of proxy advisors within corporate governance today, see Chapter 3.

[56] On this, see Chapter 9.

[57] See e.g. R. Cookson, 'Sir Martin Sorrell's £70m Pay Package Sparks Investor Rebellion', *Financial Times*, 8 June 2016; T. Macalister, J. Treanor and S. Farrell, 'BP Shareholders Revolt against CEO's £14m Pay Package', *The Guardian*, 14 April 2016.

[58] Furthermore, in 2014, the UK Corporate Governance Code was reformed so as to include (*inter alia*) a new recommendation to the effect that, where 'a significant proportion of votes have been cast against a resolution at any general meeting, the company should explain when announcing the results of voting what actions it intends to take to understand the reasons behind the vote result'. See Financial Reporting Council, *The UK Corporate Governance Code* (April 2016), Code Provision E.2.2, at www.frc.org.uk/Our-Work/Codes-Standards/Corporate-governance/UK-Corporate-Governance-Code.aspx.

somewhat gentle and unthreatening shareholder complaint might, if left unaddressed, transpire to be something of 'an iron fist in a velvet glove' from management's perspective.

Common Impediments to Effective Shareholder Engagement

It should be stressed that, in spite of what we have said above, for the most part effective shareholder engagement still remains the exception rather than the rule when it comes to prevailing institutional investor practices in general. Moreover, in view of the various structural and practical obstacles to effective shareholder engagement in widely-held corporate ownership environments (some of which have been alluded to in the previous chapter), it is not unreasonable for many investors to conclude that such efforts are simply not worth their while. Against this background, seeking to encourage effective shareholder engagement on anything more than a marginal or pocketed scale can sometimes seem like an insurmountable challenge for corporate governance policymakers.

The most obvious structural impediment to effective engagement of shareholders in public company governance has already been alluded to in Chapter 1, and indeed is one that afflicts any organizational environment featuring a large number of prospective voluntary participants. This is the classic 'free-rider' problem that occurs in large group scenarios where no one group member (in this case, an individual shareholder) can be sufficiently motivated to expend their effort on activities (e.g. managerial monitoring and/or challenge) that are prone to elicit benefits for the relevant group as a whole, in which the individual group member in question will share only to a very small and marginal extent. Accordingly, faced with this particular dilemma, an individual group member's natural inclination is simply to withdraw their efforts and remain passive. Unfortunately, this is also the individually rational response of all of her fellow members, such that in the end nothing gets done.[59]

In situations such as the corporate governance context, where the activity in question (i.e. managerial monitoring/challenge) is likely to be of collective benefit to the group (i.e. shareholders) as a whole, there arises an intractable collective action dilemma: that is to say, the particular course of action (or, more accurately, *inaction*) that is individually rational for each individual group member is curiously also the one that, from the perspective of the group's collective interest, leads to the *least* desirable overall outcome (namely unaccountable management). In this scenario, Adam Smith's classic maxim that the aggregate pursuit of individual self-interest serves the general collective interest[60]

---

[59] See Chapter 1, fn. 53 and accompanying text. On this problem generally, see M. Olson, *The Logic of Collective Action: Public Goods and the Theory of Groups* (revised ed., Harvard University Press 1971; first published 1965), 21; J.E. Parkinson, *Corporate Power and Responsibility: Issues in the Theory of Company Law* (OUP 1993), 54–55.

[60] A. Smith, *The Wealth of Nations* (Everyman 1991; first published 1776), 13.

breaks down, at least absent some form of extraneous intervention (e.g. from a publicly-spirited regulator or policymaker) geared to imposing – or, at least, facilitating – the particular outcome that is likely to enhance the subject group's welfare as a whole.

Furthermore, as likewise touched upon in Chapters 1 and 4, these difficulties are exacerbated by the typically diversified nature of most institutional investors' share portfolios, coupled with the inevitable informational deficit that afflicts most investors (even professional ones) who seek to scrutinize or challenge management on complex aspects of business policy.[61] Added to this is the common shareholder concern referred to in the last chapter about engagement giving rise to public conflict situations and consequent adverse publicity, coupled with worries about potential breach of insider dealing or market abuse laws in the event of non-public release of management knowledge. This is not to mention the abovementioned constraints on fund manager activism imposed by institutional conflicts of interest arising within large financial conglomerate firms,[62] or the potential – likewise discussed in the previous chapter – for agency problems between secondary institutional investors and fund managers in situations where the latter actors lack effective incentives to maximize the value of assets entrusted to their control.

Indeed, in light of the above issues it is unsurprising that a great many institutional investors tend to opt for conservative index-linked investment strategies, which are designed essentially to track broad macro-level movements in the stock market as a whole, as opposed to micro-level developments in individual issuer firms.[63] Curiously, the historical empirical evidence on whether those funds adopting an active securities selection policy systematically outperform (or, conversely, underperform) their so-called 'index-hugging' counterparts is both mixed and notoriously inconclusive.[64] At the very least, it can be said with reasonable certainty that – all other things being equal – there would

---

[61] On these issues, see Bainbridge, above n. 27, 243–45.

[62] On these problems generally, see Financial Services Authority, *Conflicts of interest between asset managers and their customers: Identifying and mitigating the risks* (November 2012); M. Marriage, 'Conflicts of Interest Weigh on UK Fund Managers', *Financial Times*, 19 April 2015.

[63] On index-linked investing generally, see J. Wurgler, 'On the Economic Consequences of Index-Linked Investing' in W.T. Allen, R. Khurana, J. Lorsch and G. Rosenfeld, *Challenges to Business in the Twenty-First Century: The Way Forward* (American Academy of Arts and Sciences 2011), Ch. 4.

[64] See e.g. M.C. Jensen 'The Performance of Mutual Funds in the Period 1945–1964' (1968) 23 *Journal of Finance* 389; R.S. Carlson, 'Aggregate Performance of Mutual Funds: 1948– 1967' (1970) 5 *Journal of Financial and Quantitative Analysis* 1; B. Malkiel, 'Returns from Investing in Mutual Funds 1971 to 1991' (1995) 50 *Journal of Finance* 549; M.J. Gruber, 'Another Puzzle: The Growth in Actively Managed Mutual Funds' (1996) 51 *Journal of Finance* 783; K.R. French, 'The Cost of Active Investing' (2008) 63 *Journal of Finance* 1537; E.F. Fama and K.R. French, 'Luck Versus Skill in the Cross-Section of Mutual Fund Returns (2010) 65 *Journal of Finance* 1915; D. Del Guercio and J. Reuter, 'Mutual Fund Performance and the Incentive to Generate Alpha' (2014) 69 *Journal of Finance* 1673.

appear to be no *necessarily* compelling reason for rejecting a passive index-linked fund in favour of a more actively discerning competitor product. Such macro-focused approaches to securities selection have the added bonus of mitigating the risk of a particular investment fund underperforming its peers: after all, if the market as a whole falls in value, it is likely that the performance of every index-linked investment fund will be more or less equally affected, such that no individual fund manager will appear conspicuously less competent than her peers.

THE PROBLEM OF STOCK MARKET SHORT-TERMISM

Is Short-Termism Actually a Real Problem?

In one respect stock market short-termism is not dissimilar from global warming. That is to say, for every commentator who regards it as one of the most serious and pressing problems facing the corporate and financial world today, there would appear to be another commentator equally keen to deny that it is even a material 'problem' as such at all.

Although stock market short-termism is increasingly recognized today as a definite social problem, this has not always been the case. Due to the pervasive influence of the efficient capital market hypothesis ('ECMH') within modern financial and legal scholarship, the alleged 'problem' of short-termism has customarily been dismissed by many observers as an effective non-issue, insofar as stock markets are – it is purported – innately capable of pricing companies' long-term cash-generating potential (or lack of).[65] Unfortunately, the available empirical evidence on the validity of the ECMH – while undoubtedly voluminous – has on the whole proved somewhat inconclusive on the matter.[66] Notwithstanding this fact, the proposition that short-termism is somehow an immaterial or naturally self-correcting problem – and thus not worthy of serious academic consideration – can justifiably be dismissed once the inherent logical limitations of this claim are demonstrated.[67]

The Efficient Capital Markets Hypothesis ('ECMH') and Its Limitations

In essence, the ECMH asserts that capital (and, in particular, equity) markets are notionally 'efficient', in the sense that the current market price of any security (including a corporate share) is reflective of all materially relevant

---

[65] See e.g. P. Marsh, *Short-Termism on Trial* (IFMA 1993); M.C. Jensen, 'Some Anomalous Evidence Regarding Market Efficiency' (1978) 6 *Journal of Financial Economics* 95; E.F. Fama, 'Efficient Capital Markets: A Review of Theory and Empirical Work' (1970) 25 *Journal of Finance* 383; R.J. Gilson and R.H. Kraakman, *The Mechanisms of Market Efficiency* (1984) 70 *Virginia Law Review* 549.

[66] On this, see A. Shleifer, *Inefficient Markets: An Introduction to Behavioral Finance* (OUP 2000), 5–10, 16–23.

[67] *ibid.*, 10–16.

information.[68] The most common (so-called 'semi-strong') version of the ECMH avers that all publicly available data pertaining to both historic and projected future price movements of any security will be incorporated rapidly and consistently into its present price, with the notable outcome that – barring extraordinary circumstances – no individual investor or trader can realistically hope to outperform the market by seeking to uncover fresh relevant data that has not already impacted on price.[69]

In the case of a corporate share, this means that its market-determined price will necessarily reflect everything that is publicly known about the relevant company's underlying business, to the extent that such facts will have a bearing on that company's future share price performance.[70] Given that the price of a company's share is (in theory at least) reflective of the discounted present value of future cash flows accruing to its holder, it follows that 'relevant' information for this purpose encapsulates any data that is indicative of corporate profitability whether in the immediate or longer term.[71] This includes considerations such as the company's projected future product market growth rate, the prospective implications of its long-term research and development initiatives, the impact of customer care and employee relations activities in fostering stakeholder trust and reputational capital, and – where applicable – the anticipated future challenges posed by macro-economic,[72] ecological[73] and demographical[74] factors.

In its purest form, the ECMH is premised on the (empirically dubious) assumption that investors are fully informed of all company-relevant facts, and also equipped with the computational ability to process this information effectively when making securities selection decisions. However, more recent and conceptually sophisticated variants of the theory – building on insights from behavioural economics – accept the widespread existence of informational limitations and irrational investor biases.[75] Such biases include (*inter alia*) the well-known short-termist disposition – that is, the intrinsic human tendency to attribute excessive value to choices that offer immediately satisfying outcomes, while discounting excessively the present value of initiatives that promise payoffs only over a longer time period.[76] A further and related common bias of stock markets is their collective tendency to regard relatively recent or short-term developments (e.g. market price fluctuations) as being indicative of a

---

[68] See Fama, above n. 65, 413.
[69] See Jensen, above n. 65, 96.
[70] See L. Stout, *The Shareholder Value Myth* (Berrett-Koehler 2012), 63–64.
[71] Kay, above n. 12, para. 4.4.
[72] For example, future interest rate changes and currency fluctuations.
[73] For example, the future diminution of finite resources essential for a company's productive operations.
[74] For example, future changes in the size or make-up of a company's target markets.
[75] See e.g. Jensen, above n. 65; Gilson and Kraakman, above n. 65.
[76] On this, see Kay, above n. 12, para. 1.1.

more general and sustained pattern of development, as opposed to the merely transient outcome of extraordinary or fortuitous circumstances.[77]

Notwithstanding the above factors, it is asserted that investor biases are, on the whole, prone to cancel each other out, so that – for instance – the overall price impact of investors exhibiting the above biases will ultimately be offset by the collective market decisions of those investors who, for whatever reason (e.g. excessive risk-aversion), are irrationally inclined to neglect short-term payoffs at all costs in favour of perceived longer-term benefits. The net outcome of this 'levelling out' process, therefore, would be proximately (albeit not perfectly) efficient share pricing, with market prices deviating only to a limited extent from companies' fundamental values.[78]

The weakness of the above argument, though, is its neglect of the widely acknowledged fact today that certain investor biases – including the well-known short-termist disposition – are *systematic* in nature. That is to say, such biases are both common across a significant proportion of market participants, and also tend to factor very heavily on individual investors' preferences compared to other biases. In such instances, the relevant bias is not cancelled out, and thus has a disproportionate impact on share pricing with the effect that market valuations are driven substantially out of line with fundamental values.[79]

The (Limited) Capacity of Market Arbitrage to Correct Share Mispricing

Even in situations where conflicting biases do not have the desired effect of offsetting investors' *a priori* short-termist predisposition, it can arguably be said that short-termism by its very nature contains the seeds of its own solution in the form of long-term market arbitrage opportunities.[80] Accordingly, the excessive weighting by investors of short-term outcomes at the expense of longer-term payoffs results in the systematic over-pricing of shares carrying immediate profit-making opportunities, and – correspondingly – the systematic under–pricing of those promising only anticipated long-term payoffs.

However, such under-pricing represents not just a problem but also an *opportunity*, insofar as those (generally professional) investors who have the resources and inclination to identify long-term profit opportunities (known as 'arbitrageurs') can seek to make above-normal returns by purchasing and subsequently holding the undervalued shares for a long time period, thereby exploiting the resulting capital gain when the anticipated payoffs are eventually

---

[77] See Shleifer, above n. 66, 11.

[78] See Gilson and Kraakman, above n. 65, 581; Shleifer, *ibid.*, 3.

[79] See Shleifer, *ibid.*, 12; R.J. Gilson and R.H. Kraakman, 'The Mechanisms of Market Efficiency Twenty Years Later: The Hindsight Bias' in J. Armour and J.A. McCahery (eds), *After Enron: Improving Corporate Law and Modernising Securities Regulation in Europe and the US* (Hart Publishing 2006), Ch. 1, 30.

[80] On this issue generally, see Gilson and Kraakman, above n. 65; S. Grossman and J. Stiglitz, 'On the Impossibility of Informationally Efficient Markets' (1980) 70 *American Economic Review* 393, 404.

realized. Furthermore, to the extent that the ensuing share price movements have the effect of indirectly conveying the informed investors' superior information to their less-informed counterparts, the latter group will predictably follow suit in their purchasing behaviour, thereby bringing market valuations back in line with fundamental values.[81]

As conceptually elegant as this line of argument may be, though, its validity is seriously undermined once we consider the significant structural obstacles to effective market arbitrage in the above sense. First, there is the not-infeasible possibility that professional arbitrageurs will *themselves* exhibit common irrationality characteristics (including a short-termist predisposition), in spite of their informational and computational advantages relative to uninformed (or 'noise') traders.[82]

Second, even to the extent that arbitrageurs *are* aware of the systematic under-pricing of long-term corporate profit opportunities, it is by no means clear that acting *against* the prevailing market trend in this regard is necessarily the rational course of action in such instance. Rather, it would appear that the individually rational response – at least where the same trend is likely to continue for any further length of time – may be to seek to purchase the over-valued shares of the currently successful short-term performers, with a view to exploiting any capital gains resulting from their continuing price appreciation. As long as the arbitrageur is able to exit her investment (and thereby 'lock in' her short-term gain) before the over-pricing is detected by the market generally, she will stand to make a better return (at least in the short run) than would be possible from effectively 'betting against the market'[83] over the longer term.[84]

This type of activity – known as momentum trading – is one of the principal causes of unsustainable asset price 'bubbles', insofar as it has the effect of exacerbating upward price volatility resulting from irrational market exuberance.[85]

---

[81] On this, see Gilson and Kraakman, *ibid.*, 572–79.

[82] See Gilson and Kraakman, above n. 79, 26.

[83] In effect, a trader is able to 'bet against' a rising market in a company's shares via immediate disposal of her existing (over-priced) holding in that company, coupled with the 'short-selling' of previously unheld shares. Simply put, short-selling entails a trader borrowing (from a professional counterparty, such as an investment bank) shares in a company that she expects will experience a future price drop, and subsequently selling those shares at their current market price. The investor's expectation is that, if and when the predicted price drop materializes, she will then be able to repurchase the same number of shares on the market for a lower consideration than she received on the earlier sale, and thereafter return them to the initial lender (since shares of the same class are essentially fungible commodities, it does not matter if the shares returned to the borrower are notionally 'different' from the ones borrowed). The investor's profit from the short-sale transaction (or, more accurately, *series of* transactions) is in effect the difference between (i) the earlier sale price of the shares (prior to their price drop) and (ii) their later repurchase price (after the price drop), minus any commission paid to the lender in return for their professional securities-lending services.

[84] Gilson and Kraakman, above n. 79, 23–24.

[85] On this generally, see R.J. Shiller, *Irrational Exuberance* (2nd ed., Princeton University Press 2005; first published 2000).

It is also the principal reason as to why market arbitrage is generally incapable of being relied upon as a structural mechanism for 'correcting' incidences of share mispricing resulting from noise traders' ignorance or neglect of companies' long-term earnings potential.

A third and final reason for scepticism about the effectiveness of market arbitrage as an institutional stop on stock market short-termism is that, even if one accepts the (highly tenuous) proposition that arbitrage operates in general so as to mitigate share mispricing, there are inherent limitations on the extent to which it is capable of doing so. This is on account of the fact that *substantial* share mispricing – including, where relevant, substantial undervaluation of companies' long-term profit opportunities – is a necessary trigger for arbitrage activity in the presence of significant information costs. That is to say, where (as is almost always the case) the costs[86] that prospective arbitrageurs must incur in order to inform themselves satisfactorily about potential long-term gains from any investment are *significant*, the relevant investment will only be economically viable where the projected gains arising from it are significantly above the normal market rate of return. However, in order for this to be possible, the relevant share (or other security) must be significantly undervalued *in the first place*, otherwise no compensatory arbitrage opportunity will be present.[87]

The Structural Inevitability of Stock Market Short-Termism

The net result of the above factors is that stock markets will necessarily *always* exhibit a substantial degree of informational – and, in turn, price – inefficiency (including, where relevant, the systematic undervaluation of long-term profit opportunities), to the extent that the informational costs of arbitrage have the effect of rendering private market 'correction' unviable except in the more extreme instances of asset mispricing. It can thus justifiably be concluded that, contrary to traditional belief, short-termism is a structurally *inevitable* feature of stock markets.

Of course, the systematic over-pricing of short-term (at the expense of long-term) profit opportunities by stock markets is only a recognizable problem if its effects can be shown to be socially harmful. The adverse impact of stock market short-termism on the 'internal' strategic and operational decisions of public company managers will be discussed below. Notwithstanding its negative effect on investee companies, though, short-termism can also be regarded as harmful to stock markets themselves, insofar as it is prone to elicit a direct and uncompensated transfer of wealth from future to current shareholders.

This occurs where a company's existing shareholders are either skilful or fortuitous enough to exit their investment while short-term profit opportunities are over-priced by the market, thereby locking in their gain. Correspondingly, those future investors holding the relevant shares at the point in time when

---

[86] Such costs include both data-gathering and data-processing costs.
[87] On this, see Grossman and Stiglitz, above n. 80, 404.

the over-pricing is widely detected will suffer the resulting loss in value.[88] Moreover, it can be surmised that the very possibility of such uncompensated wealth transfers occurring – to the extent that it is widely acknowledged – will have the further indirect effect of undermining public faith in stock markets, at least amongst the less informed sectors of the investor community. In social terms, the ultimate outcome will be a loss of market liquidity coupled with an increase in the cost of capital for prospective investee companies. Hence short-termism *is* an objectively problematic phenomenon, which is inherently prone to inflict long-term damage on stock markets.

The Multi-Faceted Nature of Stock Market Short-Termism

Having demonstrated that stock market short-termism is a material social problem that is highly unlikely to be structurally self-correcting, we can now consider the principal practical manifestations of the phenomenon from a corporate governance perspective. In practice, short-termism is manifested in the form of two distinct but interlocking general practices. The first of these practices is *investor* short-termism, and the second is *managerial* short-termism. As we will explain below, the second dimension of short-termism typically arises in response to the first, given the general responsiveness of public company managers to perceived stock market signals. Each of these dimensions will now be examined in turn.

Investor Short-Termism

The practice of investor short-termism can in itself take one of two general forms, namely either *speculative trading* or *earnings-based investment*. Although these two forms of investor short-termism frequently overlap to a considerable extent, they nonetheless can be said to exhibit distinct characteristics from one another, and thus ultimately each pose specific difficulties and challenges.

Speculative trading is generally acknowledged to be the most extreme form of investor short-termism. Indeed, as an activity it arguably does not even constitute 'investment' in the ordinary sense of the term, at least insofar as investment ordinarily involves the appreciation of an asset's value over a material time period.[89] In essence, speculative traders seek to generate gains by anticipating – and subsequently trading on the basis of – changing market attitudes with respect to the attractiveness of any particular company's shares. Any gains or losses to individual traders resulting from such activity are dependent on a significant and irreducible element of chance. This is because a typical

---

[88] See K. Greenfield, 'The Puzzle of Short-Termism' (2011) 46 *Wake Forest Law Review* 627, 636.

[89] On the distinction between (i) trading and (ii) investment as mutually distinct types of market activity, see Kay, above n. 12, para. 5.4 (quoting from the Investment Management Association).

speculative trader, rather than trading her shares directly on the basis of verifiable company-relevant information, will instead focus primarily on how the
collective body of market opinion (as manifested in the trading decisions of
other investors and the recommendations of stock market analysts) is likely to
perceive any new development or finding.[90]

The professional 'expertise' of the speculative trader or analyst ordinarily resides not in the field of business strategy or fundamentals, but rather
in the objectively unpredictable human chemistry of the stock market itself.
Accordingly, the research activities of speculative traders and analysts will
tend to be dedicated instead to the task of determining current and projected
trading patterns and volumes, with a view to predicting the future trajectory of
share price movements from historic trends revealed therein.[91]

The typical shareholding period of a speculative trader is extremely short, and
commonly less than a day. High-frequency traders (who collectively account
today for almost a quarter of average daily turnover in UK equity markets[92])
customarily avoid carrying material unhedged positions overnight. They will
thus be inclined to liquidate a significant proportion of holdings by close of
day's trading, in which case single-day share price movements represent the
exclusive source of trading gains. Moreover, the bulk of high-frequency equity
trading is now carried out on an automated rather than manual basis.[93]

Where speculative high-frequency trading in a company's shares is prevalent, the disjuncture between the productive and financial dimensions of the
firm is clearly at its zenith. However, the extent to which such practices impact
upon the strategies or governance practices of the underlying companies whose
shares are traded should not be overestimated. This is due to the fact that speculative trading is generally performance-neutral, in the sense that such traders
are – all other things being equal – just as likely to seek to profit from predicted
falls in a company's share price (via the practice of 'short-selling'[94]) as they are
from predicted rises.

Thus speculative traders generally do not have any innate interest in
improved corporate profitability (whether over the short or long term), so that
the main adverse effect of high-frequency trading is increased stock market volatility in both directions. For this reason, it can be said that speculative equity
trading bears no necessary direct relation to corporate financial performance.
As such, absent other complementary market factors it is not *in itself* a cause of
managerial short-termism within individual companies.

Unlike speculative trading, earnings-based investment however undoubtedly *does* have a direct impact on internal corporate strategy and governance.

---

[90] For the seminal scholarly exposition of this phenomenon in financial markets generally, see
J.M. Keynes, *The General Theory of Employment, Interest and Money* (Macmillan 1936), Ch. 6.
[91] L.L. Dallas, 'Short-Termism, the Financial Crisis, and Corporate Governance' (2012) 37
Journal of Corporation Law 264, 298.
[92] Kay, above n. 12, 38, citing data published by TABB Group.
[93] Dallas, above n. 91, 299.
[94] On this financial market practice generally, see above n. 83.

As its name suggests, earnings-based investment involves making stock allocation decisions exclusively or primarily in response to actual or anticipated changes in periodic corporate earnings. A company's 'earnings' denotes its after-tax net income, as calculated over a specified time period. In essence, a company's earnings or net income over the relevant period will comprise the difference between: on the one hand, the revenues generated from its normal business operations during this time; and, on the other, the corresponding cost of funding those activities, including labour expenses and overheads.

While a company's periodic earnings figure is an important determinant of its share price, the most crucial statistic underlying a company's share price in most cases is its 'earnings per share' or 'EPS' figure.[95] As the name suggests, this figure is essentially calculated by dividing the company's total earnings or net income over the period by the number of its ordinary shares that are in circulation. Accordingly, where a company's net quarterly income is £10 million, and the company has 2 million ordinary shares in circulation, then its quarterly EPS will be £5. In the hypothetical example, this £5 figure will (theoretically at least) be representative of the amount of earnings accruing to each individual ordinary share of the company over the period. In this way, the EPS figure (theoretically) enables the shares of companies with often radically differing business characteristics and growth profiles to be compared by investors in a like-for-like manner, on the basis of a unifying objective criterion of perceived shareholder wealth (or 'value') creation.[96]

As regards companies that are listed on the London Stock Exchange, both corporate earnings and EPS will typically be published every six months – just after, and also at the mid-point of, the financial year – and as part of the company's compulsory annual accounts and half-yearly financial reports respectively.[97] Additionally, those UK companies that have a cross-listing on a US equity market (such as the New York Stock Exchange or NASDAQ) are obliged under applicable SEC Rules to publish quarterly financial reports including a statement of quarterly earnings and EPS.[98]

Whilst quarterly financial reporting (in the form of interim management statements) was formerly also a mandatory regulatory requirement for companies traded on UK and other EU regulated markets,[99] this obligation was removed (at both EU and UK level) in 2014 amidst concerns about

---

[95] Golding, above n. 47, 167.

[96] For a detailed and authoritative statement of the criteria determining a company's EPS figure, see International Accounting Standard 33, formulated by the International Accounting Standards Board and summarized at www.ifrs.org/Documents/IAS33.pdf.

[97] Publication of these documents is mandated by the Financial Conduct Authority's Disclosure Rules and Transparency Rules, DTR 4.1–4.2.

[98] Quarterly financial reports are rendered compulsory for US listed companies under SEC Rules 13a-13 and 15d-13, which require such reports to be filed with the Securities and Exchange Commission on a prescribed form (Form 10-Q) provided for this purpose.

[99] The requirement was formerly contained in Article 6 of Directive 2004/109/EC ('EU Transparency Directive').

its impact in encouraging short-termism.[100] In spite of this development, the vast majority of UK-listed companies continue to report on a quarterly basis in conformance with established stock market norms in this regard. However, Unilever and Legal & General have in recent years sought to lead by example within the UK's corporate community by voluntarily ceasing the provision of quarterly financial statements to investors.[101] Whether other, less well-established corporate names will follow suit in this regard remains to be seen.

One notable recent beacon of hope in this regard, though, is a high-profile Action Plan recently published by the Investment Association (IA),[102] an influential representative body for UK fund managers.[103] In this document the IA is highly critical of quarterly financial reporting, which it says 'can distort management behaviour by channelling its focus on short-term fluctuations in performance, resulting in the risk of senior management increasingly focusing on managing the market rather than the business'.[104] Accordingly, the IA expresses its wish 'to see companies move away from such short-term reporting and guidance in favour of long-term metrics', together with 'improvements in reporting on the long-term drivers of sustainable value creation'.[105] The likely practical impact of the IA's recommendations in altering entrenched investor and corporate norms, particularly with respect to periodic financial reporting practices, is an intriguing question that merits continuing attention over the next few years.

The earnings estimates arrived at by analysts will ordinarily create an ongoing market expectation that a company provides a steadily increasing rate of EPS growth on a quarter-to-quarter basis, coupled with a general secondary expectation of year-on-year increases in the company's annually declared rate of dividend.[106] And, insofar as the usual principal driver of earnings (and, in turn, EPS) growth in many sectors (especially retail) is underlying growth in sales, the criterion of 'like-for-like' sales – that is, periodic returns from sales relative to the corresponding period from the previous year – customarily assumes foremost importance within management's continuing performance disclosures.[107]

---

[100] See the Transparency Directive Amendment Directive (TDAD) (Directive 2013/50/EU); Financial Conduct Authority, *Removing the Transparency Directive's requirement to publish interim management statements* (November 2014). On the centrality of informational disclosure to corporate governance generally, see Chapter 8.

[101] T. Wallace, 'Legal and General Scraps Quarterly Reporting', *The Telegraph*, 11 December 2015; 'Unilever's Paul Polman: CEOs Can't Be "Slaves" to Shareholders', *Forbes*, 20 July 2015.

[102] J. Quinn, 'UK Blue-Chip Firms Told to Stop Reporting Every Quarter', *The Telegraph*, 20 March 2016.

[103] See www.theinvestmentassociation.org/.

[104] The Investment Association, *Supporting UK Productivity with Long-Term Investment: The Investment Association's Productivity Action Plan* (March 2016), 16, at www.theinvestmentassociation.org/assets/files/press/2016/20160322-supportingukproductivity.pdf.

[105] *ibid.*

[106] Golding, above n. 47, 178.

[107] Froud *et al.*, above n. 50, 133.

The effective market 'demands' embodied in consensus earnings estimates are 'enforceable' on management by investors via the latter's actual or threatened exit from the company (by means of disposal of their holdings on a liquid market) in the event of a company's failure to conform to earnings estimates. The virtually inevitable result of such market 'enforcement' activity – where conducted on a large enough scale – is the material depreciation of the company's share price, which can potentially undermine an incumbent CEO's continuing mandate to hold office in the eyes of shareholders.[108]

The common fixation of earnings-based investors – and, in particular, professional fund managers – on regular financial-performance disclosures and estimates is attributable not just to the regulatory environment, but also to the characteristics of institutional investment chains. In the typical case, fund managers are evaluated and remunerated by institutional asset holders based on quarterly gross returns to the fund, while fund management mandates are frequently rendered terminable by asset holders on very short notice.[109]

Taken together, the above pressures in general exert a compelling discipline on corporate managers to achieve positive and consistent corporate financial performance on a quarter-to-quarter basis.[110] *How*, exactly, this discipline is manifested in the strategic and communicative practices of public company managers will be the focus of the discussion that follows.

Managerial Short-Termism

The phenomenon of managerial short-termism represents the internal response – at the business enterprise level – to the external financial-performance demands of the stock market. It can thus be regarded as the flip-side to the abovementioned notion of investor short-termism.

Managerial short-termism is based at root on a very simple mantra, which is the perceived imperative of 'giving the market what it wants to hear'. As explained above, the market's typical primary demand of an investee company is that it generates a consistently positive rate of periodic EPS growth, preferably coupled with a corresponding rise in its declared rate of dividend. From the viewpoint of investors, steady EPS and dividend growth are desirable corporate attributes for two main reasons. First, continuing dual EPS and dividend growth ensures ongoing increases in total shareholder return, whether in realized (i.e. dividend) or realizable (i.e. consequent share price appreciation) form. And, second, the same qualities are indicative of management's

---

[108] M.C. Jensen, 'Agency Costs of Overvalued Equity' (2005) 34 *Financial Management* 5, 7.

[109] On this, see Kay, above n. 12, 40–41. Kay alternatively recommends that fund management relationships be reviewed by asset holders 'at intervals of no less than three to five years'. *ibid.*, para. 7.31.

[110] As discussed above (n. 100 and accompanying text), this is notwithstanding the FCA's decision in 2014 to remove its former regulatory requirement for interim (i.e. quarterly) management statements or financial reports in publicly traded UK companies.

capacity to forestall potential turbulence in the company's trading environment, and thus are widely regarded as implicit signals of corporate stability and reliability.[111]

In graphical terms, the notionally 'ideal' EPS growth profile can be depicted in the form of an upward-sloping curve, denoting a steady rate of increase. As a general stock market practice, any significant periodic deviation by a company from this basic pattern – absent a convincing set of managerial explanations therefor – is customarily 'punished' in the form of an ensuing end-of-period share price fall.[112] From a corporate perspective, however, the stock market's general reliance upon periodic earnings estimates as a credible tool for ongoing managerial performance-evaluation is highly problematic. Whereas 'the market' tends to attach a premium to the perceived virtues of stability and predictability in corporate earnings schedules, such attributes are rarely consistent with the sales and cost profiles of business enterprises, given that contingency, volatility and occasional destabilization are intrinsic structural features of competitive product markets.[113]

Accordingly, where – as is highly likely – a company is incapable of generating earnings on a sufficiently predictable basis for the stock market's liking via its normal productive operations, it falls upon its management to seek to present to the market an effective façade of corporate income-stability. To this end, corporate managers have scope to engage in a diverse range of financial and business activities geared to 'smoothing' the company's periodic earnings figures on a continuing basis – a practice known generally as 'earnings management'.[114] The most direct and, usually, straightforward means of earnings management is creative manipulation of the numbers that are presented in a company's accounts, for instance by deferring incurred costs or losses to future accounting periods so that they do not depress the company's current-period earnings figure.[115]

Consideration for effective earnings management may also influence the timing of regulatory announcements to the market about impending business developments, such as new product launches, acquisitions or restructuring initiatives; and, vice versa, the public release of items of 'bad' news such as the possible loss of a valuable contract.[116] In some instances, even the timing of

---

[111] J.F. Houston, B. Lev and J.W. Tucker, 'To Guide or Not to Guide? Causes and Consequences of Stopping Quarterly Earnings Guidance' (2010) 27 *Contemporary Accounting Research* 143, 144.

[112] Jensen, above n. 108, 7.

[113] J. Fuller and M.C. Jensen, 'Just Say No to Wall Street' (2002) 22 *Journal of Applied Corporate Finance* 59, 62.

[114] On the phenomenon of earnings management generally, see Jensen, above n. 108, 7–8.

[115] Dallas refers to such activities as 'accounting earnings management', to be distinguished from the types of 'real' earnings management practice discussed in the following paragraph. See above n. 91, 277–78.

[116] Under the FCA's Disclosure and Transparency Rules, issuers are required to provide formal notification to the market of any information that would be likely to have 'a significant effect' on share price if used as a basis for investment decisions. See DTR 2.2.

major business activities themselves may be influenced by investor relations factors, such as where maintenance or research and development projects are delayed in order to avoiding increasing current production costs, or where product price reductions or advertising initiatives are geared specifically to enhancing a company's periodic like-for-like sales.[117]

Additionally, management has the capacity to increase artificially a company's periodic EPS figure from time to time by way of large-scale share repurchase.[118] So-called 'stock buybacks' have the intended effect of reducing the denominator (i.e. number of shares) to the company's earnings-per-share ratio, so that each share is theoretically representative of a greater proportion of total shareholder wealth created over the relevant period.[119] At the same time, stock buybacks enable management to increase directly the periodic level of total shareholder return via direct distribution of the company's free cash flow, but without bringing about a corresponding rise in its current rate of dividend. Consequently, management is able to avoid enhancing market expectations as to the trajectory of future annual dividend rate increases.[120]

Financial engineering methods of the above type are frequently supplemented by managerial communications calculated to 'manage' the expectations of analysts as to the company's forthcoming results. Thus a firmly-entrenched responsibility of public company CEOs and finance directors today is the ongoing provision of 'earnings guidance', most notably via informal profit warnings issued ahead of lower-than-expected results.[121] These communications are specifically designed and timed in order to mitigate the likely adverse impact on share price of the upcoming 'bad news', so as hopefully to effect gradual and moderate share price depreciation rather than a sharp and sudden market 'shock' at a later date.[122]

However, where any or all of the above methods fail to achieve the desired 'smoothing' effect with respect to a company's periodic numbers, management may have recourse to more extreme 'engineering' measures to ensure that the company is able to meet its consensus earnings estimates. In particular, consideration for effective earnings management may necessitate making wholesale changes to the company's underlying business strategies, even to the extent of abandoning potentially value-enhancing initiatives on the basis that they are

---

[117] Dallas, above n. 91, 279.

[118] On the role of share repurchases in corporate governance generally, see W. Lazonick, 'The Quest for Shareholder Value: Stock Repurchases in the US Economy (2008) 74 *Louvain Economic Review* 479.

[119] M. Aglietta, 'Shareholder Value and Corporate Governance: Some Tricky Questions' (2000) 29 *Economy and Society* 146, 151.

[120] J.F. Weston, J.A. Siu and B.A. Johnson, *Takeovers, Restructuring & Corporate Governance* (Prentice Hall 2001), 537.

[121] Note also the centrality to public company governance today of investor relations departments, dedicated specifically to managing investors' expectations. See Kay, above n. 12, para. 8.39.

[122] Houston *et al.*, above n. 111, 144.

likely to receive a hostile or lukewarm response from the market. Alternatively, a particular strategic policy (e.g. a high-profile acquisition or corporate restructuring) may be motivated primarily by the anticipated positive market response thereto, notwithstanding latent managerial concerns about the overall viability of that initiative in terms of its projected effect on long-term enterprise value.[123]

An especially powerful managerial incentive to engage in strategy-based financial engineering practices exists where a company's equity is substantially 'overvalued' – that is to say, where market expectations as to the company's future trajectory of earnings growth are excessively optimistic.[124] In such instances, a company's anticipated earnings growth rate will typically be unsustainable via continuing development of its existing businesses, thus compelling resort to managerial techniques that sustain the illusion of growth when viewed from the market's perspective.[125]

The most direct method of illusory earnings growth creation is corporate acquisitions,[126] which in the typical case will be implemented by using the acquiring company's inflated equity as valuable (full or partial) consideration for the target company's shares. Earnings-focused acquisitions have the immediate dual advantage of: first, enabling the company to 'buy' the sales (and consequent revenues) of the target company outright in order to enhance its group earnings statement[127]; and, second, facilitating the relatively rapid reduction of operating expenses via the systematic reduction of the target company's long-term investment activities (e.g. research and development initiatives), thereby reducing the group's consolidated cost base.[128]

In this way, a short-term acquisitions-based strategy can effectively 'buy time' for a management team that lacks ideas about how to improve a company's earnings by more conventional means. It also has the ancillary benefit of continually changing the overall scale and shape of the group enterprise, thus making it difficult for analysts to make meaningful periodic comparisons between the company and its product market competitors.[129] However, in cases where corporate acquisitions and restructurings are motivated primarily by their anticipated short-term effect on a company's periodic revenue or cost profile, there is a risk that such policies may ultimately prove to be destructive

---

[123] D. Millon, 'Why Is Corporate Management Obsessed with Quarterly Earnings and What Should Be Done About It?' (2002) 70 *George Washington Law Review* 890, 893.

[124] On the concept of overvalued equity generally, see Jensen, above n. 108.

[125] *ibid.*, 10.

[126] On the regulation of corporate acquisitions from a specific governance point of view, see Chapter 10.

[127] J. Froud, C. Haslam, S. Johal and K. Williams, 'Shareholder Value and Financialization: Consultancy Promises, Management Moves' (2000) 29 *Economy and Society* 80, 98.

[128] On this generally, see J. Froud, C. Haslam, S. Johal and K. Williams, 'Restructuring for Shareholder Value and Its Implications for Labour' (2000) 24 *Cambridge Journal of Economics* 771.

[129] Froud *et al.*, above n. 50, 120.

of shareholder wealth in the longer term. Long-term shareholder wealth destruction could ensue as a result of management increasing the acquiring or acquired company's indebtedness, diverting its attention from day-to-day enterprise considerations, or else obfuscating the group's strategic focus by expanding into activities outside of its core specialisms.[130]

In any event, where management is under pressure from the market to produce earnings growth – and particularly where the relevant company has an existing high equity valuation to sustain – managers' rational propensity in the short term is usually to favour action over inaction. This is for two main reasons. First, all other things being equal, a CEO frequently feels the need to be perceived by the market to be doing *something rather than nothing*, so that she has tangible 'progress' to report on at the end of each reporting period[131]; and, second, a stream of constant strategic activity is generally crucial to building a convincing 'narrative' of success for presentation to analysts and the press – that is, demonstrating that periodic improvements in earnings and/or share price performance are part of a deliberate and pre-conceived 'story' of corporate success or recovery, rather than (as is often the case) the merely fortuitous outcome of broader environmental or macro-economic factors.[132]

Thus one of the most common and conspicuous outcomes of earnings-based trading in a company's shares is a consequent managerial inclination towards 'hyperactivity'[133] or serial strategic 'tinkering'. This denotes the perceived managerial imperative, in response to stock market pressures, of generating a constant stream of innovation and general corporate activity, even in situations where preserving the strategic status quo may actually be the current policy most conducive to enhancing the company's long-term success and value.[134]

THE UK STEWARDSHIP CODE: ENHANCING INSTITUTIONAL SHAREHOLDER ENGAGEMENT?

The currently-fashionable notion of institutional shareholder 'stewardship' is embodied today in the Financial Reporting Council's UK Stewardship Code, first published in 2010 and most recently updated in 2012.[135] As a shareholder engagement strategy, stewardship entails institutional investors eschewing the

---

[130] Jensen, above n. 108, 8–14.

[131] The Kay Review refers to this behavioural phenomenon as a managerial 'bias towards action'. See Kay, above n. 12, para. 4.13.

[132] On the concept of corporate narrative-building generally within financialized corporate governance systems, see Froud *et al.*, above n. 50.

[133] This term is attributable to the Kay Review. See above n. 12, para. 1.2.

[134] Curiously, the phenomenon of managerial hyperactivity is opposite to the traditional assumption of managerial 'shirking' (or inactivity) that underlies standard 'agency cost' accounts of corporate governance. On the latter notion generally, see Chapter 2.

[135] See Financial Reporting Council, *The UK Stewardship Code* (September 2012), at www.frc.org.uk/Our-Work/Publications/Corporate-Governance/UK-Stewardship-Code-September-2012.pdf.

innate incentive to seek to dispose of their holdings in a company in response to concerns about its underperformance, instead seeking to resolve contentious issues via direct and ongoing communications with individual corporate managements – whether on a one-to-one or collective basis.[136] As a quasi-regulatory strategy, meanwhile, stewardship involves prompting actors at different points in the corporate equity investment chain to recognize potential long-term gains from supporting and, where appropriate, challenging directors and senior managers in an informed manner on issues of both corporate governance and business strategy.[137]

In terms of its key principles of shareholder engagement, the Stewardship Code recommends that institutional investors should: (i) publicly disclose their policy on how they will discharge their stewardship responsibilities; (ii) have a robust policy on management of conflicts of interest in relation to stewardship which should be publicly disclosed; (iii) monitor their investee companies; (iv) establish clear guidelines on when and how they will escalate their stewardship activities; (v) be willing to act collectively with other investors where appropriate[138]; (vi) have a clear policy on voting and disclosure of voting activity; and (vii) report periodically on their stewardship and voting activities.[139]

A common notable feature of the Stewardship Code – and also its longer-standing cousin, the UK Corporate Governance Code – has been their express advocacy of a discriminatory 'insider/outsider' dichotomy with respect to listed companies' shareholder engagement practices. Thus Principle E.1 of the Corporate Governance Code – on 'Dialogue with Shareholders' – expressly

---

[136] See *ibid.*, 1.

[137] On the regulatory dimension of the stewardship agenda generally, see H.-Y. Chiu, 'Turning Institutional Investors into "Stewards": Exploring the Meaning and Objectives of "Stewardship"' (2013) 66 *Current Legal Problems* 443.

[138] Interestingly, in its recently published Green Paper on corporate governance reform, the government has tentatively proposed the establishment of a 'senior shareholder committee' at individual company level, which would be responsible (*inter alia*) for scrutinizing remuneration arrangements, long-term business strategy and the directorial appointments process. At the same time, it has cautioned that '[t]he full implications of adapting any such model in the UK, however, would need careful consideration given its potential impact on our long-established unitary board structure'. See Department for Business, Energy and Industrial Strategy, *Corporate Governance Reform: Green Paper* (November 2016), para. 1.36. Additionally, two of the UK's most influential shareholder advisory groups (namely ShareSoc and the UK Shareholders' Association (UKSA)) have recently taken significant steps towards setting up an *ad hoc* committee representative of private shareholders in the Royal Bank of Scotland (RBS), with a view to enhancing the quality of the company's governance and also addressing continuing investor concerns about the running of its business operations. See B. Martin, 'RBS Investors Mount Campaign for Shareholder Committee', *The Telegraph*, 30 December 2016.

[139] Above n. 135, 5. In its recent corporate governance Green Paper (*ibid.*), the government has further mooted the idea of making disclosure of fund managers' voting records at company AGMs a *mandatory* requirement, which would presumably entail putting the Stewardship Code's current 'soft' requirement in this regard on a formal statutory footing. At the time of writing, it is unclear to what extent (if any) the government plans to advance further with this particular proposal. See *ibid.*, para. 1.35.

discriminates 'major shareholders' from other shareholders, and recommends that a company's chairman should discuss governance and strategy specifically with the former group, and also that its non-executive directors should attempt to understand major shareholders' issues and concerns while being prepared to meet with them personally on request.[140] Expanding on the FRC's major/minor shareholder dichotomy, meanwhile, the Kay Review additionally stipulates that companies should consult their 'major long-term investors' with respect to key board appointments.[141]

In a similar vein, the Stewardship Code defines effective shareholder engagement as a process of 'purposeful dialogue' with management, and, to this end, calls for collective engagement activities involving formal or informal groups of major institutions.[142] Furthermore, in a clear eschewal of the general informational equality position traditionally underpinning UK (and, moreover, European) capital markets law, the Stewardship Code expressly sanctions the corporate-managerial practice of making certain major shareholders 'insiders': as such, the latter actors can legitimately become privy to price-sensitive information on the agreed condition that they do not trade until the relevant information becomes public.[143]

The Stewardship Code's principles are enforceable on a 'comply or explain' basis in the same vein as those of the Corporate Governance Code (on the latter Code's enforcement, see Chapter 3).[144] This is formally provided for in the FCA Conduct of Business Sourcebook, which stipulates that:

> A firm, other than a venture capital firm, which is managing investments for a professional client that is not a natural person must disclose clearly on its website, or if it does not have a website in another accessible form: (1) the nature of its commitment to the Financial Reporting Council's Stewardship Code; or (2) where it does not commit to the Code, its alternative investment strategy.[145]

Accordingly, secondary institutional investors such as pension funds and insurers are expected to assess fund managers' record of compliance with the Stewardship Code's principles in determining whether to allocate or renew an asset management mandate with them. In effect, therefore, the Stewardship Code seeks to harness competitive pressures emanating from the market for asset management mandates, so as hopefully to bring about enhanced levels of engagement by fund managers in the governance of investee companies.

Whilst the theoretical rationale for the Stewardship Code's unique enforcement method is intuitively convincing, its effectiveness in practice is a more

---

[140] Above n. 58, Code Provision E.1.1.
[141] Kay, above n. 12, 13, Recommendation 5.
[142] Above n. 135, 1.
[143] *ibid.*, 7.
[144] *ibid.*, 4.
[145] *FCA Handbook*, 'Conduct of Business Sourcebook', CBOS 2.2.3 ('Disclosure of commitment to the Financial Reporting Council's Stewardship Code').

contestable issue. In addition to the practical difficulties involved in policing the accuracy of individual fund managers' disclosures under the above provision, it might further be queried how material such disclosures are to secondary institutional investors when making decisions on the allocation or renewal of mandates. In particular, it is questionable to what extent a fund manager's relatively weak commitment to the Stewardship Code's principles will be a cause of concern for her institutional investor clients, especially if the relevant agent's recent investment-performance record is otherwise highly impressive. Moreover, as Cheffins has pointed out (and as additionally alluded to earlier in this chapter), the principal intended subjects of the Code's disclosure-based enforcement machinery – namely domestic pension funds, insurers and fund managers – constitute a decreasing component of London's (increasingly foreign) investor community.[146] However, as we highlighted above, one should not be too hasty to dismiss the continuing influence of these institutions as key corporate governance actors in the United Kingdom today.

---

[146] Cheffins, above n. 4, 1024–25.

CHAPTER 6

Corporate Governance and Labour

In the previous two chapters, we examined the various respects in which share-holders are formally empowered to intervene in corporate decision-making, and also the many informal ways in which shareholders typically exercise collective governance influence over public company boards and managers on an ongoing basis. In this chapter, we temporarily shift our focus to consider an additional relational element of corporate governance, which is one of the most important in terms of ensuring the firm's continuing viability as a productive and wealth-generating entity: that is, the status of *employees* within corporate governance.

As we have previously remarked upon in this book, in view of the practical significance of human capital as both a productive and income-generating resource, it is at first sight somewhat perplexing why employees' formal status within UK corporate governance is so heavily attenuated, at least in relation to that of shareholders. In Chapter 2 we analyzed some conceptual considerations which arguably help to explain why, from a functional point of view, recognizing shareholders as the exclusive collective beneficiary of management's discretionary decision-making power is in general prone to elicit positive economic outcomes. However, as we further acknowledged, this particular claim – whilst undoubtedly influential – is also highly contestable, not least with respect to those industrial sectors in which firm-specific human capital investments are *at least as* instrumental as standard financial capital investments in securing long-term corporate sustainability and success.

Moreover, the fact that numerous other major European corporate governance systems have traditionally vested employees with a formal share of core corporate decision-making power (and, indeed, continue to do so today) suggests that, contrary to what some Anglo-American commentators have previously averred, purely shareholder-oriented models of corporate governance are – from an international standpoint – neither functionally inevitable nor innately superior to the available alternatives. Indeed, it is not readily apparent from the UK's historic industrial performance that its shareholder-centric governance framework has been conducive to any material comparative advantage over more labour-oriented 'competitor' systems. Nor would it seem that the characteristics of Britain's key industrial sectors are sufficiently distinct from those of her continental-European counterparts to justify the adoption of such a markedly differing national corporate governance paradigm, at least absent other significant operating causes.

However, as our historical discussion below will show, other operating factors in this regard have undoubtedly been present in Britain's case. Chief amongst these (somewhat curiously) has been the traditional unease of much of the British labour movement itself with the idea of European-style worker involvement in corporate decision-making. Indeed, UK trades unions – in contrast to many of their European (and, in particular, German) counterparts – for a long time exhibited a general preference for 'external' engagement of employees with employer firms independently of intra-corporate decision-making forums, via collective bargaining and other such inherently adversarial forms of industrial action. Largely (albeit not wholly) in consequence of this, organized labour in the UK has been dependent almost[1] exclusively on adversarial methods of exerting influence over management decisions, outside of core corporate decision-making processes. However, modern labour market developments – coupled with controversial recent regulatory reforms – suggest that even this fairly limited form of employee governance influence is increasingly becoming a remnant of the past, not least insofar as UK companies are concerned.

Whether this is, on the whole, a desirable social outcome is a value judgement. However, regardless of one's particular normative position on the appropriateness of direct worker involvement in corporate governance, an additional issue remains as to the likely longevity of the UK's traditionally shareholder-centric status quo in this regard. As we will show in the final part of the chapter, contemporary demographic trends in Britain provide cause to question the long-term sustainability of UK corporate governance law's exclusive shareholder focus.

Why Concentrate Specifically on *Labour* as a Relevant Non-Shareholder Constituency?

Before enquiring further as to the (limited) ways in which the interests of employees are reflected in prevailing UK corporate governance norms, there is an important preliminary issue to contend with. Some readers might reasonably query why we have opted to include a specific chapter on corporate governance and labour, as opposed to having a chapter on corporate social responsibility (or 'CSR') more generally. Relatedly, it may be asked why labour in particular merits being the subject of our attention here as a relevant non-shareholder constituency in corporate governance, in preference to other commonly-recognized stakeholder groups. Our reasons for adopting this particular approach (albeit after careful consideration) are set out below.

---

[1] This is with the exception of the very limited (indeed, virtually negligible) forms of European-style worker involvement in the UK deriving from EU regulatory initiatives over recent decades, which will be discussed below.

The Infeasibility of Dealing with Corporate Social Responsibility (or 'CSR') More Generally

First, it is extremely difficult (if not impossible) to encapsulate every possible corporate constituency that arguably merits consideration within a general CSR study, at least within the relatively limited space that we have available in this book. In addition to the so-called 'primary' stakeholder groups of shareholders, employees, suppliers and customers, there are additional 'secondary' constituencies including relevant communities, the environment and – in appropriate cases – even society more generally.[2] Moreover, defining a category as large and potentially diverse as 'communities' or 'the environment' is in itself a galling descriptive challenge, at least if one is to do so satisfactorily. In the case of the large, publicly traded business enterprises that are the subject of this study, one might include within the 'communities' category both those social groupings in geographic proximity to a corporation's main productive activities (whether domestically or internationally); and also civic, national or even global collectives more generally insofar as they stand to be materially affected by the productive, marketing and other strategic activities of such organizations.

Likewise, the notion of 'environmental' interests might be construed in a narrow sense as encapsulating only certain specific geographic localities particularly susceptible to the negative physical externalities emanating from a firm's operations. In the case of large and especially multinational corporations, however, this category can reasonably be extended so as also to include globally-relevant ecological, geological and demographical concerns. This is not to mention the sheer intractability of objectively encapsulating an interest group as vast and multifarious as 'society' more generally, especially under conditions of significant cultural, ethnic, religious and socio-economic diversity whether on a domestic or global level.

Accordingly, we believe that it is simply impossible to dedicate satisfactory attention to broader CSR issues within a book such as the present, whose principal focus is the orthodox law of corporate governance. Indeed, due in no small part to the above factors, specialized graduate modules on CSR or – to use contemporary parlance – 'corporate responsibility' are today becoming an increasingly common feature of leading universities' course offerings, and in due course we will likely see the corresponding development of dedicated CSR-focused texts to cater for the ensuing student demand. Against this background, we feel that for us to attempt to tackle such a large and growing body of material within a work such as the present would be a potentially superfluous effort, while simultaneously carrying the risk of us doing a gross injustice to CSR as an independent legal subject field in its own right. In any event, we

---

[2] On the distinction between 'primary' and 'secondary' corporate stakeholder constituencies, see R.E. Freedman, 'Stockholders and Stakeholders: A New Perspective on Corporate Governance' (1983) 25 *California Management Review* 88.

have attempted in Chapter 2 – in our critical analysis of corporate stakeholder theory – to emphasize at least those aspects of a firm's key non-shareholder relations which are of most direct relevance to corporate governance in the conventionally understood sense of the term.

The (Arguably) Special Status of Labour as a Non-Shareholder Corporate Constituency

In Chapters 1 and 2, we explained the special importance which Anglo-American corporate governance law and theory customarily attaches to the interests of shareholders over those of other corporate constituencies, in terms of the former group's perceived collective status as a uniquely 'incomplete' contractor with the firm. That is to say, a firm's ordinary shareholders are – generally speaking – in the extraordinary position of being technically unable to agree in advance on the terms of advancement of (including periodic rate of return on) their equity capital to the firm, meaning that their material welfare is exposed to managers' discretion in a qualitatively more significant way than that of any other stakeholder group. The implication is that shareholders are, in the ordinary course of business affairs, thus uniquely subjected to the corporation's internal discretionary power dynamic. This in turn purportedly justifies – by way of effective macro-level 'compensation' – having correspondingly special regard to shareholders' interests in the design and operation of prevailing corporate governance norms.

However, we would be doing something of a disservice to readers in not highlighting here the significant *questionability* of the claim that shareholders are unique in this regard, at least in relation to the analogous contractual status of labour. Indeed, it is arguable that a corporation's employees are *at least as* exposed to discretionary managerial power as its equity investors are, by virtue of the peculiar structural nature of employees' legal relation with their employer firm; which, strictly speaking, does not really take the form of a 'contractual' relationship at all in the normal juridical sense of the term. Rather, the standard employment relation (at least as it is traditionally constituted within common law jurisdictions) curiously represents the classic example of an *extra*-contractual command structure. Accordingly the employer firm, via its hierarchically senior officeholders, is legally empowered to give orders to subordinate employees or officers *without* the prior need for reciprocal negotiation concerning the content or compulsion of those decrees.

Viewing the employment relation as a coercive unilateral power relation may initially appear a somewhat quirky and politically radical notion. On the contrary, though, such a characterization is entirely consistent with the basic legal nature of the employment relation. Indeed, in his pathbreaking 1937 article 'The Nature of the Firm',[3] Ronald Coase observed how, contrary to

---

[3] R.H. Coase, 'The Nature of the Firm' (1937) 4 *Economica* 386.

what had previously been the accepted orthodoxy in economic thinking, the dual phenomena of 'firms' and 'markets' are not part of the same institutional phenomenon. Coase claimed that the firm and the market are in fact logically distinct features of a capitalist economy, and fulfil markedly separate economic functions from one another in the co-ordination of productive activity. Accordingly the entrepreneur or producer, by deciding to carry out business through the medium of a firm (whether incorporated or otherwise), in effect takes the decision to opt out of the decentralized market system and instead organize her productive activities by way of a centralized, extra-market command structure.

Coase explained how, on a formal level, the command structure within the firm is achieved by the intrinsic structural features of the common law employment relation, and – in particular – the basic and peculiar concept of employee subordination to the reasonable orders of the employer.[4] Thus the entrepreneur, rather than entering into numerous discrete contracts every time she requires a particular productive or administrative service performed, instead establishes one unifying contract 'whereby the factor [i.e. employee], for a certain remuneration (which may be fixed or fluctuating), agrees to obey the directions of [the] entrepreneur within certain limits'.[5] It follows that within the typically broad limits stated in the employment contract, the entrepreneur is free to direct and organize the employee's work in accordance with her own discretion and in light of the perceived exigencies of the business, without the need either to seek the assent of the employee to each ordered task or to negotiate the latter's compensation for each task on an ongoing basis.[6]

As Coase expressly acknowledged, this essential characteristic of the firm derives from the peculiarly vague and somewhat lopsided nature of the common law employment relation, which has its roots not in the orthodox law of (exchange) contract but rather in pre-industrial master and servant law. According to Coase:

> It is this right of control or interference, of being entitled to tell the servant when to work (within the hours of service) and when not to work, and what work to do and how to do it (within the terms of such service) which is the dominant characteristic in this relation and marks off the servant from an independent contractor, or from one employed merely to give to his employer the fruits of his labour.[7]

---

[4] For a comprehensive legal analysis of this concept from a comparative point of view, see M. Ronnmar, 'The Managerial Prerogative and the Employee's Obligation to Work: Comparative Perspectives on Functional Flexibility' (2006) 35 *Industrial Law Journal* 56.

[5] Coase, above n 3, 391.

[6] S. Deakin and F. Wilkinson, 'Labour Law and Economic Theory: A Reappraisal' in H. Collins, P. Davies and R. Rideout (eds), *Legal Regulation of the Employment Relation* (Kluwer 2000), Ch. 2, 47.

[7] Coase, above n. 3, 404.

Of course, identifying the existence of a unilateral command dynamic within the employment relation is not in itself sufficient to establish that the employee is subject to the coercive power of their employer. After all, is the employee not always at liberty to leave his present employment, and choose instead to work for an alternative employer whose terms and conditions are not so objectionable?[8] However, while this may be true in theory, the reality of labour markets presents a different and altogether more complex picture. Indeed, more often than not, unilateral termination of the employment relation by a disgruntled employee is a highly unattractive – if not entirely impracticable – option, in view of the typically high displacement costs involved for the employee, coupled with the innate structural imbalance of employer versus employee bargaining power under ordinary labour market conditions.[9]

Indeed, a typical (albeit not universal) characteristic of labour markets is the tendency to generate a surplus of supply (that is, number of prospective employees) over demand (number of prospective employers).[10] It follows that the displacement costs to employees consequent upon termination of their employment are more likely than not to exceed significantly the corresponding replacement costs to their employer firm. Such costs for the employee include the loss of regular income – and potentially even material livelihood – along with the social, psychological and other costs that loss of employment typically entails. For the employer firm, on the other hand, the ready availability of alternative personnel on the labour market has the effect of mitigating the firm's replacement costs in the event of unilateral termination of the relationship by the employee.

Accordingly, taking into account both (i) the inherently command-based nature of employment as a form of legal-organizational relation and also (ii) the characteristic structural disparity of the bargaining dynamic in labour markets in favour of employers (over employees); it becomes clear that – as a matter of both legal and economic reality – the employment relation *is* unquestionably a source of private decision-making power in the sense understood in this book. For this reason, we believe that employees (in addition to shareholders, directors and managers) merit particular consideration from a corporate governance point of view, such that any comprehensive academic account of the subject must inevitably factor labour considerations into the picture. As we will see below, however, the extent to which employees' interests figure *in practice* within corporate governance would appear to belie much of what we have just discussed.

---

[8] On this, see F.A. Hayek, *The Constitution of Liberty* (Routledge 2006; first published 1960), 105.

[9] On this, see J.E. Parkinson, *Corporate Power and Responsibility: Issues in the Theory of Company Law* (OUP 1993), 9; A. Gewirth, *The Community of Rights* (University of Chicago Press 1998), 258–59, 268.

[10] On this, see D. Ricardo, *On the Principles of Political Economy and Taxation*, (3rd ed., Murray 1821; first published 1817), Ch. 5.

SHAREHOLDERS' LEXICAL SUPREMACY OVER LABOUR WITHIN UK CORPORATE GOVERNANCE

In curious contrast to what we have said above, we believe that most directors and senior executives of UK public companies would likely regard it as trite law that, in undertaking their managerial and/or control functions, they are accountable first and foremost to their employer firm's general body of *shareholders*. This is generally perceived to demand that such officers render dutiful service to the collective shareholder interest, which ordinarily entails generating an optimal (or, at least, relatively high) financial return for shareholders whether as measured on a short- or long-term basis.

It correspondingly follows that the interests of other corporate constituencies – and, in particular, those of employees – must ultimately cede to those of shareholders in the event of conflict, such as in the scenario (described hypothetically in Chapter 2) where the cost to shareholders of maintaining some part of the firm's productive operations outweighs the private financial benefits to shareholders accruing therefrom, notwithstanding that termination of such operations (with the associated worker redundancies that this involves) will drastically reduce the relevant employees' current income-generating capacity.

However, whilst shareholders' lexical supremacy over employees from the perspective of a corporation's management is typically taken as gospel, it is at first sight rather less clear *from where* shareholders' relatively privileged governance status in this regard formally derives. In other words, how is the general governance supremacy of shareholders (particularly in relation to employees) within UK corporations *legally constituted*? As we will explain below, whilst there is no single formal legal doctrine of 'shareholder primacy' in UK company law as such, there is nonetheless an important collection of legal provisions (some of which were previously discussed in Chapter 4) which mutually establish this functionally significant corporate-managerial norm.

As we will further show, these rules and principles essentially affirm: (i) shareholders' status as the ultimate collective beneficiary of directors' fiduciary loyalty; and (ii) shareholders' exclusive collective control over the corporate voting franchise. Together, these represent the two key legal dimensions of the shareholder primacy doctrine in the sense described above. We will now proceed to examine each of these two dimensions of shareholder primacy in turn, while also highlighting the international peculiarity (and, by implication, functional inessentiality) of this doctrine when viewed from a comparative European perspective.

Section 172 of the Companies Act 2006

Undoubtedly the most overt legal component of the shareholder primacy doctrine in the UK is the director's fiduciary duty of loyalty under company law. In this regard, section 172 of the Companies Act 2006 expressly stipulates today that, in exercising his official managerial and/or control functions, '[a] director of a company must act in the way he considers, in good faith, would be most likely to promote the success of the company for the benefit of its members [i.e. ordinary shareholders] as a whole'.[11]

The section further provides that, in determining which specific course of action in any instance is most conducive to promoting the success of the company for the benefit of its shareholders, a director should have regard to a non-exhaustive list of additional 'stakeholder' criteria including, *inter alia*, 'the interests of the company's employees'.[12] However, the wording of the provision makes it equally clear that directors' mandated consideration of employee interests is not an independent corporate objective in itself, but rather merely a procedural means towards the ultimate end of enhancing business success and consequent shareholder wealth.

In our reading of the provision, it would seem that a board is expected to give due regard in its strategic deliberations to the risk that neglect of worker (or, indeed, any relevant stakeholder) welfare factors in a given scenario could have a potentially negative impact on long-run shareholder wealth. Such risk factors could potentially include the danger of proposed employee layoffs eroding valuable and irreplaceable firm-specific human capital; or the possibility of a suggested corporate downsizing or restructuring initiative reducing the perceived security and trust of the firm's continuing workforce, thereby undermining employees' general morale and productivity, and also their future incentives to develop non-readily-redeployable skills or attributes. Insofar as both these outcomes entail correspondingly adverse implications for corporate financial performance, they ultimately pose a threat to shareholder welfare and – to this extent (but no more) – thus become relevant and legitimate fiduciary concerns for boards.

As has been widely remarked on by commentators, the likelihood of either the 'shareholder' or the 'stakeholder' (including employee) elements of section 172 actually being enforced against directors is, for a variety of reasons, minimal to say the least.[13] However, whilst this may be a significant concern from an

---

[11] Companies Act 2006, s 172(1).

[12] The other additional 'stakeholder' criteria explicitly referred to in section 172(1) are 'the likely consequences of any decision in the long term'; 'the need to foster the company's business relationships with suppliers, customers and others'; 'the impact of the company's operations on the community and the environment'; 'the desirability of the company maintaining a reputation for high standards of business conduct'; and 'the need to act fairly as between members of the company'. In view of its express reference to various non-shareholder consideration, section 172 is commonly regarded as being something of a pro-stakeholder measure. However, as the following discussion should hopefully make clear, the practical significance of this aspect of the statutory duty of loyalty should not be overestimated.

[13] See e.g. A.R. Keay, 'Section 172(1) of the Companies Act 2006: An Interpretation and Assessment' (2007) 28 *Company Lawyer* 106; A.R. Keay, 'The Duty to Promote the Success of the Company: Is It Fit for Purpose in a Post-Financial Crisis World?' in J. Loughrey (ed.), *Directors' Duties and Shareholder Litigation in the Wake of the Financial Crisis* (Edward Elgar 2012), 50.

orthodox company lawyer's perspective, from a broader corporate governance standpoint – that is, in terms of calibrating appropriate managerial incentives and disciplines – it is not of direct importance. Indeed, notwithstanding the unlikelihood of enforcement action arising from breach of any of its particular doctrinal components, section 172 undeniably retains considerable 'soft' behavioural influence on an expressive or normative level at least, as a salient and authoritative public statement of the proper corporate objective in the UK.[14] Moreover, this expressive quality of the section is reinforced to the extent that it features in legal-professional advice given to corporate boards, on the permissible scope of their discretion with respect to any particular strategic matter before them.[15]

Nonetheless, from a historical standpoint section 172's express statutory statement of the British corporate objective has in general been regarded as a relatively trivial legal innovation. Indeed, the common view of both the government-appointed Steering Group that initially formulated the relevant provision,[16] and those courts which have subsequently been called upon to interpret it,[17] is that section 172 constitutes merely a codified version of the pre-existing legal position in this regard, rather than any sort of meaningful substantive reform in itself.[18] Insofar as the former (i.e. pre-2006) position of non-shareholder constituencies *other than* employees is concerned, this claim is arguably true, insofar as consideration for the welfare of a company's various non-shareholder constituencies – within reasonable bounds – has always been recognized as an implicit component of responsible business management notwithstanding the shareholder primacy doctrine.[19] However, as we will see below, with respect to the relative governance status of shareholders *and employees* in the UK, the pre-2006 legal position was somewhat different.

Comparing section 172 with (Old) section 309 of the Companies Act 1985

Contrary to the above assertions, section 172's immediate predecessor, namely section 309 of the former Companies Act 1985, was not a direct functional

---

[14] On the capacity of law to exert an indirect educative effect by making 'statements' as opposed to determining social behaviour directly, see generally C.R. Sunstein, 'On the Expressive Function of Law' (1996) 144 *University of Pennsylvania Law Review* 2021.
[15] On this, see L. Cerioni, A. Keay and J. Loughrey, 'Legal Practitioners, Enlightened Shareholder Value and the Shaping of Corporate Governance' (2008) 8 *Journal of Corporate Law Studies* 79.
[16] See Company Law Review Steering Group, *Modern Company Law for a Competitive Economy: Developing the Framework* (DTI, 2000), Ch. 2, para. 2.23.
[17] See e.g. *Re Southern Counties Fresh Foods Ltd* [2008] EWHC 2810; *Re West Coast Capital (Lios) Ltd* [2008] CSOH 72.
[18] Moreover, this assumption is even implicit in the wording of the Companies Act 2006 itself, section 170(4) of which states that '[t]he general duties [of directors] shall be interpreted and applied in the same way as common law rules or equitable principles, and regard shall be had to the corresponding common law rules and equitable principles in interpreting and applying the general duties'.
[19] See e.g. *Evans v Brunner Mond* [1921] 1 Ch 359; *Simmonds v Heffer* [1983] BCLC 298.

analogue of the current provision. For a start, old section 309 – introduced, somewhat curiously, by Margaret Thatcher's Conservative administration shortly after coming to power in 1979[20] – made reference only to employees, and did not expressly deal with other non-shareholder constituencies (although, as explained above, a reasonable degree of instrumental directorial concern for such interests was tacitly acceptable under the common law). Moreover, section 309's basic doctrinal character was notably different to that of section 172, with the former rule providing that 'the matters to which the directors of a company are to have regard in the performance of their functions include the interests of the company's employees in general, as well as the interests of its [ordinary shareholders]'.[21]

Thus, unlike in the case of section 172 today, no explicit lexical priority was afforded to the interests of shareholders over employees under section 309.[22] Accordingly, the notional 'interest of the company' which directors were expected to promote was in effect rendered an amalgam of the respective interests of shareholders and employees, with neither constituency apparently enjoying systematic fiduciary precedence over the other.[23] Admittedly, the absence in section 309 of any direct enforcement right for employees led to accusations of it being something of a 'toothless tiger' from labour's perspective.[24] Notwithstanding this obvious limitation, though, the provision at the very least offered an effective doctrinal 'shield' to directors who gave extensive consideration to employee concerns, against potential allegations of breach of duty on account of neglecting the competing interests of shareholders.[25] This is not to mention the additional normative significance of the pre-2006 provision in formally enshrining employee welfare considerations as an explicit and central element of boards' expected fiduciary remit.[26]

Against this background, it becomes apparent that section 172 – in spite of its purported intent to 'enlighten' directors as to the economic materiality of non-shareholder considerations – in effect brought about the lexical *relegation* of employees within UK corporate governance on a formal and normative level. In particular, employees' interests were notionally downgraded relative to those of shareholders, in that consideration of worker welfare factors was recognized by section 172 merely as a secondary means towards the ultimate end of shareholder wealth maximization. In comparison to the pre-2006

---

[20] See Companies Act 1980, s 46; M.F. Durham, 'The Companies Act, 1980: Its Effects on British Corporate Law' (1982) 4 *Northwestern Journal of International Law & Business* 551, 568.
[21] Companies Act 1985, s 309(1).
[22] Parkinson, above n. 9, 83; *Re Welfab Engineers Ltd* [1990] BCLC 833.
[23] *Fulham Football Club Ltd v Cabra Estates* [1992] BCC 863.
[24] One commentator notoriously referred to section 309 as being 'either one of the most incompetent or one of the most cynical pieces of drafting on record.' See L.S. Sealy, 'Director's "Wider" Responsibilities – Problems Conceptual, Practical and Procedural' (1987) 13 *Monash University Law Review* 164, 177.
[25] Parkinson, above n. 9, 84.
[26] B. Wedderburn, *The Future of Company Law: Fat Cats, Corporate Governance and Workers* (Institute of Employment Rights 2004).

position, section 172 could also be said to have relegated employees' govern-ance status in relation to other non-shareholder constituencies such as suppli-ers, customers, the community and the environment, whose interests are now formally ranked on a par with those of employees, thus depriving employees of any claim to relative governance supremacy over those groups.[27]

The Relative Status of Shareholders and Employees under the Common Law

Of course, old section 309 was in itself a fairly recent development. Its intro-duction in 1980 was a legislative response to longstanding concerns about the under-representation of employees' interests within UK company law. Indeed, *prima facie*, it would appear that English courts have historically tended to rec-ognize shareholders as the exclusive collective beneficiary of the director's duty of loyalty.[28] This is with the limited exception of 'red zone' scenarios where the company's solvency is under threat, in which event creditors assume the status of the firm's principal residual risk-bearer and – correspondingly – become the principal focus of directors' fiduciary responsibilities.[29]

Curiously, though, the main cases which are customarily cited in support of the traditional shareholder orientation of the director's duty of loyalty at common law are, on closer inspection, of somewhat questionable authority in this regard. The principal decision which commentators have tended to advance as authority for the shareholder primacy position in UK company law is the Court of Appeal's ruling in the 1951 case of *Greenhalgh v Arderne Cinemas*.[30] In this case, Evershed MR advanced the oft-cited proposition that the notion of 'the benefit of the company as a whole' – bona fide pursuit of which is customarily regarded as a director's proper fiduciary objective – should not be understood in terms of the autonomous interest of 'the company' in itself as a commercial entity, but rather as denoting nothing more than the aggregate personal inter-ests of the shareholders 'as a general body' (in the contractarian sense).[31]

As one leading commentator has observed, 'this quotation from the ruling is cited almost invariably as evidence that company law requires companies to have a profit maximizing objective, and that managers and directors have a legal duty to put shareholders' interests above all others and no legal authority to serve any other interests.'[32] However, as the same commentator points out,

---

[27] On this, see Wedderburn, *ibid*.

[28] As one esteemed commentator has posited: '[t]he correct position is … that the corporate entity is a vehicle for benefiting the interests of a specified group or groups. These interests the law has traditionally defined as the interests of the shareholders.' Parkinson, above n. 9, 77.

[29] On this, see A.R. Keay, 'The Duty of Directors to Take into Account Creditors' Interests: Has It Any Role to Play?' (2002) *Journal of Business Law* 379.

[30] *Greenhalgh v Arderne Cinemas Ltd* [1951] Ch 286.

[31] *ibid*., 291.

[32] D. Attenborough, 'How Directors Should Act When Owing Duties to the Companies' Shareholders: Why We Need to Stop Applying Greenhalgh' (2009) *International Company and Commercial Law Review* 339, 343.

those who seek to rely on the *Greenhalgh* decision as authority for the shareholder primacy position typically elide the fact that Evershed MR's comments in this case were expressly limited to 'such a case as the present',[33] as opposed to laying down any sort of generally-applicable normative proposition.[34]

Moreover, as Attenborough further highlights, the 1951 *Greenhalgh* case itself was concerned not with construction of the proper corporate objective in a directors' duties context, but rather with the very different factual (and, indeed, legal) setting of a majority versus minority shareholder dispute concerning alteration of a company's articles of association.[35] Accordingly, Evershed MR's reference to 'the benefit of the company as a whole' in *Greenhalgh* seems to pertain specifically to the judicial test for establishing the (in)equity of a proposed constitutional alteration in a private company context, where a focus on the personal interests of shareholders was not only appropriate but indeed practically necessary. However, such a scenario bears no direct relevance to the question of the propriety of the shareholder wealth maximization objective in the case of publicly traded corporations.[36] Contrarily, Attenborough asserts (in relation to the pre-2006 position at least) that '[a]s a positive matter, UK company law does not and never has imposed a legal obligation on directors to maximize shareholder value'.[37]

Furthermore, other classic English decisions which have been interpreted as affirming shareholders (over employees) as the rightful beneficiary of directors' fiduciary discretion actually have similarly limited direct bearing on this issue. For instance, the Court of Appeal's decision in the 1883 case of *Hutton v West Cork Railway Company*[38] – and, in particular, Bowen LJ's classic dictum that 'there are to be no cakes and ale [for employees] except such as are required for the benefit of the company'[39] – has subsequently been construed as authority for the principle that worker welfare may only be enhanced by directors where this is instrumental to long-term benefits for shareholders.[40] Likewise, Plowman J's refusal in the 1962 case of *Parke v Daily News Ltd*[41] to permit directors to distribute the proceeds from sale of a company's newspaper business gratuitously to certain employees has been widely construed as a pro-shareholder-primacy decision,[42] in a similar vein to the classic judicial principle established in

---

[33] Above n. 30, 291.

[34] Attenborough, above n. 32, 344.

[35] *ibid.*, 343–44.

[36] *ibid.*, 344.

[37] *ibid.*, 346.

[38] (1883) 23 Ch 654.

[39] *ibid.*, 673.

[40] For example, in their authoritative UK company law treatise, Sealy and Worthington claim that, 'in cases like *Hutton v West Cork Rly Co* and *Parke v Daily News Ltd*, generosity to employees was held to be lawful only if it could be justified by reference to the long-term interests of *the shareholders*'. See L. Sealy and S. Worthington, *Cases and Materials in Company Law* (10th ed., OUP 2013), 320 (emphasis added).

[41] [1962] Ch 927.

[42] See e.g. Sealy and Worthingon, above n. 40.

Dodge v Ford Motor Company,[43] a US case from 1919 based on not-dissimilar facts. In the latter case, the Michigan Supreme Court had held that:

> A business corporation is organized and carried on primarily for the profit of the stockholders. The powers of the directors are to be employed for that end. The discretion of directors is to be exercised in the choice of means to attain that end and does not extend to a change in the end itself, to the reduction of profits or to the nondistribution of profits among stockholders in order to devote them to other purposes.[44]

But whilst the above dictum may provide a reasonably accurate portrayal of the traditional US approach[45] to determining the fiduciary propriety of directors' decisions concerning employee welfare considerations, we would submit that – as a statement of the corresponding *English* law position in this regard (at least prior to 2006) – it is highly contestable.

It is noteworthy that the *Hutton* ('cakes and ale') case – unlike the *Dodge* case in the United States – involved the relatively peculiar incidence of a company purporting to make gratuitous payments to its outgoing directors immediately prior to the company's winding up, using funds which would otherwise have been distributable to creditors. Accordingly, the board's conduct in this case – which, curiously, was formally approved by a majority of its shareholders – entailed not just a manifest (albeit authorized) conflict of interest on the relevant directors' part, but was also at least equally detrimental to the welfare of future creditors as it was to immediate shareholder wealth,[46] involving a scenario which today would likely be dealt with (*inter alia*) under relevant aspects of insolvency legislation.

Moreover, contrary to accepted wisdom, the respective rulings in *Hutton* and also the later *Parke* case manifestly hinged not on the (assumed) general fiduciary ground that the relevant boards favoured employees' interests over shareholders' interests. Rather, they were decided on the specific doctrinal

---

[43] 170 NW 668 (1919).

[44] *ibid.*

[45] Although *Dodge v Ford* is a Michigan authority and thus, under the United States' federalist system of corporate law, formally inapplicable outside of this specific jurisidictional setting, it has generally been recognized throughout the past century as a valid authority by numerous other US States' courts including, *inter alia*, the dominant corporate law jurisdiction of Delaware. For this reason, we believe that it can, with considerable justification, be described in broad terms as a general 'US law' position as such. For a (somewhat qualified) recent reaffirmation of the basic *Dodge v Ford* position in a Delaware context, see Chancellor Chandler's ruling in the 2010 case of *eBay Domestic Holdings, Inc. v Newmark* 16 A. 3d. 1 (Del. Ch. 2010). Notwithstanding the above decisions, the long-running 'corporate purpose' debate in the United States still remains an unsettled issue to some extent, particularly amongst academic commentators. For a critical perspective on the doctrinal and normative sustainability of the *Dodge v Ford* decision in US corporate law, see L.A Stout, 'Why We Should Stop Teaching Dodge v. Ford' (2008) 3 *Virginia Law & Business Review* 163.

[46] On the relevance of concern for future creditor interests to the Court's determination in *Hutton*, see the opinion of Bowen LJ, above n. 38, 675–76.

premise that – in both instances – corporate funds were expended for a purpose which was not reasonably incidental to the relevant company's particular business objects as set out in its memorandum of association.[47] Accordingly, the payments in question were invalidated on relatively technical *ultra vires* grounds, in fundamentally the same way that the diversion of business funds to shareholders (e.g. as dividends) at a time when the company has no distributable profits would have been struck down for being outside the company's ordinary course of business.[48] Thus in both cases, the relevant court was unwilling to sanction the proposed payment because it was not conducive to furthering the interests of *the business* according to the company's pre-articulated objects; such that – in contrast to the position in *Dodge* – the issue of shareholder primacy *per se* never directly entered into the picture.

The prescriptive implication is that, under the pre-2006 *Hutton/Parke* principle, corporate funds could legitimately be devoted to shareholders and/ or employees as the directors reasonably deemed fit for the furtherance of the company's constitutionally specified line(s) of business, so long as the interests of *the business* as such were genuinely being promoted in some way. Curiously, this position is more consistent with the bipartisan 'balancing' logic of the old section 309 than with the 'lexical' rationality of the current section 172 and *Dodge* case, an observation which is reinforced by noteworthy modern judicial dictum to the effect that '[t]he duties owed by the directors are to the company and the company is *more than* just the sum total of its members'.[49] It thus further supports the view that shareholder (relative to employee) supremacy was never an established element of UK company law prior to the 2006 Act, at least with respect to questions concerning judicial determination of the proper corporate objective.

Section 172 as a Lexical Downgrading of Employees' Relative Corporate Governance Status

The above findings demonstrate that section 172 – in expressly affirming shareholders' lexical supremacy over employees in this context – has in effect

---

[47] As explained by Bowen LJ in *Hutton*, '[t]he money which is going to be spent is not the money of the majority. That is clear. It is the money of the company, and the majority want to spend it. What would be the natural limit of their power to do so? They can only spend money which is not theirs but the company's, if they are spending it for the purposes which are reasonably incidental to the carrying on of the business of the company. That is the general doctrine.' See *ibid.*, 672.

[48] Indeed, according to Bowen LJ (*ibid.*), '[t]he test … is not whether [the payment in question] is bona fide, but whether, as well as being done bona fide, it is done within the ordinary scope of the company's business, and whether it is reasonably incidental to the carrying on of the company's business for the company's benefit'.

[49] *Fulham Football Club v Cabra Estates*, above n. 23, *per* Neill LJ, 393; subsequently discussed in Attenborough, above n. 32; A. Keay, 'Enlightened Shareholder Value, the Reform of the Duties of Directors and the Corporate Objective' (2006) *Lloyds Maritime and Commercial Law Quarterly* 335, 343.

downgraded employees' formal corporate governance status not just relative to the pre-2006 statutory rule in this regard; but also in comparison to the traditional common law position concerning the relative materiality of shareholder and employee interests in determining what constitutes the notional 'benefit of the company as a whole'. The latter point is particularly significant given the 2006 Act's express provision that pre-existing case law on directors' duties remains valid as an authoritative guide to the interpretation and application of the general statutory duties (including section 172) today.[50] This seems – *erroneously*, in our view – to presuppose the functional equivalence of the pre- and post-2006 positions, an issue which could potentially pose difficulties for any future court that is called upon to adjudicate on a section 172 dispute concerning directors' alleged disregard (or, vice versa, *over*-regard) of employees' interests vis-à-vis those of shareholders.

However, irrespective of the precise doctrinal substance of the director's duty of loyalty today, company lawyers will readily testify that directors' discretion to determine what is actually conducive to promoting the success of the company for the general benefit of its shareholders is in practice largely unbounded. Although, strictly speaking, there is no explicit US-style business judgment rule applicable in the UK context, English courts have nonetheless tended to adopt a similarly deferential approach to their Delaware counterparts in evaluating subjective strategic decisions taken by directors.[51] Thus whilst – as explained above – the shareholder-oriented duty of loyalty remains influential to some extent on a 'soft' expressive or normative level (especially when coupled with supportive managerial incentive mechanisms such as performance-related pay linked to shareholder return[52]) – it is on its own of limited determinative 'bite' as a means of ingraining the shareholder primacy norm into the UK's collective corporate-managerial mindset: that is, at least relative to other, more coercive legal mechanisms in this regard.

Shareholders' Exclusive Collective Control over the Corporate Voting Franchise

In addition to the shareholder-oriented duty of loyalty under section 172 of the Companies Act 2006, shareholders typically also enjoy exclusivity over the corporate voting franchise. That is to say, a company's directors are customarily elected by – and hence owe their continuing right to hold office to – that company's body of ordinary shareholders alone. We would submit that this feature of the UK's corporate governance legal framework represents the root source of shareholders' formally privileged status within the firm.

---

[50] See Companies Act 2006, s 170(4), discussed above n. 18.
[51] See e.g. *Re Smith & Fawcett Ltd* [1942] Ch 304; *Regentcrest plc v Cohen* [2001] BCC 494. On this generally, see M.T. Moore, *Corporate Governance in the Shadow of the State* (Hart 2013), 144–57.
[52] On this, see Chapter 9.

The principle of shareholder exclusivity with respect to director appointments is a highly prevalent UK corporate governance norm, and also a characteristic feature of the Anglo-American corporate governance paradigm in general. Its primary functional consequence is that UK corporate boards – whilst formally separate decision-making organs vested with their own autonomous executive powers – are nonetheless ultimately representative of *shareholders alone*; and, correspondingly, are in no part whatsoever directly accountable to employees or indeed any other corporate constituency. Accordingly, more than any other component of the UK legal framework, exclusive shareholder enfranchisement closely accords with the shareholder-centric 'agency' model of corporate governance described in Chapter 2.

Admittedly there are a few outlying cases of UK public companies whose boards include some element of employee representation. One of the most high-profile examples of such is the British public transport operator First Group plc, which has consistently included an employee-elected (and trade-union-affiliated) director on its main group board since the firm's foundation in 1989, in addition to individual employee directors on each of its various subsidiary companies' boards.[53] However, in its extreme rarity in this regard, First Group is very much the exception that proves the rule as regards the UK's corporate community as a whole.

CO-DETERMINATION AS AN ALTERNATIVE TO EXCLUSIVELY SHAREHOLDER-ORIENTED BOARDS

The International Popularity of Co-determination

Whilst First Group's policy on employee board representation might seem somewhat radical when viewed within a purely domestic UK context, in terms of the broader international legal-institutional landscape it is, if anything, a relatively modest example of worker involvement in corporate governance. Indeed, from a comparative European perspective, the UK is very much a relative outlier in – remarkably – making *no* formal provision whatsoever for employee representation on corporate boards within its national legal framework.[54] At present, the domestic legal systems of 19 other European countries[55] provide

---

[53] G. Topham, 'Class Action: A Train Driver Stationed in the Company's Boardroom', *The Observer*, 17 July 2016. At the time of writing, First Group plc's current employee director is Mick Barker, who was appointed to the board in 2012 and is also employed as a train driver for the First Group subsidiary company First Great Western Ltd. See www.firstgroupplc.com/about-firstgroup/leadership/board-of-directors.aspx.

[54] The minority group of European countries which make no formal legal provision for worker involvement in corporate decision-making are Belgium, Bulgaria, Cyprus, Estonia, Iceland, Italy, Latvia, Liechtenstein, Lithuania, Malta, Romania and Switzerland. See A. Conchon, *Workers' Voice in Corporate Governance: A European Perspective* (London: Trades Unions Congress, 2013), 13, at www.tuc.org.uk/sites/default/files/workers-voice-in-corporate-governance_0.pdf.

a formal statutory framework for the involvement of employee representatives in high-level corporate decision-making at board level, via a practice known as 'co-determination'. Although there are significant differences between these countries in terms of the precise scope, design and operation of their respective co-determination systems, two common prevailing characteristics of the practice are: first, that it enables worker involvement in general matters of strategic policy *beyond* those specific issues pertaining directly to employee welfare, thereby enabling employee representatives to play a direct role in the overall steering of the business enterprise; and, second, that it entails a characteristically *consensual* form of board decision-making, whereby shareholder and employee representatives mutually share information and – in turn – seek to reach positions of compromise on contentious issues.[56]

The archetypical example of a national corporate governance system featuring widespread co-determination in the above sense is that of Germany, where employee representation is complementary to the country's traditional dual or 'two-tier' board structure. Accordingly, high-level business policy initiatives and executive appointments are proposed by a 'lower' management board, subsequently to be passed up for approval or veto by an 'upper' supervisory board. The composition and functioning of the German management board is in many respects similar to that of the senior executive team of a UK public company. However, the institution of the supervisory board as it exists (*inter alia*) in Germany has no real formal or functional counterpart within the British system, where public company boards are by contrast constituted almost universally on a unitary or 'one-tier' footing.

In particular, the supervisory board of any German-registered company employing between 500 and 2,000 persons must devote at least one-third of its seats to employee-elected directors, with the remaining two-thirds reserved for shareholder-representative directors. In the case of those (approximately 40) German companies with more than 2,000 employees, meanwhile, the supervisory board must feature parity (50/50) representation of shareholder/ worker representatives, albeit that the additional shareholder-elected chairman will hold the casting vote in the (extremely rare)[57] event of deadlock

---

[55] This majority group of European countries which have a so-called 'co-determination' framework in place to some extent or other includes Austria, Croatia, the Czech Republic, Germany, Denmark, Finland, France, Greece, Hungary, Ireland, Luxembourg, the Netherlands, Norway, Poland, Portugal, Sweden, Slovenia, Slovakia and Spain. However, in five of those countries (namely Greece, Ireland, Portugal, Poland and Spain) such procedures are restricted mainly to state-owned or privatized enterprises.

[56] P. Davies, K.J. Hopt, R. Nowak and G. van Solinge, 'Boards in Law and Practice: A Cross-Country Analysis in Europe' in P. Davies, P.L. Davies, K.J. Hopt, R. Nowak and G. van Solinge, *Corporate Boards in Law and Practice: A Comparative Analysis in Europe* (OUP 2013), 3, 70.

[57] It has been noted from empirical observation of co-determined boards in Germany that 'overt conflict, including the use of the chair's casting vote is rare and consensus reached after perhaps hard bargaining between the two groups is the norm'. P. Davies, 'Efficiency Arguments for the Collective Representation of Workers: A Sketch' in A. Bogg, C. Costello, A.C.L. Davies and J. Prassl (eds), *The Autonomy of Labour Law* (Hart Publishing 2015), Ch. 15, 387.

between the two groups. With the exception of trade union nominees who in any event must comprise only a minority of the worker-representative board seats, employee-elected directors must simultaneously be serving employees of the company themselves. Moreover, in Germany as in most other European countries with a co-determination framework in place, the relevant legal requirements are constituted on a *mandatory* basis such that – subject to the applicable eligibility thresholds – co-determination is an ingrained and irreversible feature of the national corporate governance landscape.

Evaluating the Economic Merits and Drawbacks of Co-determined Boards

Notwithstanding their preponderance across much of continental Europe, co-determined boards have been subject to criticism on account of their alleged economic inefficiency, particularly when viewed from an orthodox Anglo-American standpoint. In particular, critics of co-determination have claimed that including worker representatives on boards is prone to slow down corporate decision-making while also encouraging factional conflicts, which can prevent firms from responding rapidly to new product markets and technological developments.[58] On the other hand, supporters of co-determination have defended such decisional 'slowdown' as a positive outcome of the practice, insofar as putting some proverbial 'grit in the wheels'[59] provides greater time and scope for reflection on key issues, thereby curtailing the risk of boards making irresponsible or overly hasty decisions.

Relatedly, the greater range of perspectives and backgrounds brought to the boardroom by employee representatives is arguably likely to increase the cognitive dissonance of the decision-making group as a whole, particularly where it has the effect of engendering greater directorial diversity in terms of gender, race, nationality, skills base and/or socio-economic status. In this regard, co-determination has the potential to reinforce existing regulatory and policy initiatives geared to bringing about enhanced board diversity. Indeed, a diversity-based rationale for employee directors is manifest in the following statement from Theresa May's inaugural speech as incoming British Prime Minister in July 2016, where she expressed apparent support for some form of co-determination being introduced in the UK:

> In practice, [directors] are drawn from the same, narrow social and professional circles as the executive team and – as we have seen time and time again – the scrutiny they provide is just not good enough. So if I'm Prime Minister, we're going to change that system – and we're going to have not just consumers represented on company boards, but employees as well.[60]

---

[58] On this, see Davies *et al.*, above n. 56, 72.

[59] This phrase is attributable to Matt Lawrence from the Institute for Public Policy Research, as quoted in P. Inman, 'Can Theresa May Get the Wheels of British Business Turning Again?', *The Observer*, 17 July 2016.

[60] A. Sparrow, J. Elgot and R. Davies, 'Theresa May to Call for Unity, Equality and Successful Exit from EU', *The Guardian*, 11 July 2016.

In addition to its potentially positive impact on board diversity, co-determination has been said to improve informational flows to the board. This has been a particular strength of the system in Germany, where employee representatives on boards are usually also members of plant-level employee works councils.[61] Since in this latter capacity employee directors are responsible for negotiating with local management on important business matters pertaining to the workforce, they typically have a thorough knowledge of operational issues at ground level which can subsequently be brought to bear on high-level board decisions.[62] On a broader economy-wide level, meanwhile, co-determination has been advanced as an effective means of encouraging greater co-operation and compromise between industry and unions, thereby mitigating capital-labour tension and – in turn – reducing strikes and other costly forms of adversarial industrial action.[63]

However, it has been claimed that a further comparative *inefficiency* of German-style co-determined boards – especially in relation to their shareholder-centric UK counterparts – is their purported tendency to increase agency costs for shareholders. Such costs arguably emanate from the consequent dilution of shareholders' governance influence (at least relative to what it would be under a system of exclusive shareholder enfranchisement); and also from the facilitation of interest group 'coalitions' between managers and employee directors *against* the interests of shareholders, particularly in opposition to prospective corporate control changes and other potentially destabilizing policies favoured by shareholders.[64]

Expanding the agency costs line yet further, it has been argued that with the increasing globalization of corporate capital markets over recent decades, companies from jurisdictions that do not have exclusively shareholder-oriented corporate governance frameworks (e.g. Germany) will ultimately fail to attract funding from institutional investors relative to their Anglo-American competitors. Consequently – the argument goes – shareholder primacy will increasingly become the global corporate governance norm, with co-determination and other employee-oriented institutions becoming progressively extinct.[65]

In respect of the latter argument, it would appear that the persistence of significant employee-oriented governance features over recent years within most continental-European jurisdictions, in spite of the increasing influence of trans-national corporate finance over this period, demonstrates that co-determination is *not* fundamentally inconsistent with the existence of global capital markets. As regards the former argument, meanwhile, we believe that criticisms of co-determination on agency cost grounds are arguably valid to

---

[61] S. Vitols, 'Varieties of Capitalism: Comparing Germany and the UK' in P.A. Hall and D. Soskice (eds), *Varieties of Capitalism: The Institutional Foundations of Comparative Advantage* (OUP 2001), Ch. 10, 344.

[62] Davies *et al.*, above n. 56, 73.

[63] *ibid.*, 74.

[64] Davies, above n. 57.

[65] See H. Hansmann and R. Kraakman, 'The End of History for Corporate Law' (2001) 89 *Georgetown Law Journal* 439.

some extent, and the model is certainly not a panacea for the UK's corporate governance ills. On the other hand, we feel that these concerns are frequently overplayed, and moreover fail to consider the corresponding payoffs to be gained from expanding management's focus in the above way.

Indeed, the counter-argument to agency cost criticisms of co-determination is that this practice enables employee representatives to exert meaningful influence over business strategy on an ongoing basis, so as to mitigate the risk of board decisions violating pre-existing implicit contracts between management and employees.[66] In particular, co-determined boards arguably facilitate the formation of credible long-term commitments between management and employees, whereby employees in effect undertake to accept generally lower wage levels in return for correspondingly greater security of tenure. Accordingly, a strong degree of employee representation on boards empowers labour to monitor and – in effect – 'enforce' management's subsequent adherence to this notional agreement, especially in periods of economic shock when management (under pressure from shareholders) might otherwise be inclined opportunistically to renege on their prior commitments to labour in this regard.[67]

Impediments to the Voluntary Implementation of Co-determination in UK Companies

A final argument against the introduction of German-style co-determination – at least within the UK context – is that, if employee-oriented corporate governance features really were as economically advantageous as their advocates claim, then why have they not already been introduced by firms voluntarily? Indeed, as we have already remarked on above, the prevailing British norm of exclusively shareholder-elected boards has no mandatory legal basis as such in the UK, meaning that – in theory at least – it can freely be varied by individual firms so as to permit the introduction of alternative board representation norms (including, where deemed appropriate, shareholder/employee co-determination). From this point of view, it can accordingly be surmised that the apparent reluctance of the vast majority of British public companies to opt for an alternative paradigm to the shareholder exclusivity norm suggests that, on the whole, the status quo is the most efficient arrangement in this regard (at least insofar as the UK is concerned).

As against the above contention, a couple of important countervailing points can be made. First, there is the fact that constructing an effective co-determination framework is a highly complex and multi-faceted institutional challenge, involving much more than simply devoting one or more board seats

---

[66] See Davies, above n. 57, 385.

[67] *ibid.*, 388. On the economic value of credible long-term commitments by corporations to employees (and other stakeholders) generally, see C. Mayer, *Firm Commitment: Why the Corporation Is Failing Us and How to Restore Trust in It* (OUP 2013).

to nominal 'employee' directors. Rather, the existence of an underpinning network of supportive mechanisms and norms (so-called 'institutional complementarities'[68]) is practically essential in ensuring that the role of 'employee director' represents something more than just a superficial title or administrative job description. Once again the German system can be forwarded as a pertinent case in point here.

In Germany, effective co-determination is made possible not only by the formal allocation of board seats to representative officers within relevant firms, but also by a complex and longstanding institutional infrastructure supporting this arrangement. Such infrastructure includes effective nomination and election procedures for employee directors, an overlapping network of plant-level employee works councils, and also an education and training framework geared to fostering worker involvement in corporate decision-making.[69] Whilst some of those features may be susceptible to voluntary implementation by corporations, others would likely be either impracticable or cost-ineffective to implement on an individual firm basis, thereby precluding micro-level private ordering as a realistic avenue of reform irrespective of the overall collective benefits to be gained therefrom.

There is another reason as to why the substantial absence of co-determination within the British corporate environment should not necessarily be taken as *per se* evidence of its unsuitability for the UK, which concerns shareholders' existing incumbency with respect to board representation. That is to say, even in instances where exclusively shareholder-elected boards may not be the economically preferable governance norm, it is likely that shareholders' existing control over the corporate voting franchise will make it highly difficult (if not outright impossible) to displace the status quo in favour of a more employee-oriented alternative, at least absent some form of external regulatory intervention in this regard. As Davies explains:

> [A]lthough employee governance may lower the company's costs of production, it also has a distributional effect which is adverse to shareholders. In other words, shareholders may be better off with a larger slice of a smaller pie than with a smaller share of a larger pie. If they judge that to be the case, they will oppose moves on the part of the managers to introduce control sharing. Consequently, mandatory law may be necessary to achieve the introduction of control sharing over shareholder opposition for the benefit of society as a whole.[70]

Moreover, shareholders' relative positional advantage in the above respect is further buttressed today by employees' diminishing collective bargaining power

---

[68] On this notion generally, see P.A. Hall and D. Soskice, 'An Introduction to Varieties of Capitalism' in Hall and Solskice, above n. 61, Ch. 1, 17–21.

[69] Vitols, above n. 61, 344; Davies *et al.*, above n. 56, 384, 392.

[70] Davies, above n. 57, 391. Davies notes in particular that '[s]hareholders are likely to be in a strong position to oppose such voluntary moves since they would inevitably require amendment to the articles of association which, in most countries [including the UK], requires a shareholder resolution, normally on a supermajority basis'. *ibid.*, fn. 71.

vis-à-vis shareholders in the UK. This is due to a combination of factors including the significant decline of trade union membership in the UK over recent decades, the increasing fragmentation of labour markets and worker demographics flowing from globalization and technological developments, and also the growing influence of institutional investors over this period as a powerful and co-ordinated countervailing interest grouping to labour. Against this background, it can reasonably be surmised that co-determination is unlikely to be introduced on anything more than a niche or sporadic basis in the UK within the foreseeable future, irrespective of the strength (or otherwise) of the economic case for worker involvement in corporate decision-making generally: that is, at least insofar as its implementation remains dependent on voluntary corporate-managerial initiative alone. Indeed, the near-wholesale absence of employee representation in UK boardrooms today arguably bears conspicuous testament to this fact.

Does Comparative Industrial Uniqueness Explain the Absence of Co-determination in UK Companies?

It is conceivable, of course, that the UK's comparatively peculiar stance with respect to worker (non-)involvement in corporate decision-making may be explicable by factors other than the forces of institutional path dependency or interest group incumbency alone. From an alternative angle, it may be queried whether the characteristics of UK industry are so comparatively unique as to justify a qualitatively different national corporate governance paradigm from that of most other European countries. In respect of the Anglo-German comparison at least, there would indeed appear to be some degree of complementariness between: on the one hand, each country's key corporate governance norms; and, on the other, its prevalent national industrial characteristics.

In particular, it has been argued that British industry's principal comparative advantage today resides in its focus on so-called 'radically innovative'[71] markets such as IT, bio-tech pharmaceuticals, transaction-based financial services and other dynamic hi-tech sectors. In such constantly-shifting competitive and technological environments, firms arguably need the structural flexibility to move rapidly into developing new product lines and processes, and – correspondingly – to exit declining or stagnating sectors without undue delay. At the same time, by enjoying the freedom to divest (or 'spin off') a firm's non-core productive operations via systematic corporate restructuring measures, management is able to both focus on and frequently revise its core competencies. In this context, management's practical capacity to implement mass layoffs and other policies typically averse to ordinary employees' interests is arguably of foremost importance, such that the involvement of employee representatives in board-level decision-making could potentially impose a costly constraint on

---

[71] This term is attributable to Vitols, above n. 61, 350.

companies' structural flexibility, by delaying or forestalling 'painful' board decisions on such matters.[72]

By contrast, the comparative advantage of leading German industrial corporations has been attributed in large part to the 'incrementally innovative'[73] nature of their principal markets, such as automobile production, chemicals and other medium-tech manufacturing sectors. Accordingly, competition is based mainly on relatively marginal innovation and differentiation by firms within their existing product markets, such that the flexibility to divest operations and enter new product lines is not as strong. Vice versa, greater value is attached in this environment to preservation of employees' existing firm-specific human capital, especially their knowledge of and familiarity with established products and processes. Moreover, employees' incentives to develop such valuable firm-specific competencies is arguably enhanced by formal worker involvement in high-level corporate decision-making, which in effect enables management to 'bond' its promise to workers that any such investments will be protected 'come what may'.[74]

Although such functional rationalizations of different corporate governance models are intuitively convincing, one must be alert to their limitations. The above dichotomy of the respective UK and German industrial systems is ultimately a caricature, intended to emphasize each country's most prominent characteristics in this regard. Whilst this is helpful to an extent, it risks blurring over the significant outlying features of both environments which would appear to challenge these perceived archetypes. These include the UK's globally dominant mining and energy sectors; and – likewise – the significant growth of hi-tech consumer manufacturing and Anglo-American-style investment banking activities in Germany over recent decades. The ensuing implication is that, whereas shareholder-oriented and co-determined boards may arguably be appropriate to *archetypically* 'British' and 'German' industrial concerns respectively, this does not necessarily render such corporate decision-making structures *universally* appropriate within each relevant national setting.

It is further noteworthy that the UK's purported comparative advantage in hi-tech industrial sectors appears to have been a relatively recent development, following on from the progressive diminution of the UK's traditional heavy manufacturing industries throughout the latter half of the twentieth century. However, exclusively shareholder-representative boards have contrarily been a traditional and longstanding feature of the UK's corporate governance landscape, even during earlier time periods when their suitability for the prevailing product market environment of the time was not so readily apparent. This suggests that functional rationalizations of shareholder supremacy based on dominant industrial characteristics cannot in themselves explain the persistence of this corporate governance paradigm in the UK over time.

---

[72] See *ibid.*, 350–51.
[73] *ibid.*, 359.
[74] See *ibid.*, 352.

At the very least, though, the above comparative insights demonstrate the functional *inessentiality* of UK-style shareholder primacy when viewed from a broader European (and particularly German) perspective. This raises an important historical question as to *why*, then, the UK opted to take this comparatively peculiar corporate governance and industrial relations path, in the apparent absence of any fully convincing logical rationale for doing so.

HISTORIC REASONS FOR THE UK'S UNEASE WITH EUROPEAN-STYLE WORKER INVOLVEMENT

On first reflection, it is somewhat curious that the interests of labour have not figured more prominently within UK corporate governance, especially when one considers the general political disposition of the country in modern times. Throughout the course of the past century, the UK has witnessed 37 years of Labour government (or 42 years if one includes Labour's participation in the wartime coalition government). Moreover, whilst the UK is acknowledged on the whole as having a more neo-liberal (i.e. right-wing) political orientation than many of its northern European counterparts,[75] it nonetheless has a comparatively strong social-democratic (i.e. left-wing) political tradition in relation to other English-speaking and former-Commonwealth countries, at least since the Second World War.[76] It is thus not unreasonable to expect that, at some point during this time period, democratic public policy measures might have been taken to effect the direct integration of worker interests into UK corporate governance, most obviously via the regulatory implementation of some variant of German-style co-determination.

The notion of employee representation on corporate boards – known in British industrial relations parlance as 'industrial democracy' – has by no means been absent from Labour Party policy agendas in the past, and has also featured prominently in overlapping academic debates. Indeed, in the mid-to-late 1970s the imminent introduction of industrial democracy in the UK appeared to be a foregone conclusion, particularly following the publication of the 1977 Bullock Report on Industrial Democracy commissioned by James Callaghan's Labour administration.[77] In essence, the majority of the committee behind the Report recommended a so-called '2x + y' formula for achieving parity board composition in large companies as between shareholder and employee representatives. This scheme entailed equal numbers of shareholder and employee representatives on the boards of all companies employing more than 2,000 people, subject to a minimum of four directors on each side. These

---

[75] See M.J. Roe, *Political Determinants of Corporate Governance* (OUP 2002), esp. Ch. 12.

[76] See C.M. Bruner, *Corporate Governance in the Common-Law World: The Political Foundations of Shareholder Power* (CUP 2013), esp. Ch. 5.

[77] See *Report of the Committee of Inquiry on Industrial Democracy* ('the Bullock Report'), Cm 6706 (1977). For a brief discussion of the background to and content of the Committee's proposals, see B. Clift, A. Gamble and M. Harris, 'The Labour Party and the Company' in J. Parkinson, A. Gamble and G. Kelly, *The Political Economy of the Company* (Hart Publishing 2000), 51, 76–80.

two constituencies would then be supplemented by a third group of formally neutral co-opted directors, comprising an odd number of at least three so as to prevent potential deadlock. Whilst the Bullock scheme did not envisage co-determination as being a universal requirement for all companies above the relevant size threshold, it did nonetheless recommend that co-determined boards be compulsory where formally requested by a recognized trade union and subsequently approved by a majority of a company's employees.

The company and labour lawyer Paul Davies, one of the most noted academic advocates of employee board representation at the time, explained the rationale behind industrial democracy in terms which still bear strong relevance within today's British industrial relations climate. Writing in 1975, Davies claimed that '[i]n recent years the British economy has been subject to powerful and continuing pressure for "rationalisation" of productive activities', with the outcome 'that it is no longer sufficient [for employees] to be able to respond to the employment consequences of decisions already taken'.[78] Rather, argued Davies, 'it is necessary for unions and workers to be in a position to exercise control over the primary decisions whether to rationalize and by which methods, ... not only as a defensive reaction to adverse economic trends but also as part of a more positive programme aimed at securing for employees greater control over their working environment'.[79]

On the other hand, there was a conflicting body of opinion within the labour movement, which regarded the involvement of employee representatives in board decision-making as being both an unnecessary and, moreover, an *inappropriate* structural channel for the exercise of collective worker voice within the firm. This alternative school of thought, exemplified most eloquently by the academic work of the classic labour lawyer Sir Otto Kahn-Freund,[80] stressed the inherent conflict between the respective interests of shareholders and employees.[81] So fundamental was this tension, in Kahn-Freund's view, that it was simply impossible to phrase the 'interests of the company' in such a way as to enable this concept to encapsulate the particular interests of employees in those instances (e.g. proposed plant closures or mass layoffs) when the latter constituency is most in need of the protection of company law.[82] Accordingly, whilst Kahn-Freund was not entirely dismissive of the possibility of employee

---

[78] P.L. Davies, 'Employee Representation on Company Boards and Participation in Corporate Planning' (1975) 38 *Modern Law Review* 254, 254.

[79] *ibid.*

[80] See e.g. O. Kahn-Freund, 'Industrial Democracy' (1977) 6 *Industrial Law Journal* 65, 67.

[81] See *ibid.*, 75–80. Even Lord Wedderburn of Charlton, one of the most influential and respected advocates of industrial democracy in the UK, had earlier been led to concede that 'the position of [employee] directors would not be easy' insofar as they would find themselves 'either excluded from the real discussion of policy, as has been alleged to happen in Germany, or eventually distrusted by those who elected them'. K.W. Wedderburn, *Company Law Reform*, Fabian Tract 363 (1965), 16.

[82] In this regard, Kahn-Freund claimed that '[t]he so-called "interest of the company" is always identical with an interest of its shareholders, not *the* interest, but *an* interest ... [whereas] the company's interest may be irreconcilably opposed to that of each member of the employee group'. Above n. 80, 76.

representatives enjoying direct influence over managerial decisions via co-decision-making rights on the board, he was vigilant in emphasizing the necessity of such mechanisms being seen as *an extension of* the independent rights of trade unions to protect employees' interests via adversarial industrial action, as opposed to a means of submersing the particular interests of a company's workforce into the general interest of the notional 'company as a whole'.[83]

Kahn-Freund's adversarial view of industrial relations – and corresponding discomfort with the idea of employee representatives becoming co-responsible for corporate-managerial decisions with shareholder representatives – was by no means idiosyncratic for its time. On the contrary, such sceptical – or, at best, ambivalent – attitudes towards the introduction of co-determination in the UK were shared by a significant proportion of the British labour movement in the 1970s, including a number of influential figures within the Labour Party itself.[84] This hesitancy was reinforced by the common opinion of many twentieth-century British socialists that the public interest (including worker welfare considerations) would only be effectively upheld by the outright conversion of key private enterprises into government-owned public entities via nationalization: a vision that had already been realized within many public utilities and heavy industries in the UK during the post-war era. This was seen as preferable to the alternative option of effecting fundamental structural change to the private sector company itself, thereby stinting the potential for meaningful pro-worker reform of established British corporate governance norms.[85]

Consequently, the requisite political will to implement co-determination in Britain was never present, such that the Bullock reform agenda did not make it onto the statute book during Labour's five-year term of government.[86] The coming to power in 1979 of Margaret Thatcher's neo-liberal Conservative administration – whose deep-seated hostility to organized labour is well-known – signalled the effective death knell of the British industrial relations reform movement. Since then, the notion of industrial democracy in the UK has to a large extent (albeit somewhat unjustifiably) come to be associated with the notoriously confrontational industrial climate of the late-1970s, which reached its low point in the infamous 'winter of discontent' of 1978–79 characterized by seemingly constant strikes, a temporary three-day working week and frequent power blackouts. Moreover, despite 13 years of later Labour rule between 1997 and 2010 under the Blair and Brown administrations, there has been no serious or sustained political impetus in Britain for revisiting the co-determination issue over recent decades, at least on a domestic policy-making

---

[83] *ibid.*, 77. In a similar vein, Davies and Wedderburn argued in 1977 for the introduction of 'novel institutions of conflictual partnership', designed in recognition of the (then-assumed) fact that 'the reality of conflict between workpeople and capital will remain and the powers of workers organised in their trade unions seem likely to increase'. P. Davies and K.W. Wedderburn, 'The Land of Industrial Democracy' (1977) 6 *Industrial Law Journal* 197, 211.

[84] On this, see Clift, Gamble and Harris, above n. 77, 65–76.

[85] *ibid.*, 52, 81.

[86] *ibid.*, 80.

level; although – as mentioned above – the notion has somewhat curiously returned within Conservative government policy discourse lately.

THE (NEGLIGIBLE) IMPACT OF EUROPEAN WORKER INVOLVEMENT MECHANISMS IN THE UK

Granted, a brief and modest resurgence of the industrial democracy debate occurred at the beginning of the twenty-first century with the UK's implementation in October 2004 of the long-awaited EU Directive on worker involvement in the European Company.[87] This Directive made provision for the involvement of employees in board-level decision-making within any business registered as a *Societas Europaea* (SE) or European Public Limited-Liability Company.[88]

In its original guise in the 1970s,[89] the European Commission's blueprint for worker involvement in the European Company was, from a British perspective, radical to say the least. In essence, the Commission proposed a mandatory framework of employee representation at board level effective within SEs across the EU (then the European Economic Community) as a whole, based loosely on Germany's two-tier board model and featuring parity representation of shareholders and employees on an upper supervisory board in accordance with a Bullock-esque '2x + y' formula. This was to be supplemented by a mandatory system of employee consultation via plant-level works councils (likewise along German lines), with the latter bodies enjoying important co-decision-making rights in determining with management the content of so-called 'social plans' consequent upon economic restructurings.[90] Moreover, the supplementary Draft Fifth Company Law Directive, introduced in 1972, provided for the mandatory extension of employee board representation and two-tier board structures to *all* public companies incorporated throughout the EU.[91]

It would be an understatement to say that the employee representation requirements as set out in the final draft of the EU worker involvement Directive, published in 2001, were somewhat less stringent in nature.[92] Above

---

[87] See Council Directive 2001/86/EC supplementing the Statute for a European company with regard to the involvement of workers. This Directive was implemented in the UK by the European Public Limited-Liability Company Regulations 2004 (SI 2004/2326) ('the UK Regulations').

[88] On this generally, see M. Bouloukos, 'The European Company (SE) as a Vehicle for Corporate Mobility within the EU: A Breakthrough in European Corporate Law?' (2007) 18 *European Business Law Review* 535.

[89] See OJ [1970] C124/1, EC Bull. Supp. 8/1970.

[90] P.L. Davies, 'Workers on the Board of the European Company?' (2003) 32 *Industrial Law Journal* 75, 95.

[91] J. Dine and J.J. Du Plessis, 'The Fate of the Draft Fifth Directive on Company Law: Accommodation Instead of Harmonisation' (1997) *Journal of Business Law* 23, 29–30.

[92] For a detailed account of these provisions, see C. Barnard and S. Deakin, 'Reinventing the European Corporation? Corporate Governance, Social Policy and the Single Market' (2002) 33 *Industrial Relations Journal* 484, 485–88.

all there was a fundamental change in the policy impetus of the scheme, from its lofty initial ambition of seeking to mandate co-determination within SEs across the EU as a whole,[93] to the considerably more modest dual goal of: first, affording incorporators a wide ambit of flexibility in designing their own provisions for worker involvement within SEs in line with prevailing national customs;[94] whilst, second, ensuring that this flexibility is not so wide as to permit incorporators to exploit the SE framework in order to evade any more onerous employee participation requirements applicable in a founder company's 'host' Member State.[95]

Without going into further detail, it is consequently clear that an SE registered in the UK will not be required to adopt any German-style employee participation structure merely by virtue of carrying on its business in the form of an SE, except in those instances where: (i) the SE in question is formed as part of a joint venture between a British company and one or more companies registered in other EU Member States, in one of the statutorily recognized ways; and (ii) the latter company or companies is/are already subject to mandatory employee participation requirements in place within their own domestic laws (as in the case, for example, of a German or Dutch company).[96] It can reasonably be surmised that such cases will be extremely rare, an assumption which would appear to have been borne out by practice so far.

Coupled with the extremely low incidence of SE incorporations in the UK to date in general,[97] the above factors suggest that, all things considered, the EU Directive on worker involvement in the European Company is of negligible impact insofar as established British industrial relations practices are concerned. Meanwhile, the potentially more far-reaching proposals for employee

---

[93] Wedderburn, above n. 26, 45–46.

[94] In what would appear to be a stark U-turn on the European Commission's initial position on the matter, recital (5) to the 2001 Directive states that '[t]he great diversity of rules and practices existing in the Member States as regards the manner in which employees' representatives are involved in decision-making within companies makes it inadvisable to set up a single European model of employee involvement applicable to the SE'. Accordingly, both the Directive and the implementing UK Regulations make provision for the reaching of private agreement between management and employee representatives on the appropriate arrangements (if any) for employee representation on the board, with the standard legislative requirements in this regard operating on a default basis only. See above n. 87.

[95] In this regard, recital (3) to the 2001 Directive (*ibid.*) explains that, '[i]n order to promote the social objectives of the [EU], special provisions have to be set ... aimed at ensuring that the establishment of an SE does not entail the disappearance or reduction of practices of employee involvement existing within the companies participating in the establishment of an SE'.

[96] The domestic rules for employee board participation in UK-registered SEs require that, 'where the employees or their representatives of at least one of the participating companies had participation rights, the representative body shall have the right to elect, appoint, recommend or oppose the appointment of a number of members of the administrative or supervisory body of the SE, such number ... be[ing] equal to the highest proportion in force in the participating companies concerned before the registration of the SE'. See the UK Regulations, above n. 87, Sch. 3, para. 7(2).

[97] B. Hannigan, *Company* Law, (4th ed., OUP 2016), 38.

participation set out in the abovementioned Draft Fifth Company Law Directive have never been implemented,[98] and the latter Directive itself has since been abandoned.[99] Whilst the supplementary EU legislative framework on information and consultation of employees ('ICE')[100] in theory provides an additional degree of worker influence over corporate decision-making – particularly in the case of undertakings established *other than* by way of an SE – such influence is significantly limited in practice.[101] The relevant ICE requirements are applicable only conditionally upon the formal request of a sizeable number or percentage of employees of the relevant undertaking.[102] Furthermore, by nature they provide employees only with the relatively 'soft' entitlement to be informed of and consulted on managerial initiatives affecting their interests, as opposed to vesting employees with any sort of 'hard' decision-making power share in the form of partial board representation or otherwise.[103]

In any event, the continuing applicability of the European Company and ICE frameworks as a whole within the UK is now seriously in question following the country's recent (at time of writing) 'Brexit' vote, which provides further reason to discount the practical relevance of those schemes to domestic corporate governance and industrial relations norms today.

---

[98] Dine and Du Plessis, above n. 91, 25.

[99] Davies, above n. 57, 395 (fn. 84).

[100] See Directive 2002/14/EC of the European Parliament and of the Council establishing a general framework for informing and consulting employees in the European Community, as implemented in the UK by the Information and Consultation of Employees Regulations 2004 (SI 2004/3426); and Council Directive 94/45/EC on the establishment of a European Works Council or a procedure in Community-scale undertakings and Community-scale groups undertakings for the purposes of informing and consulting employees, as implemented in the UK by the Transnational Information and Consultation of Employees Regulations 1999 (SI 1999/3323).

[101] On this generally, see K.D. Ewing and G.M. Truter, 'The Information and Consultation of Employees Regulations: Voluntarism's Bitter Legacy' (2005) 68 *The Modern Law Review* 626.

[102] Where a formal employee request is made to negotiate an agreement in respect of information and consultation under the 2004 Regulations (above n. 100), Regulation 7(2) thereof provides that such a request is only valid if made by at least 10% of the employees of the undertaking in writing. If, on the other hand, an employee request is made to negotiate an agreement for a European Works Council or alternative information and consultation procedure under the 1999 Regulations (*ibid.*), Regulation 9 thereof requires that a written request be made by a minimum of either 100 employees (whether personally or representatively) in at least two undertakings or establishments in at least two different EU Member States.

[103] In this regard, the official UK government guidance on the 2004 Regulations (*ibid.*) makes clear that 'employers are not obliged to follow the [employee] representatives' opinion', and therefore that '[d]ecision-making remains the responsibility of management'. See Department of Trade and Industry, *The Information and Consultation of Employees Regulations 2004: DTI Guidance* (2005), 45. In a similar vein, Regulation 8 of the 1999 Regulations (*ibid.*) provides that, although employee works councils shall have the right to meet with management to discuss particularly pertinent labour-related issues such as relocations, closure of establishments and collective redundancies, any opinions or suggestions put forward by the works council in those respects 'shall not affect the prerogatives of central management'.

Is UK Corporate Governance Law's Exclusive Shareholder Focus Sustainable?

We remarked at the beginning of this chapter on the apparent curiosity of the fact that employees are typically afforded so little direct influence or involvement within UK corporate governance, at least in relation to the corresponding corporate governance status of shareholders. Indeed, UK corporate governance law's virtual exclusion of labour as a direct beneficiary of, or collective participant in, high-level corporate decision-making is remarkable on a number of levels. From an economic point of view, it is at least debatable whether the functional value to firms of shareholders' equity capital is sufficiently high relative to that of employees' human capital to merit a national corporate governance paradigm dedicated almost exclusively to furtherance of the former constituency's interests. From a political standpoint, meanwhile, it is a matter of note that the interests of workers have not featured more emphatically in domestic corporate governance regulatory and policy initiatives in the UK, particularly given the significant influence of labour as a general political constituency for much of the twentieth century.

But whilst – historically – employees have not garnered much direct consideration in the specific realm of UK corporate governance law, as a corporate constituency they have undoubtedly been empowered in other important respects over the past century. We explained above how a key factor underlying the British labour movement's traditional unease with German-style employee board representation has been its longstanding view that employees' interests are more effectively protected *outside of* the corporate governance process itself. Accordingly, labour has tended to exercise its collective 'voice' as such within (or, strictly speaking, *outside*) the firm on an indirect and fundamentally *non*-co-operative basis, by means of the trade-union-initiated practice of 'arm's length' collective bargaining with management on general terms and conditions of employment. Indeed, it was largely for this reason that – as recounted above – employee board representation was widely regarded (even by many vociferous supporters of worker empowerment) as an inappropriate and superfluous legal innovation, which was inherently out of sync with the basic adversarial dynamic of the British industrial relations system.

However, times have undoubtedly changed in the UK over the past four decades, with the consequence that today's national industrial relations climate bears very little resemblance to the context in which Bullock's landmark co-determination blueprint for Britain was considered (and ultimately dismissed) back in 1977–78. In the intervening period the overall level of trade union membership in the UK has fallen by approximately 50 per cent, from a peak of 12.2 million citizens in 1980 to just 6.4 million today (as of 2014),[104] such that less than 10 per cent of the UK population is now unionized. Over

---

[104] Department for Business Innovation & Skills, *Trade Union Membership 2014: Statistical Bulletin* (June 2015), 5; J. Moylan, 'Union Membership Has Halved since 1980', *BBC News*, 7 September 2012.

the same period, the percentage of the UK workforce covered by collective agreements on working terms and conditions between unions and employers (so-called 'collective bargaining density') has fallen from 82 per cent to approximately 20 per cent.[105] On a public policy level, meanwhile, recent years have witnessed the continuing decentralization and dismantling of collective bargaining structures across the UK and Europe more generally,[106] including (in the form of the Trade Union Act 2016) controversial domestic legislation aimed at heightening the legal barriers faced by unions in seeking to initiate strikes and other coercive forms of industrial action vis-à-vis employers.

Moreover, these developments have occurred within a general labour market climate characterized by increasingly 'flexible' or 'insecure' (depending on one's particular ideological perspective) working patterns including zero-hour contracts, agency work and independent contracting. Perhaps unsurprisingly in light of these factors, the British trade union movement has long abandoned its traditional antipathy to worker involvement in corporate decision-making at board level, and indeed has recently expressed support for exploring potential reform options in this regard.[107] Notwithstanding the UK Prime Minister's recent rhetorical posturing on this issue, though, it is fair to say that the chances of co-determination becoming a general feature of the British corporate governance and industrial relations landscape today seem remote, at least as things presently stand.[108]

Whether Britain's existing shareholder-centric corporate governance framework is sustainable in the long run, though, is an altogether different matter. Certainly, there is significant cause to question whether UK corporate governance law's exclusive focus on shareholders remains a relevant and legitimate position today from the standpoint of British society at large. Unlike in the United States where the notion of the 'shareholder-citizen' has fairly widespread cultural resonance amongst the general (or at least middle-class) public,[109] the UK has no comparable socio-political tradition of popular shareholder consciousness.

---

[105] K.D. Ewing, 'The Death of Social Europe' (2015) 26 *King's Law Journal* 76, 96.

[106] On this development generally (as viewed from a broader European standpoint), see *ibid.*, 87–96.

[107] See e.g. Conchon, above n. 54, 7.

[108] Indeed, at the time of writing, the government has expressly stated in its recent corporate governance Green Paper that 'we are … not proposing to mandate the direct appointment of employees or other interested parties to company boards'. Department for Business, Energy and Industrial Strategy, *Corporate Governance Reform: Green Paper* (November 2016) ('Green Paper'), 40. Instead, the government would appear to favour the encouragement of merely voluntary 'stakeholder advisory panels' to provide enhanced transparency on stakeholder concerns, but without having any direct influence over actual board decisions. See *ibid.*, 38–39. On the notion of corporate 'stakeholders' generally, see Chapter 2.

[109] On this phenomenon generally, see M. Gelter, 'The Pension System and the Rise of Shareholder Primacy' (2013) 43 *Seton Hall Law Review* 909; S. Davis, J. Lukomnik and D. Pitt-Watson, *The New Capitalists: How Citizen Investors are Reshaping the Corporate Agenda* (Harvard Business School Press 2006); A.M. Tucker, 'The Citizen Shareholder: Modernizing the Agency Paradigm to Reflect How and Why a Majority of Americans Invest in the Market' (2012) 35 *Seattle University Law Review* 1299.

Additionally, whereas in the UK (as in the US[110]) private pension wealth – generated in large part from returns on corporate equity holdings – constitutes the largest component of aggregate household wealth today,[111] it is noteworthy that private pension wealth *only* outstrips other sources of wealth for the top two deciles of the British population as determined by wealth: that is, for those citizens with total household wealth of £1,754,787 and above.[112] For the great majority of UK citizens falling below this wealth threshold, pension wealth – and thus, by implication, shareholder return – actually constitutes a small and relatively insignificant component of total household wealth, at least relative to other wealth sources such as employment income and home equity.[113] Accordingly, despite successive policy initiatives in recent decades aimed at instilling a greater collective sense of shareholder consciousness amongst the British public, the evidence suggests that relatively few working UK citizens actually have cause to identify themselves as 'shareholders' (in preference to 'workers') in any meaningful material sense.

Moreover, with seemingly increasing levels of financial disenfranchisement amongst the younger working generations today including the reduced availability and/or reliability of traditional occupational pension schemes, it may reasonably be queried whether we are witnessing the consequent *destruction* of the latent social contract on which the legitimacy – and, in turn, long-term sustainability – of the UK's shareholder-focused corporate governance framework has traditionally been predicated. Further consideration of this issue lies outside the scope of the present work. For immediate purposes, though, it suffices to say that – if this is indeed the case – then we would envisage the growth of popular support for the greater consideration and/or involvement of workers in UK corporate governance within the foreseeable future. This could, in turn, potentially encourage a revisiting by policymakers of the long-dormant debate on the merits of industrial democracy in the UK. Indeed, it is not inconceivable that the recent murmurings of co-determination within the British political arena referred to above may well represent the fledgling beginnings of such a development.

---

[110] See A. Gottschalck, M. Vornovytskyy and A. Smith, *Household Wealth in the U.S.: 2000 to 2011* (2012 United States Census Bureau), at www.census.gov/people/wealth/files/Wealth%20Highlights%202011.pdf.

[111] Office for National Statistics, *Total Wealth, Wealth in Great Britain 2010–12* (15 May 2014), 1.

[112] *ibid.*, 4–5; Office for National Statistics, *Wealth in Great Britain Wave 4, 2012 to 2014* (18 December 2015), Table 2.3 & 2.4: 'Breakdown of aggregate total wealth, by deciles and components: Great Britain, 2006/08–2010/12'.

[113] See *ibid.*

PART III

Corporate Risk Management and Oversight

CHAPTER 7

The Monitoring Board and Independent Directors

THE BOARD AND CORPORATE GOVERNANCE

In Chapter 4 we explored the board's decision-making primacy and its importance as the most fundamental legal principle of UK and, more broadly, Anglo-American corporate governance. We also emphasized board primacy as one of the most important characteristics that distinguishes corporations from other business organization forms and their governance.

However, the board's broad authority and status at the top of the corporate hierarchy also raises fundamental questions. First, as we have explained in Chapter 1, much of corporate governance is about mitigating the problems that arise as a consequence of the separation of ownership and control. The board of directors plays an important role in this regard. Given shareholders' inevitable informational limitations and collective action problems, the board becomes the main institutional mechanism to oversee the company and ensure ongoing corporate accountability. Following on from this is the crucial corporate governance question as to how to maximize the board's ability to effectively discipline senior management and other actors further down in the corporate hierarchy. In recent decades, this has led to a 'monitoring model' of the board and a strong emphasis on director independence.[1]

In addition to its monitoring function, we will see that the board is also entrusted with high-level strategic and decision-making tasks. The issue in this regard is thus how to design the board to best enable it to function and discharge its tasks effectively. This includes the question (*inter alia*) of board structure and composition.[2] In addition to director independence, which is also relevant in the decision-making context, more recent initiatives include a push for increased diversity on corporate boards, which can improve board effectiveness.

---

[1] Note, however, that according to the view we advance in Chapter 1, the separation is not just between shareholders and management, but also between shareholders and the board itself, with the latter acting as the corporation's controlling organ.

[2] Other issues in this regard – which are, however, beyond the scope of our discussion – include the length of the term of office of directors and the board's general mode of operation.

If one accepts the thesis that further enlarging shareholder rights as a conduit towards improved corporate governance is problematic,[3] 'board governance' represents a more promising focal point for corporate governance law (and, indeed, future reform measures in this area). Instead of relying on shareholders to exercise the function of corporate monitors and ultimate decision-makers, corporate accountability may well be better achieved by direct measures applicable to the board of directors itself. Decisional effectiveness can arguably be more easily maintained by upholding the division of ownership and control within corporations, as long as the problems caused by this division are countered by rules designed to ensure the optimal functioning of boards. It is also a more manageable (albeit not easy) task to control the way in which boards work, as compared to efforts to influence the enormous number of dispersed shareholders that are typically involved in a public corporation and encourage them, in turn, to influence how their firm is run. All other things being equal, well-designed board level corporate governance measures are therefore likely to be more effective than shareholder empowerment initiatives.

GROUP OR INDIVIDUAL GOVERNANCE?

At the outset, given the board's strong position as the principal corporate decision-maker, one might wonder why corporate powers are not concentrated in just *one* individual, similar to a government president, medieval king, or other autocrat. In contrast to these models, however, the Companies Act 2006 requires public companies to have at least two directors.[4] For listed public company boards, the UK Corporate Governance Code further provides that they 'should be of sufficient size that the requirements of the business can be met and that changes to the board's composition and that of its committees can be managed without undue disruption, and should not be so large as to be unwieldy'.[5] Public companies are regularly composed of multiple directors and their boards form various multi-member committees to deal with specific areas. Moreover, corporate and agency principles provide that boards take decisions collectively, while board committees or individual directors – unless they are specifically authorized – cannot by themselves act for the board.[6]

Although it is now taken for granted, we might well wonder whether the preference for boards as *collective* bodies represents the approach that best enables this institution to exercise its functions. This has led Stephen Bainbridge to ask the question, 'Why a board?'[7] Indeed, putting a group in charge of a

---

[3] See Chapter 4.

[4] Section 154 of the Companies Act 2006, which, however, allows private companies to operate with only one director.

[5] Supporting Principle B.1. See also the Code's references to collective responsibility and division of responsibilities in Principles A.1 and A.2.

[6] See, for example, article 7 of the Model Articles for Public Companies; B. Hannigan, *Company Law* (4th ed., OUP 2016), 139.

[7] S.M. Bainbridge, 'Why a Board? Group Decision Making in Corporate Governance' (2002) 55 *Vanderbilt Law Review* 1 (2002), on which the following paragraphs are based.

company, as opposed to a single individual, leads to difficulties in monitoring and measuring each team member's performance, adds problems that flow from the complexities of inter-personal team dynamics, and creates potential for free-riding on the efforts of others by certain group members. Moreover, groups are prone to fall victim to 'groupthink'.

Groupthink occurs when groups of people prioritize internal solidarity and unanimity over quality decision-making. For example, a director may be unsure whether a proposal favoured by other board members is in the best interests of the company. However, since he is not quite sure and fears that questioning the proposal may be seen as uncollegial or disruptive of the board's 'team spirit', he goes along with the option that is popular with his peers. In other words, social norms and related factors may lead boards to become complacent, sacrificing critical discussion and evaluation in favour of courtesy and 'getting along'.[8]

Such complacency can erode attentiveness and decision-making quality and as such represents a threat to the model of the collective board. Accordingly, countervailing corporate governance best practices – including the independent director model, which will be explored further below – have been developed. But would it not make sense simply to use one-person boards instead of attempting to mitigate the problems that are encountered in group settings?

As it turns out, on balance, boards indeed generally function best as a group or 'team'.[9] The board's design as a collective body is supported by experimental research by psychologists and economists, which suggests that group decision-making is often superior to decision-making by individuals. There are likely various reasons for this superiority. In particular, an important explanation may be the enhanced 'collective memory' and thus access to information by groups, which also translates into an improved ability to overcome issues of bounded rationality – that is, impediments to optimal decision-making due to cognitive and other individual human limitations. Thus, especially when forced to make decisions under complex and uncertain conditions, groups benefit from the combined inputs of their members in terms of knowledge and skills, which, moreover, also has the positive effect of reducing individual biases. As Bainbridge observes, '[i]n the corporate context, the board of directors thus may have emerged as an institutional governance mechanism to constrain the deleterious effect of bounded rationality on the organizational decision-making process'.[10]

---

[8] As Bainbridge notes: 'Highly cohesive groups with strong civility and cooperation norms value consensus more than they do a realistic appraisal of alternatives. In such groups, groupthink is an adaptive response to the stresses generated by challenges to group solidarity. To avoid those stresses, groups may strive for unanimity even at the expense of quality decision making.' Bainbridge, above n. 7, 32.

[9] See *ibid.*, 12–41. Note, however, that despite the prevalent model of collective decision-making, directors' *liability* is formulated at the individual level. *Re Westmid Packing Services Ltd, Secretary of State for Trade and Industry v Griffiths* [1998] 2 BCLC 646, per Lord Woolf MR: 'The collegiate or collective responsibility of the board of directors ... is of fundamental importance to corporate governance under English company law. That ... responsibility must however be based on individual responsibility. Each individual director owes duties to the company ....'

[10] *ibid.*, 21.

Finally, the collective board model is also useful for addressing agency costs within boards themselves. As we have seen in Chapter 4, while boards are subject to certain monitoring by shareholders and other disciplining forces, the potential for behaviour by directors that is against the interests of the company and shareholders remains. As such, it would be helpful to have a built-in monitoring mechanism at the internal decision-making level itself – which is precisely what the board, if constituted as a group and not a single individual, has to offer. In effect, a combination of social norms, legal duties and peer pressure encourages directors to monitor each other, thereby making the occurrence of misbehaviour less likely.

On aggregate, therefore, the combined advantages of a collective board appear to clearly outweigh the disadvantages. The collective board model, which has become commonplace in public companies, thus tends to be superior to a board that consists of a single individual. The collective board model with its internal delegation of tasks is also better equipped to deal with the challenges and substantial workload faced by today's public company boards.

THE FUNCTIONS OF THE BOARD

Given the board's importance, it may come as a surprise that the law provides very little guidance on its functions. While some jurisdictions provide enumerations of (sometimes non-delegable) board powers, this is not the case in the UK or the US.[11] The UK Companies Act does not directly address the board's overarching role (although it assigns various discrete duties to directors), leaving it in large part to the company and its shareholders to determine the board's role through private ordering via the company's constitution. The Model Articles for public and private companies, for their part, provide simply that '[s]ubject to the articles, the directors are responsible for the management of the company's business'.[12] Similarly, the Delaware General Corporation Law provides that '[t]he business and affairs of every corporation ... shall be managed by or under the direction of a board of directors'.[13]

The general reference to 'management' by the board would, by itself, represent a misleading or at least highly inaccurate description of what modern boards do. Delaware's reference to a company being managed 'under the direction' of the board and the UK Model Articles' provision that allows director to delegate their powers to 'such person or committee' as they think fit[14] better reflect today's situation. Public companies are for the most part not managed

---

[11] See, for example, P.L. Davies and S. Worthington, *Gower and Davies: Principles of Modern Company Law* (9th ed., Sweet & Maxwell 2012), 384, tracing this freedom to British company law's partnership origins.

[12] See article 3 of both the Model Articles for Public Companies and Model Articles for Private Companies Limited by Shares.

[13] Delaware Code Annotated, title 8, section 141(a).

[14] Article 5 of the Model Articles, above n. 12.

by the board. Rather, the board transfers managerial responsibilities to senior officers such as the Chief Executive Officer (CEO) and others. In turn, the board monitors management but also retains certain powers, including higher-level entrepreneurial tasks.

This was not always the case. During the corporation's early days, boards themselves acted as managers (albeit to varying degrees).[15] This is also reflected in the works of some of the earlier writers on corporate governance who viewed the corporate board in effect as an extension of the managerial hierarchy, with no independent function in its own right. For instance, Berle and Means referred to both the board and senior officers as the same category of 'managers' that are in charge of directing the company.[16] They believed that the board was appointed by, and therefore beholden to, managers, which led them to be sceptical about the possibility of an independent role for the board. Later, John Kenneth Galbraith similarly remarked that in 'mature' corporations, 'the board of directors is normally the passive instrument of the management'.[17] Since then, however, the board and its role have evolved dramatically.[18] First, following its early management function, the board morphed into a – rather weak – advisory body without any managerial responsibilities in the business. Boards during the managerialist era, which in the US peaked in the 1950s, were largely passive bodies that lacked the motivation or incentives to take on a meaningful governance role.[19]

In the 1970s, a combination of corporate scandals, eroding trust in corporations, and a (perceived or real) lack of corporate accountability to shareholders and the public directed renewed attention to the role of directors.[20] This environment provided a fertile ground for board reform. Thus, in an influential 1976 book on *The Structure of Corporate Law*, Berkeley Law Professor Melvin Eisenberg successfully advanced a monitoring model of the board.[21] He contended that the board should focus mainly on selecting and monitoring corporate managers as its most important tasks. Boards should not themselves get involved in managerial functions since other actors, namely managers, were better equipped to take them on. 'Under a monitoring model,' he explained generally, 'the role of the board is to hold executives accountable for adequate results (whether financial, social, or both), while the role of the executives is to determine how to achieve these results.'[22]

---

[15] See, for example, S.M. Bainbridge, *The New Corporate Governance in Theory and Practice* (OUP 2008), 158.

[16] A.A. Berle and G. Means, *The Modern Corporation and Private Property* (revised ed., Harcourt, Brace & World 1968; first published 1932), 196.

[17] J.K. Galbraith, *The New Industrial State* (Princeton University Press 1976) 186.

[18] For a concise account of this evolution in the US, see Bainbridge, above n. 15, 158–61.

[19] See J.N. Gordon, 'The Rise of Independent Directors in the United States, 1950–2005: Of Shareholder Value and Stock Market Prices' (2007) 59 *Stanford Law Review* 1465, 1511–14.

[20] See S.M. Bainbridge, above n. 15, 159–60.

[21] M.A. Eisenberg, *The Structure of the Corporation* (first published 1976, Beard Books 2006) 139–41, 165.

[22] *ibid.*

Subsequently, this interpretation of the board's role made its way into the corporate governance mainstream, and the emphasis on monitoring became the accepted essential role for boards. As mentioned above, managing the company – in a general sense – is therefore not what the modern board normally does. Rather, the board – which is in practice a part-time, intermittent decision-making body – entrusts full-time executives with most managerial tasks, including running the company on a daily basis. In turn, these managers delegate some tasks and responsibilities further down the corporate hierarchy to employees and agents at different levels. Nevertheless, the 'monitoring board' reference does not mean that the board's role is *limited* to supervision.[23] While supervision remains its chief role, today's boards will typically take on a multi-faceted role that combines supervisory and entrepreneurial elements.[24] This broad role also includes certain relational functions, which entail the management of relationships between the company and various stakeholders and may even extend to facilitating policy changes and corporate growth and innovation.[25]

The UK Corporate Governance Code attempts to capture the modern board's mix of activities and role with the following general definition:

> The board's role is to provide entrepreneurial leadership of the company within a framework of prudent and effective controls which enables risk to be assessed and managed. The board should set the company's strategic aims, ensure that the necessary financial and human resources are in place for the company to meet its objectives and review management performance. The board should set the company's values and standards and ensure that its obligations to its shareholders and others are understood and met.[26]

The G20/OECD Principles of Corporate Governance provide more detail in the form of the following list of eight specific key functions that today's boards should fulfil, and that can be collated under the broad macro function of 'control':[27]

---

[23] Although it should be noted in this context that some jurisdictions, such as Germany, have a two-tiered board structure where the company has one board with purely supervisory functions and another board with management responsibilities. On this, see Chapter 6. See also C. Gerner-Beuerle and E. Schuster, 'The Evolving Structure of Directors' Duties in Europe' (2014) 15 *European Business Organization Law Review* 191, 194–96.

[24] See, for example, D. Kershaw, *Company Law in Context: Text and Materials* (2nd ed., OUP 2012), 234–36; L.L. Dallas 'Developments in U.S. Boards of Directors and the Multiple Role of Corporate Boards' (2003) 40 *San Diego Law Review* 781. Some commentators even argue that today's boards do not exercise any meaningful managerial or advisory role anymore, reducing their function *exclusively* to monitoring. See J.R. Brown 'The Demythification of the Board of Directors' (2015) 52 *American Business Law Journal* 131.

[25] On the latter, see J.A. McCahery and E.P.M. Vermeulen, 'Understanding the Board of Directors after the Financial Crisis' (2014) 41 *Journal of Law and Society* 121.

[26] Supporting Principle A.1 of the UK Corporate Governance Code. See also Financial Reporting Council, *Guidance on Board Effectiveness* (March 2011), which among others further outlines the role of the board.

[27] OECD, G20/OECD Principles of Corporate Governance (OECD 2015), 53–57.

- Reviewing and guiding corporate strategy, major plans of action, risk management policies and procedures, annual budgets and business plans; setting performance objectives; monitoring implementation and corporate performance; and overseeing major capital expenditures, acquisitions and divestitures.
- Monitoring the effectiveness of the company's governance practices and making changes as needed.
- Selecting, compensating, monitoring and, when necessary, replacing key executives and overseeing succession planning.
- Aligning key executive and board remuneration with the longer term interests of the company and its shareholders.
- Ensuring a formal and transparent board nomination and election process.
- Monitoring and managing potential conflicts of interest of management, board members and shareholders, including misuse of corporate assets and abuse in related party transactions.
- Ensuring the integrity of the corporation's accounting and financial reporting systems, including the independent audit, and that appropriate systems of control are in place, in particular, systems for risk management, financial and operational control, and compliance with the law and relevant standards.
- Overseeing the process of disclosure and communications.

To facilitate the board's task in discharging its functions effectively, the composition of the board becomes of great importance. Specifically, some of the above tasks will be exercised by board committees and, in particular, independent directors. The latter and their functions are the subject of the following section.

BOARD INDEPENDENCE

The Rise of Independent Directors in the United States

The now prevailing monitoring model of the board was tied early on to another phenomenon, which has become a distinctive feature of public company boards: namely, the inclusion of non-executive directors and – in particular – non-executive *independent* directors.[28] As we explained in Chapter 2, in 1976 Jensen and Meckling pioneered the idea of examining the separation of corporate ownership and control through the lens of agency costs.[29] In Jensen and

---

[28] Non-executive directors (NEDs) are those that are not employed as managers of the company. Non-executive directors can be independent directors (who are sometimes referred to as outside directors) if they meet certain specific independence criteria (on this, see further below in the text). Conversely, executive directors cannot be independent directors. See for example the distinction between executive, non-executive, and independent non-executive directors in the UK Corporate Governance Code, Supporting Principles B.1.

[29] For a critique of this approach and an alternative model, see M.M. Blair and L.A. Stout, 'A Team Production Theory of Corporate Law' (1999) 85 *Vanderbilt Law Review* 247; L. Stout, *The Shareholder Value Myth* (Berrett-Koehler 2012), 36–46.

Meckling's model, the role of reducing the ensuing frictions between principals (shareholders) and agents (managers) – namely shirking, self-serving behaviour, and other conflicts of interest – was presented as predominantly the province of the firm's equity holders as its 'risk bearers', without much of the analysis being devoted yet to the precise role of boards.[30]

Subsequently, however, other economists began to place a stronger emphasis on the board and its ability to act as a mechanism to *mitigate* – and not contribute to – agency costs.[31] Eugene Fama, for instance, conceptualized the board as a market-driven check over top managers.[32] He also supported the inclusion of 'outside' (that is, non-executive) directors on boards as a means to strengthen board effectiveness in disciplining managers and to avoid 'board capture' by the corporation's executives.[33] Fama explained that while 'outsiders' can monitor 'insiders' (that is, management), there is still a check on the outsiders' own behaviour as these directors are themselves disciplined by the external market for their specialist supervisory or 'refereeing' services.

In joint work, Fama and Jensen later also argued in favour of a mix of inside and outside directors. They explained that outside directors contribute value through specialist expertise and as a 'support function' for the insiders; by acting as arbiters in disagreements among internal managers; and by carrying out tasks that involve serious agency problems between managers and residual claimants (that is, shareholders), such as determining executive remuneration and appointing new managers.[34] Nevertheless, they argued that managerial insiders should retain a minority presence on the board, principally as a source of information. Importantly, Fama and Jensen advocated for boards to maintain a clear division between decision *management* and decision *control*. This essentially reflects today's model where insiders are normally in charge of initiating and implementing strategic business decisions, while outsiders ratify and monitor managerial decisions as well as take charge of the appointment, removal and remuneration of inside directors and managers.[35] Although there is the potential for added agency costs caused by inside directors on the board, this and similar models assume that these costs can be kept in check through external market forces.[36]

---

[30] See M.C. Jensen and W.H. Meckling, 'Theory of the Firm: Managerial Behaviour, Agency Costs and Ownership Structure' (1976) 3 *Journal of Financial Economics* 305, 352, indicating (*inter alia*) that a detailed analysis of the role of the board of directors 'is left to the future'; E.F. Fama, 'Agency Problems and the Theory of the Firm' (1980) 88 *Journal of Political Economy* 288, 293–94.

[31] See M.T. Moore, *Corporate Governance in the Shadow of the State* (Hart 2013), 82–83.

[32] Fama, above n. 30, 293–94.

[33] Another (additional) way to minimize agency costs – which has become established practice – is the use of performance-related executive remuneration. On this, see Chapter 9.

[34] E.F. Fama and M.C. Jensen 'Separation of Ownership and Control' (1983) 26 *Journal of Law and Economics* 301, 314–15.

[35] See Moore, above n. 31, 85.

[36] Namely through takeovers, on which see Chapter 10.

While these writers may have been the first ones to explain the function of outside directors from an economic-contractarian perspective and embed the practice in the principal-agent model, the idea of having non-executive directors as board members was not a new concept. As Jeffrey Gordon has shown, the mean percentage of both non-executive and independent directors on large US public company boards has significantly increased between 1950 and 2005. Non-executive director representation during this period rose from approximately 50 per cent to 85 per cent, while independent directors (made up from the 'non-affiliated' individuals among these non-executives) increased from 20 per cent to 75 per cent.[37] Writing in 2008, one commentator has even observed that it is now common for US boards to have only one insider as a member, namely the CEO.[38]

In the wake of scandals such as the one surrounding Enron in 2001, the independent director model also became the subject of legislative initiatives. The Sarbanes-Oxley Act[39] required the major US stock exchanges to introduce more stringent rules relating to independent directors of listed companies. More recently, the Dodd-Frank Wall Street Reform and Consumer Protection Act (Dodd-Frank Act) further tightened these requirements.[40] Thus, companies listed on the NYSE and NASDAQ are now required – *inter alia* – to have a majority of independent directors on their boards and – building upon longer-standing requirements – to establish certain committees, such as the audit committee, that are composed only of independent directors.[41]

US stock exchange listing rules also contain detailed requirements on directors' independence. Generally, the NYSE provides that '[n]o director qualifies as "independent" unless the board of directors affirmatively determines that the director has no material relationship with the listed company (either directly or as a partner, shareholder or officer of an organization that has a relationship with the company)'.[42] In addition, there are several 'bright line' requirements that provide instances in which an individual cannot qualify as independent. These target situations such as where a director or family member is or has been employed by the company or has received payments therefrom; or where the director or an immediate family member works or has worked for the company's audit firm; or where they serve or have served as executive officer of a company in which any of the company's present executive officers at the same time serve or served on the compensation (or remuneration) committee.[43] Finally, in order to further empower these independent directors to act

---

[37] Gordon, above n. 19, 1473–75. There are comparatively fewer independent directors on UK boards; see text below on this.

[38] Bainbridge, above n. 15, 188 (referring to a 2006 survey).

[39] Public Company Accounting Reform and Investor Protection Act of 2002.

[40] See Brown, above n. 24, 132.

[41] See sections 303A.01–303A.07 of the NYSE Listed Company Manual.

[42] *ibid.*, section 303A.02, para. (a)(i).

[43] *ibid.*, 303A.02, para. (b).

as effective checks on management, the NYSE also provides that the non-management directors must meet at regularly scheduled non-executive sessions without management.[44]

Independent Directors in the UK

The UK has also experienced the rise of independent directors on boards. But in contrast to the US, where the shift to greater board independence evolved in a largely endogenous fashion over the latter half of the twentieth century, its rise to prominence in the UK has been more recent and has owed much to the visible hand of regulatory initiative.[45] UK boards today, in line with other EU countries, still tend to have fewer independent board members than their US counterparts,[46] although – at least in the UK – this may be changing.[47]

The first authoritative prompt in this direction was the Cadbury Code in 1992. The Cadbury Committee was formed as a result of corporate scandals that – not unlike Enron a few years later – involved the sudden insolvencies of major companies whose financial statements had failed to warn of their impeding downfall. Instead of only focusing on accounting and auditing, Cadbury took a bigger picture approach and identified as one of the central problems the issue of boards that were overly dominated by management.[48] Among other measures, Cadbury thus recommended that a listed company's board comprise at least three non-executive directors, a majority of whom should be formally independent – that is to say, in receipt of no income from the company besides their directors' fee, and having no relationship with the company which could materially interfere with the exercise of their independent judgement. Cadbury further recommended that boards separate the roles of chairman and CEO as well as establish audit committees staffed by a majority of independent directors.[49]

The most significant regulatory influence behind the development of the outsider-dominated board model in the UK, however, were the Higgs and Smith Committees' 2003 recommendations on reform of what is today the UK Corporate Governance Code. Going beyond previous recommendations for independent board representation, they established for the first time US-style

---

[44] *ibid.*, section 303A.03.

[45] J. Parkinson, 'Evolution and Policy in Company Law: The Non-executive Director' in J. Parkinson and others (eds), *The Political Economy of the Company* (Hart Publishing 2000), 236. As Kershaw, above n. 24, 256 notes, UK boards before the 1990s were typically dominated by executives.

[46] See D. Ferreira and T. Kirchmaier, 'Corporate Boards in Europe: Size, Independence and Gender Diversity' in M. Belcredi and others (eds), *Boards and Shareholders in European Listed Companies: Facts, Context and Post-Crisis Reforms* (CUP 2013), 191–224.

[47] See Davies and Worthington, above n. 11, 426 n. 187, suggesting that boards may be shifting towards having only one or two executive directors, similar to the situation in the US.

[48] *ibid.*, 424.

[49] The Cadbury Committee, *Report of the Committee on the Financial Aspects of Corporate Governance* (1 December 1992), paras 4.11–4.12 and 4.35.

majority-independent boards and fully independent audit committees as central norms of the British corporate governance system.[50] This step was reflected in the 2003 Combined Code on Corporate Governance and later refined, leading to today's most recent version of the UK Corporate Governance Code.

In spite of its relatively short history in the UK, the independent board paradigm has rapidly grown. It has now become a defining characteristic of the British corporate governance system, and outsider-dominated boards are presently an almost-universal fixture within larger UK listed companies. Specifically, the Code addresses non-executive and independent directors in several Principles and Provisions. Most significantly, boards of Premium Listed FTSE 350 companies ('large companies') should ensure that at least half the board, excluding its chairman, comprises non-executive directors determined by the board to be independent. For companies below the FTSE 350 ('smaller companies'), the Code recommends at least two independent non-executive directors.[51] It is additionally an important and well-established recommendation of the Code that the chairman should on appointment meet the Code's independence criteria and that a chief executive, on retirement from office, should not go on to become chairman of the same company. Rather, the chairman position should be filled by an external candidate with no previous ties to the firm or its board.[52] This means that – in effect – the Code advocates a separation between the role of chairman and that of CEO.[53]

Additionally, the Code recommends that boards should appoint one of the independent non-executive directors as the 'senior independent director', who is charged with providing a sounding board for the chairman and serving as an intermediary for the other directors and shareholders when necessary.[54] Moreover, the chairman should hold meetings with the non-executive directors without the executives present. Led by the senior independent director, the non-executive directors should meet without the chairman present at least annually to appraise the chairman's performance and on other occasions as are deemed appropriate.[55]

With regard to board committees, the Code provides that a majority of members of the nomination committee should be independent non-executive directors.[56] The board should also establish an audit committee and a remuneration committee comprising only (at least three, or in the case of smaller companies two) independent non-executive directors.[57]

---

[50] *The Higgs Report: Review of the Role and Effectiveness of Non-executive Directors* (January 2003), para. 9.5; R. Smith, Audit Committees – Combined Code Guidance (FRC 2003), para 3.1.
[51] UK Takeover Code, Provision B.1.2.
[52] *ibid.*, Provision A.3.1.
[53] *ibid.*, Provision A.2.1.
[54] *ibid.*, Principle A.4. and Provision A.4.1.
[55] *ibid.*, Provision A.4.2.
[56] *ibid.*, Provision B.2.1.
[57] *ibid.*, Provisions C.3.1. and D.2.1.

On the basic question of who qualifies as an 'independent' director, the Code does not provide a clear definition of independence. It does, however, suggest that independence pertains to 'character and judgement', which in turn may be affected by certain 'relationships or circumstances'.[58] The Code suggests that the following non-exclusive list of factors may mean that an individual is not independent, although the board may still determine that a director is independent, notwithstanding their existence. These factors, listed in Code Provision B.1.1., address situations where an individual:

- has been an employee of the company or group within the last five years;
- has, or has had within the last three years, a material business relationship with the company either directly, or as a partner, shareholder, director or senior employee of a body that has such a relationship with the company;
- has received or receives additional remuneration from the company apart from a director's fee, participates in the company's share option or a performance-related pay scheme, or is a member of the company's pension scheme;
- has close family ties with any of the company's advisers, directors or senior employees;
- holds cross-directorships or has significant links with other directors through involvement in other companies or bodies;
- represents a significant shareholder; or
- has served on the board for more than nine years from the date of their first election.

Finally, in terms of appointment and re-election of directors, the Code recommends that directors (both executive and non-executive) of FTSE 350 companies should be subject to annual re-election.[59] It also recommends that all other directors be subject to election by shareholders at the first annual general meeting after their appointment, and to re-election thereafter at intervals of no more than three years. Non-executive directors who have served longer than nine years should be subject to annual re-election.[60] The Code further stipulates that non-executive directors should be appointed for specified terms subject to re-election and to statutory provisions relating to the removal of a director. Any term beyond six years for a non-executive director should be subject to particularly rigorous review.[61]

---

[58] *ibid.*, Provision B.1.1. It is worth noting that the Code's provisions on independence are broader – that is, substantively more restrictive – than those applicable to NYSE listed companies. See Kershaw, above n. 24, 262–63.

[59] UK Takeover Code, Provision B.1.2, Provision B.7.1.

[60] *ibid.*

[61] *ibid.*, Provision B.2.3.

The Walker Report – From Independence to Expertise?

A central factor underpinning the increasing importance of director independence has been the strong emphasis that many institutional investors and corporate governance advisors have tended to place on the Code's independence criteria in assessing the relative merits of companies' governance structures. This is true despite the Code's 'comply or explain' approach and its status as a statement of best practice rather than a mandatory, rigid 'one-size-fits-all' scheme.[62] As a result, the directorial independence doctrine has over recent years increasingly become a byword for a board's accountability and effectiveness in the eyes of investors, regardless of independent boards' overall contribution to engendering improvements in business performance.[63]

Sir David Walker's influential 2009 recommendations on corporate governance in banks and other financial institutions[64] further addressed the role of independent directors, seemingly introducing a new policy shift in this regard (within the financial sector at least). Walker's suggestions in respect of non-executive directors' competencies can be said to centre principally on the perceived need for boards and shareholders to move away from inappropriately formalistic understandings of what directorial independence entails, and instead focus primarily on the 'substance' of independence in the sense of 'quality of independence of mind and spirit [and] of character and judgement'.[65]

Walker seemed to suggest that in some respects the UK Corporate Governance Code's recommendations have paradoxically served to impede the ability of non-executive directors to become effective independent monitors by preventing the development of their firm-specific knowledge and influence within the board over a reasonable time frame. In response, Walker recommended a slower rate of turnover of non-executives than has previously been the norm in listed companies so as to prevent the premature loss of valuable corporate and industry expertise, even if this entails extending directors' tenures beyond the maximum time frame for large companies (currently one year) that is recommended in the Code.[66] Walker further suggested that there is now a legitimate case for allowing former bank CEOs to serve as non-executive members of their company's board, in spite of this practice having been firmly discouraged by the Code since 2003.[67]

---

[62] On this, see Chapter 3. See also M.T. Moore, 'Whispering Sweet Nothings: The Limitations of Informal Conformance in UK Corporate Governance' (2009) 9 *Journal of Corporate Law Studies* 95, 117–25.

[63] For a discussion on the merits of board independence, see text further below.

[64] D. Walker, *A Review of Corporate Governance in Banks and Other Financial Industry Entities: Final Recommendations* (26 November 2009).

[65] *ibid.*, para. 3.6.

[66] *ibid.*, para. 3.11.

[67] *ibid.*, para. 3.7. Walker pointed to the fact that banks that appointed their former CEO as a chairman seemed to have performed relatively well during the recent financial crisis.

It remains to be seen whether Walker's comments in this regard will be sufficient to remove the stigma that institutional shareholders and corporate governance advisory agencies have tended to attach to the dual executive chairmanship position in the UK over recent years, at least insofar as banks and financial institutions are concerned. The Financial Reporting Council (FRC) for its part has challenged the suggestion, arguably implicit in the Walker reports, that the previous emphasis of the Code on ensuring the formal independence of non-executive directors may have inadvertently prevented boards from building an effective base of skills and experience by encouraging the excessive turnover of boardroom personnel.[68]

The FRC nevertheless acknowledged that independence may have been (erroneously) perceived by many boards and shareholders as the primary objective to follow when determining the appropriate composition of boards and the merits of directorial candidates. Therefore, in an attempt to mitigate such confusion, the FRC revised the former Code principle that addressed board balance and independence, now using the new broad criterion of 'Effectiveness', which recommends that the board and its committees should have an *'appropriate balance of skills, experience, independence and knowledge of the company* to enable them to discharge their respective duties and responsibilities effectively'.[69]

This revision gives effect to the FRC's express intention to emphasize that the overriding consideration in designing an effective board should not be formal independence but, rather, whether that board is on the whole fit for purpose.[70] However, the FRC ultimately decided against altering any of the established directorial independence criteria in the Code. Instead, it emphasized that investors should consider companies' application of independence norms in light of the overall need to ensure an appropriate balance of attributes on the board. Nevertheless, these relatively minor tweaks may still result in the Code contributing to mitigating the tension between independence and the long-term development of firm-specific knowledge and competencies by non-executive directors. This problem, of course, is difficult to resolve, at least as long as there is a common belief that independence of directors is a necessary component of 'good' corporate governance.

Do Independent Directors Improve Corporate Governance?

On a functional level, the basic characteristic of independence or 'externality' is to some extent intrinsic to the very concept of a 'board' in the general sense

---

[68] See Financial Reporting Council, *2009 Review of the Combined Code: Final Report* (December 2009), paras 3.12–3.13. For a critical analysis of concepts of directorial independence, see also S. Le Mire and G. Gillian, 'Independence and Independent Company Directors' (2013) 13(2) *Journal of Corporate Law Studies* 443.

[69] UK Corporate Governance Code, Principle B.1 (emphasis added).

[70] FRC, above n. 68, para. 3.17.

of the term. The essence of governance by means of a board is that it represents an exception to the orthodox hierarchical and technocratic structure of an organization, enabling high-level decisions to be made unencumbered by pre-existing bureaucratic constraints.[71] Thus board governance in many contexts generally entails the acceptance of 'outsider' input by affording membership to individuals who are not normally involved in the day-to-day running of an organization, but whose views and experience might nevertheless be valuable in providing alternative perspectives on key operational issues.[72] Outsider board governance in this sense is consequently common in many diverse fields of human activity, including charities, schools, trusts and – in the shape of the UK's Cabinet government system, for instance – even entire nations.[73]

In the business corporations context, outside or independent board members are typically argued for on grounds of their broader base of experience and lack of professional, cultural or emotional attachment to any individual company or its senior management. This renders them less at risk to the positional conflicts of interest that can constrain the objectivity and consequent effectiveness of full-time managerial personnel.[74] It also theoretically means that, as Jeffrey Gordon has suggested, independent directors are more attuned than insiders (managers) to external input, such as the opinions of securities analysts and institutional investors, meaning that they are less likely than their managerial counterparts to overestimate the viability of a company's internal capital allocation plans.[75] Therefore outside directors can be said to represent an effective strategic counterweight to a CEO or senior management team with excessive confidence in the value of its own ideas, insofar as the former are capable of 'feeding' into management's mindset external market perspectives and opinions that might challenge established ways of thinking within a firm.

Outsiders on the board may also result in potential advantages from a risk management perspective.[76] Since outside or independent directors are relatively detached from day-to-day managerial affairs and internal corporate culture, they will correspondingly be better positioned than executive officers to offer contrary or lateral opinions on prospective strategic initiatives, and

---

[71] R.J. Haft, 'Business Decisions by the New Board: Behavioral Science and Corporate Law' (1981) 80 *Michigan Law Review* 1, 3.

[72] On this, see D.C. Langevoort, 'The Human Nature of Corporate Boards' (2001) 89 *Georgetown Law Journal* 277; M.L. Mace, *Directors: Myth and Reality* (Harvard Business School Press 1971), 13–14.

[73] See S. James, *British Cabinet Government* (2nd ed., Routledge 1999; first published 1992), Ch. 5. On the history of boards generally as an organizational decision-making form, see F.A. Gevurtz, 'The Historical and Political Origins of the Corporate Board of Directors' (2004) 33 *Hofstra Law Review* 89.

[74] R.C. Nolan, 'The Legal Control of Directors' Conflicts of Interest in the United Kingdom: Non-executive Directors Following the Higgs Report' in J. Armour and others (eds), *After Enron* (Hart Publishing 2006), Ch. 11.

[75] Gordon, above n. 19.

[76] A more in-depth discussion of risk management is provided in Chapter 8.

thereby flag up any latent risk factors that might undermine their successful execution.[77] This unique 'outside' input can be especially valuable in situations where a CEO and his senior management team are driven by an irrational sense of optimism, impulsiveness or groupthink, which would otherwise encourage them to discount or even remain blind to the potential negative consequences of their decisions.[78]

Despite the various advantages provided by increased director independence, there are, however, also countervailing factors to be considered. Indeed, board independence (and other postulates of modern 'board governance', including the separation of the chairman and CEO position) can be counter-productive.[79] While it makes sense to have independent directors on a board's remuneration committee, the value of maximizing the number of independent directors (or having a majority of them) on boards generally is otherwise unclear.[80] Of course, there is no doubt that outside directors can be useful in adding new, unpreoccupied perspectives and mitigating problems related to disloyal insiders. In addition, they can provide access to valuable information and resources that would otherwise be difficult for companies to obtain. Where specific expertise is lacking within a firm, outside directors may usefully fill that gap. However, as the Walker Report has in part suggested, it should always be considered that inside directors will likely possess more firm-specific information and be more invested, on a personal level, in the company than any outsiders.[81] Reducing inside director representation on boards may therefore have unintended negative consequences. Overall, it is a matter of balancing and finding the right mix between outside and inside directors. This mix, however, will likely vary for each firm and is not conducive to a one-size-fits-all approach such as the universal requirement to have a majority independent board.

An overlooked aspect in this regard is furthermore the question as to which inside manager(s) will be appointed as executive director(s).[82] For example, a company on whose board the only inside director is the CEO (or managers that are allies of or tend to agree with the CEO) effectively disempowers other managers, who now do not have the opportunity of opposing the CEO's proposals at board level, which may result in a lack of checks and balances. Conversely, in this situation, the CEO will be more effective in executing decisions and strategies given that she will be less absorbed with internal politics and the need to overcome resistance by other senior managers who, if they sat on the board, would have been able to voice their opposition against the CEO's plans. It is

---

[77] R. Morck, 'Behavioral Finance in Corporate Governance – Independent Directors and Non-executive Chairs', Harvard Institute of Economic Research Discussion Paper No 2037 (April 2007), at http://papers.ssrn.com/sol3/papers.cfm?abstract_id=979880.

[78] On this, see Langevoort, above n. 72.

[79] In this respect, see for instance the argument for a 'minority-independent' board in E. Fogel and A.M. Geier, 'Strangers in the House: Rethinking Sarbanes-Oxley and the Independent Board of Directors' (2007) 32 *Delaware Journal of Corporate Law* 33.

[80] Given the current emphasis on board independence, this lack of certainty is surprising.

[81] See also Bainbridge, above n. 15, 189.

[82] For a discussion of this issue, see Kershaw, above n. 24, 236–38.

also important to mention in this context that the board represents an exception to the company's normal hierarchy, insofar as all members of the board (regardless of organizational rank) formally sit and vote 'as equals' during board meetings. This creates space for greater opportunities for challenge to exist within the board as compared to a company's 'top-down' chain of command.

The differing stances adopted by the Walker Report and the FRC in relation to board independence issues highlights the underlying tension between independent directors' extended risk oversight role as envisaged in recent governance reforms, and the formal doctrine of board independence as it has been developed in successive editions of the UK Corporate Governance Code over recent years. The primary fault line of this tension concerns the level of firm- and industry-specific expertise expected of non-executive directors. In one corner, the criterion of formal board independence supports regulatory measures aimed at minimizing non-executives' connections to individual firms and industries, with a view to mitigating potential conflicts of interest and preserving the broad, outward-looking focus of the proverbial 'intelligent layman'.[83] In the other corner, however, the criterion of business sustainability supports measures designed to strengthen non-executive directors' commitment to individual companies and business sectors, with a view to expanding the board's collective base of relevant expertise and consequent alertness to latent micro-level risk exposures.

Against this background, one would think it may be helpful to consider empirical data measuring the effects of board independence. Unfortunately, there are no clear answers to be found. While some studies suggest that board independence and other board governance measures have a positive effect on firm performance, others have failed to find any such relationship or even concluded that there is a negative impact.[84] For instance, two researchers found, in the US context, no strong evidence that a majority independent board is conducive to better firm performance. They concluded, however, that 'a reasonable number' of independent directors could increase firm performance.[85] Thus, while these authors 'do not doubt that independent directors are important',

---

[83] Park J coined this term in *Continental Assurance Co of London plc* [2007] 2 BCLC 287 in explaining the level of business awareness to be expected of a director. In essence, it was established that a director is expected to be capable of seeking appropriate external advice, and also framing sufficiently probing questions, to shed light on any aspects of a company's strategy or finances that appear irregular, opaque or contrary to reason. However, detailed technical or firm-specific knowledge is not ordinarily essential.

[84] For a discussion of empirical studies, see Bainbridge, above n. 15, 190–92; Kershaw, above n. 24, 274–78.

[85] S. Bhagat and B.S. Black, 'The Non-correlation between Board Independence and Long Term Firm Performance' (2001) 27 *Journal of Corporation Law* 231. A study that examined the Portuguese stock market equally casts doubt on the effectiveness of independent directors. N. Fernandes, 'EC: Board Compensation and Firm Performance: The Role of "Independent" Board Members' (2008) 18 *Journal of Multinational Financial Management* 30. Conversely, a study examining UK companies between 1989 and 1996 found increased performance in companies that adhered to Cadbury's recommendation to have at least three outside directors on boards. J. Daha and others, 'Board Composition, Corporate Performance, and the Cadbury Committee Recommendation' (2005) 42 *Journal of Financial and Quantitative Analysis* 535.

particularly in restraining self-dealing by insiders, they suggest that 'corporate governance advisors and institutional investors should support efforts by firms to experiment with different board structures and be more tentative in their advice that other countries should adopt American-style monitoring boards'.[86]

Adding further complexity, another study that examined the performance of banks between 2003 and 2008, which includes the recent financial crisis, found that companies with a greater number of independent directors fared worse than firms that had boards with greater inside director representation.[87] This coincides with commentary by some academics that boards have performed badly in the financial crisis or even contributed to it.[88] Finally, the separation of the chairman and CEO roles, a principle that is advocated by the UK Corporate Governance Code and supported by the Dodd-Frank Act in the US, can also not draw from unequivocal empirical support.[89]

What could explain the lack of a clear link between independent directors and firm performance? As we have already alluded to, it has been suggested that independent directors invest less time in their work for each firm and are less knowledgeable or informed about firm specifics than their non-independent or executive counterparts. It is arguable that, from this position of weakness, many independent directors are not able to exercise their monitoring function properly.[90] Moreover, public company boards in general still meet relatively rarely and, in order to work effectively, depend on information provided by the firm's insiders, which weakens the position of outsiders. Finally, despite more stringent independence requirements, outside directors may, even if they are nominally independent, be inclined to support and share the views of management.[91] After all, the director nomination process, which – on an informal level – tends to be driven in great part by the incumbent directors and managers, will expectedly be skewed towards individuals that are likely to be supportive of the incumbents. As such, there remains a threat of 'structural bias' that will not be removed by formal independence rules.[92]

---

[86] Baghat and Black, above n 85, 234.

[87] B.A. Minton and others, 'Do Independence and Financial Expertise of the Board Matter for Risk Taking and Performance?' (2011), at http://papers.ssrn.com/sol3/papers.cfm?abstract_id=1661855.

[88] For example W.-G. Ringe, 'Independent Directors: After the Crisis' (2013) 14 *European Business Law Review* 401; L.L. Dallas, 'Short-Termism, the Financial Crisis, and Corporate Governance' (2012) 37 *Journal of Corporation Law* 265.

[89] The evidence in this area is, again, mixed. See S.M. Bainbridge, 'Dodd-Frank: Quack Federal Corporate Governance Round II' (2011) 95 *Minnesota Law Review* 1179, 1178–99.

[90] Ringe, above n. 88. For a broader critique of independent directors and reform proposals, see also M. Gutiérrez and M. Sáez, 'Deconstructing Independent Directors' (2013) 13(1) *Journal of Corporate Law Studies* 63. Conversely, extrapolating from the study on boards of banks mentioned (above n. 87), it may also be that companies that have independent directors with specialized expertise will be led to greater acceptance of risk-levels or other strategies that may negatively affect the business.

[91] See Bainbridge, above n. 15, 193–98.

[92] See Brown, above n. 24, 133, stating that directors are not chosen primarily because of their substantive qualification but rather 'because of their predisposition toward the policies of management'.

Thus, future corporate governance rules and recommendations will have to revisit the idea that the majority independent board and other dominant board governance principles are *per se* beneficial. It seems plausible that for different firms, different constellations of board structure and composition may be appropriate, which warrants a flexible approach.[93] For instance, it appears that with respect to board composition and structure, emphasis should generally be placed on an individual's expertise (albeit keeping in mind the potential effects on risk-taking) and appropriate investment in terms of time and effort – perhaps by limiting the number of board memberships an individual is allowed to hold. In this respect, in line with the Walker Report's thrust, it may also be more desirable to add a greater number of industry experts to boards, even at the expense of a number of independent directors. Besides, greater inside representation on boards, especially in settings that empower the CEO,[94] may potentially contribute to conflicts of interest but, at the same time, may also improve the efficiency of intra-firm decision-making and policy implementation.

Board Diversity

In addition to having a collective board and an appropriate mix of insiders and independent directors, another factor that improves the substance of board decisions and the ability of board members to monitor corporate activities is to ensure that boards combine a breadth of perspectives and a variety of opinions. This relates not only to director independence but also to the push for diversity on boards.[95] Board diversity is often thought to be supported by the idea that different leadership experiences and diversity in gender, ethnicity, race, nationality and socio-economic background can provide effective means to tackle complacency, generate new ideas, and result in better risk management. As the UK Corporate Governance Code notes in its Preface:

> Essential to the effective functioning of any board is dialogue which is both constructive and challenging. The problems arising from 'groupthink' have been exposed in particular as a result of the financial crisis. One of the ways in which constructive debate can be encouraged is through having sufficient diversity on the board. This includes, but is not limited to, gender and race. Diverse board composition in these respects is not on its own a guarantee. Diversity is as much about differences of approach and experience, and it is very important in ensuring effective engagement with key stakeholders and in order to deliver the business strategy.

Recent years have seen governmental initiatives to increase one specific aspect of diversity, namely female board representation, which has been predominantly

---

[93] Indeed, it could even make sense to consider the idea of adding 'dependent' directors that represent certain stakeholders. See Ringe, above n. 88.

[94] Such as where the inside directors are composed of the CEO and his allies.

[95] Additionally, this concerns the question of employee board representation. On this, see Chapter 6.

supported by economic explanations that emphasize the business case for diversity.[96] In the UK, the first step in this respect was the 2003 Higgs Review of the Role and Effectiveness of Non-Executive Directors. The Review found that non-executives were typically middle-aged white males of British origin with previous experience as public company directors.[97] Higgs noted a striking lack of women on boards – at the time of his report only 6 per cent of non-executive director posts were held by women – and expressed the hope that future boards will be more active in appointing directors from areas 'where women tend to be more strongly represented ... such as human resources, change management and customer care'.[98]

Also in 2003, the Tyson Report on the Recruitment and Development of Non-Executive Directors reiterated the lack of board diversity and cited research showing the value of diverse corporate boards, including improved decision-making quality, reputational benefits and the ability to better manage the company's key constituencies.[99] Conversely, the Tyson Report also pointed to research on potential downsides of diversity, which may include 'lower cohesion, less trust and higher turnover within groups'.[100] As possible measures to counter these tendencies, the Report emphasized the importance of strong leader figures, coupled with appropriate board training and evaluation.

More recently, in 2011, Lord Davies of Abersoch released a government-backed report on Women on Boards.[101] The report recommended that boards of FTSE 100 companies should voluntarily aim to achieve a minimum of 25 per cent female representation on boards by 2015, doubling the 2010 representation of 12.5 per cent. In addition to the 25 per cent target, Lord Davies also recommended – *inter alia* – that companies establish policies on board diversity, disclose statistics relating to female representation in senior executive positions, and consider a broader range of potential female candidates. He also suggested that executive search firms should develop a voluntary code of conduct addressing diversity and best practices for the director recruitment process.

In the wake of these reports, and following amendments in 2010 and 2014, the UK Corporate Governance Code now provides that search for and appointment of board candidates should be conducted 'with due regard for the benefits of diversity on the board, including gender', that the annual report

---

[96] See B. Choudhury, 'New Rationales for Women on Boards' (2014) *Oxford Journal of Legal Studies* 1 (arguing for rationalizing board diversity on both economic *and* equality grounds).

[97] D. Higgs, *Review of the Role and Effectiveness of Non-Executive Directors* (Department of Trade and Industry 2003), para. 10.22.

[98] *ibid.*, para. 10.25.

[99] *Tyson Report on the Recruitment and Development of Non-Executive Directors* (London Business School 2003), 6–7.

[100] *ibid.*, 7.

[101] Lord Davies of Abersoch, *Women on Boards – February 2011* (Department of Business Innovation & Skills 2011).

should contain a description of the board's policy on diversity,[102] and that the board's annual evaluation should include a review of its diversity.[103] Also, following recent amendments influenced by EU requirements, boards of companies (other than those that are exempted by virtue of being subject to the small companies regime) are generally required to compile a strategic report that contains information including the female representation on the board and other hierarchical levels within the company.[104]

Heeding one of Lord Davies' recommendations, in 2011 the executive search industry also released a voluntary code of conduct to provide guidance on gender diversity and best practices and processes relating to director recruitment and appointments (with an enhanced code of conduct published in 2014).[105] Indeed, as the Tyson Report had also pointed out, the nature of the non-executive director recruitment process is part of the diversity problem. Board members are often selected based on informal contacts and friendships, and both companies and executive search firms tend to work with overly narrowly defined candidate profiles in considering new appointees. It was found that, as a result, the board appointment process is skewed in a manner that is unfavourable to women.[106]

Notable initiatives are also underway or have already been implemented outside the UK. For instance, various countries – including Spain, Italy and France – introduced quota for women on boards, with Norway pioneering a requirement that at least 40 per cent of a board's members are female.[107] In the US, the Dodd-Frank Act required various financial regulatory agencies to establish an Office of Minority and Women Inclusion as a means to promote diversity within the agencies themselves, businesses that supply or otherwise work with the agencies, and the financial industry entities that the agencies regulate.[108] Additionally, the United States Securities and Exchange Commission (SEC) has since 2010 required that US-listed companies disclose their policies on board diversity in the documents that they use to solicit shareholder votes on director appointments (proxy documents).[109]

---

[102] UK Corporate Governance Code, Principle B.2. and Provision B.2.4.

[103] *ibid.*, Principle B.6.

[104] See The Companies Act 2006 (Strategic Report and Directors' Report) Regulations 2014, inserting a new section 414C in the Companies Act 2006.

[105] See Department for Business, Innovation & Skills, *Women on Boards: Voluntary Code for Executive Search Firms – Taking the Next Step March 2014* (2014).

[106] See Tyson Report, above n. 99, 9.

[107] Choudhury, above n. 96, 23.

[108] Section 342 of the Dodd-Frank Act. A recently released policy statement with joint standards for assessing diversity policies and practices at the entities within their regulatory purview shows that the agencies opted for a 'light touch' approach. While the policy sets out a useful framework for promotion of diversity, it relies on a self-assessment process and voluntary disclosure of diversity measures of regulated financial industry businesses. *Final Interagency Policy Statement Establishing Joint Standards for Assessing the Diversity Policies and Practices of Entities Regulated by the Agencies* (2015), at www.sec.gov/rules/policy/2015/34-75050.pdf.

[109] See Securities and Exchange Commission, *Proxy Disclosure Enhancement*, at www.sec.gov/rules/final/2009/33-9089.pdf.

Finally, steps towards increased board diversity have also been taken at the European level. The EU's Capital Requirements Directive, effective from 2014, includes provisions to encourage diversity in management bodies of large banks and investment firms, with the aim being to improve monitoring and risk management.[110] These businesses are required to establish targets for gender representation and accompanying policies to promote those targets. Another Directive mandates that companies and groups exceeding an average of 500 employees disclose information on policies in relation to diversity, broadly defined, pertaining to their administrative, management and supervisory bodies.[111] Moreover, the EU is considering a proposed Directive that would establish a target of 40 per cent female non-executive directors on listed company boards by 2020.[112] Companies that fail to reach this target would be required to apply gender-neutral selection criteria in their selection process and give priority to the candidate of the underrepresented sex in cases of equal qualification.

At least for the time being, British companies are making progress in terms of enhanced board diversity. In a 2015 update, Lord Davies reported that FTSE 100 boards had moved close to his previously suggested 25 per cent target, finding that companies had reached the mark of 23.5 per cent female representation.[113] Davies remarked that he detected a 'profound culture change taking place on British boards' but also cautioned that an outright transformation of boards is a long-term task and that 'the job is not yet done'.[114] Female representation on boards is still lower in the US, where women hold fewer than 20 per cent of board seats in S&P 500 companies,[115] and commentators point to the slow pace of progress in this area.[116]

To conclude, it remains to be seen whether diversity will become a transformative board governance 'megatrend', comparable to board independence. It should also be noted that there is still little scholarly examination of the

---

[110] Directive 2013/36/EU of the European Parliament and of the Council of 26 June 2013 on access to the activity of credit institutions and the prudential supervision of credit institutions and investment firms (CRD IV). The Directive notes that a lack of monitoring is partly caused by groupthink, which in turn can be mitigated through diversity within management bodies (para. 60).

[111] Directive 2014/95/EU of the European Parliament and of the Council of 22 October 2014 on disclosure of non-financial and diversity information by certain large undertakings and groups.

[112] Proposal for a Directive of the European Parliament and of the Council on improving the gender balance among non-executive directors of companies listed on stock exchanges and related measures, COM(2012) 614 final (14 November 2012).

[113] Lord Davies of Abersoch, *Women on Boards – Davies Review Annual Report 2015* (2015). See also The Cranfield School of Management, *The Female FTSE Board Report 2015* (Cranfield University 2015).

[114] *Ibid.*, 3.

[115] Catalyst, *Women in S&P 500 Companies* (3 April 2015), at www.catalyst.org/knowledge/women-sp-500-companies.

[116] See e.g. B. Black 'Stalled: Gender Diversity on Corporate Boards' (2011) 37 *University of Daytona Law Review* 7.

effects of diversity on boards. Notably, the effects of diversity are difficult to capture and the few studies that have examined diversity and its impact on economic outcomes have arrived at conflicting conclusions.[117] While some studies hold that diversity on boards improves companies' financial performance or firm value, others hold that it does not. Nevertheless, diversity makes sense from the perspective of group-decision-making theory as well as based on equality considerations. Future developments will show the longevity of efforts to improve diversity and their impact on corporate governance.

---

[117] See Choudhury, above n. 96, 2–3 and 7.

CHAPTER 8

Internal Control and Risk Management

As we have seen in the previous chapter, a vital aspect of the modern corporate board's role is monitoring. This includes responsibility for what are often referred to as internal control and risk management. The following sections will discuss these concepts in greater detail, exploring their meaning and emergence in corporate governance in both the UK and the US. The chapter will subsequently examine directors' oversight liability: that is, individual board members' personal responsibility for breach of company law duties relating to risk management and oversight. To begin, however, we should note that in general the following discussion is applicable to companies operating in all industry sectors. It will therefore not solely – and, indeed, not in greater detail – be concerned with specific developments in the field of banking law and financial regulation, where risk management is particularly prevalent.[1]

INTERNAL CONTROL AND RISK MANAGEMENT – DEVELOPMENT AND DEFINITION

The term 'internal control' was historically used within the accounting profession, where it stood for a relatively minor detail of auditing practice.[2] The emergence of internal control and the related concept of risk management as important aspects of corporate governance are more recent phenomena that have continuously developed since the early 1990s.

In the UK, one of the first milestones in this regard was the seminal 1992 Cadbury Report, which contained principles directed at improving boards' control and reporting functions. Although Cadbury provided no explicit definition of 'internal control', its focus was on controls relating to accounting and

---

[1] For a discussion of these aspects, see K. Hopt, 'Corporate Governance of Banks and Other Financial Institutions after the Financial Crisis' (2013) 13(2) *Journal of Corporate Law Studies* 219; I.H.-Y. Chiu, 'Corporate Governance and Risk Management in Banks and Financial Institutions' in I.H.-Y. Chiu (ed.), *The Law of Corporate Governance in Banks* (Edward Elgar 2015) 169–95.

[2] See Committee on Law and Accounting, ABA 'Management Reports on Internal Control: A Legal Perspective' (1994) 49 *Business Lawyer* 889, 892. An early definition of internal control emerged in 1949 in a report issued by the American Institute of Certified Public Accountants. See *ibid.*, 892.

financial reporting.[3] However, Cadbury stopped short of giving any guidance on the criteria to determine an effective system of controls, or on the specific substantive matters (financial or otherwise) that should typically be included in the board's internal control statement. Cadbury took the view that it would be appropriate to rely on the accountancy profession itself to flesh out the Committee's basic recommendations on these issues in further detail.[4]

Subsequently, a working group was formed for this purpose. The group developed guidance – referred to as the Rutteman Report – on how boards could meet Cadbury's requirement to maintain an 'effective internal control system',[5] and in the process extended the concept's scope. The working group's approach, and by extension the Rutteman Report, covered all aspects of internal control, including controls to ensure effective and efficient operations and compliance with laws and regulations. It also introduced elements of risk management.[6] This approach was equally reflected in subsequent corporate governance initiatives, including the 1999 Turnbull[7] guidance on how companies should implement the internal control provisions in what would later become the UK Corporate Governance Code.

Based on the Turnbull principles, the Financial Reporting Council (FRC) began to issue its own guidelines on internal control and risk management. The most recent document is currently the FRC's Guidance on Risk Management, Internal Control and Related Financial and Business Reporting,[8] which replaced previous guidance[9] and reflects the latest Corporate Governance Code provisions.[10] The FRC Guidance takes an all-encompassing approach, combining internal control and risk management practices within a single systemic definition:

> The risk management and control systems encompass the policies, culture, organisation, behaviours, processes, systems and other aspects of a company that, taken together:
>
> • facilitate its effective and efficient operation by enabling it to assess current and emerging risks, respond appropriately to risks and significant control failures and to safeguard its assets;

---

[3] See The Cadbury Committee, *Report of the Committee on the Financial Aspects of Corporate Governance* (1 December 1992), paras 2.6., 2.7., 4.31, 5.16.

[4] *ibid.*, para. 5.16.

[5] See *ibid.*, para. 4.32.

[6] See *Internal Control and Financial Reporting: Guidance for Directors of Listed Companies Registered in the UK Issued by the Rutteman Working Group on Internal Controls in 1994* ('The Rutteman Report'); Committee on Corporate Governance, *Final Report* ('The Hampel Report') (January 1998), paras 6.10–6.13.

[7] *Internal Control: Guidance for Directors on the Combined Code* ('The Turnbull Report') (1999), para. 20.

[8] FRC, *Guidance on Risk Management, Internal Control and Related Financial and Business Reporting* (2014).

[9] Namely the FRC's 'Internal Control: Revised Guidance for Directors on the Combined Code' and 'Going Concern and Liquidity Risk: Guidance for Directors of UK Companies'.

[10] As reflected in the FRC's Boards and Risk Report and the Sharman Inquiry.

- help to reduce the likelihood and impact of poor judgement in decision-making; risk-taking that exceeds the levels agreed by the board; human error; or control processes being deliberately circumvented;
- help ensure the quality of internal and external reporting; and
- help ensure compliance with applicable laws and regulations, and also with internal policies with respect to the conduct of business.[11]

The UK's holistic approach to internal control and risk management has its roots in the US.[12] There, the most significant impulses for development of internal control originated from the National Commission on Fraudulent Financial Reporting, a private-sector initiative also known as the Treadway Commission. Formed in 1985 to study the financial reporting system in the United States, the Treadway Commission recommended in 1987 that its sponsoring organizations work together to integrate various internal control concepts and definitions.[13] As a result, another private-sector group, the Committee of Sponsoring Organizations (COSO) of the Treadway Commission, formed and undertook an extensive study of internal control to establish a common definition in view of the needs of companies, independent public accountants, legislators and regulatory agencies.

In 1992, COSO published an extensive and influential report on internal control, the Internal Control-Integrated Framework or 'COSO Report'.[14] The COSO Framework remains in place today, albeit in an updated 2013 version, and is one of the most widely recognized internal control frameworks. The COSO Report's definition of internal control, which served as the model for the corresponding definition in the UK's Turnbull guidance, is as follows:

> Internal control is a process, effected by an entity's board of directors, management, and other personnel, designed to provide reasonable assurance regarding achievement of objectives relating to operations, reporting, and compliance.[15]

Thus, the Framework distinguishes between three categories that internal control relates to, namely: (i) effectiveness and efficiency of operations; (ii) reliability of financial reporting; and (iii) legal compliance.[16] As the COSO Report explains,

---

[11] FRC, above n. 8, para. 28.

[12] See M. van Daelen, 'Risk Management from a Business Law Perspective' in M. van Daelen *et al.* (eds), *Risk Management and Corporate Governance* (Edward Elgar 2010) 69–70.

[13] National Commission on Fraudulent Financial Reporting, *Report of the National Commission on Fraudulent Reporting* (1987), 48, at http://www.coso.org/Publications/NCFFR.pdf.

[14] Committee of Sponsoring Organizations of the Treadway Commission, *Internal Control-Integrated Framework* (1992).

[15] COSO, *Internal Control – Integrated Framework: Executive Summary* (2013) 3, at http://www.coso.org/documents/990025P_Executive_Summary_final_may20_e.pdf.

[16] Similarly, the FRC has noted that while risks will differ between companies, typical examples include financial, operational, reputational, behavioural, organizational and third party risks. In addition, companies will face external risks, such as market or regulatory risk, over which the board may have little or no direct control. FRC, above n. 8, para. 28.

the first category addresses an entity's basic business objectives, including performance and profitability goals and safeguarding of resources. The second relates to the preparation of reliable published financial statements, including interim and condensed financial statements and selected financial data derived from such statements, such as earnings releases, reported publicly. The third deals with complying with those laws and regulations to which the entity is subject.[17] Internal control in this sense encompasses virtually all vital aspects of a corporation's business.

In 2004, in response to an increased focus on risk management and in addition to its existing Internal Control Framework, COSO also published the Enterprise Risk Management – Integrated Framework.[18] According to the Framework's definition:

> Enterprise risk management is a process, effected by an entity's board of directors, management and other personnel, applied in strategy setting and across the enterprise, designed to identify potential events that may affect the entity, and manage risk to be within its risk appetite, to provide reasonable assurance regarding the achievement of entity objectives.[19]

Given that according to COSO enterprise risk management should improve reporting and compliance with laws and regulations, while also mitigating reputational risks, the question arises as to the nature of the relationship between COSO's Enterprise Risk Management Framework and its Internal Control Framework. More broadly, this also raises the question as to how internal control and risk management relate to each other in general, including within a business organization.

COSO has in this respect stated that while the Enterprise Risk Management Framework and the Internal Control Framework are both useful by themselves, the Enterprise Risk Management Framework 'incorporates the internal control framework within it' and 'expands on internal control, providing a more robust and extensive focus on the broader subject of enterprise risk management'.[20] This is similar to the FRC's approach, which (as discussed above) combines internal control and risk management. Indeed, the FRC has noted that '[effective] controls are an *important element of* the systems of risk management and internal control and can cover many aspects of a business, including strategic, financial, operational and compliance'.[21] In other words, internal control is one of the components of risk management, while at the same time identification of risks is also an element of an effective internal control system.[22]

---

[17] COSO, above n 15.

[18] See COSO, *Enterprise Risk Management Framework – Executive Summary* (2004), at http://www.coso.org/documents/coso_erm_executivesummary.pdf.

[19] *ibid.*, 2.

[20] *ibid.*, Foreword.

[21] FRC, above n. 8, para. 37 (emphasis added).

[22] In practice, of course, it is not the theoretical classification that counts, but rather that adequately designed systems that cover all relevant aspects of internal control and risk management are in place.

CORPORATE DISCLOSURE AND INTERNAL CONTROL/RISK MANAGEMENT

Corporate governance as a system depends in large part on the flow of information between companies and third parties. For example, investors on primary and secondary markets as well as lenders will normally base their decision on whether or not – or under what conditions – to invest in or extend a loan on an assessment of a company's financial and operational 'health'. Consequently, in order to appropriately evaluate the risk associated with their decision and to determine the price/interest rate at which they are willing to invest or lend, these actors need reliable corporate information. A central aspect of corporate governance is therefore informational disclosure.

Following the notion that 'daylight' – in the form of transparency – 'is the best of disinfectants',[23] companies in the UK (and, of course, other jurisdictions) are subject to different layers of disclosure requirements.[24] Among others – and in part depending on an entity's size and status as a private, public or listed company – companies have to maintain adequate accounting records and publicly file periodic accounts and reports containing financial and non-financial information.[25] For instance, reporting requirements for UK listed companies now include the financial statement, strategic report,[26] directors' report, corporate governance statement[27] and directors' remuneration report, which together comprise the company's annual report. Additionally, listed companies have to publicly report certain material information and events on an ongoing basis.[28]

From an internal control and risk management perspective, the financial statement, strategic report and directors' report are of particular importance. While the financial statement includes as its essential elements a company's balance sheet and income statement, the strategic report helps to provide context and explanations to the related financial statements. It also includes a description of

---

[23] Former US Supreme Court Justice Brandeis has famously remarked that '[s]unlight is said to be the best of disinfectants; electric light the most efficient policeman'. L. Brandeis, *Other People's Money and How the Bankers Use It* (National Home Library Foundation 1933), 62.

[24] The requirements in this respect are in main part regulated by Part 15 of the UK Companies Act 2006, and (for listed companies) the FCA's Listing Rules and Disclosure Rules and Transparency Rules (DTR).

[25] Part 15 of the Companies Act 2006 distinguishes between micro-entities, small companies, medium-sized companies, unquoted public companies and quoted companies, with the complexity of reporting requirements increasing with an entity's economic size and public/quoted status. The company size classification is generally determined by thresholds relating to turnover, balance sheet total and number of employees.

[26] Introduced by the Companies Act 2006 (Strategic Report and Directors' Report) Regulations 2013.

[27] Being the statement required by rules 7.2.1 to 7.2.11 of the DTR. DTR rule 7.2.5 includes the requirement to provide a description of the main features of an issuer's internal control and risk management systems in relation to the financial reporting process.

[28] On the pervasiveness of quarterly financial reporting within UK corporate governance (in spite of recent regulatory and policy initiatives aimed at curtailing this practice), see Chapter 5.

the principal risks and uncertainties that a company faces. The directors' report includes a confirmation that, so far as the directors are aware, all relevant audit information has been disclosed to the company's auditors, with directors facing the threat of personal liability in the event of an untrue statement.[29]

Disclosure and reporting is only of value to investors, creditors and other parties if they can rely on the information provided. Given the importance of disclosure and the potential for fraudulent manipulation of financial statements by managers (also known as 'cooking the books'), the law has long required an external independent audit function to ensure the accuracy and integrity of corporate accounts and reports. As a case decided under the Companies Act 1879 noted, the requirement for audited accounts is designed, primarily, to provide shareholders with 'independent and reliable information respecting the true financial position of the company at the time of the audit'.[30] Today, Part 16 of the Companies Act 2006 contains detailed provisions regarding a company's audit obligations, including the requirement for audited accounts and its exemptions, the appointment and removal of auditors, and the function and liability of auditors. Additional requirements for listed companies are contained in the Listing Rules.

Despite these longstanding audit requirements, a series of corporate scandals, spanning roughly from the 1990s to the early 2000s, in both the UK and the US – Maxwell, Polly Peck, Enron, WorldCom and others – have made it clear that widespread problems with financial reporting and auditing existed.[31] A stark illustration in this regard is the demise of Enron. In 2001, Enron shocked investors and capital markets by unexpectedly announcing a $544 million charge against earnings and a $1.2 billion reduction in shareholders' equity. Enron also restated its financial statements for the periods from 1997 to 2001 due to accounting errors.[32] Shortly thereafter, Enron was forced to file for insolvency protection. Enron's special board committee would later find deficiencies in oversight and internal controls at both management and board levels[33] as well as a breach of professional duties on the part of the company's outside auditor,

---

[29] Section 418 of the Companies Act 2006. However, see further below in this chapter on the safe harbour provisions under section 463 of the Act.

[30] *Re London and General Bank (No 2)* [1895] 2 CH 673, Lindley LJ.

[31] In the foreword to his committee's report, Sir Adrian Cadbury noted how concerns about standards of financial reporting and accountability, heightened by corporate scandals, have kept corporate governance in the public eye. Cadbury Committee, above n. 3.

[32] W.C. Powers *et al., Report of Investigation by the Special Investigation Committee of the Board of Directors of Enron Corporation* (2002). Helpful further discussion of the Enron scandal and its impact include J.C. Coffee, 'Understanding Enron: It's About the Gatekeepers, Stupid' (2002) 57 *Business Lawyer* 1403; C.M. Elson and C.J. Gyves, 'The Enron Failure and Corporate Governance Reform' (2003) 38 *Wake Forest Law Review* 855; D. Kershaw, 'Waiting for Enron: The Unstable Equilibrium of Auditor Independence Regulation' (2006) 33 *Journal of Law and Society* 388.

[33] The committee was tasked with investigating transactions between Enron and special purpose entities created under the direction of its former Executive Vice President and Chief Financial Officer.

Arthur Andersen.[34] These multiple breakdowns had allowed Enron to report a string of misleading information to its investors and the public.

The most recent major corporate shock wave, caused by the 2007–08 financial crisis and its effects, once more triggered a renewed emphasis on the importance of board oversight. After all, board passivity in oversight and, specifically, risk management programmes is often viewed as one of the crisis' contributing elements.[35] In addition, while the financial crisis did not involve blatant financial manipulation and illegal activities,[36] it has been revealed that questionable accounting practices might have played a role in the collapse of Lehman Brothers,[37] one of the financial institutions at the centre of the crisis. As a result, not just boards' risk oversight, but also their specific responsibility to monitor accounting and general legal compliance, have once again come under closer scrutiny.

In response to Enron and other corporate scandals, regulators – internationally – took various actions. These actions included measures aimed at improving the reliability of corporate disclosures and, as a corollary, internal control and risk management. Additional impulses and regulatory initiatives were triggered by the 2007–08 financial crisis. While the resulting measures were multi-faceted and applied to various corporate actors and gatekeepers, the following sections will focus on corporate boards and changes to their internal control and risk management obligations vis-à-vis their companies and investors.[38]

THE BOARD'S EVOLVING INTERNAL CONTROL/RISK MANAGEMENT FUNCTION

Before the 2007–08 Financial Crisis

Regulatory recognition of UK company boards' internal control and risk management function began in 1992, when – as already briefly mentioned above – Sir Adrian Cadbury's corporate governance committee highlighted

---

[34] Powers and others, above n 32.

[35] See, for example, FSA, *The Turner Review: A Regulatory Response to the Global Financial Crisis* (2009), 92; D. Walker, *A Review of Corporate Governance in Banks and Other Financial Industry Entities: Final Recommendations* (26 November 2009), 220, 225–26, 231; Hopt, above n. 1, 222; S.M. Bainbridge, 'Caremark and Enterprise Risk Management' (2009) 34 *Journal of Corporation Law* 967, 968 (2009); E.J. Pan, 'Board's Duty to Monitor' (2010) 54 *New York Law School Law Review* 717; M.M. Harner, 'Ignoring the Writing on the Wall: The Role of Enterprise Risk Management in the Economic Crisis' (2010) 5 *Journal of Business & Technology Law* 45, 48–52.

[36] See B.R. Cheffins, 'Did Corporate Governance "Fail" during the 2008 Stock Market Meltdown? – The Case of the S&P 500' (2009) 65 *Business Lawyer* 1, 28–30. Of course, this does not mean that there were no instances of managerial wrongdoing in the period leading up to the crisis.

[37] See *Lehman Brothers Holdings Inc. Chapter 11 Proceedings Examiner's Report, vol 3* (2010), at http://lehmanreport.jenner.com (discussing the use of so-called 'Repo 105' transactions). Note, however, that the Report did not find colourable claims that Lehman's directors breached their fiduciary duty by failing to monitor the firm's risk-taking activities.

[38] Another aspect of board governance that has evolved over time and through various corporate crises, namely directors' independence, has already been discussed in Chapter 7.

the key importance of effective internal control for efficient company manage-ment.[39] The Cadbury Report stressed that all directors, whether or not they have executive responsibilities, have a monitoring role and are responsible for ensuring that the necessary controls over the activities of their companies are in place and working.[40] On this basis, the Report recommended that direc-tors should provide a statement in the company's annual accounts and report detailing the effectiveness of the company's system of internal control. It also suggested that the company's auditors should provide an opinion on the effectiveness of the internal control system in their annual report.[41] Consistent with Cadbury's express remit to focus on the financial aspects of governance, the Committee's exclusive concern with internal corporate controls was their effectiveness in ensuring that adequate accounting records were maintained on an enterprise-wide basis. This essentially required boards to put in place effective intra-firm monitoring systems to detect the occurrence of accounting lapses, irregularities, mis-statements or fraud at all levels within the corporate structure.[42]

Although taking the form of a disclosure obligation rather than a direct pre-scriptive requirement, and even then as enforceable on a 'comply or explain' basis only, Cadbury's recognition of the board's responsibility for internal financial controls nevertheless represented a significant corporate governance development for its time. While successive UK Companies Acts have histori-cally vested boards with ultimate collective responsibility for the preparation and approval of annual accounts,[43] it has been a comparably longstanding feature of British company law that the board of a company is at liberty to delegate executive functions (including the maintenance of intra-firm account-ing records), and in the absence of grounds for suspicion to trust that those responsibilities will be duly fulfilled.[44] Given these low standards Cadbury's acceptance of internal control as an intrinsic element of the modern board's agenda signalled a significant change and the beginning of the end for the traditional 'see no evil, hear no evil' understanding of directors' monitoring responsibilities, at least insofar as financial accounting issues were concerned.

Cadbury's recommendations on internal control were developed to a limited extent in the subsequent corporate governance enquiry led by Sir Ronnie Hampel in 1998, which prefaced the implementation of the first Combined Code on Corporate Governance in 2000. Although the subject of directo-rial risk management was not of foremost concern to Hampel, his review

---

[39] Cadbury Committee, above n. 3, para. 3.1. While Cadbury's Code of Best Practice was directed to the boards of directors of all listed companies registered in the UK, the committee encouraged other companies to also aim at meeting its requirements.

[40] Cadbury, above n. 3, para. 1.8.

[41] *ibid.*, para. 4.32.

[42] See Cadbury Committee, above n. 3, para. 4.31.

[43] These requirements are currently set out in sections 394, 399, and 414 of the Companies Act 2006.

[44] See *Re City Equitable Fire Insurance Co Ltd* [1925] Ch 407.

committee nevertheless reiterated the expectation established by Cadbury that boards 'maintain a sound system of internal control to safeguard shareholders' investment and the company's assets'.[45] Moreover, in line with the approach taken by the accountancy profession's earlier Rutteman Report, Hampel's recommendation extended not just to financial controls but also to operational and compliance controls and risk management.[46] However, as with Cadbury's earlier suggestion, Hampel left the more specific details of appropriate internal control and risk management practices to be developed elsewhere.[47]

In 1999, the accounting profession[48] established a committee to further develop the Rutteman Report and formulate guidance on internal control and risk management.[49] As mentioned above, the purpose of this guidance, which became known popularly as the Turnbull Report, was to aid boards in interpreting those principles of the forthcoming Combined Code that pertained to internal control and risk issues. In particular, Turnbull was designed to guide directors in complying with the Code requirement to provide a narrative report to shareholders on the effectiveness of the company's (or, where relevant, the overall group's) system of internal control in respect of both financial and non-financial matters.

Like its predecessor corporate governance reports, Turnbull still dedicated special attention to the issue of financial controls including the maintenance of proper accounting records, which it regarded to be crucial for ensuring that: (i) the company is not exposed to avoidable financial risks; (ii) financial information used within the business and for publication is reliable; and (iii) fraud is detected and prevented, and corporate assets safeguarded.[50] As regards the controls that were appropriate for other, particularly non-financial, risks that might typically materialize in the course of a company's business operations, however, Turnbull was deliberately unspecific. The Report also failed to provide any specific examples of risks (other than accounting-based ones) that it would be appropriate to include within the board's report on internal control. Instead, this task devolved in the first place to individual corporate compliance departments working in conjunction with their company's accountant and external auditor, with the board assuming responsibility for the final content of the report once produced.

---

[45] Committee on Corporate Governance, above n. 6, para. 2.20.

[46] *ibid.*, para. 2.20.

[47] The Cadbury and Hampel Reports' recommendations on the issue of internal control were manifested in Principle D.2 of the inaugural 2000 edition of the Combined Code on Corporate Governance, which notably provided the first affirmative recommendation that '[t]he board should maintain a sound system of internal control to safeguard shareholders' investment and the company's assets'. Principle D.2.1 expanded on this by recommending that '[t]he directors should, at least annually, conduct a review of the effectiveness of the group's system of internal control and should report to shareholders that they have done so', whilst the review itself 'should cover all controls, including financial, operational and compliance controls and risk management'.

[48] Specifically, the Institute of Chartered Accountants in England and Wales.

[49] Turnbull Report, above n. 7.

[50] *ibid.*, para. 12.

Turnbull did not consider there to be a need for companies to establish a special risk or internal control committee to handle such issues, but rather believed that boards should determine to what extent it is appropriate to delegate internal control responsibilities to existing committees – especially audit committees – depending on the nature of the matters in question.[51] However, Turnbull elided discussion as to what extent audit committees were qualified to pass judgement on the effectiveness of risk management systems unrelated to financial accounting practices.

Subsequent regulatory developments at the turn of the century provided little assistance on the above matters and, if anything, served to further emphasize the centricity of financial accounting issues within boards' risk management agenda. With the shadow of the abovementioned Enron bankruptcy in 2001 looming large over the global corporate governance horizon, regulators across both the US and Europe introduced a host of measures aimed principally at resolving the 'gatekeeper' failures – particularly those by boards and auditors – that were widely perceived to be the core cause of Enron's collapse.[52] Thus the main British regulatory response to Enron's collapse, namely the 2003 Higgs and Smith Committees' dual recommendations on revision of the (then) Combined Code – emphasized above all the need to resolve the structural conflicts of interest that had hitherto constrained the supervisory effectiveness of non-executive directors and external auditing firms.[53]

Higgs strengthened the role of non-executive directors with regards to financial controls and risk management[54] while Smith's proposals led to new provisions on board structure and auditors, including a requirement for boards to establish audit committees, composed of independent non-executive directors, with internal control and risk management responsibilities.[55] The British reform committees did not at this time suggest the establishment of mandatory risk committees. These were (and generally remain today) optional, with the default rule being that in their absence a company's audit committee or the full board will be in charge of internal control and risk management issues.[56]

---

[51] *ibid.*, para. 26.

[52] On the concept of 'gatekeepers', see J.C. Coffee, *Gatekeepers: The Role of the Professions in Corporate Governance* (OUP 2006). However, for an alternative interpretation of Enron's collapse principally as a failure of internal control over risks inherent in the company's business plan, see S. Deakin and S.J. Konzelmann, 'Learning from Enron' (2004) 12 *Corporate Governance: An International Review* 134.

[53] Deakin and Konzelmann, above n. 52, 141.

[54] See the Higgs Report: *Review of the Role and Effectiveness of Non-Executive Directors* (January 2003), 27, proposing a new Code provision A.1.4 requiring non-executive directors to satisfy themselves that financial information is accurate and that financial controls and systems of risk management are robust and defensible. In the latest version of the UK Corporate Governance Code, this is reflected in Supporting Principle A.4.

[55] See *Audit Committees: Combined Code Guidance* ('The Smith Report') (January 2003), paras 2–3. Today, this is contained in UK Corporate Governance Code Principle C.3.

[56] UK Corporate Governance Code Provision C.3.2. See, however, further below on the Walker Report's recommendations for banks and financial institutions.

In 2005, the Financial Reporting Council's review of the Turnbull Report concluded that the guidance therein had been highly successful in achieving its objectives, and had precipitated a marked improvement in the general quality of risk management and internal control.[57] Therefore, the FRC's Review Group recommended preserving the bulk of the original Turnbull guidance while suggesting only incremental amendments for the purpose of the revised 2005 edition of the Report. Over the course of the next three years, however, events were to unfold that would trigger enormous changes in the way that the corporate risk management function had conventionally been perceived by regulators and boards, in terms of its relative profile within corporate governance as a whole and also the much greater breadth of governance responsibilities that the term would come to encapsulate.

After the Financial Crisis: The Walker Report

The circumstances of the UK banking crisis that took place over much of 2007 and 2008 hardly need recounting; suffice to say that from a risk management perspective both the consequences and the causes of the corporate failures involved were truly remarkable. The consequences of the collapse (and subsequent public rescue) of institutions such as Northern Rock, RBS, HBOS and Bradford & Bingley were largely unprecedented in terms of the scale of the primary (proprietary) losses incurred by shareholders,[58] the severity of the secondary (systemic) consequences for banking liquidity and financial market stability, and the sheer breadth and longevity of the tertiary (macro-economic) consequences that followed from the UK government's extensive programmes of nationalization and cost for the public.[59]

As regards the underlying causes of the major corporate failures involved, the circumstances of the banking crisis were equally remarkable insofar as the managerial activities that brought about those failures were – in contrast to the earlier scandals around the turn of the millennium – not one-off, peripheral or rogue phenomena, such as accounting fraud, asset misappropriation or

---

[57] See *Internal Control: Revised Guidance for Directors on the Combined Code* (2005), at www.ecgi.org/codes/documents/frc_ic.pdf.

[58] The House of Commons Treasury Committee recorded that over the period from 2 April 2007 to 6 April 2009, the total market capitalization of the UK's FTSE 100 banking companies decreased from £316.9 billion to £138.1 billion, representing an astonishing 56% loss of shareholder value. See House of Commons Treasury Committee, 'Banking Crisis: Dealing with the Failure of the UK Banks' (21 April 2009), 7.

[59] Out of the nine UK banks that were in the FTSE 100 immediately prior to the onset of the crisis in March 2007, five were subsequently taken either wholly or partially into public ownership, namely Bradford & Bingley, HBOS, Lloyds TSB, Northern Rock and RBS. See also E. Avgouleas, 'The Global Financial Crisis, Behavioural Finance and Financial Regulation: In Search of a New Orthodoxy' (2009) 9 *Journal of Corporate Law Studies* 23, 25, noting the costs of public rescues and liquidity support.

other types of manifest misconduct. Nor was the bulk of the conduct involved deemed to be problematic in terms of financial regulatory compliance.[60]

Rather, as is now widely acknowledged, the major banking company failures of 2007 and 2008 were, in addition to various external factors, attributable to practices that were regarded at the time as an intrinsic and valuable part of the strategic operations of the firms involved, and a core source of their competitive advantage. In essence, these ranged from leveraged high-volume lending dependent on short-term funding from wholesale money markets; securitization and/or trading practices involving financial instruments backed by US-based sub-prime mortgages; and highly leveraged acquisitions of rival firms based on what was later perceived to be a limited degree of *a priori* due diligence.

In view of the centrality of these practices and their associated risks to the respective business models of the relevant firms, the ensuing corporate failures and wider socio-economic implications thereof would necessitate a fundamental rethink in how key risks are identified and controlled within large and complex business organizations, both in the financial services sector and beyond. Above all, a general public perception developed to the effect that 'governance failures contributed materially to excessive risk taking in the lead up to the financial crisis'.[61] With this consideration in mind, an underlying theme of the subsequent regulatory initiatives was an expectation that outside directors be equipped to provide informed contribution and challenge to a company's management on high-level strategic issues, with a view to identifying developing or latent risks in business models and proposed transactions. The major regulatory implication, as will be documented below, has been the establishment of more rigorous norms in relation to the competencies, time commitment and responsibilities of independent non-executive directors in UK listed companies, principally with a view to repositioning the board's risk oversight role.

Prior to 2007, there was arguably a tendency for companies to perceive risk management as being exclusively or mainly concerned with the 'external' or ancillary risks arising from a firm's business activities. Typical examples are the risk of incurring liability for regulatory non-compliance (including breach of capital adequacy, environmental or health and safety laws), or the risk of destroying valuable reputational capital as a result of accounting malpractice or other forms of unethical business conduct. This, in turn, led to a common perception of internal control/risk management as being a separable governance function that could be devolved to compliance departments under the

---

[60] One commentator has noted that 'though the U.S. system of corporate governance did not perform optimally during its 2008 stress test, along key dimensions it performed tolerably well under very difficult conditions. The case for fundamental reform is thus not yet made out.' Cheffins, above n. 36, 61.

[61] D. Walker, A Review of Corporate Governance in Banks and Other Financial Industry Entities: Final Recommendations (26 November 2009), 8.

supervision of independent auditors, largely in distinction from the board's 'core' responsibility for high-level strategic affairs.

However, in the context of the wider regulatory developments in this area, the board's internal control remit after the crisis can, in general, be said to have shifted from one of risk management – denoting the mitigation of the extraneous adverse effects of business activities (with limited questioning of the viability of those underlying practices themselves) – to one of risk *moderation*. Risk moderation in this sense means that the inherent riskiness of a firm's core entrepreneurial activities and management culture is placed at the very centre of its risk compass, to be independently evaluated alongside other more conventional subjects of risk-related scrutiny. Put differently, there has been a heightened focus within corporate governance on controlling the 'core' entrepreneurial risks that emanate directly from a company's business model,[62] which is in distinction from ancillary or consequential risks that arise as an indirect consequence of the firm's activities (such as accounting, compliance or reputational risk), which were the prevalent theme within pre-financial crisis regulatory initiatives.

The political switch for the post-crisis corporate governance reforms was triggered in February 2009, when the UK's then Prime Minister Gordon Brown commissioned Sir David Walker, former chairman of the Bank of England, to consult and provide recommendations on appropriate boardroom norms for the UK banking sector. The review was thereafter extended to cover all listed UK-based banks and other financial industry entities, collectively referred to as 'BOFIs'.[63] In an attempt to prevent recurrence of the types of highly risky trading and financing strategies that had led to corporate failures, Walker was given an explicit mandate by the Prime Minister to examine 'the effectiveness of risk management at board level' and 'the balance of skills, experience and independence required on the boards of UK banking institutions'.[64]

Key Implications of Walker

Walker's final recommendations were published in November 2009. Initial suggestions to put these norms on a formal legislative footing were rejected, and Walker opted instead to establish a convention of 'comply or explain' for

---

[62] On the phenomenon of 'core' or 'principal' risks as they arise in the context of non-financial and financial businesses respectively, see *ibid.*, para. 6.3.

[63] The review was initially restricted to banking corporations, but was subsequently extended to cover other major financial institutions whose activities were deemed to have comparably profound external consequences. Specifically, Walker's recommendations apply to UK-based BOFIs that either: (i) are listed on the London Stock Exchange or (ii) are subsidiaries of a parent company that is listed elsewhere. The recommendations also apply as a matter of best practice to UK-listed holding companies of unlisted FCA-authorized subsidiaries, and Walker has further suggested that other BOFIs outside of the above categories should be encouraged to take account of his recommendation. See Walker, above n. 61, para. 1.22.

[64] *ibid.*, 5.

enforcement of his recommendations.[65] Accordingly, BOFI boards are now expected to report annually on their record of compliance with the Walker recommendations and provide reasons in support of any instances of non-compliance, in a fundamentally similar manner to how the UK's mainstream Corporate Governance Code is enforced. In addition, many of Walker's recommendations have now been incorporated in financial regulation provisions.[66] As we will discuss below, the recommendations have also influenced the generally applicable principles contained in the Corporate Governance Code, thereby extending in part to non-financial companies as well.

The key recommendations of Walker in respect of boards' evolving risk oversight role concentrated on four areas: (i) improving non-executive directors' knowledge and understanding of strategic risk issues in BOFIs; (ii) greater expected time commitment of BOFI non-executive directors and chairmen; (iii) establishment of specialist risk committees on BOFI boards; and (iv) appointment of high-level chief risk officers in BOFIs.

Knowledge

First, Walker observed that the existing corporate governance regime's focus on directorial independence had come at the expense of knowledge and relevant expertise. He therefore suggested that 'financial industry experience and independence of mind' should be more important factors than simply 'formal' independence of non-executive directors.[67] For non-executive BOFI chairmen, Walker even recommended that as a general norm they should have relevant financial industry expertise, preferably as a result of a previous significant board position in the sector.[68] Walker also emphasized the importance of appropriate induction and training in the enhancement of non-executive directors' knowledge, leading him to recommend thematic business awareness sessions and the provision of dedicated internal support for non-executives.[69]

Time Commitment

Second, Walker's Final Report recommended that non-executive directors of FTSE 100 banks or life assurance companies should dedicate more time to their role than was customary in the past. While the Report did not provide specifics on the precise commitment that was seen as appropriate, a previous draft of the Report had suggested that non-executives of BOFI companies commit at least 30–36 days per year to one company and that BOFI chairmen dedicate

---

[65] *ibid.*, paras 2.15–2.19.

[66] See Chiu, above n. 1, 175, 180.

[67] Walker, above n. 61, 12. Nevertheless, Walker was alert to the danger of groupthink developing between executives and non-executives with an industry-specific background and also emphasized the importance of maintaining a degree of diversity on the board in order to encourage independence of mind and alternative perspectives. *ibid.*, para. 2.17.

[68] *ibid.*, Recommendation 8.

[69] *ibid.*, Recommendations 1 and 2.

'probably not less than two-thirds' of their time.[70] The Final Report loosened these requirements, substituting the 30–36 days guideline with a more flexible approach and changed the recommendation on the expected two-thirds time commitment for chairmen from a 'bottom end' expectation to a rough average norm.[71] Nevertheless, Walker amplified that the Chairman role should have priority over any other business time commitment.[72]

Risk Committees
Third, in addition to more stringent requirements concerning non-executive directors' competencies and time commitment, Walker recommended that BOFI boards establish a specialist risk committee to provide oversight and advice to the board on the company's or group's current risk exposures and future strategy in respect of risk.[73] The risk committee should be constituted separately from the audit committee and compliance function of the company, and should comprise a majority of non-executive directors including a non-executive chair. This was in contrast to previous British corporate governance reform committees, which – outside of the specific context of financial institutions – regarded the establishment of risk committees as optional and as a matter of discretion exercised by the full board.

A significant factor behind Walker's recommendation of dedicated risk committees in BOFIs was his recognition of the inherent complexity of the risk management task within financial institutions. Walker highlighted the distinction between measurable risks and 'other' risks (especially financial risks) that are unforeseeable or uncertain.[74] He emphasized the differences between these risks and that each type demands different institutional responses. According to Walker, measurable risks (such as changes in interest rates, inflation or currency valuations) can be predicted with reasonable dependency via *ex ante* financial probability measures based on historical experience, and not to do so would constitute a clear breach of the board's responsibilities. However, the category of 'other' risks is impossible to determine in light of past experience, either because a risk was previously unknown (such as the complete drying up of liquidity in a particular market, or the consequences of expansion into a new product market) or because a risk manifests itself in a very different or more

---

[70] See Walker's initial review consultation document, *A Review of Corporate Governance in Banks and other Financial Industry Entities* (2009) Recommendations 3 and 7, at www.ecgi. org/codes/documents/walker_review_consultation_16july2009.pdf.

[71] Walker, above n. 61, Recommendations 3 and 7.

[72] *ibid.*, Recommendation 7.

[73] *ibid.*, Recommendation 23.

[74] For the classical economic exposition of the distinction between risks and uncertainty, see F.H. Knight, *Risk, Uncertainty, and Profit* (Houghton & Mifflin 1921). Interestingly, Sir David Walker has recently stated that if he were to write his 2009 report again, he would include 'soft' risks stemming from bank culture as well as cyber crime. See 'A Banking Grandee's Rethink on the Rules of the Game', *Financial Times*, 10 December 2014, at www. ft.com/cms/s/0/e6cf88ac-7fa4-11e4-b4f5-00144feabdc0.html.

extensive way than was previously understood (for example where a stressed market environment causes the value of an asset or liability to change unexpectedly).[75] In particular, Walker highlighted the inevitable difficulty of foreseeing low-probability but high-impact occurrences.[76] Accordingly, he advocated that, in assessing current risk exposures, risk committees should draw not just on data pertaining to the current and prospective macro-economic and financial environment, but should also engage in rigorous periodic 'stress testing' aimed at determining the circumstances in which the entity may fail and the mechanisms to mitigate this risk. In essence, stress testing entails simulating a diverse range of worst-case scenarios for a business and determining appropriate countermeasures.

As a further important function of a BOFI risk committee, Walker stated its responsibility for compiling an annual risk report. This report should be separate from the annual directors' report, describing the strategy of the entity in a risk management context (including its key risk exposures), the risk tolerance of the entity, and the scope and outcome of the board's annual stress testing programme.[77] The risk committee of a BOFI also has a particular responsibility to scrutinize any major new product launch or initiative, and to report any concerns that they have about it to the full board.[78] Finally, a BOFI's risk committee should also oversee an appropriate due diligence appraisal in respect of a prospective takeover or other major asset acquisition or disposal proposed by management, so as to determine and then report to the board on whether the transaction is likely to be in the long-term interests of the company and its shareholders.[79]

Whilst the risk committee is not expected to have the same degree of up-to-date firm and industry expertise as a company's executive, the expectation is that the committee will be briefed by its chair in a succinct manner, enabling its members to focus on the major strategic issues without risk of 'information overload'. Moreover, in conformance with their duty of care, skill and diligence as directors, the risk committee's members must seek appropriate external advice in the same way that audit and remuneration committees have become accustomed to using independent auditors and remuneration consultants respectively.[80] Nevertheless, the risk committee is ultimately dependent on the company's board (and, in turn, its senior management) for information on

---

[75] Walker, above n. 61, para. 6.5. For a broader discussion of the limitations of risk management, see L. Enriques and D. Zetsche, 'The Risky Business of Regulating Risk Management in Listed Companies' (2013) 10(3) *European Company and Financial Law Review* 271, 282–88.
[76] Such as the immediate effective closure of wholesale money markets that occurred in the case of Northern Rock. See also N.N. Taleb, *The Black Swan – The Impact of the Highly Improbable* (Penguin 2008) (arguing that too much weight is placed on the odds that past events will repeat while really important events are rare and unpredictable).
[77] Walker, above n. 61, Recommendation 27.
[78] *ibid.*, para. 6.12.
[79] *ibid.*, Recommendation 26 and para. 6.23.
[80] *ibid.*, Recommendation 25.

the company's ongoing business affairs, thus inevitably restricting the committee's capacity to act as an autonomous informational hub in itself.

Chief Risk Officers

Walker's final key recommendation in respect of non-executive directors' responsibilities was that BOFI boards should be served by a specialist Chief Risk Officer (CRO), who should participate in the risk management and oversight process at the highest level on an enterprise-wide basis, and should have a status of total independence from individual business units.[81] The CRO should report to the board risk committee and have direct access to the chair of the risk committee where need arises, such as where the CRO has a difference of opinion with the CEO or finance director about the viability of a new product launch or financing method. Moreover, the CRO should have an internal reporting line to the company's CEO or finance director, and thus should be perceived as an influential high-level counterweight to a dominant senior management team. In particular, the CRO is responsible for determining whether a proposed product launch of a BOFI, or the pricing of risk in respect of a particular transaction, is consistent with the entity's risk tolerance as determined by its risk committee and board. Where the CRO is unsatisfied that agreed risk tolerance levels have been adhered to, she should have power of veto over the initiative in question irrespective of the views of the CEO or finance director. To affirm the CRO's independent and high-level status within the company's governance hierarchy, she should be removable only with the agreement of the board as a whole and her overall remuneration package should be reflective of the significance of her role.

The express seniority of the CRO office as it was set out by Walker follows from concerns that the balance of power on banking company boards had previously been set too heavily on the side of the CEO and his management team, with insufficient influence afforded to the company's risk and compliance functions.[82] Ultimately, however, the success of CROs depends on the extent to which they are viewed as an integral component of an effective entrepreneurial decision-making process, as opposed to a mere bureaucratic necessity or perfunctory impediment to management carrying out its pre-determined plans.[83] Moreover, it is essential for their effectiveness that CROs are regarded to be supportive of the board's ultimate collective responsibility for risk management, rather than part of a 'blame-shifting' strategy to deflect responsibility

---

[81] *ibid.*, Recommendation 24. Although Walker was not explicit about whether the CRO position should be regarded as an executive or non-executive position, previous practice would suggest that it is likely to entail an executive with a full-time commitment albeit with a material degree of detachment from other senior officers.

[82] The problem was summed up most succinctly by Paul Moore, former Head of Group Regulatory Risk at HBOS, who described his experience in this position as 'a bit like being a man in a rowing boat trying to slow down an oil tanker'. On this, see House of Commons Treasury Committee, above n. 58, 24.

[83] See Walker, above n. 61, para. 6.17.

for a company's key risk exposures from the CEO and other senior managerial personnel.[84]

The FRC's Post-Crisis Reforms to the UK Corporate Governance Code

Although the Walker consultation was specifically concerned with banks and other financial institutions, it left open for subsequent consideration whether the Financial Reporting Council should extend any or all of its recommendations so as to apply also to non-financial companies as part of the UK Corporate Governance Code. However, despite there being some initial expectations that the FRC would include the Walker recommendations as an annex to the main Code applicable exclusively to BOFIs, the FRC decided to maintain the generality of the Code's application and refrained from adding sectorally specific provisions. Rather, beginning with the 2010 edition, the FRC amended the Code, opting – *inter alia* – to incorporate those aspects of the Walker Recommendations that it felt were also relevant to non-financial companies, while leaving the Walker guidance itself as the primary regulatory source in respect of recommendations applicable to BOFIs.[85]

The FRC decided against adopting Walker's approach of providing an indicative time commitment for non-executive directors or chairmen, in view of its concern that this would prevent boards from being able to recruit high-quality candidates who, as a result of other commitments, are under significant time constraints. The FRC also noted that non-executives of smaller and less complex companies will likely not have the same demands placed on their time, thus making a universal norm on time commitment inappropriate outside of the BOFI sector.[86] As a more flexible alternative, the FRC introduced a new Code Principle entitled 'Commitment', which provides that '[a]ll directors should be able to allocate sufficient time to the company to discharge their responsibilities effectively'.[87]

The FRC likewise decided not to extend Walker's recommendations for the establishment of risk committees and Chief Risk Officers to non-financial companies, given the generally lower risk exposures of non-financial companies and the lesser centrality of risk management to their core business activities.[88] Instead, the FRC took the much less onerous dual step of: (i) creating a specific Code Principle on non-executive directors in order to emphasize more clearly non-executive directors' core responsibility to 'constructively challenge and help develop proposals on strategy'[89]; and (ii) extending the former Code

---

[84] See M. Power, 'Organizational Responses to Risk: The Rise of the Chief Risk Officer' in B. Hutter and M. Power (eds), *Organizational Encounters with Risk* (CUP 2005), 144.

[85] FRC, above n. 8, 2.

[86] *ibid.*, para. 3.10.

[87] UK Corporate Governance Code, Main Principle B.3.

[88] FRC, above n. 8, paras 3.49–3.50.

[89] UK Corporate Governance Code, Main Principle A.4.

Principle C.2 on internal control so as expressly to cover 'Risk Management and Internal Control'. Main Principle C.2. now states that '[t]he board is responsible for determining the nature and extent of the significant risks it is willing to take in achieving its strategic objectives', while 'maintain[ing] sound risk management and internal control systems'.

Initially, a single Code Provision accompanying Code Principle C.2 simply recommended that the board should, at least annually, conduct a review of the effectiveness of the company's risk management and internal control systems and report to shareholders that they have done so.[90] The FRC later introduced expanded Provisions, imposing greater risk management responsibilities and reporting requirements on boards, to supplement the Code's Main Principle C.2. These Provisions now read as follows:

- C.2.1. The directors should confirm in the annual report that they have carried out a robust assessment of the principal risks facing the company, including those that would threaten its business model, future performance, solvency or liquidity. The directors should describe those risks and explain how they are being managed or mitigated.
- C.2.2. Taking account of the company's current position and principal risks, the directors should explain in the annual report how they have assessed the prospects of the company, over what period they have done so and why they consider that period to be appropriate. The directors should state whether they have a reasonable expectation that the company will be able to continue in operation and meet its liabilities as they fall due over the period of their assessment, drawing attention to any qualifications or assumptions as necessary.
- C.2.3. The board should monitor the company's risk management and internal control systems and, at least annually, carry out a review of their effectiveness, and report on that review in the annual report. The monitoring and review should cover all material controls, including financial, operational and compliance controls.

Beginning from 2010, the FRC also introduced new Code provisions requiring more detailed financial and business reporting. Today, these include obligations on the part of directors to:

- state that they consider the annual report and accounts to be fair, balanced and understandable, providing the information necessary for shareholders to assess the company's position, performance, business model and strategy.
- include in the annual report an explanation of the basis on which the company generates or preserves value over the longer term (the business model) and the strategy for delivering the objectives of the company.

---

[90] UK Corporate Governance Code (June 2010), Provision C.2.1.

- state in annual and half-yearly financial statements, whether they considered it appropriate to adopt the going concern basis of accounting in preparing them, and identify any material uncertainties to the company's ability to continue to do so over a period of at least twelve months from the date of approval of the financial statements.[91]

Thus, through three major revisions (in 2010, 2012 and 2014), the Corporate Governance Code has been amended to reflect the importance of internal control and risk management, thereby heightening the board's involvement and responsibilities in this regard. In turn, more extensive reporting requirements as part of these changes have resulted in increasing amounts of information being released, which, in turn, creates new responsibilities (albeit not in a legally binding sense) on shareholders. As the FRC notes, '[f]or their part, investors will need to assess these statements thoroughly and engage accordingly'.[92] It remains to be seen in the years and decades to come whether the interplay between boards and shareholders can lead to sustainable improvements in the important internal control/risk management area.

THE BOARD'S INTERNAL CONTROL/ RISK MANAGEMENT FUNCTION IN THE US

As we have already seen above, UK internal control and risk management regulation has been influenced from the very beginning by US frameworks and developments in this area, which after Enron set the standard for many jurisdictions internationally. Still today, the US internal control/risk management framework remains highly important for the UK and other countries, in particular given its application to foreign companies that are listed or cross-listed on stock exchanges in the US.[93] It is therefore prudent to provide a short overview of the board's internal control and risk management function as it presents itself today in the United States.

US corporate law is traditionally regulated by individual States' laws. State corporate law in particular establishes directorial duties relating to internal control and risk management, which we will discuss further below. However, public companies and their directors and officers have since 1933 also been under the jurisdiction of the federal securities laws and SEC rules. The federal securities laws – whilst traditionally focused on disclosure – are increasingly establishing standards of behaviour for directors and officers and strongly influence corporate governance, including internal control and risk management. For example, the 1977 Foreign Corrupt Practices Act (FCPA)[94] requires that public corporations have adequate systems of internal accounting control.

---

[91] UK Corporate Governance Code, Provisions C.1.1.–C.1.3.
[92] UK Corporate Governance Code, Preface para. 5.
[93] For instance, companies with US-listed shares have to comply with internal control rules stemming from the Sarbanes Oxley Act.
[94] Title I of Pub. Law No. 95-213 (1977), codified in scattered sections of 15 U.S.C.

Another landmark in the federal regulation of internal control was the intro-duction of the Sarbanes-Oxley Act of 2002.[95] Passed as a response to a series of corporate scandals (including Enron, which we discussed previously), Sarbanes-Oxley and the resulting rules of the Securities and Exchange Commission (SEC) introduced – *inter alia* – new requirements pertaining to board structure and also new standards relating to corporate officers' certification responsibilities for internal controls. The obligations imposed by Sarbanes-Oxley did not go too far beyond already existing securities laws, exchange rules and best prac-tices. However, Sarbanes-Oxley gave various duties more teeth by introducing sharply increased penalties for violations of the norms that it promulgated.[96]

The core internal control related provisions in respect of Sarbanes-Oxley's tighter regulation are its sections 302 and 404. Section 302 provided in part that the SEC shall adopt rules, applicable to reporting companies, requiring a company's CEO and CFO (or their equivalents) to make in each annual or quarterly report broad certifications acknowledging their responsibility for internal controls.[97] Section 404 – a provision which has been widely criticized due to the costs related to it – required the SEC to promulgate rules to the effect that companies' annual reports contain an internal control report (to be reviewed by the company's external auditor) that states management's respon-sibility for establishing and maintaining adequate internal control structure and procedures for financial reporting, and contains an assessment of the effective-ness of the internal control structure and procedures.[98] The SEC subsequently implemented sections 302 and 404, resulting in various new rules, regulations and forms applicable to public companies.[99]

In addition to these governance and disclosure rules mandated by Sarbanes-Oxley, the Act also caused the major US stock exchanges to introduce stricter listing standards. Most notably in the internal control context, stock exchange requirements mandate that companies have an audit committee and regulate its responsibilities.[100] For example, the NYSE requires its listed companies to have an internal audit function and emphasizes the audit committee's central

---

[95] The Public Company Accounting Reform and Investor Protection Act of 2002. For a concise overview of the Act, see S.M. Bainbridge, *The Complete Guide to Sarbanes-Oxley: Understanding How Sarbanes-Oxley Affects Your Business* (Adams Media 2007).

[96] See, for example, sections 304 and 906 of the Sarbanes-Oxley Act; B.H. McDonnell, 'Sarbanes-Oxley, Fiduciary Duties, and the Conduct of Officers and Directors' (2004), University of Minnesota Law School, Legal Studies Research Paper Series, at http://ssrn.com/abstract=570321. In addition, violations of Sarbanes-Oxley are treated the same as viola-tions of other securities law provisions, which allows, for example, private class action suits for false certifications.

[97] See sections 302(a)(4)–(6) of the Sarbanes-Oxley.

[98] See *ibid.*, section 404.

[99] For an overview, see the supplementary information sections in Securities Act Release No. 33-8124 (29 August 2002) and Securities Act Release No. 33-8238 (5 June 2003).

[100] In response to the Sarbanes-Oxley Act's section 301(m) the SEC adopted Exchange Act Rule 10A-3, which directs the national securities exchanges and securities associations not to list any security where the issuer is not in compliance with certain requirements with respect to its audit committee. SEC Release Nos. 33-8220, 34-47654 (9 April 2003).

role with respect to internal control issues. The audit committee's responsibilities are described, *inter alia*, as to 'assist board oversight of (1) the integrity of the listed company's financial statements, (2) the listed company's compliance with legal and regulatory requirements, (3) the independent auditor's qualifications and independence, and (4) the performance of the listed company's internal audit function and independent auditors'.[101]

Another source that provides directors with incentives to install internal control systems is the Federal Sentencing Guidelines. A corporation that is found guilty of a crime may under federal law be sentenced to substantial fines within a range as determined under the Guidelines.[102] The Federal Sentencing Guidelines also provide that a corporation can substantially mitigate a potential fine if it can demonstrate that it had an effective ethics and compliance programme in place prior to the crime.[103] The Guidelines set out in detail certain minimum measures which a corporation should implement in order to take advantage of a possible reduction in potential fines imposed upon a conviction for criminal conduct.[104] These measures focus, among other factors, on the board's oversight with respect to the implementation and effectiveness of the ethics and compliance programme.[105]

INDIVIDUAL DIRECTORS' LIABILITY FOR OVERSIGHT FAILURES

In addition to the requirements discussed in previous sections, the board's internal control and risk management function is also covered by directors' general corporate law fiduciary duties, potentially exposing them individually to liability vis-à-vis the company (and, indirectly, its shareholders). US state courts – and those of Delaware in particular – have developed a detailed jurisprudence on boards' so-called 'oversight liability'. In the UK, directors are also subject to a duty to monitor. However, the two jurisdictions have chosen very different approaches to these types of duties. The approaches and their underlying rationales will be explored in this section.

However, it is important to note as a preliminary matter that there are various other sources that can lead to directors incurring personal liability for inadequate internal control/risk management, including aspects of securities/financial markets legislation, listing rules, tort[106] and other non-corporate laws. In the UK, notable recent developments in this regard include the new

---

[101] NYSE Listed Company Manual 303A.07.

[102] United States Sentencing Commission, Guidelines Manual, Chapter 8 (2014). As directed by Sarbanes-Oxley, the Federal Sentencing Guidelines were reviewed and amended, increasing fines for many individual and organizational defendants convicted of fraud and related offenses. See sections 805, 905 and 1104 of the Sarbanes-Oxley Act.

[103] See Federal Sentencing Guidelines, sections 8B2.1 and 8C2.5.

[104] *ibid.*, section 8B2.1(b).

[105] *ibid.*, section 8B2.1(b)(2)(A).

[106] On this, see M. Petrin, 'The Curious Case of Directors' and Officers' Liability for Supervisions and Management: Exploring the Intersection of Corporate and Tort Law' (2010) 59 *American University Law Review* 1661.

regulatory regime for senior bankers and the Bribery Act 2010. While the former creates stringent oversight liability rules for senior persons in the financial services sector,[107] the latter introduced a novel form of corporate liability for failing to prevent bribery and incentivizes companies to implement effective compliance systems and cultural norms aimed at curtailing the occurrence of corrupt practices by employees and agents.[108] A discussion of these norms is, however, beyond the scope of this section, which will focus on directors' liability based on general corporate law obligations.

Delaware's Oversight Liability

It has long been established under US state corporate law that directors have a fiduciary duty to pay attention to the ongoing business and affairs of the corporation and to supervise management. A lack of attention or utter ignorance could lead to directors' personal liability.[109] This can be illustrated by reference to a case decided in 1924,[110] in which the Supreme Court of New Jersey was faced with a director who 'never made the slightest effort to discharge any of her responsibilities'.[111] The court had no difficulties in finding a breach of fiduciary duty, holding that directors are under a continuing obligation to keep themselves informed about the corporation's activities and 'may not shut their eyes to corporate misconduct and then claim that because they did not see the misconduct, they did not have a duty to look'.[112] Yet, this and other older cases left open a critical question: is the board – beyond the duty of keeping itself informed – obliged to *proactively* monitor the conduct of subordinates and its compliance with the law through an internal control system?[113]

When first faced with this issue, the Delaware Supreme Court answered it in the negative. In *Graham v. Allis-Chalmers Mfg. Co.*,[114] the court concluded

---

[107] See I.H.-Y. Chiu, 'Regulatory Duties for Directors in the Financial Services Sector and Directors' Duties in Company Law – Bifurcation and Interfaces' (2016) 6 *Journal of Business Law* 465. Even more recently, additionally corporate offences based on failures to prevent certain scenarios have been proposed or, in the case of tax avoidance, implemented.

[108] See section 7(2) of the UK Bribery Act 2010, which provides that it is a defence for a commercial organization to prove that it had adequate procedures designed to prevent persons associated with it from bribing others with the intention to obtain or retain business (or an advantage in in the conduct of business) for the organization. For official guidance about the procedures that business can put into place, see Secretary of State, The Bribery Act 2010 – Guidance (2011), at http://www.justice.gov.uk/downloads/legislation/bribery-act-2010-guidance.pdf.

[109] See e.g. *Barnes v. Andrews*, 298 F. 614 (S.D.N.Y. 1924).

[110] *Francis v. United Jersey Bank*, 432 A.2d 814 (N.J. 1981).

[111] *ibid.*, 821.

[112] *ibid.*, 822.

[113] For an in-depth discussion, see S.M. Bainbridge *et al.*, 'The Convergence of Good Faith and Oversight' (2008) 55 *UCLA Law Review* 559, 562.

[114] 188 A.2d 125 (Del. 1963). The plaintiffs in *Graham* alleged that directors of Allis-Chalmers, a large manufacturer of electrical equipment, were liable for their failure to learn of and take steps to prevent violations of antitrust laws by company employees engaging in price fixing.

that unless presented with an event that expressly put them on notice of suspicious conduct, directors were not obliged to implement 'a system of watchfulness'.[115] This situation changed in 1996 with the seminal *Caremark* case.[116] This case concerned a proposed settlement involving claims that the directors of healthcare company Caremark violated their duty to monitor the company in connection with illegal schemes by company employees. These schemes, that had gone undetected by the board, resulted in substantial fines for the company, triggering shareholder lawsuits against directors and their alleged failures to detect and prevent the misbehaviour.[117]

The Delaware Chancery Court in *Caremark* held that directors, regardless of any notice of actual wrongdoing, had a duty to assure themselves that reasonably designed information and reporting systems exist.[118] Yet, while the standard of conduct demanded by this duty was expansive, the court formulated a narrow standard of review that severely constrained courts' authority to hold directors liable for misguided compliance decisions. According to Caremark, 'only a sustained or systematic failure of the board to exercise oversight – such as an utter failure to attempt to assure a reasonable information and reporting system exists – will establish the lack of good faith that is a necessary condition to liability'.[119]

Twenty years later, in 2006, the Delaware Supreme Court was faced with what had come to be known as a 'Caremark claim'. This case, *Stone v. Ritter*,[120] involved a shareholder derivative suit alleging that directors of a financial institution failed to implement reasonable legal compliance controls.[121] Building upon *Caremark*, the Delaware Supreme Court restated the necessary conditions for director oversight liability. As the Court explained, to recover successfully in an oversight case, a plaintiff must show that:

(a) the directors utterly failed to implement any reporting or information system or controls; or (b) having implemented such a system or controls, consciously

---

[115] *ibid.*, 130.

[116] *In re Caremark Int'l Inc. Derivative Litigation*, 698 A.2d 959 (Del. Ch. 1996).

[117] *ibid.*, 960–66. Specifically, the plaintiffs alleged that Caremark's directors failed to supervise the conduct of company employees and to institute corrective measures, exposing Caremark to substantial fines and liability as a result of civil and criminal violations of various laws applicable to health care providers. Overall, Caremark was, under its agreements with governmental agencies, required to make total payments of approximately $250 million.

[118] *ibid.*, 970.

[119] *ibid.*, 971. Applying these criteria to the case, the court concluded that the record did not indicate that the director defendants were guilty of a sustained failure to exercise their oversight function.

[120] 911 A.2d 362 (Del. 2006).

[121] Specifically, shareholders of AmSouth Bancorporation alleged that the directors had failed to implement controls that would have informed them of breaches of federal anti-money-laundering regulations that caused AmSouth and its wholly owned subsidiary to pay $50 million in governmental fines and penalties.

failed to monitor or oversee its operations thus disabling themselves from being informed of risks or problems requiring their attention. In either case, imposition of liability requires a showing that the directors knew that they were not discharging their fiduciary obligations.[122]

Thus, the Court reiterated and increased *Caremark*'s limits on liability. However, it also took the position that the fiduciary duty violated by director oversight is not the duty of care, but rather the duty of loyalty.[123] One notable consequence of this was that oversight was excluded from the category of breaches of duties that may be covered by directors' liability exculpation provisions,[124] potentially increasing directors' liability exposure. Yet, subsequent decisions affirmed Delaware's strict limits on oversight liability.

For example, later courts held that 'a very extreme set of facts' would be required to sustain a successful oversight claim[125]; that red flags are only 'useful when they are either waved in one's face or displayed so that they are visible to the careful observer'[126]; and that directors lack the necessary good faith if they not only knowingly, but also 'completely' fail to undertake their responsibilities.[127] Indeed, it is exceedingly rare for plaintiffs to succeed in oversight-based derivative actions against directors under Delaware law.[128]

In the wake of the financial crisis, Delaware was also faced with claims alleging inadequate risk management. In a notable case brought against directors and officers of Citigroup, the global financial company, plaintiffs alleged that these individuals had breached their oversight duties by failing to monitor risks stemming from Citigroup's exposure to the subprime lending market.[129] However, the Court refused to second guess the substance of the board's oversight activities, being satisfied that the board and its audit committee had done enough to make it impossible for plaintiffs to overcome the 'extremely high

---

[122] *Stone v. Ritter*, 911 A.2d 362, 370 (Del. 2006).

[123] *ibid.*, 369. This was in line with *Guttman v. Huang*, 823 A.2d 492 (Del. Ch. 2003).

[124] Section 102(b)(7) of the Delaware General Corporation Law permits a corporation to include in its certificate of incorporation:

A provision eliminating or limiting the personal liability of a director to the corporation or its stockholders for monetary damages for breach of fiduciary duty as a director, provided that such provision shall not eliminate or limit the liability of a director: (i) For any breach of the director's duty of loyalty to the corporation or its stockholders; (ii) for acts or omissions not in good faith or which involve intentional misconduct or a knowing violation of law; ... or (iv) for any transaction from which the director derived an improper personal benefit.

[125] *In re Lear Corp. S'holder Litig.*, 967 A.2d 640, 654–55 (Del. Ch. 2008).

[126] *Wood v. Baum*, 953 A.2d 136, 143 (Del. 2008).

[127] *Lyondell Chem. Co. v. Ryan*, 970 A.2d 235, 243–44 (Del. 2009).

[128] One case decided after the *Stone* decision in which plaintiffs were successful is *ATR-Kim Eng Financial Corp. v. Araneta*, 2006 WL 3783520 (Del. Ch. 2006), *aff'd*, 930 A.2d 928 (Del. 2007).

[129] *In re Citigroup Inc. Shareholder Derivative Litigation*, 964 A.2d 106 (Del. Ch. 2009).

burden on a plaintiff to state a claim for personal director liability for a failure to see the extent of a company's business risk'.[130]

As one of the few exceptions, a case involving insurance company AIG represented a rare occurrence in which a Delaware court declined to grant a motion to dismiss a claim alleging the breach of the duty of oversight.[131] However, this case was unusual in that the Court found that the pleadings supported the assertion that some of the defendants, who were inside directors of AIG, effectively led a 'criminal organization' and that the defendants were directly involved in fraudulent schemes.[132] Consequently, the court held that the plaintiffs had pleaded a claim that the defendants breached their duty of loyalty by consciously tolerating inadequate internal controls and failing to monitor legal compliance.[133]

Overall, however, Delaware has made it clear that it will maintain strict limits on *Caremark*-style oversight liability. As it stands now, plaintiffs continue to face a high burden to state a claim for directorial liability for failure to monitor, with possibly an even higher burden should these claims relate to oversight over business risks. Indeed, the lesson from a string of recent case law is that an extreme set of facts is necessary for shareholders to prevail with oversight claims. We will below provide an explanation of the reasons that motivate the Delaware judiciary to establish such a restrictive ('director-friendly') framework.

The UK's Approach to Directors' Oversight-Based Liability

As we have seen above, the Delaware approach to determining directors' oversight liability is restrictive, translating into a generous level of insulation from liability provided to boards and managers. This differs largely from the UK approach to directors' personal liability for oversight failures, which – at least in theory – is expansive and provides a substantially lower liability threshold.

Similarly to the US, directors' duties in the UK include a general obligation to actively monitor the company. This is regarded as part of the directors' duty of care, skill and diligence[134] and may also be said to follow implicitly from

---

[130] *ibid.*, 125. In contrast, in *In re Countrywide Financial Corp. Derivative Litigation*, 554 F.Supp.2d 1044 (C.D. Cal. 2008), a federal court sitting in California held that demand under Delaware law was excused for derivative claims based on the defendant directors' alleged failure to exercise oversight. The court found that shareholders sufficiently pled facts raising a strong inference of directors' scienter with respect to the mortgage company's loan origination practices and the duties of board committees to monitor high-level indicators of financial performance and credit risk. The claims in this case were subsequently dismissed after plaintiffs lost standing due to a merger between Countrywide and Bank of America.

[131] *In re American International Group, Inc.*, 965 A.2d 763, 799 (Del. Ch. 2009).

[132] *ibid.*, 777, 797–99.

[133] *ibid.*, 798–99.

[134] Section 174 of the UK Companies Act 2006. See P.L. Davies and S. Worthington, *Gower and Davies: Principles of Modern Company Law* (9th ed., Sweet & Maxwell 2012), 521; B. Hannigan, *Company Law* (4th ed., OUP 2016), 211.

the duty to promote the success of the company and thus to contain elements of directorial loyalty.[135] Additionally, although the FRC Guidance on Internal Control and Risk Management[136] and the UK Corporate Governance Code do not directly establish enforceable duties for directors, their provisions can be used as an authoritative indication of the standards that a court would require board members to meet with respect to their monitoring obligations.[137]

A leading case on directors' obligations to monitor (or exercise oversight) is a disqualification case concerning Barings Bank. Barings collapsed in 1995 after the general manager and head derivatives trader of a Barings subsidiary in Singapore, Nick Leeson, engaged in unauthorized trading that resulted in enormous losses for the bank. Leeson's rogue trading led to successful proceedings seeking to disqualify three executive directors of Barings group companies as 'unfit' to manage a company,[138] based on various shortcomings relating to internal control and risk management.[139] Specifically, the directors were found to have breached their duties by failing either to monitor Leeson or to impose risk limits or other measures to mitigate or eliminate trading risks such as the ones that materialized. They also appeared to ignore red flags, including concerns raised in an internal audit report.

On appeal by one of the directors, which was dismissed, the Court of Appeal approvingly cited the lower court's summary of directors' oversight duties:

(i) Directors have, both collectively and individually, a continuing duty to acquire and maintain a sufficient knowledge and understanding of the company's business to enable them properly to discharge their duties as directors.

(ii) Whilst directors are entitled (subject to the articles of association of the company) to delegate particular functions to those below them in the management chain, and to trust their competence and integrity to a reasonable extent, the exercise of the power of delegation does not absolve a director from the duty to supervise the discharge of the delegated functions.

(iii) No rule of universal application can be formulated as to the duty referred to in (ii) above. The extent of the duty, and the question whether it has been discharged, must depend on the facts of each particular case, including the director's role in the management of the company.[140]

---

[135] Section 172 of the Companies Act 2006.

[136] FRC, above n. 8.

[137] Gower, above n. 134, 521–22.

[138] In the sense of section 6 of the Company Directors Disqualification Act 1986.

[139] See *Secretary of State for Trade and Industry v Baker* (No 5) [1999] 1 BCLC 433; *Secretary of State for Trade and Industry v Baker* (No 6) [2001] BCC 273 (on appeal). For a succinct summary, see J. Loughrey, 'The Director's Duty of Care and Skill and the Financial Crisis' in J. Loughrey (ed.), *Directors' Duties and Shareholder Litigation in the Wake of the Financial Crisis* (Edward Elgar 2013), 21–22.

[140] *Secretary of State for Trade and Industry v Baker* (No 6) [2001] BCC 273, 283.

Contrary to what traditional case law had previously suggested, the Barings decision makes it clear that it is not enough to act only in response to warning signs[141] and that a failure on the part of directors to engage *ex ante* in meaningful internal control/risk management represents a breach of their duties.[142] While directors are still permitted to delegate tasks and rely on others, they are responsible for ensuring the latter's supervision and also the existence of adequate controls.[143] Both the extent of delegation and the implementation of internal controls will be governed by a reasonableness standard, which is measured in general against the conduct of a reasonable director carrying out the same functions as the director(s) concerned.[144]

However, in circumstances where at least some attempts to exercise oversight were made and shortcomings are less obvious – such as in case of the complex combination of factors that led to the recent financial crisis – it is less clear whether courts will find directors to be at fault.[145] Additionally, directors' liability exposure is mitigated if they can successfully argue that they properly delegated certain oversight duties to specific board members, board committees, management or advisors[146] – along the lines of Barings' guidance above – and in cases where courts apply more modest standards of care, such as based on an individual's expertise, their specific role within a company, or other circumstances.[147] For example, courts have found that directors, and to a greater degree non-executives, were not required to possess specialist accounting knowledge,[148] that non-executive directors will face lower expectations with respect to their behaviour than their full-time counterparts,[149] and that the required standards that are applied to directors will be reduced in smaller and less complex businesses.[150]

Additionally, directors' liability for oversight must be qualified by reference to section 463 of the Companies Act 2006. According to this section, a director may be liable to compensate his company for losses resulting from untrue

---

[141] *Re City Equitable Fire Insurance Co Ltd* [1925] Ch 407, 429, holding that the board can rely on the honesty of executive directors and other officials 'in the absence of grounds for suspicion'.

[142] See Loughrey, above n. 139, 23–25. For examples arising out of directors' disqualification cases, see *Re Westmid Packing Services Ltd, Secretary of State for Trade and Industry v Griffiths* [1998] 2 BCLC at 653; *Re Kaytech International plc, Secretary of State for Trade and Industry v Kaczer* [1999] 2 BCLC 351; *Lexi Holdings Plc v Luqman* [2009] EWCA Civ 117.

[143] For instance, in *Lexi Holdings Plc v Luqman* [2009] EWCA Civ 117, two directors were held liable for failing to detect fraudulent conduct by their brother and fellow director despite red flags raised in the company's books and their brother's previous deceptive actions.

[144] See section 174 of the Companies Act 2006; *Re D'Jan of London Ltd* [1994] 1 BCLC 561.

[145] Loughrey, above n. 139, 25–26.

[146] For a discussion of case law on delegation and residual supervision, see Hannigan, above n. 134, 214–18.

[147] See, for example, *Weavering Capital (UK) Limited v Peterson* [2012] EWHC 1480 (Ch).

[148] *In Re Continental Assurance Company of London plc (in liquidation) (No 4)* [2007] 2 BCLC 287.

[149] *Equitable Life Assurance Society v Bowley* [2003] EWHC 2263.

[150] *Re Produce Marketing Consortium Ltd* [1989] 5 BCC 569.

or misleading statements or omissions of required information in the strategic report, the directors' report, the directors' remuneration report, or a summary financial statement. As we have seen, these sections also contain information relating to internal control and risk management. However, section 463 includes a 'safe harbour' provision, which provides that 'no person shall be subject to any liability to a person other than the company resulting from reliance, by that person or another, on information in a report to which this section applies'. Thus, a third party (such as a lender) or even a shareholder in a direct (as opposed to derivative) action could not hold a director liable for a loss that they have suffered based on their reliance on aspects of the company's internal control or risk management system as disclosed in the relevant reports. This carve-out does not apply to liability for civil penalties or criminal offences[151] but otherwise serves to insulate directors and officers to a certain extent from oversight liability based on claims.

Indeed, it is perhaps in part due to these various hurdles that the UK has not experienced claims alleging a breach of duty by directors in the wake of the recent financial crisis: neither by shareholders, as derivative actions, nor by companies themselves in the form of direct actions that a company brings against directors on its own volition.[152] Similarly, the Libor manipulations at Barclays (and other banks) have not resulted in UK shareholders' claims alleging a breach of directors' company law duties to exercise proper oversight.[153] Indeed, judicial consideration of directors' oversight duties in the UK appears for the most part in disqualification cases, which – essentially – the government brings against directors of insolvent companies.

Nevertheless, it is important to note that UK law, as a matter of principle, does not prevent courts from finding directors to be personally liable even in complex situations or where they appear to have been only slightly negligent. This, of course, is in contrast to the corresponding law as developed in Delaware, where nothing short of conscious disregard of duties, and either an utter failure to implement internal controls or failure to monitor them can lead to directors' liability. Still, in practice the uncertainty and obstacles surrounding oversight liability claims – and derivative claims in general – act as strong deterrents to bringing claims.

Oversight Liability: Striking the Right Balance

As we have seen, UK and US law have taken different approaches to regulating oversight liability. While in the UK directors can be held responsible for any

---

[151] Section 464(6) of the Companies Act 2006.

[152] See J. Loughrey, 'Introduction' in J. Loughrey (ed.) (above n. 139), 7, noting that shareholders have (largely unsuccessful) pursued other avenues, including a claim against the government, litigation against various institutions based on misleading statements in prospectuses preceding rights issues, and claims against banks for mis-selling financial products.

[153] Note, however, that Barclays has been fined by UK and US regulators and, in addition, faced claims by investors based on US and UK securities law. Relatedly, a UBS currency trader has been criminally charged and convicted in connection with Libor rigging.

degree of negligence in discharging their monitoring obligations, Delaware case law makes it clear that there will only be liability if directors *knew* they were not discharging their fiduciary obligations.[154] Short of requiring intent to inflict harm, one can hardly imagine a more demanding liability standard. Although in practice the UK and the US regimes have thus far resulted in similar outcomes (that is, directors will only be liable when there are clear, egregious breaches), it is instructive to reflect briefly on the different approaches' respective rationales and potential effects.

In the Citigroup case, the influential Delaware Chancery Court acknowledged that 'Citigroup has suffered staggering losses' and that 'it is understandable that investors ... want to find someone to hold responsible for these losses'. However, the Court also noted that 'it is often difficult to distinguish between a desire to blame someone and a desire to force those responsible to account for their wrongdoing'. In this case, the Court found that legal and policy grounds supported its decision to reject shareholders' claims. It summarized the rationale behind its decision and its restrictive approach as follows:

> Our law, fortunately, provides guidance for precisely these situations in the form of doctrines governing the duties owed by officers and directors of Delaware corporations. This law has been refined over hundreds of years, which no doubt included many crises, and we must not let our desire to blame someone for our losses make us lose sight of the purpose of our law. Ultimately, the discretion granted directors and managers allows them to maximize shareholder value in the long term by taking risks without the debilitating fear that they will be held personally liable if the company experiences losses. This doctrine also means, however, that when the company suffers losses, shareholders may not be able to hold the directors personally liable.[155]

In contrast, the *Barings* court emphasized very different aspects of directors' liability:

> The concept of limited liability and the sophistication of our corporate law offers great privileges and great opportunities for those who wish to trade under that regime. But the corporate environment carries with it the discipline that those who avail themselves of those privileges must accept the standards laid down and abide by the regulatory rules and disciplines in place to protect creditors and shareholders. And while some significant corporate failures will occur despite the directors exercising best managerial practice, in many, too many [cases] there have been serious breaches of those rules and disciplines, in situations where the observance of them would or at least might have prevented or reduced the scale of the failure and consequent loss to creditors and investors.[156]

---

[154] *Stone v. Ritter*, 911 A.2d 362, 370 (Del. 2006).

[155] *In re Citigroup Inc. Shareholder Derivative Litigation*, 964 A.2d 106, 139 (Del. Ch. 2009.

[156] *Secretary of State for Trade and Industry v Baker (No 5)* [1999] 1 BCLC 433, 484, citing *Secretary of State for Trade and Industry v Gray* [1995] 1 BCLC 276 at 288–289 (Henry LJ).

Shareholder-led directors' duties litigation is commonly thought to serve two main goals: *ex post* compensation and, above all, *ex ante* deterrence.[157] These aspects are reflected in the Barings' court's strict approach to directorial liability, with the dual goal being in part to compensate 'creditors and investors' as well as to prevent future occurrences of similar misconduct. From this perspective, directors' and officers' liability must necessarily be as strict as possible in order to achieve these stated objectives. In such a system, however, there is a potential that the pendulum may swing to the other extreme and result in over-deterrence. Relatedly, as two commentators have observed, increasing regulation of internal control and risk management may cause courts and regulators in hindsight to label 'any business choice with adverse consequences for shareholders and/or other stakeholders a manifestation of a faulty risk management system and deem directors liable as a consequence'.[158]

In contrast, Delaware's oversight liability is largely influenced by another aspect of directors' liability. It recognizes that the potential for personal liability is a necessary check on managerial behaviour, but at the same time is wary of what is seen as a negative by-product of such liability, namely the 'threat of sub-optimal risk acceptance'.[159] Delaware's director-friendly liability rules rest on the idea that the prospect of personal liability can cause directors to be more risk-averse than the interest of diversified shareholders justifies.[160]

As there is a correlation between risk and rewards (more risks are generally thought to translate into increased profits) – and indeed taking on risks is an essential part of doing business – courts are reluctant to impose liability that could result in companies failing to take on 'healthy' levels of business risks or overinvest in safety measures. The latter may also include internal control, monitoring and risk management systems that are not optimal from a cost-benefit perspective (their cost is higher than the losses that they help avoid), which from the perspective of diversified shareholders is undesirable.[161] In a somewhat ironic and roundabout way, therefore, insulating boards from liability could be seen as a device to protect shareholders from themselves, in that it allows boards to take risks that will ultimately benefit shareholders as a class.

In sum, liability rules governing failures in exercising oversight, which includes internal control and risk management, are – like directors' liability in

---

[157] See e.g. J.C. Coffee and D.E. Schwartz, 'The Survival of the Derivative Suit: An Evaluation and a Proposal for Legislative Reform' (1981) 81 *Columbia Law Review* 261, 302–04; D.M. Ibrahim, 'Individual or Collective Liability for Corporate Directors?' (2008) 93 *Iowa Law Review* 929, 951–56 (2008).

[158] Enriques and Zetsche, above n.75, 290.

[159] See *Gagliardi v. Trifoods Int'l, Inc.*, 683 A.2d 1049, 1052 (Del. Ch. 1996).

[160] *ibid.*, 1052. See also *Joy v. North*, 692 F.2d 880, 885–86 (2d Cir. 1982).

[161] *See* Bainbridge *et al.*, above n. 113, 578. To be sure, opting out of internal controls will usually not make sense in the important area of accounting. Maintaining precautions in that particular area is often relatively cost-efficient and not having such controls could hardly be justified. Conversely, the case for controls that monitor business risks is more complex. See Enriques and Zetsche, above n. 75.

general – intended (at least in part) to deter misconduct and enable investors to be compensated for losses in firm value caused by negligent monitoring. As such, these policy goals demand that suitable tools are available to ensure that directors are held liable (in appropriate instances) and oversight liability is critical in this respect. However, personal liability for directors may also result in negative effects, such as increased costs and over-deterrence. Liability rules in this area, and particularly risk management, touch upon the issue of 'risk-taking' as a core issue at the heart of business. While liability rules that are too lax may lead to disaster, overly stringent rules threaten to unduly restrict otherwise beneficial business activities. Courts and legislators alike are therefore charged with the difficult task of striking the correct balance between these two competing considerations.

PART IV

Managerial Incentives and Disciplines

CHAPTER 9

Design and Control of Executive Remuneration

In the previous two chapters, we examined the board of directors' key monitoring and risk oversight functions within public companies. In this chapter we explore another concern that is central to the effectiveness of the board's role in supervising management, namely its capacity to determine the remuneration (or pay) of the company's senior executive officers. As we will see below, the level and forms of pay awarded to top-level corporate managers are crucial in providing such officers with powerful incentives to promote the success of the company for the benefit of its shareholders: in particular, by taking entrepreneurial risks that might otherwise put managers outside of their personal comfort zone. However, such incentives should not be so pervasive as to drive managers to undertake irresponsible levels of risk. This latter concern is especially pertinent in the banking and financial services sector where, as is now well-known, the systemic repercussions of unsuccessful risk-taking are potentially seismic both for shareholders and wider society.

Of course, how directors – and, in particular, independent non-executive directors – are *themselves* paid is, in turn, important in conditioning board members for their abovementioned monitoring and risk oversight roles. For this reason, any effective system of executive remuneration design must be sensitive not just to the pay conditions of those individuals fulfilling high-level managerial functions within the firm, but also to those charged with monitoring managers' continuing performance of those functions, while also overseeing the level of risk to which the firm is consequently exposed. Moreover, to the extent that certain senior executive officeholders (e.g. the CEO or finance director) will normally also be directors of their employer company, both the executive and directorial components of a company's overall remuneration policy will likely prove to be mutually reinforcing. Accordingly, the discussion that follows will focus on the design and control of directors' remuneration in addition to the remuneration of senior executives.

At the same time, how the pay of a company's senior executives and directors is determined is crucial to ensuring that the firm is able to attract the right candidates to undertake its key managerial and governance functions in the first place. That is to say, as well as incentivizing incumbent officeholders an effective remuneration policy must also be designed to attract suitably qualified and skilled *new* recruits to the firm, by offering sufficiently compelling inducements to prospective managerial and directorial candidates. However, as we will see below these two objectives – on the one hand, attracting suitable new managerial and directorial appointees and, on the other, incentivizing continuing performance on the part of existing appointees – are not always consistent with one another. This presents an additional challenge to those responsible for the design and control of executive remuneration policies and practices, whether in a strategic or regulatory capacity.

Finally, it is increasingly the case today that, within large and high-profile corporations at least, attracting suitable talent and incentivizing managerial performance are not the only aims of an effective executive remuneration policy. Additionally, those responsible for the design and control of executive remuneration must ensure that prevailing levels of executive pay are not significantly out of kilter with corresponding standards of social reasonableness or decency, so as to mitigate adverse public and/or political opinion pertaining to perceived pay inequality or unfairness. This is especially important in the contemporary regulatory and civil society climate, where executive pay transparency has become a central expectation and feature of corporate governance in practice, and a salient focus for activist shareholders, media and pressure groups alike. The potentially adverse consequences for corporations of a public 'black-listing' on their executive pay practices – including reputational damage and also the danger of enhanced regulatory intervention in this regard – call for remuneration designers to be sensitive to a diverse range of social considerations that have traditionally not been reflected in instrumental 'pay-for-performance' models.

AGENCY COSTS AND THE PAY-FOR-PERFORMANCE CHALLENGE

Within modern regulatory policy on corporate governance, the notion of ensuring effective managerial and directorial 'pay-for-performance' is afforded pivotal importance. In large part, this is due to widespread concern about the dangers of encouraging so-called 'rewards for failure' in public companies, where directors and/or senior executives are granted seemingly exorbitant remuneration packages in return for levels of managerial performance that are at best average or unremarkable, and – at worst – sub-average or even downright dismal.

For instance the landmark 1995 Greenbury Report, in setting out the seminal policy rationale for the regulation of directorial pay-setting arrangements in UK public companies under the (then) Combined Code on Corporate Governance, already emphasized as 'key themes' of its approach 'the alignment of Director and shareholder interests, and improved company performance'.[1] According to Greenbury, '[t]he key to encouraging enhanced performance by Directors lies in remuneration packages which *link rewards to performance*, by

---

[1] Directors' Remuneration: Report of a Study Group Chaired by Sir Richard Greenbury (17 July 1995) ('The Greenbury Report'), 7 ('Chairman's Preface').

both company and individual; and *align the interests of Directors and shareholders* in promoting the company's progress'.[2]

In a similar vein, the present-day edition of the same Code recommends – as one of its Main Principles – that '[e]xecutive directors' remuneration should be designed to promote the long-term success of the company', and moreover that '[p]erformance related elements [of executive pay] should be transparent, stretching and rigorously applied'.[3] Likewise the UK's (then) Business Secretary Vince Cable, in setting out the policy rationale for enhanced shareholder 'say on pay' voting[4] in British public companies in 2013, premised his case on the observation that 'the pay of our top executives has quadrupled but ... has not always been an indication of how well a particular company has performed', thereby justifying (*inter alia*) a new regulatory regime for 'improved disclosure on the performance conditions used to assess variable pay of directors', including the requirement for 'an illustration of the level of awards that could pay out for various levels of performance'.[5]

On a theoretical level, how performance-based pay functions within the broader context of the corporate governance framework is arguably best understood in terms of the central agency costs problem explained in Chapter 2. From this perspective, performance-related executive remuneration is an *ex ante* 'gap-filling' mechanism in the notional corporate governance 'contract' between a firm's shareholders and managers. Accordingly, given shareholders' inability to anticipate all (or even nearly all) of the diverse circumstances and challenges to which the firm's business will be exposed in future, together with the multifarious decisions and actions that its management will consequently be required to take, it is wholly impractical to expect these two constituencies to agree on a set of specific terms to govern the future direction of the business.

Against the above background, a suitably designed system of performance-related executive remuneration – which, above all, seeks to align periodic levels of individual managerial pay with the corresponding level of residual wealth earned by the firm and its shareholders as a whole – will instil a proactive discipline in managers to seek to maximize shareholder (and, in turn, personal) wealth at all times. In this way, shareholder 'principals' are given the credible assurance that their managerial 'agents' are at all times driven to look out for their best interests, notwithstanding the principals' incapacity to exert direct contractual or even supervisory control over their agents on a continuous basis.[6]

---

[2] *ibid.*, para. 1.15.

[3] Financial Reporting Council, *The UK Corporate Governance Code* (April 2016) ('UKCGC'), Main Principle D.1, at www.frc.org.uk/Our-Work/Codes-Standards/Corporate-governance/UK-Corporate-Governance-Code.aspx.

[4] On this, see below.

[5] UK Department for Business, Innovation & Skills, 'Sweeping Reforms to Directors' Pay and Narrative Reporting Come into Force' (press release, 30 September 2013).

[6] M.C. Jensen and K.J. Murphy, 'Performance Pay and Top-Management Incentives' (1990) 98 *Journal of Political Economy* 225, 225–26.

In view of the above factors, performance-related (and, in particular, equity-based) managerial pay has in modern times been widely regarded as one of the main structural 'solutions' to the central agency problem at the heart of the Anglo-American public company.[7] On a basic level, by (theoretically at least) ensuring that the loss of any pound of shareholder wealth is reflected to a material extent by a corresponding drop in managers' personal income, equity-based pay can be said to mitigate the personal incentives that managers would otherwise have to engage in 'shirking', 'empire-building' or other latent (and thus largely undetectable) forms of shareholder wealth destruction.[8]

On a more advanced level, meanwhile, linking managerial pay to a firm's ongoing share price performance can be said to reduce the ongoing agency costs to shareholders arising from managers' natural risk aversion. To explain further, whereas (as explained in Chapter 2) the liquid equity capital invested in the firm by shareholders is uniquely diversifiable, by contrast managers' invested human capital is inherently non-diversifiable, given the natural limitations on the number of firms for which a manager can work at any one time (in the typical case, just one). It follows that the failure of an individual employer firm represents a potentially catastrophic outcome for a manager (as it would for any other employee of the firm), with the likely effect that managers will – absent powerful incentives to the contrary – be dissuaded from taking risks concerning the future development of the firm's business, even where they promise positive risk-adjusted returns for shareholders. However, by offering managers the inducement of significant personal wealth gains in the event of such risks 'paying off' from a general shareholder perspective, equity-based pay can go some way towards counteracting such *ex ante* risk aversion on managers' part.[9]

Of course an equity-based pay structure, no matter how well-designed, will never succeed in *exactly* replicating shareholders' incentives in the mindset of managers, given that managers – unlike shareholders – are inherently incapable of hedging against their downside risk of lost personal wealth via diversification of their human capital. Thus whereas, from the perspective of a typical (individual or institutional) shareholder, a loss-making entrepreneurial project represents – at worst – an incremental portfolio loss; from the perspective of a manager whose pay is based entirely on the periodic performance of her employer firm's share price, the same loss-making initiative constitutes imminent personal financial disaster.[10]

---

[7] On this problem generally, see Chapter 2.

[8] On this, see Jensen and Murphy, above n. 6; M.C. Jensen and W. Meckling, 'Managerial Behavior, Agency Costs and Ownership Structure' (1976) 3 *Journal of Financial Economics* 305.

[9] *ibid.*, 226.

[10] J.C. Coffee, 'Shareholders Versus Managers: The Strain in the Corporate Web' in J.C. Coffee, L. Lowenstein and S. Rose-Ackerman (eds), *Knights, Raiders & Targets: The Impact of the Hostile Takeover* (OUP 1988), Ch. 6, 80.

For the above reason, a manager requires a substitute protective 'cushion' against downside risk, in place of the effective risk protection that shareholders enjoy via their capacity for diversification. In practice, this cushion is provided in the form of a material fixed component to managers' periodic income – ordinarily in the form of a contractually specified salary – which provides managers with the baseline assurance of a certain periodic financial return on their human capital throughout their period of tenure, notwithstanding the performance of the firm over this time. Therefore, contrary to what might first appear to be the case, a remuneration policy that aligns managers' pay entirely (i.e. 100 per cent) with periodic shareholder returns is unlikely to be conducive to optimal risk-taking incentives on managers' part. Rather, the notionally 'optimal' managerial performance-pay package will in practice involve a combination of variable and fixed components, with the precise ratio adopted in any particular case likely to vary in accordance with the specific circumstances of the firm and market sector in question.

Furthermore, whichever balance in this regard is optimal in any instance from an *incentive* perspective will not necessarily be optimal from a *recruitment* point of view. For example, a firm whose executive remuneration policy renders the vast majority of its top managers' personal income contingent on meeting a highly onerous benchmark level of annual corporate earnings would likely provide its existing officeholders with very powerful incentives to maximize (or at least increase) shareholder wealth. However, the same remuneration policy might make it difficult for the firm to attract many high-calibre candidates for future managerial and/or directorial vacancies, and may even drive away some of its high-performing incumbent officeholders to more attractive positions elsewhere, such that the overall effect of that policy on the firm's performance is *negative*.[11]

Designing an effective remuneration policy thus involves striking an appropriate balance between these potentially conflicting concerns.[12] Moreover, the difficulties involved in successfully attracting and retaining high-quality managerial and directorial personnel have arguably been enhanced by the present-day corporate governance environment, where the demands placed on managers and directors by investors and other key civil society actors – together with the associated potential liabilities and other personal costs – appear to be steadily increasing. Moreover, the overall optimal remuneration arrangement

---

[11] In this regard, the recent (at time of writing) government Green Paper on corporate governance reform asserts that '[i]t is right that our major companies should be able to attract and retain top management talent, recognising that many of the leaders of our most successful companies are recruited from outside the UK'. See Department for Business, Energy and Industrial Strategy, *Corporate Governance Reform: Green Paper* (November 2016) ('Green Paper'), 16.

[12] This challenge is recognized by the UK Corporate Governance Code, which expressly recommends that '[t]he remuneration committee should determine an appropriate balance between fixed and performance-related, immediate and deferred remuneration'. Above n. 3, Sch. A.

in this regard under any given circumstances will likely depend as much on the risk appetite of the individual appointee in question, as on that of the appointing firm itself.

An additional consideration operating against the extensive use of equity-based pay as an inducement to enhanced managerial risk-taking is that, from an incentive-conditioning point of view, the suggested remedy can sometimes be worse than the original disease. This is because performance remuneration linked to short-term corporate profitability or share price appreciation – especially when combined with managers' (like shareholders') limited liability in the event of firm failure – can in some instances be a cause of what economists call 'moral hazard'. In essence, this denotes a situation where the private payoffs (in this case, to shareholders and managers) of a risky course of action are out of kilter with the general public payoffs (i.e. to society as a whole) thereof, such that the pursuit of what is *individually* rational from the decision-maker's (i.e. manager's) perspective is collectively *irrational* once the wider negative externalities of that decision are factored into the overall risk calculus.[13]

The above problem is illustrated vividly by the circumstances prefacing many of the well-documented banking collapses that occurred during the 2007–08 financial crisis, where the capacity of equity-remunerated corporate managers to generate continuing short-term wealth gains for shareholders (and, in turn, themselves) was dependent to a significant extent on their pursuit of highly risky policies that – ultimately and collectively – led to the implosion of global credit and mortgage markets as a whole, necessitating the extensive intervention of national governments at considerable cost to the taxpaying public.[14] This provides further cause for scepticism about the apparent economic optimality of heavily equity-based executive remuneration policies, at least in contexts (such as the above) where the propensity for managerial moral hazard is especially serious.

Principal Forms of Executive and Director Remuneration

Having set out the primary theoretical rationale for performance-related executive remuneration, and also some of the main practical challenges involved in the design and control of the corporate pay-setting process within public companies, we will now turn to examine the principal *forms* of remuneration typically awarded to senior executives and directors of UK public companies. For purposes of this analysis it should be noted that, insofar as the top managerial officers of most UK public companies tend also to be members of their employer company's board of directors, it follows that any references to (i) *executive* and (ii) *director* remuneration practices have dual relevance with respect to such individuals.

---

[13] On this, see S.L. Schwarcz, 'Misalignment: Corporate Risk-Taking and Public Duty' (2016) 92 *Notre Dame Law Review* 1.

[14] M.T. Moore, 'The Evolving Contours of the Board's Risk Management Function in UK Corporate Governance' (2010) 10 *Journal of Corporate Law Studies* 279, 288–89.

Furthermore, since the dominant forms of remuneration are for the most part determined privately by companies themselves, there will inevitably be a significant degree of variation amongst prevailing practices in this regard. For this reason, the list below cannot claim to be exhaustive. Likewise, the extent to which each of the main pay components factor into any particular officer's remuneration package will likely differ depending on the characteristics of the firm, the market sector and the candidate concerned. Subject to the above provisos, the following provides a general outline of the most common remuneration norms.

Basic Director's Service Fee

The director's service fee is the basic remuneration that is due to a company director in return for fulfilling their official directorial functions. This is distinct from any further functions carried out by a director for the company in an additional capacity, such as a senior executive office. In public companies, directorial functions typically include attending and participating in periodic board meetings and any associated board committee meetings, assessing relevant documentation both during and in advance of meetings, acquiring any requisite expertise or knowledge in advance of meetings, and – where necessary – consulting with relevant third parties such as professional legal and financial advisors.

The director's service fee will ordinarily be paid in the form of a fixed salary. In the case of a director who simultaneously holds a paid executive position in the same company (e.g. as Chief Executive Officer, Finance Director or Chief Operating Officer), the director's service fee may be of purely nominal value. However, in the case of non-executive directors (NEDs), the service fee will normally constitute the exclusive source of remuneration from an employer company, particularly in light of the UK Corporate Governance Code's influential recommendation that NED remuneration ordinarily should not include share options or other variable, performance-related elements.[15]

Executive Salary

This is the basic annual contractual pay due to an executive officer in return for fulfilling their official managerial functions. In the case of a senior executive who holds an additional office as director of the company, the executive salary (rather than director's service fee) will usually constitute the more significant component of basic remuneration, with the director's service fee being purely nominal in nature. In the case of Chief Executive Officers (CEOs) and other senior executives of larger publicly traded companies, executive salary will frequently comprise a minority of total remuneration received in any year; with

---

[15] See UK Corporate Governance Code, above n. 3, Code Provision D.1.3. On this, see further below.

the variable, performance-related components of pay providing the majority of the executive's overall annual award.

Bonus Payments

A bonus payment is an additional increment on pay, normally awarded on an annual basis. The word 'bonus' suggests an element of unexpectedness on the part of the recipient. Notwithstanding, in practice the frequent receipt of bonuses is both customary and entirely expected within many corporate environments. A bonus can be contractual in nature, in which case its award will be triggered by the relevant employee meeting a pre-specified periodic performance target. Alternatively, a bonus can be discretionary in nature, in which instance it may be awarded on the initiative of the employer additionally to, and also independently of, an employee's pre-specified forms of contractual remuneration.

In many market sectors including banking and financial services, annual employee bonuses are a traditionally common practice at most levels within the organization. Furthermore, in the case of employees fulfilling senior executive functions within public companies (and, in particular, CEOs), the award of an annual pecuniary bonus in recognition of exceptional (or, at least, satisfactory) corporate performance has become a culturally ingrained expectation today. Whilst it was traditionally common practice for executive bonuses to be paid in cash form, in the case of larger public companies it is now increasingly the case that bonuses are paid in the form of shares in the employer company, or as restricted share grants.[16]

Shares and Restricted Share Grants

The rationale for remunerating senior executives in the form of shares in their employer company has already been explained above: that is, to provide managerial officeholders with a direct pecuniary incentive to seek to maximize shareholder wealth, thereby mitigating anticipated agency costs in the relationship between shareholders and management.[17] In recent years, concern about the apparent freedom enjoyed by many executives – particularly in banks – to liquidate personal shareholdings in their employer company in advance of share price falls has prompted growing scepticism about the effectiveness of unrestricted shares as a form of remuneration.[18] Consequently (and largely in response to ensuing regulatory developments[19]), *restricted* share grants have

---

[16] On this, see below.

[17] See above n. 8 and accompanying text.

[18] See e.g. L.A. Bebchuk and J.M. Fried, 'Paying for Long-Term Performance' (2010) 158 *University of Pennsylvania Law Review* 1915; L.A. Bebchuk, A. Cohen and H. Spamann, 'The Wages of Failure: Executive Compensation at Bear Sterns and Lehmann 2000–2008' (2010) 27 *Yale Journal on Regulation* 257.

[19] On this, see below.

become increasingly popular as a form of executive remuneration (especially for the payment of annual bonuses) within larger publicly traded companies, and most notably in the case of banks.

In essence, such schemes prohibit the disposal of some or all shares granted thereunder for a contractually pre-determined period of time. The relevant time period could be a specific number of years, or else could be determined by reference to a specified event such as the retirement of the relevant office-holder or the company's satisfaction of a particular financial-performance target. Alternatively, restrictions on share disposal may be disapplied on a phased basis over the length of the recipient employee's tenure in office, with disapplication of restrictions rendered contingent on the satisfaction of periodic performance objectives. Insofar as restricted share grants are designed to align managers' personal monetary incentives with the long-term performance of their employer firm, they are commonly referred to in practice as a type of long-term incentive scheme (or 'LTIS').

Executive Share Options

Executive share options (or, to use the more common US terminology, 'stock options') have undoubtedly been the dominant form of executive performance pay within Anglo-American public companies in recent decades. Share options are designed to provide a more powerful pecuniary incentive on the part of executives to elicit improvements in shareholder wealth (as reflected in the market price of a company's shares) in comparison to standard share grants. Essentially, a share option is a realizable right to purchase a share in a company at a future date, and at a price that is customarily set at the time the option is granted (known as the exercise or 'strike'[20] price of the option).

In its most straightforward (so-called 'vanilla') form, the exercise price will be the market price of the underlying share on the date of granting of the option (known in shorthand as 'at-the-money'[21]). This means that, to the extent that the market price of the underlying share on the eventual date of exercise of the option is greater than the market price on the earlier grant date, the option holder will be able to make a corresponding profit on exercising the option and then immediately sell the underlying share (known as 'unwinding'[22] of the option). Where a large number of options to acquire shares in the one company are unwound simultaneously, the resulting personal profit for the options holder can be considerable due to the powerful effect of options in 'leveraging' prospective equity gains. In a more sophisticated variant on the standard vanilla option, the exercise price might alternatively be set at a price

---

[20] This term is attributable to L.A. Bebchuk, J.M. Fried and D.I. Walker, 'Managerial Power and Rent Extraction in the Design of Executive Compensation' (2002) 69 *University of Chicago Law Review* 751.

[21] *ibid.*

[22] *ibid.*

materially above the market price on the grant date (i.e. 'out-of-the-money'[23]), with the intended effect of eliciting increased levels of devotion by managers to improving share price performance.

The main motivational value of share options resides in the fact that – unlike the case with standard share grants (which are essentially 'free' awards of shares) – the realization of share options entails the options holder making a financial outlay in order to acquire the underlying shares. Hence share options provide a specific incentive to increase a company's share price over and above the relevant options' exercise price. Otherwise, the options holder stands to make no pecuniary gain whatsoever. This is in contrast to (standard or restricted) share grants, where *any* instance of share price appreciation after the grant date (even in the context of a broader pattern of price depreciation) is of some material benefit to the grant beneficiary.

Like restricted share grants (described above), share options are a common form of long-term incentive scheme (or 'LTIS'). However, the extent to which any option scheme is actually conducive to aligning its beneficiary's personal incentives with long-term firm performance depends on the specific design of the scheme itself. Where options can be readily exercised, and the shares obtained thereunder readily disposed of on an unrestricted basis, the intended long-term incentivizing effect of the scheme in question will be undermined. In more extreme cases, share options might even be artificially manipulated via a practice known as options 'backdating', whereby the specified grant date is falsely set at a date earlier than the options' actual grant date, so as to enable their holder to benefit from fortuitous market developments in the interim period. Therefore remuneration committees and external consultants must consider carefully the ease (or, conversely, difficulty) with which options can be unwound by their recipients under alternative future market conditions.

Notably, the UK Corporate Governance Code recommends that, unlike their executive counterparts, non-executive directors ordinarily should not receive share options or other forms of equity-based award as part of their remuneration.[24] This is because, as a key element of their risk management and oversight function discussed in the previous chapter, NEDs are responsible for offering constructive challenge on management's strategic initiatives. In particular, a high-quality NED is expected to exploit their 'inside' monitoring position to identify any latent risk factors or other problems relating to the company's business or financial strategy, which have not yet been identified by 'outside' stock market actors such as institutional investors or market analysts.

Where any such undiscovered issues exist, it is likely that the company's shares will in effect be 'overvalued', at least until such time as the market becomes generally aware of the relevant matters.[25] In these circumstances, the

---

[23] *ibid.*

[24] See above n. 15.

[25] On the notion of overvalued equity generally, see M.C. Jensen, 'Agency Costs of Overvalued Equity' (2005) 34 *Financial Management* 5.

effective NED's role is to bring their concerns in this regard to management as soon as possible, with a view to ensuring either their rectification or – at least – the orderly disclosure of such to the market. However, where a NED stands to profit personally from overvalued shares via option holdings or other equity-based forms of remuneration, their incentive to identify and challenge the underlying causes of any such overvaluation is reduced or even eliminated outright. This danger was illustrated by the catastrophic collapse of the US utilities giant Enron in 2001, where the company's NEDs were apparently encouraged to overlook latent accounting failures and risk management lapses within the organization over a prolonged time period, at fear of undermining the (artificially inflated) value of their personal interests in Enron shares.[26]

For the above reasons, minimizing NEDs' personal exposure to their employer company's ongoing share price performance is today regarded as a key safeguard of such individuals' independence and objectivity of judgement, in the context of UK listed companies at least. This is notwithstanding the traditional (and, it may be said, increasingly outmoded) view that a director who proverbially refuses to 'put their skin in the game' by acquiring a material shareholding in their employer company is somehow showing disloyalty towards that firm or a lack of faith in its current management.

Pension Allowance

In addition to basic salary and further performance-related components, a senior executive compensation package will also customarily include a pension allowance. In the standard case, this will be calculated on a defined benefit basis as a contractually specified proportion of the officeholder's final salary.

Gratuities

A gratuity is essentially a discretionary payment made to an employee (most commonly a senior executive officeholder) independently of any pre-existing contractual undertaking on the part of the employer to do so. The most common and well-known forms of gratuity are inducement payments (so-called 'golden handshakes') and severance payments (so-called 'golden parachutes'). A golden handshake is a (normally one-off) discretionary payment made to a new recruit in order to entice them initially to take up a vacancy. A golden parachute is a (likewise normally one-off) discretionary payment made to an outgoing employee as part of the agreed termination of their employment. In this context, a severance payment serves the dual function of: (i) from the *employer's* perspective, encouraging the outgoing employee to acquiesce in the

---

[26] On the Enron debacle generally, see Chapter 8. On the significant conflicts of interest afflicting Enron's board members generally prior to the company's implosion, see S. Deakin and S.J. Konzelmann, 'Learning from Enron' (2004) 12 *Corporate Governance: An International Review* 134, 139.

termination of their employment on generally cooperative terms, so as to preclude any future dispute between the parties; and (ii) from the *employee's* perspective, mitigating the likely short-term financial blow from loss of office, thereby metaphorically facilitating a 'soft landing' from the initial 'fall' of job termination.

Expenses and Perquisites

A further notable but relatively inconspicuous component of senior executive remuneration in public companies is the common general entitlement to indirect and/or non-pecuniary benefits of office. These include the right to charge reasonable expenses incurred in fulfilment of official executive functions to the employer, with the bounds of 'reasonableness' for this purpose often defined in somewhat liberal terms to include such particulars as business class air travel and fairly lavish corporate hospitality. Additionally, an executive's monetary remuneration may be supplemented by the direct receipt of various non-pecuniary benefits of office, such as the use of a company-owned car or free accommodation in a company-owned apartment. Whilst not impacting directly on measurable levels of pecuniary pay, such 'soft' entitlements nonetheless tend to be important components of a senior executive officeholder's overall remuneration package.

WHO DETERMINES THE REMUNERATION OF SENIOR EXECUTIVES AND DIRECTORS?

Fundamental Principles

As the supreme decision-making body within the internal corporate hierarchy, the board of directors has ultimate responsibility for determining enterprise-wide remuneration policy, and also for ensuring that such policy is implemented throughout the organization. In large-scale public companies or groups, administrative exigency normally dictates that the vast majority of decisions concerning the practical application of enterprise remuneration policy to individual employees are delegated by the board to subordinate managerial or human resources personnel. In such instances, the board's input is typically restricted to 'arm's length' oversight only. However, where determination of the pay of senior executive officers is concerned, the board naturally has a more compelling incentive to play an active role in the process.

From a governance point of view, the determination of senior executive pay gives rise to certain unique and significant positional conflicts of interest. Not least amongst these is the fact that many senior executives – most notably CEOs, CFOs and COOs – are typically members of the board of directors themselves. Moreover, such individuals – and, in particular, CEOs – frequently wield considerable personal influence over boards due to a combination of hierarchical, informational, personal and psychological factors.[27] For these reasons, absent countervailing legal and/or regulatory controls on their decisions, the objectivity and functional independence of boards with respect to executive remuneration issues is a major cause for concern.

Additionally, there remains the outstanding question of who determines the pay of the board members themselves, particularly the nominally 'independent' non-executive directors who have no complementary managerial position in their employer company. To this, the answer is at once both simple and counterintuitive: it is that *the board itself* conventionally has ultimate formal responsibility for determining the pay of its members, by virtue of its more general constitutional authority over corporate managerial affairs (which ordinarily includes decisions on employee remuneration policy).[28]

Furthermore, companies' articles of association customarily entrust boards with a broad ambit of discretion as to the specific forms and design of remuneration awarded to directors. Indeed, articles normally permit any form or level of pay deemed appropriate for the relevant individual's contribution to the company, whether in a 'pure' directorial or, alternatively, a dual executive-directorial capacity.[29] The only standard procedural constraint in the articles with respect to potential positional conflicts is that any director whose pay is in question should not be counted as participating and voting in the relevant board meeting.[30] With the (limited) exception of this provision, though, articles are typically silent on the matter.

The (Limited) Role of the Courts

Likewise limited is the capacity of the courts to exert external judicial control over directorial and executive pay-setting in UK public companies, whether from a substantive or procedural perspective.

The most obvious potential basis for substantive judicial control over remuneration is the director's duty of loyalty under section 172 of the Companies Act 2006. As discussed in Chapter 6, section 172(1) requires generally that a director, in discharging his official functions, acts in a way that he considers, in good faith, would be most likely to promote the success of the company for the benefit of its shareholders as a whole. Any director found to be in contravention of this section, whether as a result of an individual or collective (board) decision that they were involved in, will in principle be civilly liable to the company (and, indirectly, its shareholders) for breach of duty.

---

[27] On this issue generally, see D. Langevoort, 'The Human Nature of Corporate Boards: Law, Norms and the Unintended Consequences of Independence and Accountability' (2001) 89 *Georgetown Law Journal* 797.

[28] See The Companies (Model Articles) Regulations 2008 (SI 2008/3229), Schedule 3 ('Model Articles for Public Companies'), article 3. On the board's ultimate managerial authority within the company generally, see Chapter 4.

[29] *ibid.*, article 23.

[30] *ibid.*, article 16.

Notwithstanding this fact, the prospect of section 172(1) being success-fully invoked against a public company board that approves an allegedly exces-sive executive remuneration award is highly unlikely for a number of reasons. First, given the basic fiduciary nature of the director's equitable duty of loyalty (from which the section 172 duty is historically derived), the ambit of discre-tion afforded to directors under the section is very broad to say the least.[31] The innately subjective status of the duty means that, so long as a defendant direc-tor's purported honest commitment to promoting the company's success is irrefutable, it follows that the propriety of any specific strategic or operational decisions that they make is beyond judicial reproach.[32] The only conceivable situation outside of the self-dealing context where a remuneration decision might put a board in breach of section 172 is where an approved award is so egregious under the circumstances that no intelligent and honest person could reasonably have deemed it conducive to advancing the company's interests.[33] Even then, determining a specific threshold of pay 'excess' for this purpose would likely be a virtually intractable judicial task, and it would certainly be a bold bench that sought to posit an authoritative view on this matter.[34]

A more likely scenario where the duty of loyalty could potentially be invoked in the remuneration context is where a company's board approves an argu-ably exorbitant executive remuneration package at a time when the company's solvency is threatened. In this regard, section 172(3) expressly retains the pre-2006 common law duty of directors to take account of creditors' interests in addition to those of shareholders, in situations where a company is either insolvent or facing an imminent risk to its continuing solvency.[35] This requires,

---

[31] On this, see A.R. Keay, 'Good Faith and Directors Duty to Promote the Success of the Company' (2011) 32 *The Company Lawyer* 138.

[32] See *Re Smith and Fawcett* [1942] Ch 304 (CA); *Regentcrest plc v Cohen* [2001] BCC 494.

[33] Pennycuick J's so-called 'intelligent and honest man' test arguably provides a basic objec-tive component to the (otherwise subjective) director's duty of loyalty, with the outcome that a decision which is simply incapable of being deemed conducive to advancing the company's interests by any reasonable estimation will put a director in breach of his duty of loyalty irre-spective of whether absence of good faith on his part has been established. See *Charterbridge Corp v Lloyds Bank* [1970] Ch 62, 74.

[34] Interestingly, while English courts have been notoriously reluctant to confront this issue directly, the Delaware courts in the United States have made tentative inroads into determining the propriety of arguably exorbitant executive remuneration awards under the auspices of the judicial doctrine of 'corporate waste', which denotes 'an exchange of assets [including the remu-neration of employees] for consideration so disproportionately small as to lie beyond the range at which any reasonable person might be willing to trade'. See *Lewis v Vogelstein* 699 A 2d 327 (Del Ch 1997), 366, per Chancellor Allen. For a high-profile instance where this test was (ulti-mately unsuccessfully) applied in practice with respect to a remuneration award, see *Brehm v Eisner* 746 A 2d 244 (Del 2000). While there is no explicit 'waste' doctrine in English company law, the above 'intelligent and honest man' test (see *ibid.*) could be said to elicit broadly similar outcomes in determining the propriety of board remuneration approval decisions.

[35] On this aspect of the director's duty of loyalty, see *West Mercia Safetywear v Dodd* [1988] 4 BCC 30 (CA); *Kinsela v Russell Kinsela Pty* (1986) 10 ACLR 395 (NSW CA); A.R. Keay, 'The Duty of Directors to Take into Account Creditors' Interests: Has It Any Role to Play?' (2002) *Journal of Business Law* 379.

in particular, that the board refrains from dissipating the company's cash flows on discretionary business expenses (including exorbitant executive remuneration arrangements) without at least giving prior consideration to the alternative option of preserving such funds in the company, in order to mitigate the potential losses to unsecured creditors in the event of its future liquidation.[36]

Due to their concentrated and largely autonomous control over an insolvent company's affairs, coupled with the absence of restrictive rules of standing governing liquidator (as opposed to shareholder) initiated enforcement actions against directors,[37] liquidators tend to be much better positioned than shareholders to act as a prospective claimant in actions for breach of directorial duty. For this reason, it is conceivable that the collective interests of a company's *creditors*,[38] rather than its shareholders, may in practice turn out to be the more common criterion by which the fiduciary propriety (or otherwise) of boards' remuneration approval decisions under section 172 is judicially determined in practice.

Besides the director's general duty of loyalty, an additional (albeit structurally limited) substantive judicial control over exorbitant remuneration awards was identified in the case of *Re Halt Garage (1964) Ltd*.[39] Here it was established that a company director, whose pay was significantly and manifestly out of keeping with her corresponding contribution to managing the company's business, could not genuinely claim to be receiving the money in question as remuneration for directorial services. Rather, on the given facts it was more appropriate, in the court's view, to regard the payments received as an effective disguised gift to the director in her alter capacity as a company shareholder. Since the company in question did not have sufficient distributable profits at the relevant time to cover those payments, the court consequently found ground to strike down the awards in question as improper payments to a shareholder out of capital.

Whilst the *Halt Garage* decision could be construed as a creative judicial attempt to impose an uppermost limit on remuneration awards (at least where the director or executive in question is simultaneously a company shareholder), its significance in this regard for public companies should not be overestimated. Not only was the *Halt Garage* case concerned with the very different context of a family-owned private company, but it involved the somewhat extreme scenario of a director who had effectively carried out no material functions for the company at all over a number of years (albeit on account of ill health). Hence

---

[36] However, in more serious cases of corporate financial instability, where there exists no reasonable prospect of the company avoiding going into insolvent liquidation, it is incumbent upon the board to cease the company's trading operations entirely, and thereafter to take all reasonable efforts to mitigate the potential losses to creditors. This is the essence of the wrongful trading rule under section 214 of the Insolvency Act 1986.

[37] See Insolvency Act 1986, s 212 ('Summary remedy against delinquent directors, liquidators, etc.').

[38] Or, at least, the *unsecured* segment of its creditors whose collective interests the liquidator is formally appointed to safeguard.

[39] [1982] 3 All ER 1016.

this case should be understood as having a very marginal impact on public company remuneration practices at best, and as doing little to limit the customarily broad sphere of discretion vested in boards with respect to the design and approval of remuneration awards.

Alongside the above substantive judicial controls on directorial and executive remuneration, there exists some (limited) further scope for *procedural* control by courts over the board's pay-setting practices. Strictly speaking, remuneration awards could be said to constitute the most common and obvious instance of a directorial conflict of interest, insofar as the relevant officer's personal interest in receipt of the award is directly averse to his fiduciary responsibility to ensure compensation of labour by the company on the most cost-effective available terms. However, unlike other forms of conflicted interest transaction, which should be formally declared by the relevant director to the board,[40] conflicts arising from the terms of directors' service contracts (including pay arrangements) are exempted from this requirement where (as is customary) they are already susceptible to consideration by the board or a formally appointed committee of directors (e.g. a remuneration committee).[41] This is subject to the important common law proviso that the board's constitutional powers to determine the remuneration of directors will – on account of the manifest conflicts of interest at play – be construed strictly and narrowly by the courts, so as to preclude directors from exercising discretion in this regard outside the bounds of their formal mandate from shareholders under the articles.[42]

Remuneration Committees

Ordinarily the board is freely entitled under the articles to delegate any of its powers to specialized committees.[43] Moreover, in public companies today, the delegation of key board functions to sub-board committees is generally perceived as a practical imperative, in terms of improving the functionality of directorial decision-making and also mitigating particular conflicts of interest. Executive remuneration is almost universally regarded today as being one such issue on which the input of a specialized sub-committee of directors is indispensable.

There is no express statutory requirement for remuneration committees in the UK, whether generally or for any specific category of companies. However, the UK Corporate Governance Code recommends that FTSE 350 companies

---

[40] This general procedural requirement is imposed by sections 177 and 182 of the Companies Act 2006. The former provision establishes the director's duty to declare an interest in a proposed or existing transaction, whilst the latter sets out the corresponding requirement for a director to declare an interest in a pre-existing transaction or arrangement.

[41] See Companies Act 2006, ss 177(6)(c) and 182(6)(c).

[42] On this, see *Guinness plc v Saunders* [1990] 2 AC 663 (HL).

[43] See Model Articles, above n. 28, article 5(1)(a).

should establish a specialized remuneration committee comprising at least three independent non-executive directors.[44] Under the Code, independent remuneration committees are forwarded as the principal structural means for achieving the important policy objective to the effect that '[n]o director should be involved in deciding his or her own remuneration'.[45] Accordingly, by requiring the absence of any executive presence on the body that is formally entrusted with responsibility for determining senior executive remuneration arrangements, the Code seeks to ensure that this problematic scenario is avoided. To this end, the Code further recommends that remuneration committees be vested with delegated responsibility for setting remuneration for all executive directors and the chairman, including pension rights and any compensation payments for loss of office.[46] The committee is also expected to recommend and monitor the level and structure of remuneration for at least the first layer of senior management below board level,[47] for example the relevant organization's functional divisional heads.

In addition, the committee should take responsibility for the appointment of any independent remuneration consultants to provide external advice on executive pay arrangements, so as to mitigate the obvious conflict of interest that would otherwise arise where executives have a direct influence over such appointments.[48] To ensure as best as possible that the deliberative dynamic of the remuneration committee does not replicate that of the full board, it is recommended that the chairman of a company's board does not simultaneously act as chair of the remuneration committee (although she may still be a member of the committee).[49]

Whilst there are no specific requirements with respect to the skills or expertise that should be possessed by remuneration committee members in non-banking companies, the expectations of bank remuneration committee members in this regard are notably more onerous. Under the Prudential Regulation Authority's Remuneration Code, remuneration committees in the banking sector must be sufficiently equipped to exercise competent and independent judgement on a firm's remuneration policies and practices, with particular regard to the incentives created for managing risk, capital and liquidity.[50] Bank remuneration committees must be particularly alert to any decisions on remuneration that have implications for the firm's overall risk exposure and/or risk management,

---

[44] In the case of UK-listed companies below FTSE 350 level, the corresponding recommendation is for the establishment of committees consisting of at least two independent NEDs. See above n. 3, Code Provision D.2.1.

[45] *ibid.*, Main Principle D.2.

[46] *ibid.*, Code Provision D.2.2.

[47] *ibid.*

[48] *ibid.*, Supporting Principle D.2.

[49] *ibid.*, Code Provision D.2.1.

[50] See *Prudential Regulation Authority Rulebook*, 'CRR firms: remuneration', Principle 7.4(1), at www.prarulebook.co.uk/rulebook/Content/Part/292166/10-01-2017 ('PRA Remuneration Code').

which should ultimately be referred for approval by the group board as a whole as part of its general strategic remit (although, in such instances, the committee retains responsibility for initially preparing the decision in question for referral to the full board).[51]

A further unique demand that is placed on remuneration committees in banks today is their regulatory responsibility to take directly into account in their decision-making not only the long-term interests of shareholders (as is the case with committees in non-banking companies), but also the interests of the bank's other stakeholders (most notably its depositors) together with the public interest as a whole.[52] This places a broad and onerous responsibility on bank remuneration committees today, with the implication that serving on such a committee in the post-crisis era is by no means a job for the uninformed or light-hearted.

In the case of banks and other financial industry entities (so-called 'BOFIs'), the 2009 Walker Report[53] recommends that BOFI remuneration committees should furthermore assume responsibility for determining the overall structure and framework of remuneration policy across the entity as a whole, with particular regard to the risk factors affecting prospective performance outcomes in different parts of the business.[54]

In performing this broad and important function, a BOFI remuneration committee should have particular regard to the pay conditions of any 'high end' employees in the company, meaning those individuals performing a significant influence function in the entity or whose activities or decisions could have a material impact on the entity's risk profile.[55] This is in acknowledgement of the fact that, somewhat extraordinarily in the case of banks, many of the most influential employees from an enterprise risk perspective – such as senior traders – are commonly positioned below the board or senior managerial levels of the corporate hierarchy, meaning that they fall outside the scope of the remuneration committee's purview as it is conventionally understood and defined. However, for pragmatic reasons bank remuneration committees are not expected to determine the specific pay arrangements of individual employees below top executive level, which remains within the remit of responsible managerial personnel.[56]

---

[51] *ibid.*, Principle 7.4(3).

[52] *ibid.*, Principle 7.4(4). Interestingly, the government's current (at time of writing) corporate governance Green Paper proposes the introduction of a general (i.e. non-bank-specific) regulatory requirement for remuneration committees to consult both shareholders *and the wider workforce* prior to preparing its executive pay policy, on the basis that '[t]his could allow a much broader range of views to be heard from across all areas of a large public company'. See above n. 11, 28.

[53] On the Walker Report (and associated review) generally, see Chapter 8.

[54] See D. Walker, *A Review of Corporate Governance in Banks and Other Financial Industry Entities: Final Recommendations* (26 November 2009), 108, para 7.7 and Recommendation 28.

[55] *ibid.*, 109–10, paras 7.8–7.10 and Recommendation 29.

[56] *ibid.*, para. 7.

Due in no small part to the abovementioned regulatory developments, remuneration committees are now a virtually universal element of UK public company board structures, both in the banking sector and also more generally. Whilst such committees have undoubtedly played a crucial role in increasing the objectivity and formal legitimacy of the executive pay-setting process in public companies, they are by no means the governance panacea insofar as directorial conflicts of interest are concerned. The basic fact remains that remuneration committee members, in spite of their formally independent status, are – like any director – ultimately employed and remunerated by the company itself, under the ultimate leadership of its board and senior management.

Against this background, a remuneration committee that adopts an apparently overzealous stance to constraining perceived executive pay excess could risk alienating itself from other board members, thereby undermining the board's collective decision-making dynamic and – in turn – destabilizing the committee members' position within the company. It is thus essential that the remuneration committee is supplemented by other legal and institutional mechanisms that are designed to ensure the effective alignment of executive remuneration levels with the corresponding levels of performance of the officers in question.

Determination of Non-Executive Directors' (NEDs') Remuneration

Since the remuneration committee is typically composed entirely of independent non-executive directors, it would obviously be improper for the committee to determine the pay of the non-executive members of the board. Accordingly, responsibility for determining NEDs' remuneration is – under the UK Corporate Governance Code – vested in the board as a whole, or alternatively the shareholders where the articles make provision to this effect.[57] Exceptionally, a company is permitted under the Code to appoint a specialized committee for this purpose,[58] although it is unlikely that a committee with any more than a minority of non-executive representatives would be deemed acceptable for this purpose from the point of view of a company's institutional shareholders.

The Code further recommends that levels of remuneration for NEDs should reflect the time commitment and responsibilities of the role.[59] Crucially, though, remuneration for NEDs should not include share options or other performance-related elements.[60] This is in view of the risk – explained above – that NEDs with a vested personal interest in a company's share price performance might be discouraged from raising concerns about latent enterprise risk exposures, which might in turn have an adverse impact on share price if publicly exposed.

---

[57] See UK Corporate Governance Code, above n. 3, Code Provision D.2.3.
[58] *ibid.*
[59] *ibid.*, Code Provision D.1.3.
[60] *ibid.*

The Code does, however, provide exceptional dispensation to grant share options to a NED where this is deemed necessary for recruitment, retention or incentivization purposes. In such instance, shareholder approval should be sought in advance of the options award, and any shares acquired by the exercise of the options should be held until at least one year after the relevant NED leaves the board.[61] It is additionally specified that the holding of share options could be deemed relevant to the determination of a NED's independence for the purposes of the Code,[62] thereby insinuating that investors and proxy advisory agencies should be particularly cognizant of this fact when evaluating a company's annual regulatory disclosures.

Directors' Service Contracts Open for Inspection by Shareholders

It should finally be noted that – alongside the above rules governing the determination of senior executive and directorial remuneration in public companies – there is the additional statutory requirement that a company keeps available for inspection a copy of every director's service contract (including those relating to subsidiaries of the company).[63] The contracts should normally be accessible at the company's registered office,[64] and each contract should remain accessible until at least one year after the relevant director leaves office.[65]

Any shareholder of the company is entitled to inspect the directors' service contracts – including any remuneration provisions included therein – without charge.[66] Furthermore, any shareholder is entitled to be provided by the company with any or all of the directors' service contracts on request,[67] and failure by the company to make such provision within seven days will render any officers of the company responsible for the default liable to a fine.[68] There is no minimum share ownership threshold for the purpose of triggering either of these entitlements. Therefore it is technically possible for an individual to purchase a single share in a public company for the purpose of gaining access to contractual information pertaining to directors' remuneration arrangements.

Since most meaningful data on directorial pay in public companies will be specified in the annual statutory directors' remuneration report[69] in any event, the practical value to shareholders of the above provisions today is somewhat limited. Notwithstanding, they still provide an extra layer of transparency for

---

[61] *ibid.*

[62] *ibid.*

[63] See Companies Act (CA) 2006, s 228(1).

[64] CA 2006, s 228(2)(a).

[65] CA 2006, s 228(3).

[66] CA 2006, s 229(1).

[67] CA 2006, s 229(2).

[68] CA 2006, s 229(3)-(4).

[69] On this, see below.

shareholders with respect to a company's high-level remuneration policy and practices, particularly where a shareholder – for whatever reason – requires immediate access to such information before publication by the company of that year's remuneration report.

THE DIRECTORS' REMUNERATION REPORT AND 'SAY ON PAY' VOTE

Historical Background

The last two decades of the twentieth century witnessed a stratospheric rise in general levels of executive pay in UK public companies, fuelled in part by the spate of large-scale privatizations, and subsequent flotations, of former public utilities. A particular cause of concern in the recessionary years of the 1990s was the abovementioned 'rewards for failure' issue, where lucrative pay awards to senior executives in many instances appeared to be unreflective of corresponding corporate performance levels.

The principal industry response to these concerns was the landmark Greenbury Report on directors' remuneration, which was published in 1995.[70] Initially, the Report took the form of a self-regulatory body of principles promulgated by an industry-representative Study Group. However, many of Greenbury's key recommendations were subsequently incorporated within the inaugural Combined Code on Corporate Governance[71] (now the UK Corporate Governance Code[72]), whereupon they fell under the regulatory purview of the UK's main corporate governance regulatory body, the Financial Reporting Council.

One of the central themes that emanated from the original Greenbury Report – and also its more recent incarnations – is the significance of effective transparency in combatting perceived directorial' pay excess. Hence Greenbury professed to 'attach the highest importance to full disclosure of directors' remuneration as a means of ensuring accountability to shareholders and reassuring the public'.[73] To this end, Greenbury recommended that companies furnish their shareholders with 'all the information they may reasonably require to enable them to assess the company's general policy on executive remuneration and the entire remuneration packages of individual Directors'.[74] It was recommended that this information be included within a report of the remuneration committee, provided on behalf of the board, and to which shareholders would be invited to give their approval at any General Meeting where this was deemed by the board to be appropriate.[75]

---

[70] See above n. 1.
[71] See The Combined Code: Principles of Best Practice and Code of Best Practice (May 2000).
[72] See above n. 3.
[73] Above n. 1, para. 5.2.
[74] *ibid.*, para 5.3.
[75] *ibid.*, para 5.4.

The Greenbury Study Group strongly favoured providing companies with considerable flexibility regarding how they implemented its recommendations on pay transparency, and correspondingly disfavoured a formal legislative approach to the matter.[76] However, this position became increasingly untenable as the new millennium approached, due to perceived poor standards of compliance with the original 'soft law' framework, coupled with a fresh spike in exposed pay levels triggered by the bull market of the late 1990s.[77] In view of these factors, the Department for Trade and Industry (now Department for Business, Energy and Industrial Policy) deemed it necessary to put Greenbury's main recommendations on pay transparency on a formal statutory footing, in the form of the Directors' Remuneration Report Regulations 2002.[78]

The Regulations placed a mandatory obligation on quoted[79] company boards to prepare a directors' remuneration report for each financial year, to be laid before shareholders alongside the company's standard annual accounts and reports.[80] Furthermore, shareholders were given the opportunity to pass an advisory (i.e. non-legally-binding) approval resolution on the report (known in US terminology as a 'say on pay' vote) in each Annual General Meeting.[81]

The Revised (Post-2013) Two-Tier Procedure for 'Say on Pay' Voting

The original 'say on pay' model introduced by the 2002 Regulations operated for a decade thereafter, until its replacement in 2013 with a more complex 'two-tiered' framework of remuneration reporting and voting. This was influenced in large part by a perception that the original system had failed to curb the continually spiralling rate of public company executive pay, and also the longstanding malaise of 'rewards for failure' within many firms.[82] Furthermore, it was widely felt by commentators that – if anything – the greater scope for cross-company pay comparisons facilitated by 'say on pay' disclosures over the previous decade had actually prompted a further general 'ratcheting up' of

---

[76] See *ibid.*, para. 1.13.

[77] C. Villiers, 'Controlling Executive Pay: Institutional Investors or Distributive Justice?' (2010) 10 *Journal of Corporate Law Studies* 309, 317.

[78] See SI 2002/1986 ('the Regulations'); Department of Trade and Industry, *Directors' Remuneration: A Consultative Document* (July 1999).

[79] For this purpose, 'quoted' companies include all UK-registered companies which are traded either on the London Stock Exchange, any other regulated market in the European Economic Area, the New York Stock Exchange or the Nasdaq market. See CA 2006, s 385. For the sake of consistency we will in general continue to use the term 'public' company in the discussion that follows, subject to this proviso.

[80] Directors' basic statutory obligation in this regard is set out today in section 420 of the Companies Act 2006.

[81] See CA 2006, s 439.

[82] See Department for Business Innovation and Skills ('BIS'), *Directors' Pay: Consultation on Revised Remuneration Reporting Regulations* (June 2012), para. 12.

executive pay levels.[83] Consequently, in the government's view, more stringent legislative action in this area was needed.[84]

Under the revised post-2013 framework,[85] the directors' remuneration reporting (and corresponding voting) system now comprises two separate components. These are: (i) a legally-binding shareholder vote (and corresponding report) on a company's reported general *policy* for annual directorial remuneration-setting, which must be administered by quoted companies at least once every three years[86] ('the policy report')[87]; coupled with (ii) an annual, non-binding[88] advisory vote by shareholders on the company's ongoing *implementation* of its directorial

---

[83] See A. Dignam, 'Remuneration and Riots: Rethinking Corporate-Governance Reform in the Age of Entitlement' (2013) 66 *Current Legal Problems* 401, 410. Indeed, directly in response to this acknowledged problem, the most recent (2016) edition of the UK Corporate Governance Code recommends that whilst '[t]he remuneration committee should judge where to position their company relative to other companies [on pay] ... they should use such comparisons with caution, in view of the risk of an upward ratchet of remuneration levels with no corresponding improvement in corporate and individual performance, and should avoid paying more than is necessary'. See above n. 3, Supporting Principle D.1.

[84] See BIS, above n. 82, 5 ('Foreword from the Secretary of State').

[85] See CA 2006, ss 226A–226F, 439A; The Large and Medium-sized Companies and Groups (Accounts and Reports) Amendment Regulations 2013, substituting new Schedule 8 to the previous Companies and Groups (Accounts and Reports) Regulations 2008.

[86] That is unless interim changes to an existing remuneration policy are proposed, in which case a vote on those changes should be held either at the company's next AGM, or at a specially convened General Meeting beforehand. Furthermore, in its recently published Green Paper on corporate governance reform, the government has mooted the idea of requiring the executive pay policy vote to be held *more frequently* than a tri-annual basis, particularly in companies that have recently experienced significant changes to their business model or executive team, thereby calling into question the continuing suitability of their existing policies in this regard. See above n 11, 24.

[87] CA 2006, ss 226A(1), 439A(1). The policy report should contain (*inter alia*): (i) a description of each of the components of directors' remuneration package which are comprised in the company's remuneration policy; (ii) how each component supports the short and long-term strategic objectives of the company (or, where the company is a parent company, the group); (iii) an explanation of how that component of the remuneration package operates; (iv) the maximum that may be paid in respect of that component; (v) a description of the framework used to assess performance including a description of any performance measures which apply; and (vi) an explanation as to whether there are any provisions for the recovery of sums paid or the withholding of the payment of any sum. See The Large and Medium-sized Companies and Groups (Accounts and Reports) Regulations 2008, Sch. 8, paras. 25–26 (as substituted by The Large and Medium-sized Companies and Groups (Accounts and Reports) Amendment Regulations 2013) ('Revised Regulations').

[88] Although, in its recent (at time of writing) corporate governance Green Paper, the government has tentatively raised the issue of additionally subjecting all or at least some of the company's annual policy implementation report to a legally-binding shareholder vote, on the premise that '[t]here would [consequently] be clear and immediate consequences flowing from an adverse shareholder vote, rather than the current situation where the annual vote on the remuneration report is merely advisory'. In the alternative, the government has proposed a so-called 'escalation process' whereby significant minority shareholder opposition to a pay award (e.g. in the range of 20%–33%) could trigger the application of a binding vote regime in future. See above n. 11, 22–23.

remuneration policy, as reported on by the board at the end of each year ('the implementation report').[89] In promulgating this new two-tiered 'say on pay' system, the government expressly envisaged that the reforms would encourage remuneration committees and external consultants to take a longer-term strategic approach when developing a company's remuneration policy, based on an extended three-year (as opposed to annual) time horizon.[90]

Crucially, a company is prohibited under the new system from making a remuneration payment to a director in breach of its own pre-established remuneration policy.[91] Any contractual arrangement entered into with a director for the future receipt by her of such a payment will have no legal effect,[92] unless the relevant payment is specifically authorized by shareholders via a resolution to this effect.[93] Consequently, remuneration committees must ensure that any major shareholder concerns in relation to pay are recognized and addressed proactively at the initial policy design stage.

Under the post-2013 framework, moreover, special attention is afforded to the controversial issue of directorial severance payments or 'golden parachutes' (on which, see above). A company's policy on severance payments must be clearly set out in its tri-annual remuneration policy report.[94] Any such payments can now only validly be made within the ambit of the company's pre-existing policy in this regard,[95] or – failing that – with the formal approval of shareholders thereto.[96]

Notably, the board's annual implementation report is required to show (*inter alia*) a single total remuneration figure for every director each year, comprising: salary, benefits, pension, bonus, plus earnings from any long-term incentive scheme.[97] This figure should cover only remuneration actually received by a director during the previous year,[98] and is calculable by reference to an official formula that has been developed by the Financial Reporting Council's Financial Reporting Lab, based on consultation with investors and industry.[99] The implementation report must also provide a graphical correlation of CEO remuneration with recent company performance, highlighting the extent to which periodic variations in a CEO's pay are reflective of corresponding variations in the total shareholder return generated by her employer company.[100]

---

[89] Revised Regulations, above n. 87, para. 21.

[90] See BIS, above n. 82, para. 15.

[91] CA 2006, s 226B(1)(a).

[92] CA 2006, s 226E(1).

[93] CA 2006, s 226E(1)(b).

[94] Revised Regulations, above n. 87, para. 16.

[95] CA 2006, s 226C(1)(a).

[96] CA 2006, s 226C(1)(b).

[97] Revised Regulations, above n. 87, paras. 4–10.

[98] *ibid.*, para. 7. Although it should additionally cover any amounts of remuneration that remain receivable as a result of the directors' achievement of performance measures and targets relating specifically to the previous year. *ibid.*, para. 7(1)(c).

[99] See Financial Reporting Lab, *Lab project report: a single figure for remuneration* (June 2012).

[100] Revised Regulations, above n. 87, para. 18.

Evaluating the Impact of the 2013 Reforms

We envisage that the recent partial upgrading of the directorial remuneration vote onto a legally-binding footing is in itself likely to have only a marginal effect on prevailing standards of board accountability with respect to remuneration matters. However, the reforms will almost certainly give rise to a materially higher degree of compliance and contracting costs, as companies seek to insure against the risk of individual directors' contracts being rendered invalid, and thus legally ineffective, on the ground of substantive non-compliance with a firm's currently-applicable remuneration policy.

A further and related cause of concern is the reduced flexibility afforded to remuneration committees, who must refrain from making any extraordinary awards to new or continuing officeholders outside the bounds of a company's remuneration policy, at least without first convening a General Meeting of shareholders (or, alternatively, awaiting the company's next AGM) in order to obtain the necessary formal approval. This could potentially make it more difficult for UK public companies to attract high-quality leaders from overseas jurisdictions (especially the United States) where the regulatory obstacles in this regard are generally less onerous.

An additional important question concerns the actual legal mechanics of how the new procedure will work, particularly in cases where a payment awarded to a director is deemed invalid on the ground of non-compliance with a company's remuneration policy. Significantly, shareholders are for the first time entrusted with the formal legal power to *strike down* director remuneration awards that are inconsistent with the company's applicable remuneration policy.[101] The intended civil consequences in such cases are specified under section 226E of the Companies Act 2006. Under this provision, any director in receipt of such a payment is deemed to hold the relevant payment on trust for the company.[102]

It is not automatically clear, though, who will have legal capacity to initiate an action for recovery of the invalid payment on the company's behalf. Where there is a subsequent change of control or business failure, this will presumably be the new board, or liquidator, respectively. However, where the existing board remains in control, it would appear that recovery action in respect of the improper remuneration payment will have to be instigated by a disgruntled minority shareholder via a derivative claim, on the ground that the payment in question amounts either to a 'default' or to a 'breach of trust' within the meaning of section 260(3) of the Companies Act 2006.

Since the key information necessary to prompt such an action is likely to be contained in the company's annual implementation report, remuneration committees must be vigilant in ensuring that there are no possible grounds for an awarded payment to be seen as in breach of the company's current remuneration policy. At

---

[101] See CA 2006, ss 226B(1), 226E(1).

[102] CA 2006, s 226E(2). This provision additionally states that any director who authorized the payment in question is jointly and severally liable to indemnify the company for any loss resulting from it.

the very least, in instances where a material non-compliance risk exists it falls upon the committee (and, in turn, the board) to ensure that an appropriate approval resolution is sought from shareholders at the company's next General Meeting.

Where a company is subject to a takeover involving a wholesale transfer of control over its share capital, the outgoing shareholders (rather than the company itself) will collectively be entitled to recover any exit payment received by an outgoing director as part of the takeover arrangements, in the event that such payment fails to comply with the company's currently-applicable remuneration policy and was unauthorized by shareholders.[103] Presumably, the right to initiate a recovery action in this regard against the recipient ex-director will be vested in each individual former shareholder as an effective beneficiary of the payment held on trust by the defendant.[104]

Finally, the intended effect of the above reforms in encouraging enhanced periodic evaluation of the directorial pay-performance nexus could be said to sit somewhat uneasily alongside the UK government's contemporaneous policy objective (as emphasized most recently in the Kay Review[105]) to combat short-termism in UK equity markets, in particular by removing structural impediments to long-term strategic planning by managers.[106] Frequent directorial pay evaluation necessarily entails the corresponding evaluation of ongoing managerial performance, especially where (as within a company's annual implementation report) CEO pay and total shareholder return are explicitly and graphically correlated with one another each year.[107] This could potentially increase the incentives of some CEOs to engage in creative earnings management practices[108] aimed at proactively 'correcting' expected pay-performance non-correlations, so as to legitimize year-on-year pay increases in the eyes of investors and their corporate governance advisors. As an aside, moreover, the special attention afforded to CEO pay within the proposed implementation report arguably risks 'individualizing' the monitoring focus of investors, thereby detracting from the inherently *collective* nature of the board's responsibility for overseeing the company's business strategy and key risk exposures.[109]

---

[103] CA 2006, ss 226C, 226E(4)(b).

[104] Although note that, under s 226E(5), a defendant director in such an action will be entitled to discretionary relief from the court against prospective civil liability under this section (whether wholly or partially, and whether vis-à-vis the company itself or its former shareholders) if he can demonstrate that he has acted honestly and reasonably and, having regard to all the circumstances of the case, ought to be relieved as such.

[105] See J. Kay, *The Kay Review of UK Equity Markets and Long-Term Decision Making: Final Report* (July 2012), para. 3.17. On this, see Chapter 5.

[106] On this, see M.T. Moore and E. Walker-Arnott, 'A Fresh Look at Stock Market Short-Termism' (2014) 41 *Journal of Law and Society* 416, 433–34.

[107] On this requirement, see above n. 100 above and accompanying text.

[108] On managerial earnings management practices generally, see Chapter 5.

[109] On the collective nature of the board's responsibility, see UK Corporate Governance Code, above n. 3, Main Principle A.1, which states that '[e]very company should be headed by an effective board which is collectively responsible for the long-term success of the company'. On the parallel common law position in this regard, see *Re Westmid Packing Services Ltd (No. 3)* [1998] BCC 836.

REGULATORY CONTROLS ON THE *SUBSTANCE* OF EXECUTIVE AND
DIRECTOR REMUNERATION AWARDS

With the exception of the very limited instances outlined above, UK company
law has traditionally been silent regarding the appropriate structure and design
of directorial and executive remuneration contracts, which were regarded as
private concerns within the discretionary remit of boards. Since the 1990s,
though, the discretion conventionally enjoyed by boards over questions
of executive pay policy and practice has been progressively undercut by an
expanding body of influential non-statutory principles. Moreover, in the aftermath of the 2007–08 financial crisis the regulatory treatment of banking and
non-banking companies respectively in this regard has diverged along largely
different paths. Accordingly, banks are now subject to a growing deluge of
highly complex, industry-specific requirements from which their non-banking
counterparts are exempt.

The considerably greater scope of regulatory control over executive
pay-setting in banks today is attributable principally to the impact of the abovementioned PRA Remuneration Code,[110] which first came into force in 2010.
Whilst the Code is non-statutory in nature, as part of the PRA Rulebook its
provisions are potentially subject to administrative enforcement by the government's Prudential Regulation Authority. Thus, unlike the corresponding
provisions of the UK Corporate Governance Code, the Remuneration Code's
requirements are formally binding on firms, in effect rendering the latter Code
'hard law' in nature. Where any provision of a remuneration agreement is
deemed to contravene any requirement of the Remuneration Code, the relevant provision will be rendered void.[111] Consequently, any payment (or transfer
of non-pecuniary property) made under that provision will be recoverable by
the employer firm which, moreover, *must* take reasonable steps with a view to
recovering the payment in question from its recipient.[112]

Fundamental Principles

As regards the UK's listed company community in general, the UK Corporate
Governance Code stipulates that '[e]xecutive directors' remuneration should
be designed to promote the long-term success of the company', and that
'[p]erformance-related elements should be transparent, stretching and rigorously applied'.[113] Moreover, in banking companies, boards must balance
these general concerns with their sector-specific requirement under the PRA
Remuneration Code to establish, implement and maintain remuneration policies, procedures and practices that are consistent with and promote sound and

---

[110] Above n. 50.
[111] *ibid.*, Principle 16.9.
[112] *ibid.*, Principle 16.14.
[113] Above n. 3, Main Principle D.1.

effective risk management, and do not encourage risk-taking that exceeds the firm's level of tolerated risk.[114]

This is in recognition of the typically greater degree and scope of risk to which banking companies are exposed relative to their non-bank counterparts, including the unique systemic interdependencies between (formally independent) firms in the banking sector, and the consequent risk of a sector-wide 'contagion effect' in the event of any one firm's failure or financial instability. Thus, whilst maintaining the relative attractiveness of remuneration awards to prospective executive candidates, and also ensuring effective incentives for executive officeholders to maximize shareholder wealth, are by no means irrelevant considerations for banking companies; such considerations must not undermine the board's potentially countervailing responsibility to ensure that key managerial decision-makers are not incentivized to pursue enhanced firm profitability at the expense of the relevant company or group's longer-term financial sustainability.

Regulatory Controls on Bonus Payments

Despite their recent public and political unpopularity, bonus payments remain a prominent element of the executive pay culture in public companies today, in banking and non-banking companies alike. The general corporate governance principles with respect to bonus payments are relatively straightforward. The UK Corporate Governance Code recommends simply that directors' eligibility for annual bonuses should be assessed by the remuneration committee, which should ensure that performance conditions attached to bonuses are relevant, stretching and designed to enhance shareholder value.[115] The Code further stipulates that bonuses should be subject to defined and transparent upper limits.[116]

In the case of banking companies, the wide discretion formerly enjoyed by boards over matters of bonus policy has been bounded considerably by regulation over recent years, with the outcome that determining the form and level of bankers' bonuses today has become a highly complicated and specialized governance function in itself. This is due to the fact that in the immediate aftermath of the 2007–08 financial crisis a number of serious problems were revealed in the ways in which banks had customarily awarded bonuses to their senior executive personnel. In consequence, the responsibilities of bank remuneration committees have become much more onerous in the post-crisis era, demanding a correspondingly greater range of competencies on the part of committee members.

In this regard, a particular theme of the PRA Remuneration Code is its focus on mitigating the formerly common banking sector practice of paying

---

[114] Above n. 50, Principle 6.2.
[115] Above n. 3, Schedule A.
[116] *ibid.*

'straight' cash bonuses to senior employees without any longer-term provisos attached. Accordingly, banks today must ensure that a substantial portion (and, in any event, at least 50 per cent) of any variable remuneration (including bonus) payable to a relevant employee consists of an appropriate balance of (i) shares in the employer firm and (ii) appropriate debt instruments that adequately reflect the employer firm's current credit quality.[117] Furthermore, at least 40 per cent of the variable remuneration (including bonus) payable to any employee fulfilling senior management functions in a bank must be deferred for a period of at least seven years, so as to align senior managerial decision-makers' personal financial incentives with the long-term success and sustainability of the business policies and practices that they are responsible for.[118]

Additionally, and in what might initially appear a somewhat counter-intuitive step (given recent public controversy about alleged banker pay excess), the PRA Remuneration Code requires that banks ensure an appropriate balance between the fixed and variable components of a relevant employee's remuneration; and, in particular, that the fixed component of remuneration is sufficiently *high*.[119] The logic here is that, where an annual bonus or other form of variable remuneration constitutes the dominant part of an employee's typical pay package, non-receipt of that payment in any given year will be likely to have a considerably detrimental impact on their overall personal income. In such circumstances, the employer firm will likely face greater pressure to retain bonus entitlements even where not strictly justified by employee performance, leading the relevant employee(s) in turn to regard receipt of a bonus as an ordinary entitlement for fulfilling their basic functions, rather than as an extraordinary reward for truly exceptional individual or firm performance. Hence a relevant employee's fixed remuneration should be sufficiently high to permit a 'fully flexible' policy on bonuses and other variable remuneration components.[120]

The regulator initially refrained from specifying any precise uppermost ratio between the fixed and flexible components of a relevant employee's remuneration, stipulating only that the former element of pay should be sufficiently high as adjudged by the employer firm. However, on 1 January 2014 the Remuneration Code was amended to incorporate the requirements of the EU Capital Requirements Directive IV ('CRD IV'),[121] which in effect implemented the Basel III Accord within the European Union. Undoubtedly the most controversial provision of the Directive, at least from a UK perspective, has been its prescription of a mandatory 'bonus cap' applicable to EU-based (including UK) banks. The 'cap', which is now in force at domestic level under the PRA

---

[117] Above n. 50, Principle 15.15.

[118] *ibid.*, Principle 15.17. Where the overall amount of variable remuneration awarded in any individual case is £500,000 or over, or the recipient is a director of a particularly large or organizationally complex banking firm, the relevant percentage threshold for this purpose is 60%. *ibid.*, Principle 15.18.

[119] *ibid.*, Principle 15.9(1)-(2).

[120] *ibid.*

[121] See Directive 2013/36/EU.

Remuneration Code, prohibits the annual variable remuneration (including bonus) of a relevant employee from exceeding 100 per cent of that individual's annual fixed (e.g. salaried) remuneration.[122]

The only permissible exceptions to the above rule are: (i) that the relevant percentage threshold may be raised to 125 per cent where the additional 25 per cent of variable pay is deferred for a period of least five years from the date of payment[123]; and (ii) that the relevant percentage threshold may be raised to 200 per cent where this is approved by a supermajority of at least 66 per cent of the company's shareholders (where at least 50 per cent of shareholders attend the relevant General Meeting), or by a higher supermajority of at least 75 per cent (where less than 50 per cent of shareholders attend the relevant General Meeting).[124]

The so-called 'banker bonus cap' represents a landmark development insofar as executive remuneration culture in UK banks is concerned, given the previous sectoral norm of paying bonuses that were frequently many times the level of an employee's base salary. Somewhat predictably, the reform has been subject to vociferous criticism from many quarters, not least on account of the fact that its intended downward impact on banker pay can be readily counteracted by raising the fixed remuneration levels of relevant employees accordingly.[125] Insofar as this leads to reduced reliance by banks on performance-sensitive pay, and – correspondingly – an increased risk of underperforming employees receiving 'rewards for failure', its overall impact on corporate governance quality within the sector will likely be negative. In any event, the continuing application of the banker bonus cap at domestic level is now seriously in question following the recent Brexit vote, and especially so in light of the UK's vociferous and outspoken opposition to the policy at the time of its initial formulation.[126]

Regulatory Controls on Long-Term Incentive Schemes

So-called long-term incentive schemes (or 'LTISs') – including share options[127] and restricted share grants[128] – are a highly popular form of variable executive

---

[122] See PRA Remuneration Code, above n. 50, Principle 15.9(3).

[123] *ibid.*, Principle 15.13.

[124] *ibid.*, Principle 15.10–15.11.

[125] J. Treanor, 'Barclays Aims to Dodge EU Bank Bonus Cap with New Top-Up Payments to Staff', *The Guardian*, 23 October 2013.

[126] H. Jones and W. Schomberg, 'Britain Challenges Banker Bonus Cap in New Clash with EU', *Reuters*, 25 September 2013. Notably, in September 2013, the UK government lodged a legal challenge to the EU bonus cap in the European Court of Justice, based on a number of alleged administrative defects with respect to the provision's introduction and subsequent application. However, in November 2014, the UK's challenge was withdrawn following publication of an opinion by the ECJ Advocate General Niilo Jaaskinen that the action was unlikely to be successful. See A. Barker, S. Schafer and G. Parker, 'George Osborne takes EU to Court over Bank Bonus Cap', *Financial Times*, 25 September 2013; 'Osborne Abandons Challenge to EU Cap on Bankers' Bonuses', *BBC News*, 20 November 2014.

[127] On share options generally, see above.

[128] On restricted share grants generally, see above.

remuneration in public companies. However, in designing the specific terms of such schemes, boards and remuneration committees must be mindful of some important corporate governance rules that operate as mandatory constraints on their discretion in this regard.

For a start, all UK-listed companies are required as a compulsory listing condition to ensure that any LTIS (including any share option or restricted share grant scheme) is approved by an ordinary resolution of shareholders in General Meeting before it is adopted.[129] Such a scheme may exceptionally be offered to an incoming or incumbent director without prior shareholder approval where this is deemed necessary to facilitate, under unusual circumstances, the recruitment or retention of that individual. However, where this occurs, the company must later provide its shareholders with a formal explanation as to why the circumstances in which the arrangement was established were unusual.[130] The most obvious example of 'unusual' circumstances meriting dispensation with the need for prior shareholder approval of an LTIS would be the sudden resignation of a company's CEO, necessitating immediate action on the part of the company to recruit a suitable successor on sufficiently attractive terms. In addition, UK Listing Rules prohibit companies from issuing share options 'at a discount': that is, where the relevant options' specified exercise price is *below* the market value of the underlying shares at the time the options are issued, thereby entitling their recipient to an immediate 'windfall' irrespective of performance factors.[131]

There are some further important recommendations with respect to LTISs contained in the UK Corporate Governance Code, albeit that these are applicable on a non-binding, 'comply or explain' basis.[132] Most notably, boards and remuneration committees should ensure that traditional ('vanilla') share option schemes are weighed against other more exacting kinds of LTISs,[133] such as 'out-of-the-money' options and performance-conditional restricted share (or option) grants.[134] Also, in normal circumstances, shares granted or other forms of deferred remuneration should not vest, and options should not be exercisable, in less than three years.[135] In the case of banks, this latter Corporate Governance Code recommendation reinforces the abovementioned

---

[129] See *FCA Handbook*, 'Listing Rules', LR 9.4.1.

[130] *ibid.*, LR 9.4.2(2).

[131] *ibid.*, LR 9.4.4.

[132] On this generally, see Chapter 3.

[133] Above n. 3, Schedule A.

[134] On these generally, see above.

[135] Above n. 3, Schedule A. In its recent (at time of writing) corporate governance Green Paper, the government has suggested the possibility of the Code's minimum holding requirement for executive stock options (in the case of banking and non-banking companies alike) being raised to five years, on the purported premise that 'a three year holding period for shares is not sufficient to deter executives from avoiding long-term expenditures that may negatively impact on the share price' (see above n. 11, 33). Whether this proposed reform is ultimately adopted by the Financial Reporting Council remains to be seen.

PRA Remuneration Code rule with respect to mandatory deferral of a significant component of relevant employees' variable remuneration.[136]

In the case of banks, since LTISs – like bonus payments – constitute a form of variable executive remuneration, they are likewise subject to the same regulatory restrictions applicable to annual bonus payments (on which, see above). Nonetheless, restricted share grants are still a particularly common form of bonus payment in banking companies today, not least as a means of meeting the regulatory imperative for banks to defer at least 40 per cent (or, in appropriate cases, 60 per cent) of a relevant employee's variable remuneration for three to five years.[137] Moreover, banker bonuses paid by way of restricted share (or option) grant, like cash bonuses, will also be subject to the EU bonus cap. Therefore the total value of any shares (or options) granted under such a scheme must similarly not exceed the recipient employee's annual fixed remuneration for the relevant year, unless appropriate shareholder approval is obtained.[138]

In light of the above factors, it should be readily apparent why restricted share (or option) grants are – from a regulatory perspective – regarded as the preferred form of variable remuneration for senior banking company executives today. In consequence, the pervasive pre-crisis remuneration culture in banks of unrestricted cash bonuses is becoming an increasingly outmoded norm. Notwithstanding, the general employee expectation of incrementally expanding annual awards (albeit in increasingly complex LTIS form) would appear to remain as culturally entrenched in the banking sector as ever, especially within the uppermost echelons of management.[139]

Regulatory Controls on Severance Payments ('Golden Parachutes') and Pension Allowances

Severance payments (or 'golden parachutes') present one of the most galling corporate governance dilemmas in practice. In view of the typically short tenure of senior executive positions within larger public companies today,[140]

---

[136] On this, see above n. 118 and accompanying text. In this regard, the Corporate Governance Code additionally recommends that pay-outs or grants under all incentive schemes should preferably be made on a phased basis rather than awarded in one large block (see *ibid.*).

[137] On this, see above n. 118 and accompanying text.

[138] On this, see above nn. 122, 124 and accompanying text. However, where the specified period of restriction under such a scheme is five years or more, the shares (or options) granted thereunder may together contribute an additional 25% of variable remuneration over and above the recipient employee's normal capped level. On this proviso, see above n. 123 and accompanying text.

[139] In this regard the former RBS chairman, Sir Philip Hampton, notably remarked that, in the banking sector, 'the expectation of a bonus has become embedded in the past 10 to 15 years', thereby creating an 'expectation that the bonus will be high, come what may'. See High Pay Centre, *Pay for Performance – Does It Work?* (12 November 2013), at http://highpaycentre. org/blog/pay-for-performance-does-it-work.

[140] In 2012, average CEO tenure in FTSE 100 companies was recorded at 5.91 years, and 6.35 years across the broader FTSE 350. These figures are attributable to research carried out by Thorburn McAlister in conjunction with the University of Southampton.

it is frequently necessary to offer new appointees to such positions the security of a fixed term contract or notice period. This will, in effect, entitle the relevant officeholder to contractual compensation in the event of unilateral termination of their service contract (i.e. 'firing') prior to expiration of their agreed term or notice.[141] At the same time, though, contractually-determined severance payments risk acting as a protectionist measures for underperforming executives, on the basis that the anticipated expense of compensating an officeholder for loss of position might render their dismissal cost-ineffective. It follows in such circumstances that retention of the relevant officeholder until the expiry of their term may potentially represent the most cost-effective (or, rather, least cost-ineffective) option from the employer firm's perspective.

An equally troubling issue is that of discretionary (i.e. non-contractually-agreed) severance payments that are offered with a view to eliciting an outgoing officer's acquiescence in their own effective dismissal.[142] Whilst the practical benefits of such arrangements for the employer firm are understandable, it might reasonably be queried what long-term corporate benefit is achieved by such payments, given that the recipient of the payment is intended to have no future involvement with the company. Hence the performance-based rationale for discretionary pay is entirely absent in these circumstances.

The above problems posed by severance or 'golden parachute' payments, whilst perhaps most publicly conspicuous in the banking sector over recent years, are by no means specific to this category of companies. Rather, they are very much a common governance challenge for public companies in general. In response, the legal and regulatory protections available to companies and their shareholders in this regard have been both expanded and tightened considerably over recent years. Accordingly, under sections 188–189 of the Companies Act 2006, no directors' service contract may be made to run for a period of more than two years without prior shareholder approval in General Meeting. Otherwise the terms of the relevant agreement will be rendered void, whilst the agreement as a whole will be deemed terminable by the company at any time on the giving of reasonable notice.

This basic statutory rule is overlaid by supplementary provisions of the UK Corporate Governance Code, which recommend in particular that notice or contract periods for directors should be set at the more stringent threshold of one year or less.[143] In exceptional circumstances where a longer term or notice period is necessary in order to attract a new outside recruit to the board, the applicable period should reduce to one year or less after expiry of that individual's initially agreed term or notice.[144]

---

[141] It is notable in this regard that, whilst a company's shareholders are statutorily empowered to dismiss any or all of its directors without cause, this expressly does not deprive the outgoing director(s) of any compensation payable to them in respect of the dismissal. See CA 2006, s 168(5).

[142] On this generally, see above.

[143] Above n. 3, Code Provision D.1.5.

[144] *ibid.*

Meanwhile, under the Companies Act any discretionary termination payments that are intended to be made to outgoing directors must be submitted for prior approval by a company's shareholders in General Meeting.[145] Otherwise, the recipient will be regarded as holding the payment on trust for the company, thereby entitling the company (or, potentially, any of its shareholders via a derivative claim) to seek recovery of the relevant sum therefrom.[146] In addition, any directors who authorized the unapproved payment will be held jointly and severally liable to indemnify the company for any outstanding loss resulting from the payment, regardless of whether they personally benefitted from it.[147]

A particular cause of concern in the wake of the well-publicized RBS/Fred Goodwin controversy is the arrangements for provision of pension allowances to outgoing directors or executives, especially following early termination of the outgoing officer's tenure. To this end, the UK Corporate Governance Code today recommends that, as a general norm, only a director's basic salary should be pensionable.[148] The implication is that discretionary pension provision of the type observed in the RBS/Goodwin case should be avoided, at least in the absence of extraordinary circumstances. It is further recommended that remuneration committees consider the pension consequences and associated costs to the company of basic salary increases and any other changes in directors' pensionable remuneration.[149] This is particularly so in the case of directors close to retirement,[150] for whom late-career pay increases can have long-term implications for the relevant officers' entitlements under final salary, defined benefit pension schemes. Finally, in the specific case of banking companies, the PRA Remuneration Code further requires employer firms to ensure generally that any payments to relevant employees relating to the early termination of their employment contract reflect performance achieved over time, and are designed in a way that does not reward failure or misconduct.[151]

Requirement for Banks to Adopt 'Clawback' and Unilateral Pay-Reduction Provisions

Once again in the particular case of banks, a final important regulatory control on executive pay today is the requirement to put in place so-called 'clawback' arrangements. These contractual provisions, as mandated by the PRA Remuneration Code, in effect empower banking companies to demand that a

---

[145] CA 2006, ss 215–217.
[146] CA 2006, s 222(1)(a).
[147] CA 2006, s 222(1)(b).
[148] Above n. 3, Schedule A.
[149] *ibid.*
[150] *ibid.*
[151] Above n. 50, Principle 15.14.

relevant employee repays a specified proportion of variable remuneration previously received from the firm in the event of: (i) the employer firm incurring significant losses for which that employee was responsible or participated in; and/or (ii) that employee failing to meet appropriate standards of fitness and propriety for their position in the firm.[152]

In addition, banks are required to make provision for the future unilateral reduction of any unvested variable remuneration due to a relevant employee where, as a minimum: (i) there is reasonable evidence of employee misbehaviour or material error; (ii) the firm or the relevant business unit suffers a material downturn in its financial performance; or (iii) the firm or the relevant business unit suffers a material failure of risk management.[153] Notably, any such contractual pay-reduction provision should be designed so as to apply not just to prospective cash bonus awards, but also to any non-pecuniary forms of variable remuneration that are payable to a relevant bank employee in future, including deferred share or option grants.[154]

PAY RATIO REPORTING: BEYOND PAY-FOR-PERFORMANCE?

In general, the various regulatory provisions documented above, whilst no doubt costly and onerous from a corporate compliance point of view, are not necessarily inconsistent with the standard pay-for-performance model of executive remuneration control.[155] That is to say, the majority of these measures are designed with a view to improving the ongoing alignment between: on the one hand, managers' and directors' periodic levels of pay award; and, on the other, the corresponding long-term financial performance and sustainability of the companies in question.

Admittedly, some of the key requirements applicable to executive remuneration in banks today, such as the mandatory deferral of variable pay awards for extensive time periods, appear to be motivated at least as much by concern for the wider social externalities arising out of major banking company failures, as by orthodox financial-performance concerns. However, even the most ardent proponents of the narrow principal-agent understanding of corporate governance[156] will no doubt accept the need for such occasional publicly-oriented regulatory interventions, in the interest of mitigating the potential adverse impact on third parties and society of irresponsible managerial risk-taking.

Notably, though, recent years have seen a conspicuous shift in policymaking emphasis in response to the surrounding social and political climate of the times. It is common knowledge that levels of senior executive – and, in particular, CEO – remuneration in public companies have risen at a stratospheric

---

[152] *ibid.*, Principle 15.21.
[153] *ibid.*, Principle 15.22(1).
[154] *ibid.*, Principle 15.22(2).
[155] On this, see above.
[156] On this, see Chapter 2.

rate over recent decades, not least in the United Kingdom.[157] This trend has undoubtedly been a cause of widespread public outcry, both in itself and on account of its alleged role in contributing to increased social inequality more generally. Whilst successive UK governments of recent times have consistently refrained from taking any significant steps to tackle pay inequity concerns arising in the context of corporate governance, we have nonetheless witnessed some interesting domestic regulatory developments on this front lately.

For instance, the UK Corporate Governance Code today recommends that, in setting the level of executive pay awards in public companies, remuneration committees should 'be sensitive to pay and employment conditions elsewhere in the group, especially when determining annual salary increases'.[158] Moreover, in 2013, Britain's (then) coalition government introduced a mandatory statutory requirement for quoted[159] UK companies to report annually on any periodic percentage increases in CEO remuneration and average worker pay respectively. This was with a view to enabling ready exposition of the ongoing correlation (or lack of) between the respective year-on-year variations in each figure within individual companies.[160]

In a similar vein, the government has recently proposed following the example of the United States[161] by introducing a mandatory pay ratio reporting

---

[157] In this regard, it has been recorded that, over the past three decades, the average annual pay of a FTSE 100 CEO has increased from £115,000 (in 1980) to £4.3 million (in 2012). Correspondingly, the ratio of CEO to average worker pay over the same period has increased by 900%, from an initial figure of 18:1 (against an average UK worker's salary of £6,500 in 1980) to 162:1 (against an average salary of £26,500 in 2012). Since the turn of the twenty-first century alone, FTSE 100 CEO pay has seen a more than four-fold increase, vastly outstripping the corresponding rate of growth in the FTSE 100 Index and also UK retail price inflation over the same period. Particularly controversial has been the continuing rapid growth of public company CEO pay since the 2007–08 financial crisis, a period which in general has simultaneously witnessed declining or at least stagnating real wages, contributing to falling material living standards for the great bulk of the UK population. See Office for National Statistics (ONS), 'Annual Survey of Hours and Earnings', cited in High Pay Centre, *Reform Agenda: How to Make Top Pay Fairer* (2014), 7. See also High Pay Commission, *Cheques with Balances: Why Tackling High Pay Is in the National Interest* (2012), 23.

[158] Above n. 3, Supporting Principle D.1.

[159] On this term, see above n. 79.

[160] See Revised Regulations, above n. 87, para. 19. These Regulations additionally require that the directors' remuneration policy contains a statement of how pay and employment conditions of non-directorial employees of the company (or, where relevant, group) were taken into account when setting the company's policy for directors' remuneration, setting out (*inter alia*) whether (and, if so, how) employees were consulted during the formulation of this policy. See *ibid.*, paras 38–39.

[161] See Securities and Exchange Commission (SEC), *Pay Ratio Disclosure: Proposed Rule* (18 September 2013), introduced under section 593(b) of the Dodd-Frank Wall Street Reform and Consumer Protection Act of 2010. Notably, though, section 443 of the new federal Financial Choice Act of 2016 (which, at the time of writing, is currently before Congress) if implemented will significantly amend the US statutory 'say on pay' requirement, such that a shareholder vote need only take place each year in which there has been 'a material change' to a company's executive remuneration arrangements from the previous year.

regime in the UK, which would require annual disclosure of the ratio between: (i) the overall pay received by a company's CEO during the relevant financial year; and (ii) the average or median level of general employee pay within the relevant company or group as a whole.[162] It is presently uncertain whether such a requirement will become law in the UK; and, if so, to which companies it will apply. Moreover, the practical value of pay ratio reporting from a corporate governance perspective is a contentious issue. On the one hand, pay ratio reporting could potentially improve general levels of board accountability and firm performance in the UK by enabling investors to identify more readily any instances of genuinely excessive executive pay awards, thereby mitigating the risk of managerial rewards for failure. On the other hand, implementing an effective pay ratio reporting regime presents a number of significant challenges on a practical level.

A particular cause of unease is the arguably crude and simplistic nature of the resulting arithmetical ratio, which in itself is insensitive to important contextual factors. These considerations include differing general levels of pay between different industrial sectors and geographic localities, and also the extent to which reporting firms outsource productive functions involving low-paid work to entities outside of their formal corporate or group structure.[163] Additionally there is concern about the arguably questionable practical relevance of pay ratios to many institutional investors, who might conceivably discount the value of such disclosures on the basis of their perceived irrelevance to the risk-return profiles of corporate equities.[164]

No doubt the above debate will roll on, at least pending this proposal's ultimate implementation (or otherwise). In the meanwhile, we will leave readers to form their own opinions as to whether, on balance, pay ratio reporting is likely to be an overall force for good within UK corporate governance.[165]

---

[162] See Green Paper, above n. 11, 29.

[163] *ibid.*, 30.

[164] In this regard, a group of commentators from the US corporate law advisory community – responding to the SEC's 2013 proposal in this regard – have claimed to be 'unaware of any evidence correlating corporate performance to the ratio of CEO pay to median employee pay', with a further group of respondents remarking that, '[w]hile [pay ratio reporting] may be of general interest to some investors for different purposes, it is unclear how [it] will be material for the reasonable investor when making investment decisions'. See quotes from, respectively, Group of Executive Compensation Lawyers and Group of Trade Associations, cited in SEC, above n. 161, 96.

[165] On this issue generally, see M.T. Moore, 'Corporate Governance, Pay Equity, and the Limitations of Agency Theory' (2015) 68 *Current Legal Problems* 431, esp. 449–61.

CHAPTER 10

Regulation of the Market for Corporate Control

INTRODUCTION

At the outset of the book, in Chapter 1, we discussed how corporate power – in addition to being subject to limits imposed by laws and regulations – is also subject to various disciplining market pressures imposed by customers, suppliers, employees and investors. We also described the phenomenon of the separation of ownership and control and the problems that it may cause. Chapter 5 explored institutional investors and shareholder engagement as one particular aspect of the web of forces that constrain managers, while Chapter 9 looked at executive remuneration and its potential to help align shareholders' and managers' interests. This last chapter will focus on another external mechanism that may influence corporate decision-making and counteract problems stemming from the separation between ownership and control – that is, the market for corporate control.

The expression 'market for corporate control' was famously coined by Henry Manne, a US law professor and pioneer of the law and economics movement. It relates to transactions by which a party (typically a company) – referred to as the 'bidder', 'acquirer' or 'offeror' – acquires or tries to acquire another company (the 'target' or 'offeree'). These transactions can be either 'friendly' (negotiated) or 'unfriendly' ('hostile'; not negotiated). In the latter case – which is most relevant for Manne's thesis – the acquisition is opposed by the target company's board.[1] In the following discussion, we will use the term 'takeover' more broadly as reference to any type of corporate acquisition,[2] although *hostile* takeovers of *publicly* traded companies are the paradigmatic cases.

The following sections will begin by critically evaluating the main theoretical rationales for an active market for corporate control, looking at the

---

[1] An offer can also initially start off as hostile but subsequently – with the target board's approval – turn into a friendly, negotiated offer/acquisition.

[2] Note that while in the UK an acquisition by way of a public offer to shareholders is commonly referred to as a takeover, in US parlance it can be called either a takeover or a tender offer. Conversely, a tender offer in the UK is a specific type of offer subject to special rules under the Takeover Code.

hostile takeover threat as a managerial disciplinary mechanism as envisioned by Manne. The chapter will further explore the role of private equity leveraged buyouts and consider competing arguments for and against the proposition that they are a positive spur to improved corporate performance. The discussion will then proceed to assess how the law resolves disputes between shareholders and boards concerning the merits of accepting/rejecting takeover offers, comparing the contrasting positions taken in the UK and the US respectively. Finally, the chapter will briefly highlight the political dimensions of takeovers by reference to the role of national governments in deciding the outcome of cross-border takeover bids.

TAKEOVERS AS A MANAGERIAL DISCIPLINARY MECHANISM

Efficient Markets and Agency Costs

There are a host of potential reasons, several of which may apply simultaneously, as to why a party would wish to acquire a company or business. For example, a bidder can use the target to expand its own business activities or geographic reach; there may be vertical integration (such as where a target will be integrated into the acquirer's supply chain) or horizontal integration (where the target produces competitive or complementary products); or various synergies. While these types of consideration describe what would normally motivate a strategic buyer to buy another company, a takeover could also serve a financial buyer's investment purposes, in which case the focal point will be a target's potential return on investment as compared to other investment opportunities. Finally, an acquisition could be motivated (at least in part) by the potential to increase 'efficiency' or, in other words, the buyer's perceived opportunity to reduce inefficiencies – a point to which we will return below. First, however, some brief remarks on the pricing of takeover offers are in order.

In Chapter 5 we explained how the so-called efficient capital markets hypothesis or 'ECMH' (in its most common 'semi-strong' form) posits that all publicly available information that affects a company is reflected in its share price. However, in the takeovers context this raises a difficult question. In order to attract sufficient shareholder support, a takeover bidder will almost invariably offer the target shareholders a significant premium over the current market price of the target company's shares. Yet, assuming that a company's share price is already 'efficiently' or 'correctly' priced (reflecting the true value of the business), why would an acquirer pay more than the market price? Although a takeover may be motivated by any or several of the basic rationales mentioned above, the commonality that they share is that the target is more valuable to the acquirer of a *controlling* interest (which itself can be seen as a valuable asset) than it is to its current shareholders, which explains why the price offered to shareholders in takeovers normally includes a premium over the market price.

The difference in value for the present and the future controlling shareholder can exist because the bidder expects to use the target in a manner that unlocks or results in additional value, such as via access to an established distribution system or the creation of synergies that boost the bidder's profits. Additionally, an important consideration for the market for corporate control is that the information that is said to be reflected in share prices includes instances of managerial incompetence, misbehaviour, or – more generally – inadequate corporate governance norms that are disadvantageous for investors.[3] If, for instance, capital market participants are made aware of substandard managerial skills or self-dealing transactions, the market will take this information into account and discount the affected company's share price. In effect, in these cases, the market adjusts for agency costs,[4] which in turn creates opportunities for outside buyers. Such buyers may take over the company with the aim of reducing the existing inefficiencies.

The classic exposition on the subject of the hostile takeover threat and its effect on corporate managers is Henry Manne's seminal 1965 article 'Mergers and the Market for Corporate Control'.[5] The basic proposition, as Manne describes it, is 'that the control of corporations may constitute a valuable asset; that this asset exists independent of any interest in either economics of scale or monopoly profits; that an active market for corporate control exists; and that a great many mergers are probably the result of the successful workings of this special market'.[6] An important driver of this market are agency costs. As Manne states:

> A fundamental premise underlying the market for corporate control is the existence of a high positive correlation between corporate managerial efficiency and the market price of shares of that company. As an existing company is poorly managed – in the sense of not making as great a return for the shareholders as could be accomplished under other feasible managements – the market price of the shares declines relative to the shares of other companies in the same industry or relative to the market as a whole.[7]

Thus, incompetent management results in a decreased share price, which can turn the company into an attractive takeover target. Acquirers who believe that they can eradicate agency costs and manage the company more efficiently can purchase a large enough amount of shares to allow them to take control of a company by voting in a new board of directors and subsequently replacing the incumbent management team and/or effectuating other changes. The

---

[3] See F.H. Easterbrook and D.R. Fischel, *The Economic Structure of Corporate Law* (Harvard University Press 1991), 18–19.

[4] On agency costs as a lens through which to conceptualize corporate governance generally, see Chapter 2.

[5] H.G. Manne, 'Mergers and the Market for Corporate Control' (1965) 73 *Journal of Political Economy* 110. For further background and historical insights, see also J. Armour and B. Cheffins, 'The Origins of the Market for Corporate Control' (2014) 5 *University of Illinois Law Review* 1835.

[6] Manne, above n. 5, 112.

[7] *ibid.* (footnote omitted).

measures that they introduce should, of course, increase the value of the bidder's investment to a level that justifies having had to pay a premium to gain control in the first place.

Thus, takeovers can create value by lowering agency costs, both *ex post* and, because of managerial incentives to stay in power and prevent hostile takeovers, *ex ante*. As such, the market for corporate control – in conjunction with laws and regulations that protect investors – may benefit dispersed shareholders who would otherwise not be in a position to reduce agency costs.[8] Accordingly, one can argue that an active market for corporate control, including the mere threat of, or potential for, a takeover's occurrence, lessens the scope for agency costs and lowers the likelihood that incompetent management will be able to retain control of a company in the longer term.

Limitations

We highlighted in Chapter 5 how, despite its prominence, the ECMH is still just that: a *hypothesis*, i.e. a proposed explanation. Indeed, events such as the recent financial crisis, the occurrence of 'bubbles' in the stock markets, and behaviour on the part of investors that – at least in hindsight – is difficult to reconcile with fully rational behaviour cast doubt on the view that markets are (at all times) fully efficient.[9] Nevertheless, it is safe to say that public information, including agency costs, is normally in some manner – albeit not perfectly – reflected in share prices, and many market participants quickly act on such information.

Even assuming that the ECMH holds true, though, the disciplining effects of the market for corporate control are constrained. For example, agency costs may remain undetected and thus fail to become incorporated in share prices; they may not amount to a large enough share price discount to justify a costly bid by a potential acquirer; or the underlying causes for the agency costs may not be perceived as reversible by outsiders.[10] Additionally, hostile takeovers are rare and – as we will see below – corporate boards can to varying degrees defend against takeovers, thereby effectively shielding themselves and managers against removal from their positions. Commenting on the situation in the US, one scholar observed 'that a top manager who shirks his responsibilities by playing golf when he should be working is undoubtedly more likely to be struck by lightning while on the course than to be fired after a hostile takeover'.[11]

---

[8] According to Manne, the market for corporate control is even more important – and effective – than regulatory enforcement or shareholders' derivative actions. See *ibid.*, 113.

[9] On this, see B. Clarke, 'Where Was the Market for Corporate Control When We Needed It?' in W. Sun *et al.* (eds), *Corporate Governance and the Global Financial Crisis: International Perspectives* (CUP 2012), 75–94.

[10] See J.C. Coffee, 'Regulating the Market for Corporate Control: A Critical Assessment of the Tender Offer's Role in Corporate Governance' (1984) 84 *Columbia Law Review* 1145.

[11] S.M. Bainbridge, *The New Corporate Governance in Theory and Practice* (OUP 2008), 151.

The market for corporate control's beneficial effects are also difficult to prove.[12] Studies commonly test the effect of managerial entrenchment on share value, the effect of takeovers on share prices, or managerial turnover, which, however, does not directly address the question of takeovers' effects on agency costs (either those that were eliminated or those that were prevented in the first place). Nevertheless, some studies show that measures to insulate boards and managers from takeovers correlate with negative returns for shareholders and suggest that takeovers are beneficial, although this effect seemed to disappear during the most recent financial crisis.[13] Conversely, two studies from the UK found that takeovers had no disciplining effect and that they were not normally aimed at underperforming companies.[14] In short, the effects of the market for corporate control – although accepted broadly as a valuable theoretical model – remain difficult to capture empirically, in particular as they are influenced by a host of extraneous factors, including regulatory and macroeconomic effects.

THE ROLE OF PRIVATE EQUITY

Private Equity and Leveraged Buyouts

Important players in the area of corporate acquisitions are private equity firms.[15] Emerging in the 1970s,[16] private equity firms are typically organized as general or limited liability partnerships or – in the US – limited liability corporations. These firms essentially pool investments in various funds. Traditionally, the investors are institutional investors and high-net-worth individuals, although more recently several large private equity firms have become listed on stock exchanges, thereby at least partially opening up to the public. The private

---

[12] See e.g. L. Enriques, 'European Takeover Law: The Case for a Neutral Approach' (2011) 22 *European Business Law Review* 623, 625: 'Their [takeovers'] positive effects on managerial agency costs are impossible to quantify, if only because it is the mere possibility of a takeover that aligns managers' interests to those of shareholders. While these benefits may be substantial, the available empirical evidence shows that hostile takeovers that do occur are not targeted at underperforming companies' (footnotes omitted); B. Clarke, 'Articles 9 and 10 of the Takeovers Directive (2004/25) and the Market for Corporate Control' (2006) *Journal of Business Law* 355, 357–62. Nevertheless, the market for corporate control theory has broad appeal and is, among others, one of the drivers of the EU's Takeovers Directive. On this, see the discussion further below in this chapter.

[13] For a helpful recent discussion on this, including an overview of the empirical literature, see J. Kesten, 'Managerial Entrenchment and Shareholder Wealth Revisited: Theory and Evidence from a Recessionary Financial Market' (2010) 2010 *Brigham Young University Law Review* 1609. See also A.J. Davis, 'The Institutional Appetite for "Quack Corporate Governance"' (2015) 2015 *Columbia Business Law Review* 1, 29–42

[14] See C. Mayer and J. Franks, 'Hostile Takeovers and the Correction of Managerial Failure' (1996) 40 *Journal of Financial Economics* 163; J. Frank et al., 'Who Disciplines Management in Poorly Performing Companies?' (2011) 10 *Journal of Financial Intermediation* 2009.

[15] Well-known firms include Kohlberg Kravis Roberts (KKR), Blackstone Group and 3i.

[16] On this, see S. Davidoff Salomon, 'The Failure of Private Equity' (2009) 82 *Southern California Law Review* 489–93.

equity funds themselves (as opposed to the firms that manage them) are typically organized as limited partnerships, established for a fixed amount of time and with the aim of raising a pre-determined, fixed and non-redeemable (for the life of the relevant fund) investment amount. The private equity firm acts as a fund's general partner and manages the fund and its investments, while the investors as limited partners provide the bulk of the capital. Private equity firms receive management fees from the investors and, additionally, are entitled to a share in fund profits.[17] Investments that are raised through the funds are then used to take control of other companies, building a portfolio of businesses in the process. The target companies can be private or public, although in the latter case a company would normally be de-listed and taken private after the acquisition, resulting in a 'public to private transaction'.[18]

Private equity firms aim to improve the acquired business' profitability. The general changes that are applied can be summarized under the headings of financial, governance, and operational engineering.[19] All of these changes tend to be implemented rapidly, driven by the pressure on the private equity fund to increase value and, subsequently, divest portfolio companies within a relatively short time-frame.[20] Thus, once the target business has been successfully 'revitalized', private equity investors exit by selling the shares of the portfolio company either to another private owner or to the public at large by way of an initial public offering (IPO).

Financial measures in private equity firms commonly emphasize managerial incentive structures. These include substantial grants of shares and options that let managers participate in their company's upside, but also requirements that managers maintain equity investments in their companies to ensure that there is a downside risk for them. Additionally, as private equity companies – as we will see below – are leveraged and need to repay debt and make interest payments, managers are focused on tight cash flow management, which reduces the potential for wasteful uses of cash liquidity. Governance measures, in turn, include the private equity firm's control over board appointments in portfolio companies, small and active boards, and the tendency to swiftly replace underperforming managers.[21] Finally, from an operational

---

[17] For further reading on private equity and its mechanisms, see S.N. Kaplan and P. Strömberg, 'Leveraged Buyouts and Private Equity' (2009) 23 *Journal of Economic Perspectives* 121; B.R. Cheffins and J. Armour, 'The Eclipse of Private Equity' (2008) 33 *Delaware Journal of Corporate Law* 1; R.W. Masulis and R.S. Thomas, 'Does Private Equity Create Wealth? The Effects of Private Equity and Derivatives on Corporate Governance' (2009) 76 *University of Chicago Law Review* 219; House of Commons Treasury Committee, *Private Equity – Tenth Report of Session 2006–07*, Vol. I (2007); M. Moore and A. Rebérioux, 'From Minimization to Exploitation: Re-Conceptualizing the Corporate Governance Problem' (2009) 5 CLPE Research Paper 16/2009, Vol. 5, No. 3, 10–13.

[18] Private equity is also used to invest in start-up companies, in which case it is often referred to as 'venture capital'.

[19] Kaplan and Strömberg, above n. 17, 130–32.

[20] Cheffins and Armour, above n. 17, 14.

[21] As two commentators have noted, '[t]he most commonly cited argument for private equity creating value is that these transactions lead to improved corporate governance and therefore agency-cost reductions'. Masulis and Thomas, above n. 17, 227.

standpoint, private equity firms often specialize in certain industries, using their specific expertise and skills in these areas to implement changes such as strategic repositioning, enhanced productivity, managerial changes and cost reduction measures.

Private equity firms often engage in transactions referred to as 'leveraged buyouts' (LBOs).[22] In an LBO, the private equity buyer typically acquires a majority stake in a target company using only a relatively small amount of equity and a relatively large portion of outside debt financing.[23] Thus, the private equity firm will normally use its own funds to pay between 10 per cent and 40 per cent of the purchase price while the majority is paid by using borrowed money from banks, other institutional investors, and bonds or mezzanine debt. This acquisition structure is chosen because debt acts as a 'lever' and can – in addition to the abovementioned operational and other drivers – increase the investor's return on investment and cash-on-cash returns.[24] A further characteristic of an LBO is that the loans used to finance the purchase are secured against the target company's assets, while the interest and capital repayments on the debt are paid with cash flows generated by the target. The new controllers may also sell off target assets for the same purpose.[25] In effect, the acquired business thereby largely 'pays for itself'.

Perspectives on Private Equity

The recent financial crisis and the resulting difficulties in obtaining debt financing once more underlined the 'boom and bust' pattern that private equity follows: successful years with large transaction volumes are regularly followed by periods of very low activity.[26] Yet, as private equity has survived the crisis and is returning to old strengths, the focus can now return to fundamental, longer-standing issues. Indeed, despite the fact that private equity has been in existence for several decades, questions surrounding its economic value and broader effects have not been answered decisively and remain the subject of an ongoing debate.

---

[22] Although 'private equity' is sometimes used as a synonym for LBOs, LBOs are just one (particularly high-profile) category of private equity, which, however, also covers other categories of activity including both venture and distressed/rescue capital funding.

[23] Kaplan and Strömberg, above n. 17, 121.

[24] A purchase through debt finance provides a tax shield as interest on debt is deductible. On this, see A. Knauer et al., 'How Much Do Private Equity Funds Benefit from Debt-Related Tax Shields?' (2014) 26 Journal of Applied Corporate Finance 85. Leveraged acquisitions are also beneficial as increases in company value go to the equity holders as debt is paid down, while debt holders' claims are fixed.

[25] After an acquisition, an investor may split up the company and sell parts of it – such as specific assets or business divisions – in order to pay back some of the debt (which is known as a 'bust-up' bid).

[26] See Kaplan and Strömberg, above n. 17, 137–41; see also Davidoff Solomon, above n. 16 (focusing on the structural weaknesses in private equity contractual arrangements).

In 1989, prominent financial economist Michael Jensen noted the following in a *Harvard Business Review* article entitled 'Eclipse of the Private Corporation':

> New organizations are emerging in [the place of private corporations] – organizations that are corporate in form but have no public shareholders and are not listed or traded on organized exchanges. These organizations use public and private debt, rather than public equity, as their major source of capital. Their primary owners are not households but large institutions and entrepreneurs that designate agents to manage and monitor on their behalf and bind those agents with large equity interests and contracts governing the use and distribution of cash.[27]

Jensen was, of course, referring to the private equity model. In his view, this model would lead to economically superior results and soon eclipse the public corporation. As Jensen contended, private equity was able to resolve 'the central weakness of the public corporation – the conflict between owners and managers over the control and use of corporate resources' and make 'remarkable gains in operating efficiency, employee productivity, and shareholder value'.[28] Although he still saw a future role for the public corporation, he noted its tendency for 'widespread waste and inefficiency' and predicted that the '[t]he conventional twentieth-century model of corporate governance – dispersed public ownership, professional managers without substantial equity holdings, a board of directors dominated by management-appointed outsiders' would be pushed back to a smaller section of the economy.[29]

Today, more than 20 years later, Jensen's prognosis has not materialized, and it remains unclear if it ever will. Curiously, while private equity has many supporters, even the seemingly basic question of whether LBOs improve a company's performance is still an open one.[30] Moreover, the private equity model has been severely criticized. Among others, some commentators – ranging from various academics to politicians – have argued that private equity increases default risks and systemic risks, unduly emphasizes short-term results, reduces growth and innovation, leads to conflicts of interest between firms and investors, disadvantages employees, and suffers from a lack of transparency and public accountability.[31] Even Jensen's fundamental idea of private equity as an

---

[27] M.C. Jensen, 'Eclipse of the Public Corporation' (1989) 67 *Harvard Business Review* 61, at https://hbr.org/1989/09/eclipse-of-the-public-corporation.
[28] *ibid.*
[29] More recently, Larry Ribstein highlighted the increasing importance of unincorporated firms, including private equity firms, which he perceived in many ways as representing a superior governance model. See L.E. Ribstein, *The Rise of the Uncorporation* (OUP 2010).
[30] See e.g. Masulis and Thomas, above n. 17, 219; D. Kershaw, *Company Law in Context: Text and Materials* (2nd ed., OUP 2012), 753 n. 153 (both referring to the openness of the debate but agreeing with the view that private equity does create long-term value).
[31] These and other criticisms are described in more detail in E. Ferran, 'Regulation of Private Equity – Backed Leveraged Buyout Activity in Europe' (2007) ECGI Law Working Paper 84/2007, 7–12, at http://ssrn.com/abstract=989748; Moore and Rebérioux, above n. 17, 12–13; Kaplan and Strömberg, above n. 17.

agency cost-reducing device, in the general vein of the market for corporate control, has been disputed. William Bratton, for example, argues that, due to the substantial fees involved, private equity structures create a net surplus of agency costs. In this context, Bratton points to studies that 'show that buyout firms take so much of the gain that [investors] in buyout funds would be better off investing in market indices'.[32]

Contrary to these critical views, (other) empirical evidence tends to paint a more nuanced picture. For example, a study conducted by Kaplan and Strömberg found that the default (insolvency) rate for companies that were subject to an LBO was lower than the average default rate of other businesses,[33] with the authors also noting that '[t]he empirical evidence on the operating performance of companies after they have been purchased through a leveraged buyout is largely positive'.[34] Still other studies indicate that amongst newly established companies, private equity owned firms experience stronger growth than similarly placed *non*-private equity owned firms, and that in certain contexts private equity ownership can in fact contribute to a firm's innovation.[35] With regards to employment, some empirical studies[36] suggest that employment declines in portfolio companies are mainly restricted to the retail sector. In other areas, however, private equity owned companies were found to have experienced job growth, albeit at a slower rate than other comparable businesses. Finally, yet another study produced 'neutral' results that were not consistent with LBOs creating or destroying jobs.[37]

Given these conflicting perspectives on private equity, its future is indeed difficult to predict. Bratton, for example, acknowledges that the private equity model 'appears to work within its own limited durational framework'[38] but concludes that it will not eclipse the public corporation with its unlimited term equity capital and option for investors to easily exit an investment. In a similar vein, Cheffins and Armour predicted in a 2008 article that not the public corporation, but rather the traditional version of private equity will be eclipsed,[39] opining that private equity could be disrupted by deteriorating market and regulatory conditions.[40] Alternatively, they contend, should these conditions remain favourable, future models of private equity will see

---

[32] W.W. Bratton, 'Private Equity's Three Lessons for Agency Theory' (2008) 3 *Brooklyn Journal of Corporate Financial and Commercial Law* 1, 3.

[33] Kaplan and Strömberg, above n. 17, 129.

[34] *ibid.*, 132.

[35] See N. Torres, 'Private Equity Can Make Firms More Innovative', Harvard Business Review (June 2015), at https://hbr.org/2015/06/private-equity-can-make-firms-more-innovative.

[36] For an overview, see Kaplan and Strömberg, above n. 17, 133–34.

[37] K. Amess and M. Wright, 'Barbarians at the Gate? Leveraged Buyouts, Private Equity and Jobs' (2007), at http://papers.ssrn.com/sol3/papers.cfm?abstract_id=1034178.

[38] Bratton, above n. 32, 27.

[39] Cheffins and Armour, above n. 17.

[40] Particularly the availability of credit and, on the regulatory side, developments in antitrust, corporate, securities and tax law.

private equity transform to broadly based, publicly traded financial groups, even if they continue to engage in public-to-private transactions. Indeed, this transformation to a publicly traded model is now seen in a few private equity firms that are publicly listed. Nevertheless, the continuance of this trend is dependent on private equity firms being able to attract sufficient interest from public market investors, which remains challenging if these investors, as has been the case thus far, cannot be convinced that these types of investment will reward them with more favourable returns than investments in other sectors.[41]

In sum, the private equity market is alive but in flux. Indeed, after more than seven years since the devastating credit and financial crisis, private equity now seems to be returning to its old strengths.[42] Nevertheless, challenges remain. For example, on the market side, private equity buyers struggle with high assets valuations and increased competition for buyout targets. Additionally, the prospect of rising interest rates may, among other effects, increase the cost of debt.[43] In terms of regulation, it also appears that more pressure is building. First, the UK has seen a push for increased transparency by private equity firms and portfolio companies that resulted in the (voluntary) 2007 Walker Guidelines.[44] This was followed by the EU's Alternative Investment Fund Managers Directive, which, *inter alia*, now provides for a broad range of transparency and disclosure requirements for private equity fund managers and portfolio companies.[45] Meanwhile, in the US, the 2010 Dodd-Frank Act requires that private equity fund managers register with the Securities Exchange

---

[41] See 'Stephen Schwarzman of Blackstone Feels the Agony of Victory', *New York Times*, 4 September 2015.

[42] After reaching a high watermark in the record-breaking period between 2005 and 2007, the LBO market came to an abrupt halt in the second half of 2007 when credit markets were severely affected by the crisis in debt and financial markets, which marked the beginning of a private equity 'bust' period between 2008 and 2009. See T. Maynard, *Mergers and Acquisitions – Cases, Materials, and Problems* (3rd ed., Wolters Kluwer 2013), 73–75. Thereafter, the private equity market picked up again, swelling from modest levels of activity to a rebound in numbers in globally announced deals and deal values, which in 2013 and 2014 were at the highest level since the financial crisis. See Preqin, *2015 Preqin Global Private Equity and Venture Capital Report*; Bain and Company, *Global Private Equity Report 2015*; M. Moszoro and A. Koscielecka, 'Private Equity – Ripples of a Fourth Wave' (2013) 130 *IDEAS* 21.

[43] Bain and Company, above n. 42.

[44] D. Walker, Guidelines for Disclosure and Transparency in Private Equity (2007). In 2014, Part V of the Guidelines was amended by Guidelines Monitoring Group, Guidelines for Disclosure and Transparency in Private Equity, Part V (2014).

[45] Directive 2011/61/EU of the European Parliament and of the Council of 8 June 2011 on Alternative Investment Fund Managers and Amending Directives 2003/41/EC and 2009/65/EC and Regulations (EC) No 1060/2009 and (EU) No 1095/2010, *Official Journal of the European Union* 2011 L 174/1. On this, see E. Ferran, 'After the Crisis: The Regulation of Hedge Funds and Private Equity in the EU' (2011) 12 *European Business Organization Law Review* 379; J. Payne, 'Private Equity and Its Regulation in Europe' (2011) 12 *European Business Organization Law Review* 559.

Commission and has given the SEC enhanced powers to regulate private equity,[46] which most recently led to SEC investigations and charges pertaining to the fee structures and disclosure practices of several private equity firms.[47]

Financial Assistance Prohibition

In addition to the more recent regulatory developments mentioned above, UK company law has long contained a substantial hurdle for private equity transactions.[48] In line with EU law, the Companies Act 2006 makes it illegal – subject to certain exceptions – for a public company to provide 'financial assistance' towards the purchase of its shares.

Section 678(1) of the Act states in this respect:

> Where a person is acquiring or proposing to acquire shares in a public company, it is not lawful for that company, or a company that is a subsidiary of that company, to give financial assistance directly or indirectly for the purpose of the acquisition before or at the same time as the acquisition takes place.

Section 678(3) further provides that where a person has already acquired shares in a company and a liability has been incurred for the purpose of the acquisition, the company or its subsidiaries may not give financial assistance towards reducing that liability if, when the assistance is given, the target company is a public company. Additionally, section 679 extends the prohibition against financial assistance to assistance given by a public company towards the acquisition of shares in its private holding company. A violation of these principles may result in the company that gives assistance, as well as its directors, incurring civil and criminal penalties. The transaction that provides the assistance is also void.

Financial assistance within the meaning of the Companies Act prohibition is broadly defined. It includes any monetary assistance given, such as gifts, loans, guarantees, waivers, releases, indemnities, etc.[49] In terms of policy considerations, this extensive type of financial assistance prohibition is based on the legislature's conviction that it is abusive to finance a takeover by a loan and use the target's assets to secure the loan, while also using target cash flows and assets to repay and service the debt.[50]

---

[46] Among others, section 404 of the Dodd-Frank Wall Street Reform and the Consumer Protection Act of 2010 requires advisors to private equity funds with more than $150 million in assets to register with the SEC and report basic organizational and operational information about the funds.

[47] 'Blackstone to Pay $39m over SEC Probe into Fees', *Financial Times*, 7 October 2015.

[48] For a detailed discussion of the financial assistance regime, see E. Ferran and L. Chan Ho, *Principles of Financial Regulation* (2nd ed., OUP 2014), 232–68.

[49] Section 677 Companies Act 2006. Sections 678–682 contain exceptions to the prohibition.

[50] For a discussion of the policy objectives behind the rule, see Ferran and Chan Ho, above n. 48, 234–39; S. Mercouris, 'The Prohibition on Financial Assistance: The Case for a Commercially Pragmatic Interpretation' (2014) 35 *Company Lawyer* 321, 322–24.

This negative view of leveraged transactions is also reflected in the House of Lords' *Chaston* decision, in which Lady Justice Arden referred to the 'general mischief' of using target company assets to assist a purchaser in acquiring the target.[51] Referring to the potential negative effects of such practices, she noted that '[t]his may prejudice the interests of the creditors of the target or its group, and the interests of any shareholders who do not accept the offer to acquire their shares or to whom the offer is not made'. In *Chaston*, the prohibited assistance consisted of the subsidiary paying for accounting work carried out in the context of an acquisition of its parent company. This was held to be a violation of financial assistance prohibitions (under the version of the Companies Act in place at the time of the decision).

In effect, the financial assistance prohibition therefore targets (*inter alia*) private equity leveraged buyouts of public companies. Due to the applicable provisions, it is not permissible to borrow against a target company's assets, since that would include guarantees and other assistance. Nor is it permissible to use the target's cash flow to repay a loan or make interest payments. Nevertheless, the ban's effect on private equity has not been as severe as one might think, in part because the prohibition is normally restricted to the acquisition of public companies and because practitioners have found ways to work around the prohibition.[52] As an example, the most straightforward way to avoid the ban is to reconstitute the acquired entity as a private company following acquisition, thereby enabling the acquirer to provide assistance to the acquirer retrospectively. Still, the prohibition is today broadly opposed by academics and regulators alike. It remains on the books principally due to EU corporate law, which continues to demand provisions against financial assistance.[53]

TAKEOVER DEFENCES

Takeovers implicate the enduring question of which corporate constituency should have the ultimate power to decide whether a takeover offer will be accepted or rejected. Should the target's board be allowed to take defensive measures against a hostile takeover or, alternatively, should it be solely up to shareholders to decide on the offer? As we will see, the traditional UK approach is not to allow boards to 'frustrate' takeovers. It is thought that a takeover offer is only between the bidder and the target shareholders, and that the board should not interfere. Conversely, the US position is generally to give boards largely unfettered powers to block unfriendly takeover attempts. In this section we will discuss the legal framework and underlying policy considerations that govern takeover defences.

---

[51] *Chaston v SWP Group Plc* [2003] BCC 140.
[52] See Ferran, above n. 31, 20–28 (discussing the prohibition's limits and techniques to escape the scope of the ban; Mercouris, above n. 50, 324–25.
[53] Kershaw, above n. 30, 754; Mercouris, above n. 50, 321. See Art. 25 of the Second Company Law Directive 2012/30/EU.

The Role of General Company Law

Given the potentially drastic consequences of a takeover for the company and its stakeholders (in particular the shareholders and employees, but also the directors and managers), a target board may have strong incentives to oppose, and thus attempt to defend against, hostile takeovers. Whether or not it is permissible for boards to do so is, in part, decided by general company law. Particularly pertinent statutory provisions in this regard are sections 171 and 551 of the Companies Act 2006.

Under section 171, directors must act in accordance with the company's constitution and only exercise the powers delegated to them for the purposes for which they are conferred. Conversely, using their powers for other, 'improper' purposes constitutes a breach of duty. This 'improper purpose doctrine' also extends to takeovers,[54] as defensive measures by the board may be improper in this sense, and thus represent a breach of duty on the part of the directors concerned.[55] Under the older leading cases *Hogg v. Cramphorn Ltd.*[56] and *Howard Smith Ltd. v. Ampol Petroleum Ltd.*[57] boards may not, without shareholder approval, engage in actions whose primary purpose is to block a takeover, independent of the directors' motivations (which may be well-intentioned) for doing so.[58] This is in line with later decisions that emphasize the directors' duty to 'ensure that the offer and any competing offers are put to the members so that they can decide for themselves whether to accept or reject the best bid available'.[59]

However, the current state of the law is not entirely clear as some cases have indicated that the principle of almost absolute protection of shareholders' right to decide may be softening. In particular, the decision in *Criterion Properties plc v. Stratford UK Properties LLC*[60] suggests the possibility of an emerging willingness by courts to take into account 'commercial realities' and allow boards to defend against takeovers that they believe would lead to severely negative consequences for their company.

Alternatively, even if such a change in the law should not materialize, certain board actions that make it more difficult for a company to be taken over could be regarded as proper even under the traditional case law. This could be true in

---

[54] For an in-depth analysis, see Kershaw, above n. 30, Chapter 11 and (on directors' duties in takeovers generally) D. Kershaw, *Principles of Takeover Regulation* (OUP 2016), 297–321.

[55] Which does not necessarily, however, mean that such measures are invalid as against a third party.

[56] [1967] Ch 254.

[57] [1974] AC 821 (Privy Council).

[58] See also *Eclairs Group Ltd v JKX Oil & Gas plc* [2015] UKSC 71 for a more recent Supreme Court affirmation of the proper purpose doctrine.

[59] *Arbuthnott v. Bonnyman and Ors* [2015] EWCA Civ 536 at [50], referring in part to *Dawson International Plc v Coats Patons Plc* [1990] BCLC 560 and *Heron International Ltd v Lord Grade* [1983] BCLC 244.

[60] Decided by the House of Lords in [2004] UKHL 28. For the improper purpose doctrine's application to takeover defences, however, the lower courts' decisions are equally relevant. See [2002] EWCH 496 (Ch); [2003] 1 WLR 2108.

situations where such actions are not *primarily* intended to serve a defensive purpose but – incidentally – have such an effect. For instance, one can think of various potentially legitimate actions that make it more difficult or less attractive to acquire a company, but can be explained as being motivated by commercial reasons, such as the assumption of additional debt or distributions to shareholders. While such actions can often be explained as purely business decisions, they may also render a target less attractive in the eyes of potential bidders. Nevertheless, the proper purpose doctrine – for premium listed companies in conjunction with the Listing Rules[61] – continues to present an important hurdle for unilateral (without shareholders' approval) board defences against unwelcome bids to acquire a company.

Another company law provision that restricts defensive measures is section 551 of the Companies Act. This section, together with section 549, provides that shareholder approval is needed for decisions by directors of public companies to issue shares, unless they are already empowered to do so by the articles. Directors also need shareholder approval in order to grant rights to subscribe for securities or to grant rights to convert securities into shares. Section 551, in conjunction with the proper purpose doctrine in section 171, makes it extremely difficult for a UK company to prevent hostile takeover bids by using US-style 'poison pills'.

Poison pills are based on schemes that provide existing target company shareholders the right to purchase additional shares at a discounted price (below market price) provided that someone – a third party bidder – attempts to take over the target and surpasses a certain threshold of shareholding in the target.[62] If shareholders were then to exercise their right, this would substantially dilute the bidder's holding and make a takeover financially unattractive, and therefore unlikely. Although such poison pills are not expressly prohibited under UK company law, they are subject to section 171 and the proper purpose doctrine. Importantly, however, directors cannot implement these schemes unilaterally. As section 551 provides, shareholders have to approve plans involving options to subscribe for or convert securities into company shares, either through a vote in each specific instance or globally via the articles.[63] Additionally, the requirement

---

[61] Listing Rule 10.5 requires shareholder approval in case of transactions that exceed certain value thresholds. This precludes a board from unilaterally defending against a takeover by selling certain key company assets. Financial Conduct Authority, *FCA Handbook*, 'LR Listing Rules', at https://www.handbook.fca.org.uk/handbook.

[62] For details on the poison pill defence, as developed in US law, see further below. Note, however, that particularly non-US commentators may use the term 'poison pill' generally as a reference to any type of defensive tactic against takeovers.

[63] See also section 549(1). For a detailed discussion, D. Kershaw, 'The Illusion of Importance: Reconsidering the UK's Takeover Defence Prohibition' (2007) 56 *International and Comparative Law Quarterly* 267; C. Gerner-Beuerle, D. Kershaw and M. Solinas, 'Is the Board Neutrality Rule Trivial? Amnesia about Corporate Law in European Takeover Regulation' (2011) 22 *European Business Law Review* 559, 569–82. As the latter work explains, because the Companies Act 2006 in section 561(3) applies pre-emption rights to the grant of an option but not in relation to the allotment of shares in exercise of the option, pre-emptive rights are not a concern in this respect. Additionally, in terms of other defensive mechanisms, an equity restructuring defence involving the issuance of shares to a friendly third party would equally face substantial legal and practical hurdles.

to have shareholder approval thus limits UK boards' leeway in using poison pills and similar defences based on the target's equity or debt securities.

Another way to fend off takeovers is for a company to implement a capital structure with multiple voting shares or non-voting shares, that is shares that have no right to vote at the General Meeting and/or shares that have more than one vote attached to them. Both share types may help concentrate control in a group of insider shareholders, such as the company's founders or management: they can either hold multiple voting rights (examples for which are Facebook and Google's parent company Alphabet) or, alternatively, issue a certain proportion of non-voting shares to outside shareholders (such as in the case of the proposed initial public offering of Snap), which allows them to exercise control despite their relatively – compared to regular shareholders – small economic investment in the company. Consequently, if the insider shareholders decide not to sell their shares, a bidder will not be able to gain control of the company. This is true because unless these often large blocks of voting rights are acquired, the bidder is unlikely to obtain a sufficient number of voting rights required for a successful takeover.

Multiple voting rights are allowed under UK company law, although there are severe restrictions for companies with a premium listing on the London Stock Exchange.[64] However, the effect of such shares can be temporarily circumvented in companies where shareholders opt in to Article 11 of the EU Takeovers Directive.[65] Article 11 contains a 'break-through rule', which allows a bidder to break through defensive measures based on multiple or non-voting shares or share transfer restrictions. Shareholders can opt in,[66] in which case the special voting rights will be rendered ineffective for the purposes of defending against a takeover. Therefore, if there is opting-in by shareholders, this may allow for control transactions that would otherwise not be possible.

The Takeover Code's Board Neutrality Rule

The Companies Act provisions discussed thus far limit, but do not prohibit outright, defensive measures by target company boards. However, more restrictive rules are contained in the UK's City Code on Takeovers and Mergers (the 'Takeover Code' or 'Code'), which in great part is responsible for developing and enforcing the framework for corporate control transactions in the UK.[67] The Code is applicable from the point in time when a target board has reason to believe that a bona fide offer for its company might be imminent.[68]

The Code is based on the belief that a takeover offer is between the offeror and the target's shareholders, while the target board should not be able to

---

[64] See Chapter 4.

[65] Directive 2004/25/EC on Takeover Bids, Article 11(2)–(4).

[66] See sections 966–969 of the Companies Act 2006.

[67] The Panel on Takeovers and Mergers, *The Takeover Code* (September 2016), at http://www.thetakeoverpanel.org.uk/the-code/download-code. On the Code's scope, see its Introduction, A3; see also sections 952–956 of the Companies Act 2006.

[68] Takeover Code, Rule 21.

interfere with or even block the offer. In the UK, this 'non-frustration' or 'board neutrality' approach has been in place since the late 1960s, implemented as a response to what had been seen as unwarranted rejections of take-over bids by target boards in previous years.[69] The rule was introduced at the time of the Takeover Panel's formation and, in keeping with emerging UK Takeover Regulation during this period, represented a self-regulatory approach by the City of London's financial industry representatives.[70] The board neutrality approach later also inspired the EU Takeovers Directive, which – subject to Member States' right of non-implementation – has adopted this approach as its default rule on takeover defences.[71]

Board neutrality is now expressed in General Principle 3 and Rule 21 of the Takeover Code. General Principle 3 (corresponding to Article 3(c) of the Takeovers Directive) provides that the board 'must act in the interests of the company as a whole and must not deny the holders of securities the opportunity to decide on the merits of the bid'. Rule 21.1 provides more detailed restrictions on actions that might frustrate a takeover bid. Such actions are therefore only allowed if there is shareholder consent[72]:

> During the course of an offer, or even before the date of the offer if the board of the offeree company has reason to believe that a bona fide offer might be imminent, the board must not, without the approval of the shareholders in general meeting:
> (a) take any action which may result in any offer or bona fide possible offer being frustrated or in shareholders being denied the opportunity to decide on its merits; or
> (b) i. issue any shares or transfer or sell, or agree to transfer or sell, any shares out of treasury or effect any redemption or purchase by the company of its own shares;
>   ii. issue or grant options in respect of any unissued shares;
>   iii. create or issue, or permit the creation or issue of, any securities carrying rights of conversion into or subscription for shares;
>   iv. sell, dispose of or acquire, or agree to sell, dispose of or acquire, assets of a material amount; or
>   v. enter into contracts otherwise than in the ordinary course of business.

---

[69] On the board neutrality rule's origins in the UK and the EU, see Gerner-Beuerle *et al.*, above n. 63, 559–61; Kershaw, above n. 54, Ch. 3.

[70] *ibid.*

[71] See Article 12 of the Takeovers Directive (pertaining to board neutrality and breakthrough rules). Nevertheless, companies still need to be granted the right to opt in and make these provisions applicable on an individual (company-level) basis. Notably, Germany (among others states) has not implemented the board neutrality system. See the table on implementation of the Takeovers Directive in J.A. McCahery and E.P.M. Vermeulen, 'The Case against Reform of the Takeover Bids Directive' (2011) 22 *European Business Law Review* 541, 549–50.

[72] See also Article 9(2) of the Takeovers Directive, which provides that 'the board of the offeree company shall obtain the prior authorisation of the general meeting of shareholders ... before taking any action, other than seeking alternative bids, which may result in the frustration of the bid and in particular before issuing any shares which may result in a lasting impediment to the offeror's acquiring control of the offeree company'.

Additionally, the Takeover Code's Rule 21.2 (except with the consent of the Panel) prohibits a target company from entering into any 'offer-related arrangement' during an offer period or when an offer is reasonably in contemplation. Offer-related arrangements are defined as 'any agreement, arrangement or commitment in connection with an offer, including any inducement fee arrangement or other arrangement having a similar or comparable financial or economic effect'. Therefore, insofar as the Takeover Code applies, a UK target company board may not employ deal-protection devices such as a promise to compensate a bidder in the event that shareholders reject its offer ('break fees'), commit to refrain from discussing a potential transaction with other parties ('no-talk provisions'), or undertake not to solicit competing bids ('no shop provisions').

Thus, General Principle 3 and Rule 21 of the Takeover Code play a central role in entrenching shareholder sovereignty as the foremost position of UK law with regard to takeovers (but, as we have seen in Chapter 4, not in other areas of corporate governance). Indeed, absent shareholder consent, the Code's non-frustration rule reduces the major defensive tactics available to target companies to essentially three categories. First, boards can try to convince shareholders that their future is better assured with the incumbent management and that they should not accept an offer because they would be worse off. Second, they may try to persuade competition authorities that a bid should not be allowed based on competition law concerns. Finally, they could attempt to encourage a 'white knight' to come forward: that is, a third party who makes an alternative offer and is deemed by the board to be better suited as a potential new controller of the company than the original hostile bidder.[73]

Delaware's Board-Centric Approach

As we have seen, the UK's default position, at least in regulation that is geared specifically towards takeovers, is to disallow defensive measures against hostile acquisitions of a company unless shareholders, which are given the ultimate power to decide, approve such measures. This solution stands in stark contrast to the managerially- and judicially-centric approach of Delaware law in the US. Indeed, the contrast between UK (and EU) law and Delaware law on this point is among the most notable trans-Atlantic differences from a comparative corporate governance perspective.

The extent to which boards of Delaware companies can defend against takeovers is limited by their duties and the extent to which courts can review their actions. Generally, as a principle of Delaware corporate law, courts will not review board decisions based on the 'business judgment rule'. This rule

---

[73] It should be noted, however, that, given the hurdles in general UK company law, the Takeover Code's board neutrality regime appears to be far less consequential – perhaps even 'trivial' – than it is often thought to be. See the detailed analysis in Gerner-Beuerle *et al.* above n. 63, 569–82.

provides that 'directors' decisions will be respected by courts unless the directors are interested or lack independence relative to the decision, do not act in good faith, act in a manner that cannot be attributed to a rational business purpose or reach their decision by a grossly negligent process that includes the failure to consider all material facts reasonably available'.[74]

However, the business judgment rule does not provide a suitable fit for reviewing directors' decisions – namely in terms of defensive measures – in the takeover context. As one case has noted, since directors' have a personal interest in opposing a takeover (in order to protect their positions), there is an 'omnipresent specter that a board may be acting primarily in its own interests' in takeover situations.[75] Thus, the business judgment rule, whose protective ambit does not apply in situations where directors are self-interested, is ill-suited for the takeover context. Courts have therefore altered the rule and developed alternative tests for assessing takeover defences taken by boards.

One of the most prominent cases is *Unocal Corporation v. Mesa Petroleum Co.*,[76] decided by the Delaware Supreme Court. The case arose after an investor with a reputation as a corporate 'raider' attempted to take control of a target company, Unocal. The investor, through his company Mesa Petroleum, launched a takeover bid, the terms of which included offering more valuable consideration for target shares that were tendered early, and less valuable consideration (so-called 'junk bonds') for those tendered later.[77] This structure was intended to encourage target shareholders to accept the offer early, thus allowing the bidder to gain control quickly. In response, and in order to stop the takeover, Unocal made an offer for its own shares, stating that if Mesa acquired a majority of Unocal stock, Unocal would purchase the remaining shares from shareholders other than the hostile bidder. In doing so it would offer a high, above-market price that would lower Unocal's value and make it unattractive as a target. Mesa then brought a lawsuit against Unocal's board, alleging that the directors were in breach of their fiduciary duties by not treating all shareholders alike, that is offering only to buy back shares not held by the hostile bidder.

The court found that Mesa's bid was coercive (given its two-tiered structure) and inadequate, and that Unocal was allowed to defend against the takeover. As Unocal's exclusion of Mesa from its offer to buy its own shares was essential for its defensive strategy's effectiveness, the directors were found not to be in breach of their duties. Importantly, the court then went on to formulate a test for assessing the legality of defensive measures by a target board. Under the *Unocal* test, directors who adopt defensive tactics in a

---

[74] *Brehm v. Eisner*, 746 A.2d 244, 264 n.66 (Del. 2000). See also S.M. Bainbridge, 'The Business Judgment Rule as Abstention Doctrine' (2004) 57 *Vanderbilt Law Review* 83, 88.

[75] *Unocal Corp. v. Mesa Petroleum Co.*, 493 A 2d 946 (Del. 1985).

[76] *ibid.*

[77] This form of bidding is prohibited under the UK's Takeover Code.

takeover scenario must show that: (i) the board (based on good faith and reasonable investigation) had reasonable grounds for believing that a danger to corporate policy and effectiveness existed; and (ii) the board believed that its defensive actions were a reasonable response to the threat posed, meaning that the response must be proportionate to the threat. Given the facts of the case under consideration, the court was satisfied that the board had met these conditions.

The *Unocal* standard of review remains the prevailing standard to assess the legality of defensive measures in Delaware corporations. This includes situations where target boards implement poison pills based on a 'shareholder rights plan'.[78] While the courts tend to grant deference to the board's assessment of whether a bid constitutes a threat in the sense of *Unocal*, and may allow poison pills and other defences, a recent high-profile decision described the limits of what will be permissible as follows:

> A board cannot '*just* say no' to a tender offer. Under Delaware law, it must first pass through two prongs of exacting judicial scrutiny by a judge who will evaluate the actions taken by, and the motives of, the board. Only a board of directors found to be acting in good faith, after reasonable investigation and reliance on the advice of outside advisors, which articulates and convinces the Court that a hostile tender offer poses a legitimate threat to the corporate enterprise, may address that perceived threat by blocking the tender offer and forcing the bidder to elect a board majority that supports its bid.[79]

Interestingly, *Unocal* allows boards to consider the impact of their decisions on non-shareholder constituencies – including employees, customers, creditors, communities and others – when they assess the bid and its effects on the corporation.[80] There is some speculation as to the extent to which this allows (if at all) for a departure from the 'shareholder wealth maximization' approach. Indeed, some scholars have interpreted the reference to non-shareholder interests as supportive of Corporate Social Responsibility (CSR) considerations by boards, while others have argued that taking account of other stakeholders' interests must – at least in the long run – still coincide with a duty to advance the interests of shareholders. However, in light of more recent case law, it seems

---

[78] The plan offers existing shareholders an option to purchase target company shares at a deep discount over the market price when a hostile bidder reaches a certain percentage threshold of shares in the target, thereby diluting the bidder. The first case in which the Delaware Supreme Court upheld a poison pill defence was *Moran v. Household International, Inc.*, 500 A.2d 1346 (Del. 1985). Additionally, it is also possible to devise poison pills with a 'flip-over' feature that allows target shareholders to acquire bidder shares at a discount. Further details on poison pill defences can be found in Kershaw, above n. 63; J.P. Lowry, '"Poison Pills" in US Corporations – A Re-Examination' (1992) *Journal of Business Law* 337.

[79] *Air Products and Chemicals, Inc. v. Airgas, Inc.*, 16 A.3d 48, 54 (Del. Ch. 2011). The court's reference to a bidder's option to elect a board majority supportive of its bid refers to a shareholder's option to engage in a 'proxy contest'. On this, see Chapter 4.

[80] *Unocal Corp. v. Mesa Petroleum Co.*, 493 A.2d 946, 955 (Del. 1985).

clear that a complete abdication of shareholder value maximization would not be permissible as a matter of Delaware law.[81]

Finally, it should be noted that Delaware also recognizes certain situations when directors may not only *not* block a takeover, but where they must maximize the value of their company by selling it to the highest bidder. The landmark decision in this regard (establishing these so-called 'Revlon duties' of boards) is *Revlon, Inc. v. MacAndrews & Forbes Holdings, Inc.*,[82] as modified by subsequent decisions. In one of them, *Paramount Communications v. Time*, the Delaware Supreme Court stated that 'generally speaking and without excluding other possibilities', the two circumstances which may implicate Revlon duties are: (i) 'when a corporation initiates an active bidding process seeking to sell itself or to effect a business reorganization involving a clear break-up of the company'; or (ii) when 'in response to a bidder's offer, a target abandons its long-term strategy and seeks an alternative transaction also involving the breakup of the company'.[83] In another important case, *Paramount Communications, Inc. v. QVC Network, Inc.*,[84] the Delaware Supreme Court added that a change of control, in the sense of a transition from dispersed to concentrated ownership (by a majority shareholder), also constitutes a triggering event for *Revlon* duties.

WHO SHOULD DECIDE?

As we have seen, the law in the UK and the EU reflects the idea that a takeover bid is solely between the bidder and the target company's shareholders. Shareholders should be free to transfer their shares to anybody whose offer they wish to accept. Therefore, there are strong restrictions against defensive measures, and shareholder approval is needed for effectively preventing a takeover bid. On the other hand, in the US (Delaware), a target board may often block a hostile takeover bid, taking advantage of various defensive mechanisms that directors can implement unilaterally: that is, without shareholder consent. Having thus described pertinent aspects of the legal framework governing takeover defences, this chapter's final part will deal with the normative question of which corporate constituency *should* decide whether a hostile takeover bid for a company may proceed and will be accepted.

---

[81] See *eBay Domestic Holdings, Inc. v. Newmark*, 16 A.3d 1 (Del. Ch. 2010). Additionally, this position was also established in *Revlon, Inc. v. MacAndrews and Forbes Holdings, Inc.*, 506 A.2d 173 (Del. 1986).

[82] 506 A.2d 173 (Del. 1986). As the court put it in this case, given the triggering circumstance, '[t]he directors' role changed from defenders of the corporate bastion to auctioneers charged with getting the best price for the stockholders at a sale of the company'. *ibid.*, 82.

[83] 571 A.2d 1140 (Del. 1990). See also *Barkan v. Amsted Industries, Inc.*, 567 A.2d 1279 (1989), which allows boards to approve a transaction without an active survey of the market when directors possess a body of reliable evidence with which to evaluate the fairness of a transaction.

[84] 637 A.2d 34 (Del. 1994).

The Case for Board Neutrality

A first argument in favour of board neutrality is that leaving the shareholders in charge of accepting or declining takeover offers may promote the board's accountability and performance incentives – or at least this is what proponents of the market for corporate control would argue. In other words, board neutrality may reduce inefficiencies and lead to better managed companies due to the disciplining effects of the potential threat of efficiency-enhancing measures imposed by a new controlling shareholder.[85]

Relatedly, a board neutrality rule also avoids the problem of creating a conflict of interest, such as where boards defend against a takeover but are primarily motivated to do so by a desire to preserve their own positions instead of seeking the best possible outcome for shareholders. However, if the board simply does not have the ability to prevent a takeover without shareholder approval, a conflict of interest problem is less likely to arise or will at least be far less consequential (in that, for example, the board advises shareholders for selfish reasons against an offer, but does not prevent it).

Indeed, in the experts' report that the EU Commission relied on as the basis for preparing the Takeovers Directive (hereinafter the 'Winter Report'), the principle reasons for the experts' support of a non-frustration rule was the danger of directorial conflicts of interest. As the report noted:

> Most importantly, managers are faced with a significant conflict of interests if a takeover bid is made. Often their own performance and plans are brought into question and their own jobs are in jeopardy. Their interest is in saving their jobs and reputation instead of maximising the value of the company for shareholders. Their claims to represent the interests of shareholders or other stakeholders are likely to be tainted by self-interest. Shareholders should be able to decide for themselves and stakeholders should be protected by specific rules (e.g. on labour law or environmental law).[86]

Additionally, the Winter Report mentioned various other factors that informed its decision to recommend a board neutrality rule. Thus, the experts emphasized that shareholders have a right to decide the outcome of a bid based on their contribution of 'risk capital' (in the form of share capital) and highlighted the substantial costs of takeover defences, the potential financial benefits of takeovers (in the form of synergies and premiums paid to target shareholders), the disciplining effect on management, and the need to create a 'level playing field' in the area of takeover regulation among EU Member States.[87]

---

[85] See, however, above for factors limiting the market for corporate control thesis. See also Kershaw, above n. 54, 341–47 on the potential case for board neutrality based on the need to protect shareholders from sub-optimal decisions by their fund managers.

[86] Report of the High Level Group of Company Law Experts on Issues Related to Takeover Bids (2002) ('Winter Report') 16.

[87] See ibid., 18–19.

In terms of the level playing field that the experts and, by extension, the EU Takeovers Directive wished to advance, important reservations remain. From an intra-EU perspective, this goal was not achieved due to the possibility for Member States to opt out of the relevant takeover defence provisions. Moreover, the question remains whether the contrast between approaches in the EU and the US can be justified given the lack of a level playing field between these jurisdictions. Is it defensible to maintain a situation in which, for instance, UK boards cannot unilaterally decide to use 'poison pills' in order to effectively defend against hostile bids by a US bidder, but this same US company's board could use such tools in fending off a UK company's hostile takeover bid?

The authors of the Winter Report believed that this trans-Atlantic divergence was justified. The experts pointed to more intense pressure on US boards to focus on their companies' 'performance on the capital markets' (which presumably refers to the share price), the heightened liability risk of directors and the US courts' superior ability to deal with claims in the takeover context. The experts also found that the EU legal framework prevents certain abusive bids that in the US may need to be defended against; that European companies have still been able to take over US companies; and that the EU context requires reduced hurdles to takeovers in order to achieve an integrated internal market.[88] Additionally, other commentators have more recently noted that despite the UK and the EU's non-frustration rule, it is not a simple matter to conduct hostile takeovers. Various hurdles, practical and legal in nature, remain, making the regime less bidder friendly than it might seem on paper.[89]

Nevertheless, while there may be factors that explain or to some extent mitigate the lack of a level playing field in the trans-Atlantic context, and even considering that the differences may not be as stark as they first seem, the fact remains that the diverging legal frameworks put US companies in a more favourable position. From this perspective, the Winter Report's suggestion to explore a restriction of the EU's non-frustration/board neutrality approach only to takeover bids *between* EU companies, but to disapply the principle in case of a bid by a party from another jurisdiction, seems to potentially offer an interesting middle-ground approach that merits further consideration.

The Case for Board Primacy

Alternatively, there are also good arguments that support a universal shift towards a 'board primacy' approach, in which the directors of a target company are

---

[88] *ibid.*, 40–42.
[89] See L.E. Strine, 'The Soviet Constitution Problem in Comparative Corporate Law: Testing the Proposition that European Corporate Law Is More Stockholder-Focused than U.S. Corporate Law' (2016) 89 *Southern California Law Review* 1239; M. Gatti, 'The Power to Decide on Takeovers: Directors or Shareholders, What Difference Does It Make?'(2014) 20 *Fordham Journal of Corporate and Financial Law* 73.

empowered to decide whether or not to block a hostile bid and, if so, to take the necessary defensive actions. Indeed, the Winter Report's unequivocal support of, and arguments for, board neutrality – and the board neutrality rule or non-frustration principle as such – raise various questions. They also stand, as will be shown below, in stark contrast to the general thrust of debates among US academics.

As a preliminary observation, with regards to concerns as to conflicts of interest – such as those that were quite strongly expressed by the Winter Report's authoring group of company law experts – it should be recognized that a board primacy rule does not mean that the board can 'just say no', or that the door is wide open to self-interested behaviour by boards. As discussed above, Delaware courts clearly recognize the 'omnipresent specter' of self-interested actions in the takeover context. The solution to this problem is to tie directors' freedom to act without shareholder approval to certain conditions, as expressed for instance in the *Unocal* test. Boards thus do not possess unfettered discretion and still have to meet certain objective criteria. Additionally, the combined forces of market pressures and the continuing shift towards greater representation of independent directors on boards, as well as performance-based remuneration, together serve to ameliorate concerns about directors' self-interested conduct.

Moreover, while the Winter Report noted in 2002 that giving boards the power to defend against takeovers was controversial in the US, most US academics today are generally supportive (albeit to varying degrees) of board primacy in the takeover context. Even strong shareholder rights proponents are prepared to support the board's engagement in defensive tactics, albeit only for a limited time. Commenting on the current state of the debate, Guhan Subramanian has recently pointed to a new consensus, stating that '[n]o academic commentator today questions … [the] right of a target board to maintain a [poison] pill for a limited period of time, in order to identify a higher-value buyer or to inform shareholders about the bid'.[90]

In favour of a board primacy approach it may be argued that granting the board broad powers to block takeovers allows directors to protect shareholders from inadequate, coercive, or otherwise unsuitable bids, such as offers that undervalue the company or fail to provide a viable long-term strategy for target. The board should have the most intimate knowledge of the company, its plans and potential, which at least in theory puts it in a superior position to decide the fate of the company and whether or not a change in ownership would be beneficial. Conversely, many smaller shareholders will have neither the information, expertise, time nor inclination to thoroughly investigate and assess an offer, making it advantageous for them to defer to the board's judgement. In this respect, one can argue that the principle of board primacy – as discussed more generally in Chapter 4 – should also apply in the important context of takeovers.

---

[90] G. Subramanian, 'Bargaining in the Shadow of Takeover Defences' (2013) 113 *Yale Law Journal* 621, 655. The literature on this topic is ample and will not be further explored in this chapter.

Having the power to block an offer also enables the board, if it is agreeable to a sale of the company in principle, to negotiate more effectively for the benefit of shareholders. Thus, the ability to block or delay hostile takeovers can convert such bids into negotiated acquisitions processes, which assists boards to maximize the offer's value.[91] Additionally, boards that have the power to defend against hostile takeovers are better equipped to take into account non-shareholder interests, such as those of employees. For instance, a board could decide against supporting a bid if the negative consequences for employees or other stakeholders are thought to outweigh potential benefits.[92] Alternatively, the board could seek to include specific terms that address its concerns in this regard in a negotiated transaction.

Finally, the power to implement defensive measures mitigates concerns that boards may be too responsive to shareholder demands. Fearing that they may lose their positions if shareholders decide to sell their shares to a new controlling shareholder, boards could develop an undue focus on short-term goals. As a counter-argument to the market for corporate control and its disciplining effect on management, it can be said that insulation from such pressures may contribute to longer-term, sustainable corporate governance that is less constrained by the public markets' focus on quarterly or short-term results and short-term share price fluctuations.

Regulating in the Face of Empirical Uncertainty

Given the diverging views on the role of the board in takeovers, and given that both board neutrality and board primacy have various advantages, it seems as if a suitable way to decide the controversy is through reliance on empirical data. However, thus far neither board neutrality nor board primacy proponents can point to clear empirical evidence to bolster their claims. Measuring the long-term economic effect of takeover defences (which is linked to measuring the effect of hostile takeovers) is a challenging task.[93] Existing studies that have attempted to do so have produced mixed results, without providing a clear answer.[94]

---

[91] See A.O. 'Chip' Saulsbury IV, 'The Availability of Takeover Defenses and Deal Protection Devices for Anglo-American Companies' (2012) 37 *Delaware Journal of Corporate Law* 115 (comparing US and UK approaches).

[92] See e.g. *Unocal Corp. v. Mesa Petroleum Co.*, 493 A 2d 946 (Del. 1985), which allows boards to consider such interests in defending against a hostile bidder. Conversely, this type of reasoning was rejected by the EU's High Level Group of Company Law Experts. See Winter Report, above n. 86, 16.

[93] One commentator, writing in 2000, found that many of the empirical studies available at the time examining the effect of takeover defences on company value were scientifically flawed. J. Coates, 'The Contestability of Corporate Control: A Critique of the Scientific Evidence on Takeover Defenses' (2000) 39 *Texas Law Review* 271.

[94] Kershaw, above n. 63, 303. But cf. S.M. Bainbridge, *Corporate Governance after the Financial Crisis* (OUP 2012), 25, stating that there is 'clear evidence that hostile takeovers increase shareholder wealth'; Clarke, above n. 12, 363, who acknowledges that 'the empirical evidence is often contradictory' but concludes that the majority of evidence appears to support the hypothesis that defensive actions reduce shareholder value and are devices for management entrenchment.

A recent study for instance suggests that the effect of anti-takeover measures on firm value may change over time and can have unintended consequences.[95] For the period from 2000 to 2014, the study finds that 'firm value is increasing in takeover susceptibility' and '[s]hareholders ... appear to value the disciplinary market for corporate control'.[96] However, the authors also find evidence that susceptibility to hostile takeovers reduces takeover premiums, supporting the link between takeover defences and managerial bargaining power. The study concludes that '[i]n terms of economic magnitudes, the negative effect [of takeover protections] on firm value and the positive effect on takeover premiums are roughly offsetting'.[97]

Given these uncertainties, the question once more arises as to how regulators should approach takeover defences. In this context, Luca Enriques has argued that because it is impossible to predict in advance whether a particular takeover will enhance or decrease value, the law should take a neutral approach in the form of regulation that neither promotes nor hinders takeovers. Instead, individual companies should be able to decide how contestable their control is, including whether or not adopting defensive measures is desirable.[98] In effect, this reasoning suggests that current EU and UK approaches, which contain various limitations on defensive measures, go too far and should be revisited. In a similar vein, based on an in-depth analysis of the cases for and against board neutrality, David Kershaw has argued in favour of making stronger takeover defences mechanisms available to UK boards, which among other measures would include the abolition of the Code's non-frustration rule.[99]

Governmental Interventions

Apart from the discussions surrounding the economic effects of takeover defences, primarily as expressed in shareholder value, we should note that the power to prevent takeovers can also have broader societal and political dimensions. This is particularly significant in the case of cross-border acquisitions of so-called 'flag-bearer' companies: that is, businesses of special importance or strategic interest to their host country. In these instances, not only boards but also governments may have an interest in taking an active role in deciding the outcome of – and, if necessary, preventing – an acquisition. Some notable recent examples of such scenarios include the takeover of iconic British confectioner Cadbury by Kraft or the attempted (but unsuccessful) takeover of pharmaceutical producer AstraZeneca by Pfizer.

In the Kraft-Cadbury takeover, the then-Business Secretary Lord Mandelson suggested that the UK government would oppose unsuitable buyers, echoing

---

[95] M.D. Cain *et al.*, 'Do Takeover Laws Matter? Evidence from Five Decades of Hostile Takeovers' (2015), at http://papers.ssrn.com/sol3/papers.cfm?abstract_id=2517513.

[96] *ibid.*, 5.

[97] *ibid.*

[98] Enriques, above n. 12.

[99] As he notes, aside from neutrality rule's historical policy reasons, 'the case for reform in the UK is very one-sided'. Kershaw, above n. 54, 369, detailed analysis at 338–362.

concerns in political circles and the public about an American takeover of one of Britain's most famous brands.[100] However, legally, the government's options were – and at least for now continue to be – severely limited, and 'the government did not take any action to prevent the bid, or secure commitments from Kraft to protect British factories or jobs'.[101]

Indeed, the UK belongs to those countries that take a relatively market-liberal approach to governmental interventions.[102] Mergers and takeovers are by default only scrutinized by the competition authorities (who may have to refer a case to the European Commission, depending on the outcome of a turnover test), whose mandate extends to an examination of whether a transaction has or may be expected to result in a 'substantial lessening of competition'.[103] The government, through the Secretary of State, may only intervene where an acquisition gives rise to certain specified public interest concerns, namely issues of national security; media quality, plurality and standards; and financial stability.[104] Additionally, the Secretary of State may seek Parliament's approval for the recognition of a further category of public interest considerations, which, if granted, would need to be consistent with EU law. However, the EU Commission is reluctant to recognize individual governments' new public interest grounds for interventions, given the potential conflict with the principles underlying the EU merger control system and the single market's free movement of capital principle.[105] This rather restrictive definition of public interest issues – coupled with (pre-Brexit) constraints under EU law – prevents the UK government from blocking, through strictly legal channels, takeovers that they do not approve of as a matter of policy. Although the Cadbury takeover triggered changes in the Takeover Code, neither this episode (with heated debates following a factory closure by Kraft) nor the discussions surrounding the failed attempt to acquire AstraZeneca (where there were concerns about research activities being transferred abroad) led to a broader public interest test.[106]

---

[100] See J. Wiggins, 'The Inside Story of the Cadbury Takeover', *Financial Times*, 12 March 2010, at http://www.ft.com/cms/s/2/1e5450d2-2be5-11df-8033-00144feabdc0.html.

[101] *ibid*. Note, however, the Takeover Code's new provisions on post-offer intention statements and post-offer undertakings, the latter of which can be enforced by the Takeover Panel. UK Takeover Code, Rules 19.7–19.8. Although these may ameliorate some concerns that arise in connection with bids for flag-bearer companies, they are far weaker than a potential governmental intervention right.

[102] See Kershaw, above n. 54, 363–366. Similarly, in the US, review of foreign transactions is limited. See Strine, above n. 89, 77–77.

[103] See, among other provisions, section 22 of the Enterprise Act 2002.

[104] *ibid*., section 58; A. Seely, House of Commons Library, Business and Transport Section, 'Takeovers: The Public Interest Test' (2015), 4. The financial stability ground only applies if the merger is not subject to EU jurisdiction, although the UK may seek to have the competition issue referred back to for domestic review.

[105] See Seely, above n. 103, 14; Slaughter and May, 'Pfizer's Approach for AstraZeneca and the Outlook for Government Intervention in Takeovers' (30 May 2014), at 105 https://www.slaughterandmay.com/media/2165095/pfizers-approach-for-astrazeneca-and-the-outlook-for-government-intervention-in-takeovers.pdf

[106] See Seely, above n. 103, 11–29.

The effects of the lack of a tool for governmental intervention are further exacerbated by the UK's board neutrality rule. This has led Leo Strine, the Chief Justice of the Delaware Supreme Court, to comment that '[i[n Kraft's takeover of the iconic Cadbury, long-standing UK law tilted decidedly in favor of stockholder interests, but UK politicians found the logical consequences of their own settled law dismaying'.[107] Strine contrasts this with other countries, in particular Canada, where the government has the statutory powers to block a foreign takeover based on far broader 'national interests', including when they believe that the acquisition would be detrimental to the domestic economy. In Canada, the law provides the government with 'a naked grant of power'[108] as it can intervene and prevent a transaction by a foreign investor if the government is not satisfied that the investment is likely 'net beneficial' to Canada.[109]

Going forward, an alternative option to the current UK system may well be to emulate a system similar to the one found in Canada. Thus, the government could prevent a transaction by a foreign investor – or demand certain representations and undertakings – if it is not satisfied that the investment is likely to be of 'net benefit' to the country as a whole. However, there are legitimate questions to be asked about the wisdom of such a mechanism. After all, while some negative effects may be avoided, blocking a takeover may also forgo potential gains. Thus, any broader governmental powers in this area would have to be carefully designed, together with procedures and criteria to be used to assess a proposed acquisition. *Inter alia*, a core consideration would be an in-depth cost-benefit analysis of the transaction in question.[110] This would be akin to the current practice of regulatory impact analyses in the legislative arena, although this practice comes with its own difficulties.[111] In this respect, it should also be noted that available empirical evidence on the various economic effects of foreign ownership (as measured by metrics such as firm performance, productivity, job creation, wage levels, R&D, innovation, etc.) tends to be mixed, suggesting that decisions on interventions would have to be made on a case-by-case basis and would likely involve considerable degrees of political judgement.

In sum, against the background of the UK system with its company law restrictions on board-administered defensive measures against takeovers, there might be a case for a 'safety valve' in the form of stronger (post-Brexit) governmental powers in reviewing bids in light of the perceived public interest. Indeed, tackling this problem more openly – by way of clear statutory

---

[107] L.E. Strine, 'Our Continuing Struggle with the Idea that For-Profit Corporations Seek Profit' (2012) 47 *Wake Forest Law Review* 135, 156.

[108] *ibid.*

[109] Investment Canada Act, R.S.C. 1985, c. 28 section 16.

[110] On this, see also Kershaw, above n. 54, 366–67 (noting that there are good reasons to doubt the efficacy and legitimacy of direct interventions by the government).

[111] On this, see M. Petrin, 'Regulatory Analysis in Corporate Law' (2016) 79 *Modern Law Review* 537.

powers – would be preferable compared to cases where governments, due to a lack of proper legal tools, resort to exercising hidden economic protectionism. While foreign takeovers of domestic companies evoke intuitive reactions, it is important for the government to regulate carefully and on the basis of robust academic research in order to find the most beneficial solution for the economy, corporate stakeholders and the public at large.

Although the UK has so far stayed its market-liberal course, it remains to be seen how future cross-border takeovers and changes in government policies or political conditions will affect the status quo. The first signs of possible reform are on the horizon. In the aftermath of the Brexit vote, the current Prime Minister has expressed a desire to formalize and further develop the procedures for vetting acquisitions of UK companies by foreign investors.[112] Although it is not clear whether this would entail changes to the current grounds for governmental intervention, this could well turn out to be the case.

---

[112] 'May and the Case for Vetting Foreign Deals', *Financial Times*, 11 October 2016, 14.

BIBLIOGRAPHY

J. Armour and J.A. McCahery (eds), *After Enron: Improving Corporate Law and Modernising Securities Regulation in Europe and the US* (Oxford, UK: Hart Publishing 2006).

J. Armour and D.A. Skeel, 'Who Writes the Rules for Hostile Takeovers, and Why? – The Peculiar Divergence of US and UK Takeover Regulation' (2007) 95 *Georgetown Law Journal* 1727.

S.M. Bainbridge, 'Director Primacy: The Means and Ends of Corporate Governance' (2003) 97 *Northwestern University Law Review* 547.

S.M. Bainbridge 'Director Primacy and Shareholder Disempowerment' (2006) 119 *Harvard Law Review* 1735.

S.M. Bainbridge, *The New Corporate Governance in Theory and Practice* (New York, NY: Oxford University Press 2008).

S.M. Bainbridge, *Corporate Governance after the Financial Crisis* (New York, NY: Oxford University Press 2012).

L.A. Bebchuk, 'The Case for Increasing Shareholder Power' (2005) 118 *Harvard Law Review* 833.

L.A. Bebchuk and J.M. Fried, 'Paying for Long-Term Performance' (2010) 158 *University of Pennsylvania Law Review* 1915.

L.A. Bebchuk, J.M. Fried and D.I. Walker, 'Managerial Power and Rent Extraction in the Design of Executive Compensation' (2002) 69 *University of Chicago Law Review* 751.

A.A. Berle, 'For Whom Corporate Managers *Are* Trustees: A Note' (1932) 45 *Harvard Law Review* 1365.

A.A. Berle and G. Means, *The Modern Corporation and Private Property* (New York, NY: Harcourt, Brace & World 1968).

M.M. Blair, *Ownership and Control, Rethinking Corporate Governance for the Twenty-First Century* (Washington, DC: Brookings Institute 1995).

M.M. Blair and L.A. Stout, 'A Team Production Theory of Corporate Law' (1999) 85 *Vanderbilt Law Review* 247.

W.W. Bratton and M.L. Wachter, 'The Case against Shareholder Empowerment' (2010) 158 *University of Pennsylvania Law Review* 653.

C.M. Bruner, *Corporate Governance in the Common-Law World: The Political Foundations of Shareholder Power* (Cambridge, UK: Cambridge University Press 2013).

L. Cerioni, A. Keay and J. Loughrey, 'Legal Practitioners, Enlightened Shareholder Value and the Shaping of Corporate Governance' (2008) 8 *Journal of Corporate Law Studies* 79.

B.R. Cheffins, *Company Law: Theory, Structure and Operation* (Oxford, UK: Oxford University Press 1997).

B.R. Cheffins, *Corporate Ownership and Control: British Business Transformed* (Oxford, UK: Oxford University Press 2008).

B.R. Cheffins, 'Did Corporate Governance "Fail" during the 2008 Stock Market Meltdown? – The Case of the S&P 500' (2009) 65 *Business Lawyer* 1.

B.R. Cheffins and J. Armour, 'The Eclipse of Private Equity' (2008) 33 *Delaware Journal of Corporate Law* 1.

B.R. Cheffins and J. Armour, 'The Past, Present and Future of Shareholder Activism by Hedge Funds' (2011) 37 *Journal of Corporation Law* 51.

R.H. Coase, 'The Nature of the Firm' (1937) 4 *Economica* 386.

L.L. Dallas, 'Short-Termism, the Financial Crisis, and Corporate Governance' (2012) 37 *Journal of Corporation Law* 264.

P.L. Davies and S. Worthington, *Gower: Principles of Modern Company Law* (10th ed., London, UK: Sweet & Maxwell 2016).

S. Deakin, 'Anglo-American Corporate Governance and the Employment Relation: A Case to Answer' (2006) 4 *Socio-Economic Review* 155.

S. Deakin and S.J. Konzelmann, 'Learning from Enron' (2004) 12 *Corporate Governance: An International Review* 134.

E.M. Dodd, 'For Whom Are Corporate Managers Trustees?' (1932) 45 *Harvard Law Review* 1145.

F.H. Easterbrook and D.R. Fischel, 'The Corporate Contract' (1989) 89 *Columbia Law Review* 1416.

F.H. Easterbrook and D.R. Fischel, *The Economic Structure of Corporate Law* (Cambridge, MA: Harvard University Press 1991).

M.A. Eisenberg, *The Structure of the Corporation* (Frederick, MD: Beard Books 2006).

L. Enriques, 'European Takeover Law: The Case for a Neutral Approach' (2011) 22 *European Business Law Review* 623.

E.F. Fama, 'Agency Problems and the Theory of the Firm' (1980) 88 *Journal of Political Economy* 288.

E.F. Fama and M.C. Jensen, 'Separation of Ownership and Control' (1983) 26 *Journal of Law and Economics* 301.

E. Ferran and L. Chan Ho, *Principles of Financial Regulation* (2nd ed., Oxford, UK: Oxford University Press 2014).

A.M. Fleckner and K.J. Hopt, *Comparative Corporate Governance: A Functional and International Analysis* (Cambridge, UK: Cambridge University Press 2013).

R.E. Freedman, 'Stockholders and Stakeholders: A New Perspective on Corporate Governance' (1983) 25 *California Management Review* 88.

J.K. Galbraith, *Economics and the Public Purpose* (Boston, MA: Houghton Mifflin 1973).

J.K. Galbraith, *The New Industrial State* (Princeton, NJ: Princeton University Press 1976).

C. Gerner-Beuerle, D. Kershaw and M. Solinas, 'Is the Board Neutrality Rule Trivial? Amnesia about Corporate Law in European Takeover Regulation' (2011) 22 *European Business Law Review* 559.

J.N. Gordon, 'The Rise of Independent Directors in the United States, 1950–2005: Of Shareholder Value and Stock Market Prices' (2007) 59 *Stanford Law Review* 1465.

B. Hannigan, *Company Law* (4th ed., Oxford, UK: Oxford University Press 2016).

H. Hansmann and R. Kraakman, 'The End of History for Corporate Law' (2001) 89 *Georgetown Law Journal* 439.

J.G. Hill and R.S. Thomas (eds), *Research Handbook on Shareholder Power* (Cheltenham: Edward Elgar 2015).

P. Ireland, 'Company Law and the Myth of Shareholder Ownership' (1999) 62 *Modern Law Review* 32.

M.C. Jensen and W.H. Meckling, 'Theory of the Firm: Managerial Behaviour, Agency Costs and Ownership Structure' (1976) 3 *Journal of Financial Economics* 305.

M.C. Jensen and K.J. Murphy, 'Performance Pay and Top-Management Incentives' (1990) 98 *Journal of Political Economy* 225.

M. Kahan and E.B. Rock, 'Hedge Funds in Corporate Governance and Corporate Control' (2007) 155 *University of Pennsylvania Law Review* 1021.

S.N. Kaplan and P. Strömberg, 'Leveraged Buyouts and Private Equity' (2009) 23 *Journal of Economic Perspectives* 121.

J. Kay and A. Silberston, 'Corporate Governance' (1995) *National Institute Economic Review* 84.

A. Keay, 'Company Directors Behaving Poorly: Disciplinary Options for Shareholders' (2007) *Journal of Business Law* 656.

D. Kershaw, *Principles of Takeover Regulation* (Oxford, UK: Oxford University Press 2016).

D. Kershaw, *Company Law in Context: Text and Materials* (2nd ed., Oxford, UK: Oxford University Press 2012).

R. Kraakman et al., *The Anatomy of Corporate Law: A Comparative and Functional Approach* (2nd ed., Oxford, UK: Oxford University Press 2009).

R. La Porta, F. Lopez-de-Silanes, A. Shleifer and R. Vishny, 'Corporate Ownership around the World' (1999) 54 *The Journal of Finance* 471.

R. La Porta, F. Lopez-de-Silanes, A. Shleifer and R. Vishny, 'Investor Protection and Corporate Governance' (2000) 58 *Journal of Financial Economics* 3.

J. Loughrey (ed.), *Directors' Duties and Shareholder Litigation in the Wake of the Financial Crisis* (Cheltenham, UK: Edward Elgar 2013).

I. MacNeil and X. Li, '"Comply or Explain": Market Discipline and Non-Compliance with the Combined Code' (2006) 14 *Corporate Governance: An International Review* 486.

H.G. Manne, 'Mergers and the Market for Corporate Control' (1965) 73 *Journal of Political Economy* 110.

C. Mayer, *Firm Commitment: Why the Corporation Is Failing Us and How to Restore Trust in It* (Oxford, UK: Oxford University Press 2013).

M.T. Moore, *Corporate Governance in the Shadow of the State* (Oxford, UK: Hart Publishing 2013).

M.T. Moore, 'Private Ordering and Public Policy: The Paradoxical Foundations of Corporate Contractarianism' (2014) 34 *Oxford Journal of Legal Studies* 693.

M.T. Moore and A. Rebérioux, 'Revitalizing the Institutional Roots of Anglo-American Corporate Governance' (2011) 40 *Economy and Society* 84.

J.E. Parkinson, *Corporate Power and Responsibility: Issues in the Theory of Company Law* (Oxford, UK: Oxford University Press 1993).

J. Parkinson, A. Gamble and G. Kelly (eds), *The Political Economy of the Company* (Oxford, UK: Hart Publishing 2000).

M. Petrin, 'Reconceptualizing the Theory of the Firm: From Nature to Function' (2013) 118 *Penn State Law Review* 1.

M.J. Roe, *Political Determinants of Corporate Governance* (New York, NY: Oxford University Press 2002).

L. Stout, *The Shareholder Value Myth* (San Francisco, CA: Berrett-Koehler 2012).

O.E. Williamson, *The Mechanisms of Governance* (New York, NY: Oxford University Press 1999).

INDEX